The Tricontinental Revolution

The Tricontinental Revolution provides a major reassessment of the global rise and impact of Tricontinentalism, the militant strand of Third World solidarity that defined the 1960s and 1970s as decades of rebellion. Cold War interventions highlighted the limits of decolonization, prompting a generation of Global South radicals to adopt expansive visions of self-determination. Long associated with Cuba, this anti-imperial worldview stretched far beyond the Caribbean as activists struggled to unite international revolutions around programs of socialism, armed revolt, economic sovereignty, and confrontational diplomacy. Linking independent nations with nonstate movements from North Vietnam through South Africa to New York City, Tricontinentalism encouraged marginalized groups to mount radical challenges to the United States and the inequitable Eurocentric international system. Through eleven expert essays, this volume recenters global political debates on the priorities and ideologies of the Global South, providing a new framework, chronology, and vocabulary for understanding the evolution of anti-colonial and decolonial politics.

R. Joseph Parrott is Assistant Professor of History at The Ohio State University. He is a historian of diplomacy, transnational activism, and US-Africa relations, with an emphasis on the intersection of decolonization, race, and domestic politics.

Mark Atwood Lawrence is Professor of History at the University of Texas at Austin. He has written extensively on twentieth-century America and especially American foreign relations. His most recent book is *The End of Ambition: The United States and the Third World in the Vietnam Era* (2021).

Cambridge Studies in US Foreign Relations

Edited by

Paul Thomas Chamberlin, *Columbia University*

Lien-Hang T. Nguyen, *Columbia University*

This series showcases cutting-edge scholarship in US foreign relations that employs dynamic new methodological approaches and archives from the colonial era to the present. The series will be guided by the ethos of transnationalism, focusing on the history of American foreign relations in a global context rather than privileging the US as the dominant actor on the world stage.

Also in the Series

Aaron Donaghy, *The Second Cold War: Carter, Reagan, and the Politics of Foreign Policy*

Amanda C. Demmer, *After Saigon's Fall: Refugees and US-Vietnamese Relations, 1975–1995*

Heather Marie Stur, *Saigon at War: South Vietnam and the Global Sixties*

Seth Jacobs, *Rogue Diplomats: The Proud Tradition of Disobedience in American Foreign Policy*

Sarah Steinbock-Pratt, *Educating the Empire: American Teachers and Contested Colonization in the Philippines*

Walter L. Hixson, *Israel's Armor: The Israel Lobby and the First Generation of the Palestine Conflict*

Aurélie Basha i Novosejt, *"I Made Mistakes": Robert McNamara's Vietnam War Policy, 1960–1964*

Greg Whitesides, *Science and American Foreign Relations since World War II*

Jasper M. Trautsch, *The Genesis of America: US Foreign Policy and the Formation of National Identity, 1793–1815*

Hideaki Kami, *Diplomacy Meets Migration: US Relations with Cuba during the Cold War*

Shaul Mitelpunkt, *Israel in the American Mind: The Cultural Politics of US-Israeli Relations, 1958–1988*

Pierre Asselin, *Vietnam's American War: A History*

Lloyd E. Ambrosius, *Woodrow Wilson and American Internationalism*

Geoffrey C. Stewart, *Vietnam's Lost Revolution: Ngô Đình Diệm's Failure to Build an Independent Nation, 1955–1963*

Michael E. Neagle, *America's Forgotten Colony: Cuba's Isle of Pines*

Elisabeth Leake, *The Defiant Border: The Afghan-Pakistan Borderlands in the Era of Decolonization, 1936–1965*

Tuong Vu, *Vietnam's Communist Revolution: The Power and Limits of Ideology*

Renata Keller, *Mexico's Cold War: Cuba, the United States, and the Legacy of the Mexican Revolution*

The Tricontinental Revolution

Third World Radicalism and the Cold War

Edited by

R. JOSEPH PARROTT

The Ohio State University

MARK ATWOOD LAWRENCE

University of Texas at Austin

CAMBRIDGE
UNIVERSITY PRESS

CAMBRIDGE
UNIVERSITY PRESS

University Printing House, Cambridge CB2 8BS, United Kingdom

One Liberty Plaza, 20th Floor, New York, NY 10006, USA

477 Williamstown Road, Port Melbourne, VIC 3207, Australia

314–321, 3rd Floor, Plot 3, Splendor Forum, Jasola District Centre,
New Delhi – 110025, India

103 Penang Road, #05– 06/07, Visioncrest Commercial, Singapore 238467

Cambridge University Press is part of the University of Cambridge.

It furthers the University's mission by disseminating knowledge in the pursuit of
education, learning, and research at the highest international levels of excellence.

www.cambridge.org
Information on this title: www.cambridge.org/9781316519110
DOI: 10.1017/9781009004824

© R. Joseph Parrott and Mark Atwood Lawrence 2022

First published 2022

A catalogue record for this publication is available from the British Library.

ISBN 978-1-316-51911-0 Hardback

Contents

Figures

Maps

Contributors

Pierre Asselin is Professor and Dwight E. Stanford Chair in American Foreign Relations at San Diego State University. He is author of *A Bitter Peace: Washington, Hanoi, and the Making of the Paris Agreement* (University of North Carolina Press, 2002), winner of the 2003 Kenneth W. Baldridge Prize; *Hanoi's Road to the Vietnam War, 1954–1965* (University of California Press, 2013), winner of the 2013 Arthur Goodzeit Book Award; and *Vietnam's American War* (Cambridge University Press, 2018). His many articles have appeared in journals such as *Cold War History*, *The Journal of Cold War Studies*, and *Diplomatic History*.

Jeffrey James Byrne is Associate Professor of History at the University of British Columbia. He works on decolonization and revolutionary movements, principally in Africa and the Arab world. He is the author of the award-winning *Mecca of Revolution: Algeria, Decolonization, and the Third World Order* (Oxford University Press, 2016). He is currently writing a book on the morality of war in anti-colonial liberation struggles.

Paul Thomas Chamberlin is Associate Professor of History at Columbia University. His first book, *The Global Offensive: The United States, the Palestine Liberation Organization, and the Making of the Post-Cold War Order* (Oxford University Press, 2012), is an international history of the Palestinian liberation struggle. His next book, *The Cold War's Killing Fields: Rethinking the Long Peace* (HarperCollins, 2018), is a global history of the bloodiest encounters of the Cold War. His articles have appeared in *Cold War History*, *Middle Eastern Studies*, and *Diplomatic*

History, and he has published op-eds with *The New York Times* and the *Christian Science Monitor*.

Eric Covey is a Visiting Assistant Professor of History at Grand Valley State University and former Fulbright U.S. Scholar to Nigeria, where he taught at the University of Abuja. He is the author of *Americans at War in the Ottoman Empire: US Mercenary Force in the Middle East* (I.B. Tauris, 2019) and is working on a new project that examines literary, legal, and political responses to mercenary force in Nigeria after 1960.

Jeremy Friedman is Associate Professor of Business Administration in the Business, Government, and International Economy Unit at the Harvard Business School. His book *Shadow Cold War: The Sino-Soviet Competition for the Third World* was published by the University of North Carolina Press in 2015. His current book project, *Ripe for Revolution: Building Socialism in the Third World*, covers the evolution of the socialist project in Asia, Africa, and Latin America from the 1940s to the 1980s and is due to appear with Harvard University Press in 2021. His work has also been published in the *Journal of Cold War Studies*, *Cold War History*, and *Modern China Studies* and in media outlets including *The Washington Post*, *The National Interest*, *The Diplomat*, and *The Moscow Times*.

Eric Gettig teaches Latin American studies and international history as Deputy Chair for Western Hemisphere Area Studies at the Foreign Service Institute of the US Department of State and as Adjunct Professor in the School of Foreign Service at Georgetown University. He earned his PhD in history from Georgetown University in 2017.

Rafael M. Hernández is the Chief Editor of *Temas*, Cuba's leading social sciences journal. He has been Professor at the University of Havana; Director of US Studies at the *Centro de Estudios sobre América* (a think tank of the Cuban Communist Party Central Committee); and a senior research fellow at Havana's *Instituto "Juan Marinello."* His books include *U.S.–Cuban Relations in the 1990s* (Westview, 1989); *Culturas encontradas: Cuba y los Estados Unidos* (Harvard, 2001); *Looking at Cuba: Essays on Culture and Civil Society* (Florida, 2001); *Vietnam, China and Cuba Foreign Policies towards the United States* (IDE, 2015); *The History of Havana* (Palgrave, 2006); and *Play Ball! Debating US-Cuban Relations* (Routledge, 2015).

Jennifer Ruth Hosek is Professor in the Languages, Literatures and Cultures Department at Queen's University in Ontario. She earned her PhD in Comparative Literature at the University of California at Berkeley and was a postdoctoral fellow at Stanford. One of her foci is transnational German cultural and film studies, which featured prominently in her first book, *Sun, Sex, and Socialism: Cuba in the German Imaginary* (University of Toronto Press, 2012). She publishes broadly and has garnered substantial research support. Dr. Hosek's current larger project investigates non/petrocultural urban movement and includes the codirected, award-winning documentary *Rodando en La Habana: Bicycle Stories* (2015). She created and runs www.LinguaeLive.ca, a free, open-access, student language exchange platform.

Ryan Irwin is Associate Professor of History at the State University of New York-Albany and author of *Gordian Knot: Apartheid and the Unmaking of the Liberal World Order* (Oxford University Press, 2012).

Mark Atwood Lawrence is Professor of History at the University of Texas at Austin. He is author of *Assuming the Burden: Europe and the American Commitment to War in Vietnam* (University of California Press, 2005), *The Vietnam War: A Concise International History* (Oxford University Press, 2008), and *The End of Ambition: The United States and the Third World in the Vietnam Era* (Princeton University Press, 2021).

Anne Garland Mahler is Associate Professor at the University of Virginia, and author of *From the Tricontinental to the Global South: Race, Radicalism, and Transnational Solidarity* (Duke University Press, 2018). Mahler studies transnational solidarity movements, with a focus on the Global South. Her book in progress, *South-South Solidarities: Racial Capitalism and Political Community from the Americas to the Globe*, is supported by a 2020–21 American Council of Learned Societies Fellowship.

Michelle D. Paranzino is Assistant Professor in the Department of Strategy and Policy at the US Naval War College. She is the author of *The Cuban Missile Crisis and the Cold War: A Short History with Documents* (Hackett, 2018), and her work has appeared in *The International History Review*, *The Journal of Cold War Studies*, and several edited volumes. She is currently working on a book about the War on Drugs and the Reagan administration.

R. Joseph Parrott is Assistant Professor of Transnational and Diplomatic History at The Ohio State University. His publications have appeared in *Race & Class*, *Modern American History*, and *Radical History Review*. He is currently revising a manuscript that considers Portuguese decolonization in Africa as a component in the transformation of the US left and Western engagement with the Global South.

Preface

The Tricontinental Revolution explores the history of Tricontinentalism, a political project that gained influence in the Global South as decolonization and interventions by the Cold War superpowers dramatically altered life in Asia, Africa, the Middle East, and Latin America. The authors of the assembled essays are primarily international and transnational historians with expertise in individual states and movements during the 1960s and 1970s. We generalize from the cases examined in those chapters to highlight global – what some might call lateral – connections rather than delve into detailed vertical histories of the countries concerned. We lack the space to explore the fascinating questions of how national and international projects affected individuals on the ground, reshaped their societies, and represented the desires and interests of the governed, but we recognize the importance of these issues and acknowledge them where possible.

The book is an outgrowth of a conference held at the University of Texas at Austin in 2016, the fiftieth anniversary of the Tricontinental Conference. We regretted at the time that we lacked the funding to involve more experts from the Global South. The incorporation and recognition of their scholarship and perspectives have greatly enriched historical studies over the past decades, and we contribute to this effort in the chapters that follow. We hope these essays will encourage a better understanding of the complex history of the Third World, anti-imperial solidarity, and their relationships to the protracted experiences of decolonization and the Cold War.

During the five years it took to complete this volume, we have benefited from the support of numerous institutions and the intellectual generosity of many scholars. We are indebted to all the organizations at the University of Texas that provided support for "The Transnational

Revolution: Tricontinentalism at 50," the conference held in April 2016. These organizations include the UT-Austin History Department, the Institute for Historical Studies, Robert S. Strauss Center for International Security and Law, Clements Center for National Security, Center for European Studies, E3 W, Lozano Long Institute of Latin American Studies, College of Liberal Arts, Department of American Studies, and Center for Russian, East European, and Eurasian Studies. Besides the authors in this volume, contributors to the conference included Minkah Makalani, who moderated discussion, and Jonathan Brown and Robyn Spencer, who gave excellent presentations that informed the way we thought about Tricontinentalism. Barbara Harlow played a major role encouraging the conference and book before her death in 2017; we remember her as an incredibly thoughtful and supportive colleague, mentor, and scholar-activist.

We also want to express our thanks to our authors for their wonderful contributions, attention to many emails, and patience with the publication process. In particular, we would like to thank Anne Garland Mahler, Paul Thomas Chamberlin, Jeremy Friedman, Michelle D. Paranzino, and Pierre Asselin for their attentive feedback to the proposal, introduction, and various aspects of the project. Additionally, Joe would like to thank the many scholars who provided feedback on the introduction, which greatly improved the final product. These include Lydia Walker, his wonderful colleagues at The Ohio State History Department (especially Alice Conklin, David Steigerwald, Joan Flores-Villalobos, Mitchell Lerner, Jennifer Siegel, and Stephen Kern), Thomas Field and the participants of the LSE-Sciences Po Seminar in Contemporary International History (especially Erin O' Halloran, Tom Meinderts, and Mario Del Pero), Maurice Labelle, and Christopher Dietrich. The graduate students in History 7500 at Ohio State suffered through early articulations of ideas in the introduction. Questions and comments from Patrick Nash, Leyla Tiglay, Michael Corsi, Victoria Gurevich, and Seth Andre Meyers were especially helpful in clarifying these ideas.

Joe also extends thanks to Tanya Harmer and Jonathan Holloway, who separately helped him consider his work on Africa through the lens of Tricontinentalism, and Michele Louro, whose discussions of the League Against Imperialism helpfully framed the Anti-Imperial Project. Finally, friends and colleagues contributed to the conceptualization of this study through conversations and shared insights; these include Cindy Ewing, Timothy Nunan, Zoe LeBlanc, David Stenner, Philip Muehlenbeck, Natalia Telepneva, Paul Adler, Robert Rakove, Stephen Macekura,

Wen-Qing Ngoei, and Lorenz Lüthi. Mark would like to acknowledge the colleagues and students who have done so much to deepen his understanding of the Cold War in the 1960s. Besides the authors in this collection, these scholars include Carl Forsberg, Robert J. McMahon, Brian McNeil, Robert Rakove, and Jeremi Suri.

We also want to thank the first-rate team at Cambridge University Press who made the publication process run smoothly, especially Paul Thomas Chamberlin, Lien-Hang T. Nguyen, Debbie Gershenowitz, and the two anonymous reviewers who provided insightful, supportive feedback. Our editor, Cecelia Cancellaro, has been helpful throughout the process while offering much-appreciated patience. Lincoln Cushing graciously provided images from Cuban and Chinese poster collections throughout the project, including the majority of those that appear in this book. All of them can be found on his website of Docs Populi and in two publications: *Revolucion! Cuban Poster Art* (Chronicle Books, 2003) and (with Ann Tompkins) *Chinese Posters: Art from the Great Proletarian Cultural Revolution* (Chronicle Books, 2007).

Finally, we would be remiss if we did not thank our families. Mark owes a huge debt of gratitude to his wife, Stephanie Osbakken, and their daughters, Maya and Bryn, who showed boundless good cheer despite the long hours he spent at his desk. Joe would like to thank his parents, Ray and Pat, and his wife, Julie, for their support. Julie helped make the original conference work and patiently accommodated many writing weekends and unsolicited explanations of connections between Third World political movements babbled at lightspeed.

Abbreviations

AAPSO	Afro-Asian People's Solidarity Organization
ANC	African National Congress
CONCP	Conference of Nationalist Organizations of the Portuguese Colonies
CPC	Coloured People's Congress
CPSU	Communist Party of the Soviet Union
DRV	Democratic Republic of Vietnam
FLN	National Liberation Front (Algeria)
FNLA	National Liberation Front of Angola
FRG	Federal Republic of Germany
GDR	German Democratic Republic
IPC	International Preparatory Committee of the Tricontinental
LADLA	Anti-Imperialist League of the Americas
LAI	League Against Imperialism and for National Independence
MK	uMkhonto weSizwe
MLG	Liberation Movement of Guinea
MPLA	People's Movement for the Liberation of Angola
NAM	Non-Aligned Movement
NATO	North Atlantic Treaty Organization
NIEO	New International Economic Order
NLF	National Liberation Front (South Vietnam)
OAS	Organization of American States
OAU	Organization of African Unity
OLAS	Organization of Latin American Solidarity
OPEC	Organization of Petroleum Exporting Countries

OSPAAAL	Organization of Solidarity with the Peoples of Africa, Asia, and Latin America
PAC	Pan Africanist Congress
PAIGC	African Party for the Independence of Guinea and Cabo Verde
PLO	Palestine Liberation Organization
PRC	People's Republic of China
SACP	South African Communist Party
UAR	United Arab Republic
UF	United Front
UN	United Nations
UNCTAD	United Nations Conference on Trade and Development
UNITA	National Union for the Total Independence of Angola
VWP	Vietnamese Worker's Party
WPC	World Peace Council

INTRODUCTION

Tricontinentalism and the Anti-Imperial Project

R. Joseph Parrott

Lights glowed brightly from the Hotel Habana Libre on the first day of January 1966. Built by Hilton seven years earlier for wealthy American tourists to enjoy the expat playground that was Havana, the building's facade now featured hundreds of bulbs sketching an image of an out-stretched arm gripping a rifle and holding a stylized globe. Thus did Fidel Castro's regime welcome its guests to the first Tricontinental Conference uniting revolutionary Asians, Africans, and Latin Americans.[1] Hundreds of delegates from Indonesia, India, Iran, Guinea, the United Arab Republic, Kenya, China, the Soviet Union, and elsewhere filled the streets of Havana for the next two weeks. Their goal was to define a vision of Third World solidarity that could combat the threats of imperialism, colonialism, and neocolonialism that Castro saw embodied in the former life of the 25-floor casino hotel. Joining heads of state and diplomats were representatives of armed revolutionary movements from both European colonies and independent states, ranging from the Rebel Armed Forces of Guatemala (FAR) to the recently founded Palestinian Liberation Organization (PLO).[2] At the center of this loose coalition of governments and activists was a radical vision of self-determination. The majority of attendees championed armed revolt, socialism, the creation of cultural and economic institutions to resist foreign domination, and a new focus

---

[1] *Souvenir of the First Conference of Solidarity of the Peoples of Africa, Asia, and Latin America*, 1966, Arquivo Mário Pinto de Andrade, Fundação Mário Soares, online at Casa Comum: http://casacomum.org/cc/visualizador?pasta=08035.001#!1.
[2] General Secretariat of OSPAAAL, *First Solidarity Conference of the Peoples of Africa, Asia, and Latin America* (Havana: 1966), 183–186.

on the "common enemy of North American imperialism."[3] The Havana conference reflected a radical worldview justifying Third World revolution, which is best termed Tricontinentalism.

Secular, socialist, and militant, Tricontinentalism aimed to empower the states of Latin America, Asia, and Africa and mount a revolutionary challenge to the Euro-American dominated international system in the 1960s and 1970s. While the organizers of the Havana meeting described the conference as a continuation of the search for solidarity begun a decade earlier by Afro-Asian organizers at Bandung, they also insisted that their gathering constituted "a new stage in the common struggle."[4] The incorporation of Latin America, heightened concern about economic neocolonialism, and a commitment to internationally contentious revolts in Vietnam, Palestine, and the Congo all demonstrated that solidarity had evolved in radical directions. No longer was it sufficient for Afro-Asian heads of state to collaborate diplomatically to denounce nuclear war and explore new forms of economic cooperation, as earlier examples of Third World cooperation had proposed.[5] A decade of mostly pro-Western coups showed the fragility of postcolonial governance as well as the rising threat of American-led interventionism. New forms of action seemed necessary.

Delegates to the Havana meeting concluded that armed revolts by stateless groups, the creation of new coalitions, and the embrace of radically socialist domestic and international agendas were necessary to defeat global imperialism and empower decolonization. Conspicuous support for this agenda came from the Soviet Union and – initially – China, both of which championed anti-imperialism, claimed linkages to and sometimes membership in the Third World, and offered aid to help balance disparities of power.[6] The Tricontinental Conference thus broke with Bandung's self-conscious neutralism by, in the words of one organizing document, reuniting "the two currents of world revolution … the socialist revolution of October and that of the national liberation revolution."[7] Cuba's role as

---

[3] International Preparatory Committee of the First Solidarity Conference of the peoples of Africa, Asia and Latin America and the Cuban National Committee, *Towards the First Tricontinental* (Havana: 1966), 6.
[4] Ibid., 7.   [5] Ibid., 6.
[6] China initially positioned itself as first among equals in the Third World. While never claiming Third World membership, the Kremlin used its Central Asian republics (acquired by czarist Russia in order to join the European empire club) to identify with non-Europeans and deepen its anti-imperial bona fides when diplomatically beneficial.
[7] *Towards the First Tricontinental*, 12.

FIGURE O.1 The OSPAAAL publication *Tricontinental* regularly included posters highlighting specific movements and their relationship to the larger anti-imperial struggle, a practice that established both a roster and an iconography of revolutionary radicalism. This poster captures a common theme related to solidarity with the African American struggle, but it also points to the revolutionary logic uniting state and nonstate actors. OSPAAAL, artist unknown, 1967. Offset, 52x31 cm. Image courtesy Lincoln Cushing / Docs Populi.

conference host was symbolic of this new unity of purpose. The agenda laid out at Havana refined and promoted a new current of anti-imperial activism that had percolated for years and would shape international affairs for a decade.

Tricontinentalism recast the Third World agenda while energizing the Cold War, but its history reveals broader dynamics of anti-imperial solidarity politics within the Global South. In an attempt to recover the complexity of the ongoing challenge to the Euro-American dominated international system, *The Tricontinental Revolution: Third World Radicalism and the Cold War* offers a revised framework and chronology of Third World internationalism by challenging the idea of a single, evolving movement. Third World solidarity emerged during the Cold War, as political scientist Robert Vitalis has argued, from a series of overlapping ideologies and movements that promoted different forms of cooperation as postcolonial countries grappled with political, economic, and social challenges.[8] Adjusting Vijay Prashad's idea of a "Third World Project" pursued by the "Darker Nations," it might be more accurate to talk of a century-long *Anti-Imperial Project* that existed in the overlapping goals of these diverse movements and which informed the Third World idea as it evolved in the context of the Cold War.[9] This project encompassed an array of sometimes competing ideologies and alliances that collectively hoped to achieve sufficient unity to advance the shared interests of the Global South, or the regions of Asia, Africa, and Latin America that shared historic experiences of empire, economic disparity, and resistance. Using the term "Anti-Imperial" consciously recognizes that this negative opposition to Western imperialism provided a sense of common purpose and inspired transnational cooperation, but Southern actors often diverged – sometimes dramatically – in their visions for the positive programs that would replace it. Although one ideology never triumphed, certain strands of thought rose to prominence within this Anti-Imperial Project at different points in time. From the 1960s through the late

---

[8] Robert Vitalis, "The Midnight Ride of Kwame Nkrumah and Other Fables of Bandung," *Humanity* 4:2 (Summer 2013): 261–288.

[9] The Anti-Imperial Project captures the complexity of Global South collaboration against Euro-American hegemony, which predated but also informed the post-1945 theorization of the Third World. Prashad offers a more unitary vision with his Third World Project. Vijay Prashad, *The Darker Nations: A People's History of the Third World* (New York: New Press, 2008), xv–xviii.

1970s, Tricontinentalism was arguably the most influential of these competing visions, ushering in an era in which militant anti-imperialism became a prominent part of the global zeitgeist.

Tricontinentalism gained traction as a radical alternative to the relatively reformist agendas of the first generation of postcolonial leaders. In many places, these politicians inherited fractious societies while facing a hostile international system. Promises of economic development built primarily on adaptations of capitalist and socialist modernization schemes faltered as the 1960s dawned, reinforcing inequitable ties to an international commercial system upheld by Western governments and corporations. Potential allies within the Global South shared problems and interests but embraced a variety of political, ideological, and economic orientations. Superpower interventions further constrained the autonomy of the Third World actors. The sheer economic, political, and military power wielded by the United States and the Soviet Union circumscribed options for economic and political sovereignty by empowering specific socioeconomic agendas aligned with Cold War camps, sometimes undermining governments that aggressively championed independent nationalist programs.

In this setting, armed revolution and confrontational diplomacy became attractive alternatives for Third World elites frustrated by the slow pace of change. Repressed nationalists and diasporic peoples that continued to chafe under Euro-American preponderance championed aggressive, transnational responses that challenged Bandung's emphasis on diplomatic cooperation between independent states.[10] The Cuban, Algerian, and North Vietnamese governments that came to power through armed conflict offered visions of a militant, socialist anti-imperialism.[11] Revisiting earlier ideas and associations, these and sympathetic states like Egypt spoke openly of revolution and flirted

[10] See, for example, Brenda Gayle Plummer, *In Search of Power: African Americans in the Era of Decolonization, 1956–1974* (New York: Cambridge University Press, 2012); Paul Thomas Chamberlin, *The Global Offensive: The United States, the Palestine Liberation Organization, and the Making of the Post-Cold War Order* (New York: Oxford University Press, 2012); Laura Pulido, *Black, Brown, Yellow, and Left: Radical Activism in Los Angeles* (Berkeley: University of California Press, 2006).
[11] See Jonathan C. Brown, *Cuba's Revolutionary World* (New York: Oxford University Press, 2017); Jeffrey James Byrne, *Mecca of Revolution: Algeria, Decolonization, and the Third World Order* (New York: Oxford University Press, 2016); Judy Tzu-Chun Wu, *Radicals on the Road: Internationalism, Orientalism, and Feminism during the Vietnam Era* (Ithaca, NY: Cornell University Press, 2013).

with new alliances such as the increasingly militant Afro-Asian People's Solidarity Organization (AAPSO). By the late 1950s, the radical anti-imperialism present at the Havana conference began to differentiate itself from the neutralism of Bandung. These radical impulses gained momentum as ambitious but measured Third World programs faltered and military coups upended governments in Brazil, Ghana, and Indonesia. Scholars have recognized this shift, describing it vaguely as a "second generation" of Third World leadership and noting "the vogue of revolution in poor countries."[12]

This volume contends that Tricontinentalism provides an essential framework for understanding and analyzing this phenomenon and the era it helped define. At its core was the idea that countries in the Global South shared histories of Euro-American colonization, which gave them reason to seek coordinated, militant strategies of resistance and empowerment in the hostile context of an international system created by empires. International meetings and publications such as *Tricontinental* from the Havana-based Organization of Solidarity with the Peoples of Africa, Asia, and Latin America (OSPAAAL) became forums for revolutionaries to articulate and debate specific programs. Texts, conferences, and diplomatic exchanges integrated diverse ideas of political, economic, and cultural revolution into a common agenda inspired by and reflected in the oft-referenced armed struggles in Vietnam, Cuba, Algeria, South Africa, and elsewhere. Though Third World leaders used the term inconsistently, Tricontinentalism captures how many militant parties and movements described their visions of self-determination and national development as part of a global community of likeminded peers. This "dynamic counter-modernity," in the words of scholar Robert J. C. Young, challenged Western imperialism at multiple levels with interrelated African, Asian, and Latinx

---

[12] Mark T. Berger and Heloise Weber, *Rethinking the Third World: International Development and World Politics* (New York: Macmillan, 2014), 71–72. Forrest D. Colburn, *The Vogue of Revolution in Poor Countries* (Princeton: Princeton University Press, 1994). Odd Arne Westad refers to them as "new revolutionary states" in Westad, *The Global Cold War: Third World Interventions and the Making of Our Times* (New York: Cambridge University Press, 2005), 158. Samantha Christiansen and Zachary A. Scarlett speak of the "second wave" of Third World struggles that began in the mid-1960s, "Introduction" in Christiansen and Scarlett, eds., *The Third World in the Global 1960s* (New York: Berghan Books, 2013).

internationalisms.[13] It also proved more attentive to the demands of a wide array of international actors than had prior iterations of the Anti-Imperial Project, articulating an expansive anti-imperialism that directed popular ire at the capitalist West and its client states in the Global South.

Given the diversity of its adherents, Tricontinentalism is best understood as a worldview. It was a way of understanding how the international system worked and laid down specific goals for marginalized, often impoverished states to achieve genuine self-determination. Eschewing strict dogmatism, this worldview led countries with similar assessments of comparable problems toward a set of best practices for achieving independence that were adapted and negotiated to address local circumstances and insecurities. The ultimate objective was the destruction of colonial and international structures favoring Western interests and their replacement with more egalitarian states and institutions. This perspective and the policy choices it suggested borrowed heavily from socialism, which invited Western reaction and threatened to pull states into the Sino-Soviet competition. The most assertive advocates adopted violence and expanded alliances with the communist powers as the logical response to Euro-American interventions. This leftward revolutionary shift effectively differentiated Tricontinental advocates from moderate postcolonial peers, creating what members argued was the vanguard of a global Third World revolt during the 1960s and 1970s.

THE HISTORIOGRAPHY OF TRICONTINENTALISM

Despite its influence, Tricontinentalism remains an underappreciated concept because anti-imperial internationalism has only recently become a popular subject for scholarly study. The global history of the later twentieth century has long been dominated by the Cold War. To the extent researchers have considered the foreign relations of Third World governments, the majority have done so in terms of superpower conflict: how the great powers perceived their interests, and how actors in the ostensible periphery reacted to intervention.[14] Only in the last two

[13] Robert J. C. Young, *Postcolonialism: An Historical Introduction* (Malden, MA: Wiley-Blackwell, 2001), 2.
[14] For example, Gabriel Kolko, *Confronting the Third World* (New York: Pantheon, 1988); Thomas Borstelmann, *The Cold War and the Color Line* (Cambridge: Harvard University

decades has the international turn led scholars to seriously question this dominant narrative. Many now argue for the equal importance of decolonization, which transformed the international system by adding dozens of new states in Africa, Asia, and Latin America. Scholarship initially focused on metropolitan retreat has shifted to consider how decolonization empowered the Global South to challenge the Eurocentric international system.[15] South-South alliances and material exchanges encouraged struggles for self-determination during a period of increased superpower attention to these regions.[16] So too did Southern states collaborate to establish new institutions and economic ideologies in attempts to create a fairer international system.[17] Such scholarship is informing new histories of Third World international relations and solidarities that opposed – or even predated or existed independently from – the Cold War.

Though the historiography has expanded to reflect the experience of nations from the Global South in the twentieth century, scholars are still working to understand the complex realities of Third World internationalism – its alliances, ideologies, chronologies, and terminologies. Most

Press, 2001); Robert J. McMahon, ed., *The Cold War in the Third World* (New York: Oxford University Press, 2013); Salim Yaqub, *Containing Arab Nationalism: The Eisenhower Doctrine and the Middle East* (Chapel Hill: University of North Carolina Press, 2006).

[15] For the former, see Martin Shipway, *Decolonization and Its Impact: A Comparative Approach to the End of the Colonial Empires* (New York: Wiley-Blackwell, 2008). For the latter, Westad, *The Global Cold War*; Adom Getachew, *Worldmaking After Empire: The Rise and Fall of Self-Determination* (Princeton: Princeton University Press, 2019); Christopher Kalter, *The Discovery of the Third World: Decolonization and the Rise of the New Left in France, c.1950–1976* (New York: Cambridge University Press, 2016).

[16] For examples, see Matthew Connelly, *A Diplomatic Revolution: Algeria's Fight for Independence and the Origins of the Post-Cold War Era* (New York: Oxford University Press, 2002); Piero Gleijeses, *Conflicting Missions: Havana, Washington, and Africa, 1959–1976* (Chapel Hill: University of North Carolina Press, 2003); Jeremy Friedman, *Shadow Cold War: The Sino-Soviet Competition for the Third World* (Chapel Hill: University of North Carolina Press, 2015); David Stenner, *Globalizing Morocco: Transnational Activism and the Postcolonial State* (Palo Alto: Stanford University Press, 2019); South Africa Democracy Education Trust, *The Road to Democracy in South Africa: Volume 5, African Solidarity, Parts 1 & 2* (Pretoria: UNISA Press, 2013, 2014).

[17] Christopher R. W. Dietrich, *Oil Revolution: Anticolonial Elites, Sovereign Rights, and the Economic Culture of Decolonization* (New York: Cambridge University Press, 2017); Giuliano Garavini, *The Rise and Fall of OPEC in the Twentieth Century* (New York: Oxford University Press, 2019).

histories of the Third World fall into one of two categories: studies like Odd Arne Westad's influential *Global Cold War* that highlight connections to the superpower conflict and others that detail the foreign relations of noteworthy countries or individuals from the Global South.[18] A smaller third category considers diplomatic conferences as windows into the broad project, with an emphasis on Bandung in historical circles and Non-Aligned Movement summits in political science.[19] Although these latter works are pivotal to our understanding of politics in the Global South, Prashad's polemical exploration of the rise and frustration of the Third World Project remains the primary overarching narrative from which many scholars draw.[20] Prashad hints at the diversity of visions that existed within the movement, but he generally describes the efforts of a continuous, if decentralized, leftist anti-imperial ideology.

In collapsing solidarity politics into a single phenomenon, Prashad and other scholars have yet to fully grapple with the diversity of the Anti-Imperial Project. This is especially true among historians, for whom an exaggerated or mythic version of Bandung and Afro-Asian solidarity orients most studies.[21] The 1955 meeting assembled twenty-nine Afro-Asian

[18] See Westad, *The Global Cold War*; McMahon, *The Cold War in the Third World*; Robert B. Rakove, *Kennedy, Johnson, and the Nonaligned World* (New York: Cambridge University Press, 2012). Scholars of Global South diplomacy continue to privilege the Cold War, though this is changing. See Connelly, *A Diplomatic Revolution*; Gleijeses, *Conflicting Missions*; Renata Keller, *Mexico's Cold War: Cuba, the United States, and the Legacy of the Mexican Revolution* (New York: Cambridge University Press, 2015); Lien-Hang T. Nguyen, *Hanoi's War: An International History of the War for Peace in Vietnam* (Chapel Hill: University of North Carolina Press, 2016).

[19] See footnote 21 for histories of Bandung. For political-science oriented studies of the NAM, see Peter Willetts, *The Non-Aligned Movement: The Origins of the Third World Alliance* (London: Frances Pinter Publishers, 1978); Robert A. Mortimer, *The Third World Coalition in International Politics* (London: Prager, 1980); S. W. Singham and Shirley Hune, *Non-Alignment in an Age of Alignments* (London: Lawrence Hill, 1980). Recent historical studies include Rinna Kullaa, *Non-Alignment and Its Origins in Cold War Europe: Yugoslavia, Finland, and the Soviet Challenge* (London: I.B. Tauris, 2012) and Jürgen Dinkel, *The Non-Aligned Movement: Genesis, Organization and Politics* (Leiden: Brill, 2018).

[20] Prashad, *Darker Nations*; Vijay Prashad, *The Poorer Nations: A Possible History of the Global South* (New York: Verso, 2013).

[21] See Christopher J. Lee, ed., *Making a World After Empire: The Bandung Moment and Its Political Afterlives* (Athens: Ohio University Press, 2010); Jamie Mackie, *Bandung 1955: Non-Alignment and Afro-Asian Solidarity* (Paris: Didier Millet, 2005); Seng Tan and Amitav Acharya, eds., *Bandung Revisited: The Legacy of the 1955 African-Asian Conference for the International Order* (Singapore: National University of Singapore Press, 2008); see also various articles on Bandung and superpower responses to it including Augusto Espiritu, "'To Carry Water on Both Shoulders': Carlos P. Romulo, American

states (Map o.1) in the Indonesian city of Bandung, where they sought collaboration in support of self-determination, economic development, and peaceful coexistence. The vague conclusions of the final statement reflect the fact it was a relatively staid gathering of mostly independent Asian countries, but the "Bandung Spirit" promised much more. Contemporary reporters (and later revolutionaries) cited Bandung to critique an expansive list of global inequalities between and within nations that sometimes diverged from the actual proceedings. Thus, the conference earned a symbolic association with key issues of Third World transnationalism and revolution that more closely align with other iterations of the Anti-Imperial Project such as Tricontinentalism.[22] As a result, even historians of African revolutions and nonstate movements – the vast majority of which had barely a presence at Bandung – feel obliged to connect their studies to the 1955 conference.[23]

Lost in this universalization of the Bandung Spirit are the ways Third World actors devised new forms of solidarity to confront contingent global challenges. The extended process of decolonization, Cold War interventions, the proliferation of multinational businesses, the rise of neo-capitalism, and geostrategic conflicts within the Global South all strained the inclusive vision of solidarity present at Bandung. These multiplying challenges compelled advocates of anti-imperialism to consider

Empire, and the Meanings of Bandung," *Radical History Review* 95 (Spring 2006): 173–190; Jason Parker, "Cold War II: The Eisenhower Administration, the Bandung Conference, and the Reperiodization of the Cold War," *Diplomatic History* 30:5 (November, 2006). In addition to a focus on the Bandung conference, some literature situates the Non-Aligned Movement as the natural successor to the Afro-Asian impulse. See H. W. Brands, *The Specter of Neutralism* (New York: Columbia University Press, 1990); Natasa Miskovic et al., eds., *The Non-Aligned Movement and the Cold War: Delhi – Bandung – Belgrade* (New York: Routledge, 2014).

[22] The conflation grows from reporting on Bandung that speculated widely on what it *could* mean for non-white peoples. Brian Russell Roberts and Keith Foulcher, eds., *Indonesian Notebook: A Sourcebook on Richard Wright and the Bandung Conference* (Durham: Duke University Press, 2016).

[23] Michele Louro, *Comrades against Imperialism: Nehru, India, and Interwar Internationalism* (New York: Cambridge University Press, 2018); Jason Parker, *Hearts, Minds, Voices: US Cold War Public Diplomacy and the Formation of the Third World* (New York: Oxford University Press, 2016); John Munro, *The Anticolonial Front: The African American Freedom Struggle and Global Decolonization, 1945–1960* (New York: Cambridge University Press, 2017). It is illustrative of the phenomenon that recent attempts to move beyond Bandung have felt obliged to refract their scholarship through the conference. See Su Lin Lewis and Carolien Stolte, "Other Bandungs: Afro-Asian Internationalisms in the Early Cold War," *Journal of World History* 30:1–2 (June 2019): 1–19.

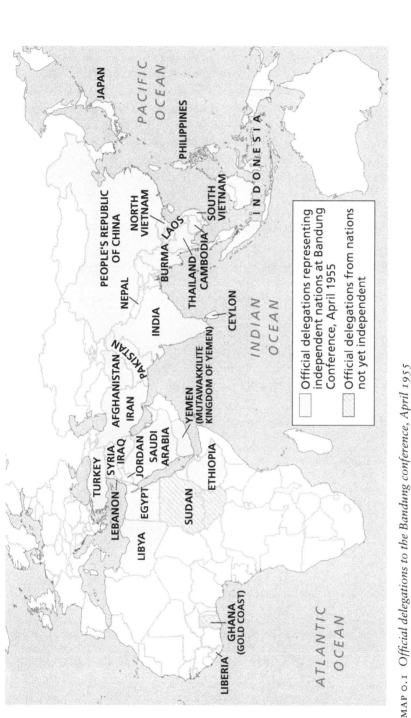

MAP 0.1 *Official delegations to the Bandung conference, April 1955*

Twenty-seven independent states sent official delegations as did Sudan and Ghana, which were moving toward self-rule. Yemen refers to the Mutawakkilite Kingdom of Yemen.

Source: Final Communiqué of the Asian-African Conference of Bandung, April 24, 1955.

radical solutions. Ironically, it has been these Tricontinental elements –
including an explicit militancy, vocal opposition to racism, and inclusion
of transnational movements – that often typify the mythologized Bandung
Spirit and give it explanatory power.[24] This conflation of both Cold War
Third Worldism and the larger Anti-Imperial Project with elements specific to the radical, leftist internationalism of the 1960s obscures complex
internal dynamics, not just in the radicalization of Tricontinental states
after Bandung but also the mobilization of anti-imperial ideas by such
diverse actors as authoritarian Brazil and Islamist Iran.[25] Many countries
pursued shared goals of the Anti-Imperial Project and claimed legitimacy
by citing common precedents such as Bandung. Yet because they adhered
to discrete ideologies, states clashed politically and sometimes militarily
even as they cooperated uneasily in ventures such as the Non-Aligned
Movement (NAM) or the pursuit of a New International Economic Order
(NIEO).

Tricontinentalism deserves attention as a distinct worldview within the
Anti-Imperial Project – one example of Vitalis's discrete ideologies.[26]
A handful of scholars have been attentive to this outlook, especially the
ways in which it linked Cuban foreign policy to US radicalism.[27] But alongside this approach has emerged a broader reading of Tricontinentalism as
a "framework for understanding ... global, antiracist, and anti-imperialist

---

[24] This phenomenon owes much to later radicals, including those at the Tricontinental, who
referred back to Bandung as they promoted liberation struggles that had minimal relation
to the content of the conference and conflicted with the priorities of organizing states such
as India and the Colombo Powers.

[25] See Jerry Davilla, *Hotel Tropico: Brazil and the Challenge of African Decolonization,
1950–1980* (Durham: Duke University Press, 2010); Timothy Nunan, "'Neither East Nor
West', Neither Liberal Nor Illiberal? Iranian Islamist Internationalism in the 1980s,"
Journal of World History 31:1 (March 2020): 43–77.

[26] Recently, the Afro-Asian Networks Research Collective began to consider a new chronology of Third Worldism, centered around the transition from Bandung to
Tricontinentalism, asking "questions about how imperialism functioned, what freedom
and liberation actually looked like, and how to achieve these goals animated these
networks across the temporality of 'Bandung' or the 'Tricontinental.' Is there a moment
at which one ends and the other begins?" Afro-Asian Networks Research Collective,
"Manifesto," *Radical History Review* 131 (May 2018): 179.

[27] See Teishan A. Latner, *Cuban Revolution in America: Havana and the Making of a United
States Left, 1968–1992* (Chapel Hill: University of North Carolina Press, 2018); John
A. Gronbeck-Tedesco, *Cuba, the United States, and Cultures of the Transnational Left,
1930–1975* (New York: Cambridge University Press, 2015); Sarah Seidman,
"Venceremos Means We Shall Overcome: The African American Freedom Struggle and
Cuban Revolution, 1959–79" (PhD diss., Brown University, 2013). See also the *Journal of
Transatlantic Studies* (September 2009), which devoted an issue of loosely related articles
to the theme of Tricontinentalism.

politics," which Besenia Rodriguez argues better explains some of the more expansive black internationalist traditions used in the United States than do ethnonationalist forms of Pan-Africanism alone.[28] Yet as Robert J. C. Young argues, Tricontinentalism drew inspiration and meaning beyond the Americas, articulating a radical challenge to the global status quo that integrated Marxism and anti-imperial nationalism. Young's proposal that a universalized form of Tricontinentalism better explains the academic discourse of postcolonialism muddies historical relationships and timelines, but he successfully outlines a canon of radical thinkers including Mao Zedong, Frantz Fanon, Che Guevara, and Amílcar Cabral that laid its intellectual foundations. They adapted elements of Marxism to create a global vision of empire that united movements across cultures and informed a Third World "nationalist internationalism" positioning militant revolution against the systemic economic and racial inequalities created by capitalist imperialism.[29]

An improved historical understanding of Tricontinentalism therefore promises to help explain both the long history of anti-imperialism and a pivotal period within the Cold War. Indeed, consideration of the ideologies and transnational solidarities built by this "second generation" of Third World leaders has been at the heart of a number of important studies over the past decade, but disciplinary silos and the challenges of multicontinental research have militated against the creation of a common vocabulary. Related phenomena that fall under the umbrella of Tricontinentalism have been variously described as radical Third World Politics (Quinn Slobodian), the Third World Left (Cynthia Young), Anti-imperialism (Jeremy Friedman), and a component of Prashad's Third World movement.[30] Anne Garland Mahler, who wrote the first book-length history of

---

[28] Besenia Rodriguez, "'De la Esclavitud Yanqui a la Libertad Cubana': U.S. Black Radicals, the Cuban Revolution, and the Formation of a Tricontinental Ideology," *Radical History Review* 92 (Spring 2005): 63; Besenia Rodriguez, "Beyond Nation: The Formation of a Tricontinental Discourse" (PhD diss., Yale University, 2006); R. Joseph Parrott, "Boycott Gulf! Angolan Oil and the Black Power Roots of American Anti-Apartheid Organizing," *Modern American History* 1:2 (2018): 195–220.

[29] Young, *Postcolonialism*, 4–5, 305.

[30] Rodriguez, "Beyond Nation"; Quinn Slobodian, *Foreign Front: Third World Politics in Sixties West Germany* (Durham: Duke University Press, 2012); Cynthia A. Young, *Soul Power: Culture, Radicalism, and the Making of the U.S. Third World Left* (Durham: Duke University Press, 2006); Friedman, *Shadow Cold War*; Parker, *Hearts, Minds, Voices*. Other examples that consider similar ideas include Wu, *Radicals on the Road*; Pulido, *Black, Brown, Yellow, and Left*; Robeson Taj Frazier, *The East is Black: Cold War China in the Black Radical Imagination* (Durham: Duke University Press, 2014); Gregg A. Brazinsky, *Winning the Third World: Sino-American Rivalry during the Cold War* (Chapel Hill: University of North Carolina Press, 2017).

Tricontinentalism and contributes to this volume, helps unite these various discussions by providing a globally applicable definition of the Tricontinental worldview reflected in but independent of Cuban policy. Emphasizing its roots in black internationalist thought, she describes a discourse that envisioned anti-imperial, anti-capitalist transnational solidarity "as a rehearsal for the eventual realization of a new global social relation."[31] This volume mirrors and builds on this expansive concept of Tricontinentalism, linking it to the diverse discussion of Third World politics occurring in international history circles. It seeks to capture the wide manifestations of this phenomenon while exploring the political and diplomatic alliances it sought to create. In the process, it reveals the fraught and fluid nature of anti-imperial solidarity, and why it proved difficult to translate powerful ideas into an effective challenge to deep-seated global inequalities.

ELEMENTS OF THIRD WORLD REVOLUTION

The volume explores the content and historical context of Tricontinentalism by bringing together some of the top scholars of Third World international politics. Representing a variety of disciplines, linguistic skills, and regional expertise, our contributors have written eleven intersecting case studies with an emphasis on the contributions of prominent nations and liberation groups to the Tricontinental project. Taken together, the chapters reveal how revolutionaries developed militant, anti-imperial solidarity in the 1960s and established semiformal networks to empower states and organizations from the Global South against what they regarded as an unjust world system. The book's agenda goes beyond simply considering the 1966 Havana conference or regional internationalisms. Specific programmatic aspects united diverse polities under the umbrella of Tricontinentalism, which inspired the foreign policies of nations and movements from Southeast Asia to Latin America as well as the agendas of civil society groups in Europe and the United States. Cuba features prominently in these studies as arguably the most committed state advocate of Tricontinentalism, the home of OSPAAAL, and a consistent proponent of integrating Latin American revolutions into

---

[31] Anne Garland Mahler, *From the Tricontinental to the Global South: Race, Radicalism, and Transnational Solidarity* (Durham: Duke University Press, 2018), 11. See also, Anne Garland Mahler, "The Global South in the Belly of the Beast: Viewing African American Civil Rights Through a Tricontinental Lens," *Latin American Research Review* 50:1 (2015): 95–116.

the Afro-Asian tradition. So too does the Cold War play a role, with the militant shift encouraged by the Sino-Soviet split empowering advocates of the socialist-inflected Tricontinental worldview even as the United States sought to contain radicalism. But the principal goal of the volume is to provide a perspective on Third World solidarity that accounts for the array of visions and policy prescriptions offered by small states and political movements seeking to assert their independence via radical anti-imperialism.

The overlapping visions revealed in each chapter enable us to see the core elements of Tricontinentalism. Although it fits within a longer Anti-Imperial Project that championed political independence and greater economic equality for Southern nations, a unique combination of elements made it distinct. First, it was militant in its goals, aiming for a wholesale restructuring of the international system that promoted complete self-determination and economic justice between global North and South. The most dramatic tool for achieving this transformation was military struggle, which became the preferred method in the 1960s for nationalists unable to evict colonial powers and foreign economic control through negotiation or United Nations (UN) mediation. While armed revolt became a kind of political totem by the 1970s, chapters in this volume show nationalists adopted militancy as a direct response to interventions by colonial and Western powers – specifically the Cold War United States. Tricontinental advocates used negotiations and economic coercion to pursue their goals, but armed revolt provided a powerful bargaining chip and necessary last resort for redressing rigid systemic inequalities.[32]

Second, Tricontinentalism emphasized an expansive form of anti-imperialism. Recalling critiques of the international system proposed by earlier organizations such as the League Against Imperialism (see below), advocates opposed not only political control by European empires but also subtler forms of economic and cultural domination.[33] This agenda owed much to the centrality of a socialist-inflected worldview, which saw the international system as intertwined with a Euro-American capitalism that also explained the preponderant influence of Western culture. Regularly defined in the mid-1960s as opposition to neocolonialism, this line of thinking marked a shift from an emphasis on anti-colonialism against European metropoles to an anti-imperialism against creeping US

[32] See chapters by Hernandez and Hosek, Mahler, Asselin, Irwin, Paranzino, and Covey.
[33] See chapters by Mahler, Paranzino, and Friedman.

preponderance. As Michael Goebel argues, this shift was necessary for meaningful Tricontinental solidarity; decolonization allowed Afro-Asian states to recognize and identify with the threat of dollar diplomacy that long inspired resistance in Latin America.[34] Tricontinentalism – cohering as it did in the wake of decolonization's supposed triumph – required an ambitious program to combat pernicious forms of foreign domination that lingered in the wake of "flag" independence.

The broad definition of imperialism meant that Tricontinentalism exhibited hostility not just to states of the Global North but also to Southern governments deemed insufficiently revolutionary.[35] Participation in the Anti-Imperial Project bestowed an element of legitimacy on stateless nationalist parties throughout the twentieth century, which they used against both metropoles and political opponents when claiming authority as governments-in-waiting.[36] But the fight against neocolonialism added a new wrinkle. Rejecting Bandung's notion of "unity in diversity" that made room for an array of states with competing ideologies, Tricontinentalism defined a loose ideological litmus test based on commitment to militant confrontation, socialist redistribution of economic wealth, and anti-imperial foreign policies. This approach defined an exclusive but ideally more unified vision of Southern solidarity. A coalition of vanguard parties and states led a movement that would grow as moderate Third World states either aligned with the ideology or suffered radical revolutions. This approach opened the door for participation by insurgent revolutionary parties to play a vital role in Tricontinentalism, opposing colonialism and occasionally Southern governments that radicals claimed were complicit with imperialism.[37]

Third, the Tricontinental reading of anti-imperialism sought to wed the program of Southern sovereignty with Marxism. Anti-imperialists found common cause with the Soviet Union from its founding, but the

---

[34] Michael Goebel, "Forging a Proto-Third World?" in Michele Louro, Carolien Stolte, Heather Streets-Salter, and Sana Tannoury-Karam, eds., *The League Against Imperialism: Lives and Afterlives* (Leiden: Leiden University Press, 2020), 72. See "Introduction" in Thomas C. Field Jr., Stella Krepp, and Vanni Pettinà, *Latin America and the Global Cold War* (Chapel Hill: University of North Carlina Press, 2020), 5.

[35] See Kwame Nkrumah, *Neo-Colonialism: The Last Stage of Imperialism* (New York: International Publishers, 1966); Jean-Paul Sartre, *Colonialism and Neocolonialism*, Steve Brewer, trans. (New York: Routledge, 2006).

[36] In this volume, Asselin argues for this tendency in North Vietnamese diplomacy, Parrott in Guinea-Bissau.

[37] Authenticity was important for exiled or minority revolutionary movements. See chapters by Asselin, Paranzino, Irwin, and Parrott.

dogmatism of international Communism and its inability to fully integrate either the national or racial questions prevented a wholesale merging of the movements. These divisions – along with Moscow's ill-timed promotion of peaceful coexistence and China's perception of the Soviet Union as an imperial power – fueled the Sino-Soviet split and complicated the construction of solidarity. Nonetheless, Tricontinentalism spread precisely because it sought to address problems specific to Third World states using a worldview based on Marxist structural analysis. The movement, in short, shared a sense that underdevelopment, racial inequality, and cultural marginalization grew from capitalist exploitation without accepting a single model of action or political mobilization. Tricontinentalists did not abandon European communism because most never fully adhered to it. Rather, major theorists including Castro and Cabral argued Southern states were building on earlier Communist victories by leading a new stage in the anti-imperial revolution that addressed lingering inequalities.

Most Tricontinental states defined their socialism as distinct from Soviet communism in two ways that made it better suited for the postcolonial context. First, they wedded it to the creation of sovereign nation-states that would collectively combat racism and change the international system; second, they eschewed classical definitions of class warfare in favor of a colonized (South) versus colonizer (North) mentality, wherein the colonized occupied the role of the masses and the colonizing imperialists a sort of global bourgeois.[38] This formulation allowed for a greater emphasis on national unity in the anti-imperial struggle – both before and after independence – while opening avenues for broad solidarity.[39] More

---

[38] Like Tricontinentalism, the North-South terms were used inconsistently, but other terminologies – exploiters-exploited, center-periphery – captured similar dichotomies. Young, adjusting Anour Abdel-Malek, argues the adaptation of Marxist thought to colonial subjectivity and non-Western cultures (ideas tied to the South) informed Tricontinentalism, though Mahler contends a "resistant imaginary" to capitalism inspired Tricontinental color politics and informed the Global South idea. I do not see these as mutually exclusive, though I define North-South mainly along historic/geographic lines created by industrialized imperialism, with the diaspora concept explaining political and cultural linkages across the flexible North-South divide. Effectively, shared experiences of/resistance to empire and exploitation led diverse constituencies to identify with Tricontinental thought, which increasingly reflected Mahler's ideologically inflected color politics from the late 1960s as racial minorities in the North and sub-Saharan African revolutions gained prominence in the movement broadly and Cuban policy/cultural production in particular. Young, *Postcolonialism*, 175; Mahler, *From the Tricontinental to the Global South*, 6.

[39] See chapters by Mahler, Parrott, and Paranzino.

problematically, it cast the small middle classes of the Third World as outsiders or minor imperialists and encouraged party leaders to dismiss even legitimate dissent as the product of external influence. The result was ideologically-based identities – both in terms of local nationalism and global anti-imperialism – that were fungible. Assimilated or educated classes in the Global South, Northern Diasporas, and even Euro-Americans could all align with the revolution, so long as they adopted sufficiently anti-imperial identifications and political programs.[40]

Fourth, Tricontinentalism effectively picked sides in the Cold War but created few permanent institutions for both ideological and practical reasons. Third World nationalists were committed to non-alignment and independent foreign policies, but the communist bloc offered models for politico-economic reinvention, material assistance, and diplomatic protection from Western intervention. After early attempts to formalize a radical Third World alliance faltered due to limited resources and superpower hostility, many Tricontinental states looked East for help. Cooperation with communist countries – particularly the Soviet bloc – provided an avenue for moderating power disparities between small iconoclastic states and a Western-dominated international system hostile to revolutions. The Sino-Soviet split complicated these alliances, but competition for the preeminent role in the world revolution encouraged both communist powers to expand their involvement in the Third World.[41] Aggressive, agrarian Maoism contrasted with Soviet preferences for gradual revolution, peaceful coexistence with the United States, and orthodox Marxism. The Maoist brand of socialism influenced and more fully aligned with the Tricontinental worldview, but China's emphasis on opposing the Soviet Union (and Moscow's Third World allies) ultimately reduced Beijing's influence. By contrast, the Soviet Union accommodated itself to the heterodox socialism where revolutionary movements proved effective, and industrialized Eastern countries could offer more aid than agrarian China. Radical Third World relations with Moscow were not always warm, but sufficient ideological affinities and the need for material assistance made Soviet bloc linkages vital for Cuba, Vietnam, and many African liberation movements. The result was a diplomatic balancing act, but one which

---

[40] See chapters by Hernandez and Hosek, and Parrott. Mahler and Rodriguez both highlight the extent to which Tricontinentalism merged ideological conviction with color politics, discussed more below.

[41] See chapters by Friedman and Paranzino; Friedman, *Shadow Cold War*.

leaned toward the Soviet Union by the late-1960s and developed further in the next decade.

The combination of ideological and strategic considerations explains why Tricontinentalism remained loosely organized and states non-aligned, even as they collectively leaned left. International institutions and major post-Havana conferences threatened to exacerbate Third World or Sino-Soviet tensions and could possibly invite Western intervention. This last issue highlights the reality that as much as Soviet (and to a lesser extent Chinese) aid assisted revolutions and radical states, the communist ability to project military power trailed the West into the 1970s. Tricontinentalists thus relied upon flexible ad hoc alliances to advance their goals. OSPAAAL provided a clearinghouse for information, but there were no bylaws or regular summits as occurred with the NAM. Rather, the UN and NAM became forums for Tricontinental cooperation and negotiation. Aid came mostly via bilateral relationships with communist states and regional Third World allies, with many parties also making broad appeals for assistance from sympathetic Western audiences and progressive European governments.

Fifth, Tricontinentalism hinged on non-white racial identity, but in a specific way. This tendency sprang from two factors: its distinct opposition to a US-championed form of imperialism overlaid with Anglocentric race connotations and the historic attempt to bridge Marxist and nationalist visions of revolution. Unlike Bandung's implicit racial solidarity and Non-Alignment's conscious attempt to transcend the issue, Tricontinentalism used racialized rhetoric to mobilize support and to focus attention on deep-seated social inequalities closely associated with empire and identity. Political movements incorporated cultural renovation projects that often balanced sub-national, national, and pan-ethnic identities by selectively redeploying local traditions and regional affinities under the umbrella of anti-imperial socialist revolution.[42] Racial identification thus became a fluid, often symbolic element within Tricontinentalism. Rather than a static biological category, "color" sat at the intersection of programs meant to combat political, economic, and cultural disparities. It became shorthand for

---

[42] See chapters by Mahler, Parrott, and Covey. Tricontinentalism envisioned culturally distinct continents and peoples forming a common struggle against the shared threat of imperialism, with the balance between racial/cultural distinction and shared interests/programs directly informing iconography and ideology. Thus, black, brown, or Pan-Asian movements would unite in pursuit of radical self-determination.

a politico-ideological affinity associated with the Global South, what Mahler describes as a "metonymic color politics."[43] Tricontinental definitions of non-white races stretched to incorporate light-skinned elites in North Africa and Latin America, and they allowed cultivation of white Euro-Americans as anti-imperial allies and even members of nationalist movements in Mozambique and South Africa. Tensions existed because the line between race pride and race hate was fungible, but most theorists argued racism was anathema to the egalitarian Tricontinental movement. Indeed, emphasis on specific racial identities threatened to divide the diverse anti-imperial coalition if used as the sole foundation of political unity. A generalized claim to non-whiteness thus became a powerful rhetorical and symbolic representation of historic oppression as well as a rallying cry that empowered and connected movements.

Sixth, all these elements encouraged Tricontinentalism to make greater space for nonstate movements. Nearly 40 percent of Havana conference delegations came from anti-colonial liberation parties or leftist opposition operating in independent Southern states (see Map 0.2). And Tricontinentalism arguably proved most beneficial to such groups as the African National Congress (ANC) and South Vietnam's National Liberation Front ("Viet Cong"), which could claim legitimacy as authentic revolutions when recognized by Third World allies and operate with funds from benefactors like the Soviet Union. Treated essentially as governments-in-waiting, these groups were important components of the successful Anti-Imperial Project since they weakened imperial and collaborationist states from within (see Figure 0.1). Additionally, the ideological and racial flexibility of Tricontinentalism encouraged appeals to all "progressive" forces, which included Western domestic organizations that opposed the policies of sitting governments.[44] However, the process of identifying authentic revolutionary movements and sufficiently progressive allies in Western states was a complicated one that nominally considered ideology, identity, and geography but revolved heavily around personal connections. Publications such as OSPAAAL's *Tricontinental*, conferences like the Sixth Pan-African Congress of 1974, and various diplomatic junkets sponsored by countries such as North Vietnam and Cuba identified groups and built networks between them. But membership in the Tricontinental movement was fluid and its decentralized nature

---

[43] Mahler, *From the Tricontinental to the Global South*, 13.
[44] See chapters by Hernandez and Hosek, Asselin, Parrott, and Paranzino.

militated against clear leadership, so there was not always agreement on which parties represented authentic revolutions or allies.

Nonetheless, this flexibility and transnational appeal was vital to Tricontinentalism's popularity. Marginalized peoples in places as diverse as the United States and Palestine gained inspiration from this global challenge to the status quo, defining fictive transnational kinships within the Third World framework as a way of building domestic momentum on foreign successes.[45] OSPAAAL literature and the writings of Tricontinental personalities such as Mao, Fanon, Nkrumah, Cabral, and Guevara were pivotal in building this solidarity. New critiques of domestic systems evolved by reproducing and adapting the Marxist worldview, ideas of self-determination, and ideological solidarity central to Tricontinentalism. In Western democracies, this most often inspired "Third World" pride movements and the rise of New Left politics, though a few groups – such as the Black Panthers or the Baader–Meinhof Gang – adopted either the trappings or tactics of armed revolt.[46] Violent uprisings were more common in the West's Southern allies, such as those waged by the PLO and Naxalite Movement in India. Since Tricontinental legitimacy came in part from the ability to wage revolution, internal competition within these movements rewarded aggressive factions with expanded membership (at least temporarily), a trend that partially explains the terrorist tactics of groups like the PLO.[47]

Finally, Tricontinentalism proved attractive because it produced tangible results, if never on the scale that ardent advocates desired. The most obvious concrete benefit was material aid – educational, medical, and military. Military assistance was vital to revolutions in Africa, Asia, and Latin America because their legitimacy required them to wage armed struggles, but providing aid – in whatever form – also legitimized benefactors' commitment to redressing global inequalities. Generally, there existed two primary avenues, either involving regional assistance or the import of arms from the communist world (especially Czechoslovakia, China, and the Soviet Union). Regarding the former, anti-imperial states

---

[45] Komozi Woodard, "Amiri Baraka, the Congress of African People, and Black Power Politics from the 1961 United Nations Protests to the 1972 Gary convention," in Peniel Joseph, ed., *The Black Power Movement: Rethinking the Civil Rights-Black Power Era* (New York: Routledge, 2006), 62.

[46] See Pulido, *Black, Brown, Yellow, and Left*; Cynthia Young, *Soul Power*; Joshua Bloom and Waldo E. Martin, Jr., *Black against Empire: The History and Politics of the Black Panther Party* (Berkeley: University of California Press, 2016); Max Elbaum, *Revolution in the Air: Sixties Radicals turn to Lenin, Mao and Che* (New York: Verso, 2002).

[47] See Chamberlin, *Global Offensive*.

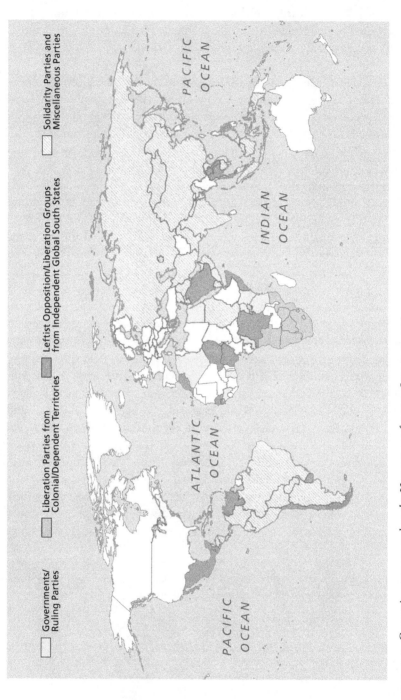

MAP 0.2 *Countries represented at the Havana conference, January 1966*
Governments/ruling parties: Algeria, Republic of Congo (Brazzaville), Cuba, Ghana, Guinea, Kenya, United Arab Republic,

Governments/
Ruling Parties

Liberation Parties from
Colonial/Dependent Territories

Leftist Opposition/Liberation Groups
from Independent Global South States

Solidarity Parties and
Miscellaneous Parties

PACIFIC
OCEAN

INDIAN
OCEAN

ATLANTIC
OCEAN

PACIFIC
OCEAN

Democratic Republic of Vietnam, Tanzania, Uganda. **Liberation parties from colonial/dependent territories:** South Africa, South-West Africa, Angola, Lesotho, Botswana, Guiana, Guinea-Bissau, Mauritius, St. Thomas and Prince Island, Mozambique, Palestine, Puerto Rico, Swaziland (Eswatini), South Yemen, Zimbabwe. **Leftist opposition/liberation groups from independent Global South states:** Burundi, Congo-Lusaka, Chile, Guatemala, Haiti, Laos, Lebanon, Morocco, Mexico, Niger, Nigeria, Saudi Arabia, Senegal, Thailand, Uruguay, Venezuela, Somaliland. **Solidarity parties:** Argentina, Bolivia, Brazil, Cambodia, Colombia, (North) Korea, Costa Rica, China, Cyprus. Ecuador, El Salvador Guadeloupe, (French) Guiana-Cayenne, Honduras, India, Indonesia, Iran, Iraq, Jamaica, Japan, Jordan, Malaya, Martinique, Mongolia, Nepal, Nicaragua, Oman, Pakistan, Panama, Paraguay, Peru, Dominican Republic, Rwanda, Syria, Sudan, Trinidad and Tobago, South Vietnam, USSR, Yemen.
Source: Proceedings, First Solidarity Conference of the Peoples of Africa, Asia, and Latin America, 1966.

such as Egypt set the standard by supplying arms to liberation movements in nearby countries in the early years of the Cold War. Later, Algeria and Cuba exported weapons and expertise to neighboring states in attempts to spread revolution across their respective continents, and the North Vietnamese provided shelter to the Khmer Rouge during its formative years.[48] Southern intercontinental exchanges were rarer for both practical and political reasons, which explains the need for alliances with the communist superpowers and states like the arms-exporting Czechoslovakia. After setbacks in the 1960s in the Congo and Cuba, the Eastern bloc increased its capacity to deliver assistance and such aid became increasingly important to revolutionary movements, especially in Africa.[49] Cuba, the Eastern bloc, and Western civil society groups also sponsored educational exchanges and provided medical assistance, enabling liberation movements to reinforce their legitimacy by providing social services during and after the revolutionary period.

Of equal if not greater importance was the political power of Tricontinentalism. Nascent revolutions and isolated states gained confidence through association with other successful movements, or what Ryan Irwin calls in Chapter 5 the power of "analogies." External comparisons and solidarity helped revolutionaries define their movements, legitimize specific agendas, and imagine future successes that seemed unlikely in the present. Even where these connections did not produce revolution, the emergence of transnational discourses popularized once provocative ideas such as economic nationalization and legitimized liberation organizations to the point where they gained hearings at the UN and other supranational organizations.[50] These analogies also operated outside the Third World, providing avenues through which disaffected Westerners found the language of anti-imperialism necessary to challenge the Cold War excesses of their own governments. The result was the rise of the vocal political opposition in the North that sympathized or identified with the Global South, most often associated with the New Left and Black Power movements.[51] Widespread

---

[48] See Paranzino and Irwin in this volume; Connelly, *A Diplomatic Revolution*; SADET, *The Road to Democracy in South Africa*.

[49] See Natalia Telepneva, "Saving Ghana's Revolution: The Demise of Kwame Nkrumah and The Evolution of Soviet Policy in Africa, 1966–1970," *Journal of Cold War Studies* 20:4 (Fall 2018): 4–25.

[50] See chapters by Irwin, Chamberlin, Asselin, and Byrne; Dietrich, *Oil Revolution*, 133–138, 154–157.

[51] See chapters by Parrott, and Hernandez and Hosek. See also, Mahler, *From the Tricontinental to the Global South*; Slobodian, *Foreign Front*; Elbaum, *Revolution in the Air*; Bloom and Martin, *Black against Empire*.

solidarity allowed for the imagining of ambitious Southern agendas while increasing the potential repercussions (international and domestic) of Western interventions in Vietnam, Angola, and elsewhere. Tricontinentalism allowed marginalized nations and parties to feel less isolated as they challenged historic Euro-American linkages and sought to remake their societies in hopeful but frequently disruptive ways.

SITUATING THE TRICONTINENTAL ERA WITHIN THE ANTI-IMPERIAL PROJECT

In recognizing the Tricontinental era as distinct from the earlier Bandung moment, it is worth considering in greater detail how Tricontinentalism fit into the longer history of anti-imperial politics in the Global South. Tricontinentalism represented a single strand of thought, but it pulled from earlier manifestations of the Anti-Imperial Project. Neither an evolutionary process nor inherently radical, this project took shape as competing visions of anti-imperialism coexisted, jockeyed for support, and borrowed from each other.[52] Shared worldviews rose to prominence when leaders in the Global South adopted similar approaches to deal with contingent but comparable problems and opportunities. Specific ideologies or strategies gained influence when structural changes to imperial practice and the international system invested Southern actors with increased cultural, economic, or political power that allowed them to pursue more ambitious programs. Yet Northern – and specifically Western – power proved robust, meaning the distance between imagined possibilities and realities has remained frustratingly persistent. The result was an alternation between pragmatic compromise and radical challenges, which gradually chipped away at Northern preponderance but rarely at the pace or to the extent desired by anti-imperialists. Tricontinentalism represented one of the radical swings of this pendulum.

Localized resistance challenged European expansion from its beginnings into the twentieth century, but pan-civilizational programs informed the first attempts to forge Southern solidarity. The most diplomatically powerful cohered around independent states such as Japan and the Ottoman Empire, which championed Pan-Asianism and Pan-Islamism, respectively. Cemil Aydin argues they offered "a corrective

---

[52] For this phenomenon in the Middle East, see Nathan Citino, *Envisioning the Arab Future: Modernization in US-Arab Relations, 1945–1967* (New York: Cambridge University Press, 2017).

critique of the world order" by universalizing Western notions of civilization while celebrating non-Western traditions, undermining the racialized
hierarchy that informed Euro-American claims to superiority.[53] Yet in key
ways, these were reformist movements. The Pan-Asian and Pan-Islamic
projects essentially claimed equal status alongside the world's modern
empires rather than seeking to upset the system itself.[54] Though more
ambitious, they were comparable to the efforts of the Indian National
Congress and what became the South African ANC, which redeployed
imperial claims in order to increase the authority of a mostly educated,
Westernized elite in colonial governance. Even Pan-Africanism bent to the
limitations of the era, though its opposition to the interrelated policies of
American segregation and European colonialism transcended regional
borders and the need for state sponsorship to offer a radical intellectual
challenge to empire. For example, most speeches and conclusions of the
1900 Pan-African Conference in London, where DuBois powerfully
articulated the twentieth century's greatest problem as that of a global
"color line," primarily demanded equality and a greater role for an
educated black elite within government.[55] These pan-civilizational campaigns imagined cross-border solidarity and struck at the cultural and
racial hierarchies of Northern imperialism. But their end goals involved
participation in the existing system, and many successful examples
deployed their own paternalistic and/or chauvinistic assumptions even
as they challenged Western imperialism.

While cultural and pan-projects influenced Tricontinentalism, the
worldview owed much to interwar organizing, as Anne Garland
Mahler notes in Chapter 1. World War I weakened European claims to
superiority and, with the October Revolution demonstrating the

---

[53] Cemil Aydin, *The Politics of Anti-Westernism in Asia: Visions of World Order in Pan-
Islamic and Pan-Asian Thought* (New York: Columbia University Press, 2019), 7–8. For
a comparable theory of this process at the national level, see Partha Chatterjee, *Nationalist
Thought and the Colonial World: A Derivative Discourse* (London: Zed Books, 1983),
50–51, 54–81.

[54] Michel Gobat argues anti-imperialism also informed Latin American identity when faced
with a rising United States. Gobat, "The Invention of Latin America: A Transnational
History of Anti-Imperialism, Democracy, and Race," *American Historical Review* 118:5
(December 2013): 1345–1375.

[55] W. E. B. DuBois, "To the nations of the world," Series 1A General Correspondence, W.E.
B. DuBois Papers, University of Massachusetts Amherst: https://credo.library.umass.edu
/view/full/mums312-b004-i321. See also Marika Sherwood, *Origins of Pan-Africanism:
Henry Sylvester Williams, Africa, and the African Diaspora* (New York: Routledge,
2011), chapter 6; Hakim Adi, *Pan-Africanism: A History* (London: Bloomsbury, 2018),
19–23.

feasibility of revolution, initiated a radical interwar period that moved beyond calls for reform. Communism did not inspire this radical turn; indeed, myriad local frustrations and anti-colonial networks formed before World War I and fueled major revolts during the conflict.[56] But, as Robert J. C. Young notes, "[Marxist] political discourse constituted an instrument through which anti-colonial struggles could be translated from one colonial arena to another."[57] Lenin's formulation of empire as the highest stage of capitalism provided a global framework for under-standing Western hegemony and mobilizing non-industrialized popula-tions, ultimately legitimizing alliances with anti-colonial nationalists as first steps toward socialist revolution. Intra-imperial migration and urbanization helped spread Marxist thought, aided by the foundation of the Comintern in 1919 and attempts to integrate Asia into a global vision of revolution. The result was a flurry of organizing. The less closely policed metropolitan cities of Paris, London, Berlin, and New York became hubs linking global anti-imperial networks, joining established regional centers such as Cairo, Delhi, Shanghai, Tokyo, and Mexico City. Communist parties offered some of the strongest critiques of empire, racism, and fascism, expanding membership from Lisbon to the US South and becoming centers for nationalist revolt when colonial crackdowns weakened alternative parties.[58] Communist networks offered subject and marginalized peoples the freedom and funds to explore radical forms of resistance and exchange ideas on social reforms at home, connecting Asia, Africa, Europe, and (intermittently) Latin America behind a common worldview.

Yet like Tricontinentalism, this era's brand of leftist anti-imperialism achieved its broadest impact by moving beyond the strict appeal of Soviet-style communism. The Comintern and Berlin-based League Against Imperialism (LAI) provide examples. Launched in 1927 with Comintern funds, the LAI became a meeting place for a variety of left-leaning dissi-dents, ranging from the francophone African communist Lamine Senghor

---

[56] See, for example, Heather Streets-Salter, *World War One in Southeast Asia: Colonialism and Anticolonialism in an Era of Global Conflict* (New York: Cambridge University Press, 2017).

[57] Young, *Postcolonialism*, 169.

[58] See Parrott and Mahler in this volume; Sophie Quinn-Judge, *Ho Chi Minh: The Missing Years, 1919–1941* (Berkeley: University of California Press, 2003); Robin D. G. Kelley, *Hammer and Hoe: Alabama Communists during the Great Depression* (Chapel Hill: University of North Carolina Press, 1990); Michael Goebel, *Anti-Imperial Metropolis: Interwar Paris and the Seeds of Third World Nationalism* (New York: Cambridge University Press, 2015).

28   R. Joseph Parrott

to Jawaharlal Nehru.[59] The Marxist worldview provided a useful conceptualization of empire, but the racial and cultural inequities that justified
colonialism and segregation led them to define Southern liberation – not
a proletariat-led emancipation – as driving forces of global socialism.[60]
This strained relations with Moscow, whose decision to prioritize class
warfare in 1928 mixed with Comintern inflexibility to gradually alienate
nationalists and anti-racist activists. But this break encouraged the
redeployment of Marxist ideas in creative ways, reflecting Oleksa
Drachewych and Ian McKay's argument that the Comintern served less
as "prison-house" than "seed-bed" for revolutionary ideas.[61] Always
quite heterogenous, local parties and relationships created through groups
like the LAI inspired a diverse, decentralized network beyond Moscow's
control. Circulation and adaptation of leftist programs encouraged anti-
imperialists generally to strengthen their commitment to social justice
programs and nationalists to break completely with imperial metropoles.
Thus, a socialist worldview influenced Nehru's organizing for *Purna
Swaraj* (self-rule) and later INC foreign policy, while also helping con-
vince exiled Algerian Messali Hadj to embrace independence from France
by merging leftist anti-imperialism with an Islamist form of Arab
nationalism.[62]

It is important to recognize, however, that leftist anti-imperial influence
was just one factor promoting this radical turn in the interwar period.
Pan-projects informed some of the most popular movements of the early
1920s, notably the Indian Khilafat and Marcus Garvey's black nationalism. The Wilsonian Moment proved fleeting, but non-leftist radicals
adopted the language of nationalism to demand clean breaks from
European control. Specific visions linking cultural renewal with independent nations motivated some of the most successful interwar movements.

---

[59] See Michele Louro et al., "The League Against Imperialism: Lives and Afterlives," in
Louro et al., *The League Against Imperialism*.
[60] Minkah Makalani – after Mignolo – argues this "heretical intellectualism" emerged from
the inability of Eurocentric, modernist Marxism to fully conceptualize the Southern
experience of empire. Makalani, *In the Cause of Freedom: Radical Black
Internationalism, 1917–1939* (Chapel Hill: University of North Carolina Press, 2011),
8; Walter D. Mignolo, "Delinking: The Rhetoric of Modernity, the Logic of Coloniality
and the Grammar of De-coloniality," *Cultural Studies* 21:2–3 (2007), 483–484.
[61] Oleksa Drachewych and Ian McKay, "Left Transnationalism?" in Drachewych and
McKay, eds., *Left Transnationalism: The Communist International and the National,
Colonial, and Racial Questions* (Montreal: McGill-Queen's University Press, 2020), 32.
[62] See Michele Louro, "An Anti-Imperialist Echo in India" and Dónal Hassett, "An
Independent Path: Algerian Nationalists and the League Against Imperialism," in Louro
et al., *The League Against Imperialism*.

Perhaps most famously Gandhi's vision for India set out in *Hind Swaraj* rejected foreign rule, Western civilization, and aspects of modernization in ways that contrasted with pre-war Pan-Asian movements and frustrated allies like Nehru. In the Middle East, suspicion of secularism meant local and Pan-Arab nationalists radicalized the anti-imperial movement in Syria and Egypt. Even the Baath Party, which cohered around Paris-trained radicals, adopted a specifically Arabic view of socialism that did not seriously incorporate Marxist elements until the Tricontinental era.

Socialist anti-imperialism clearly did not dominate every interwar movement, but it proved important for efforts to knit movements together. Alternative anti-imperial networks did exist – notably the authoritarian, anti-liberal modernism that connected Nazi Germany, India, and the Middle East – but leftist internationalism provided the most effective and widely adopted foundation for building solidarity across regions and cultures.[63] Its revolutionary worldview was universal, allowing adaptation (with or without Comintern permission) within a variety of circumstances and political formations. This latter point is especially important given Frederick Cooper's reminder that the nation-state was not the inevitable result of decolonization.[64] Southern applications of socialism legitimized everything from progressive pan-civilizational movements to what Gary Wilder has called "postimperial and postnational federation" that ideally transcended North-South divides.[65]

The combination of universality and adaptability explains why the socialist worldview became so important to interwar anti-imperialism. Adapting Marxist conceptions of empire provided activists with a consistent logic for situating local struggles within larger contexts, reimagining both national and pan-projects in more progressive ways while stitching them together across regional and identarian lines.[66] The resulting framework informed nascent Afro-Asianism and later Tricontinentalism. One can see this process in Pan-African politics of the era. Minkah Makalani argues Asian challenges to Eurocentric

[63] David Motadel, "The Global Authoritarian Moment and the Revolt Against Empire," *American Historical Review* 124:3 (June 2019): 843–877.

[64] Fredrick Cooper, "Possibility and Constraint: African Independence in Historical Perspective," *Journal of African History* 49:2 (2008): 167–196.

[65] Gary Wilder, "Decolonization and Postnational Democracy," in Andrew Arato et al., eds., *Forms of Pluralism and Democratic Constitutionalism* (New York: Columbia University Press, 2018), 54.

[66] Both Goebel and Carolien Stolte note the continuing importance of pan-projects to national and radical solidarity. See Stolte, "Towards Afro-Asia," in Louro et al., *The League Against Imperialism*, 348–350; Goebel, *Anti-Imperial Metropolis*, chapter 8.

communism helped open the movement to black radicals such as George Padmore and Garan Kouyaté, who sought new associations after the Comintern proved an unsuitable vehicle to address the race question.[67] This coincided with the leftward drift of traditional leaders like DuBois now disillusioned with calls for gradual, elite-driven change. A powerful black radicalism formed at the intersection, integrating race consciousness into a Transatlantic movement against empire and racism that also high-lighted avenues for broader collaboration. Hakim Adi notes the program-matic and personal connections linking the Pan-African and Subject People's Conferences of 1945 illustrate how Southern socialist anti-imperialisms encouraged the emergence of Afro-Asian solidarity.[68] DuBois recognized the reality of a global color line separating North and South decades prior, but interwar leftist networks translated solidar-ity from the realm of thought into concrete politics.

The Bandung era built on this Afro-Asian unity, but the new possibil-ities offered by postcolonial diplomacy moderated the thrust of the Anti-Imperial Project. After Indian independence in 1947 launched the process of decolonization, the proliferation of dozens of new countries created an opportunity to build formal diplomatic alliances without having to oper-ate through colonial administrative centers or European-controlled organizations like the LAI. It also compelled revolutionaries to become statesmen responsible for the management of diverse, often underdevel-oped nations. The process of establishing stable governments and reinfor-cing sovereignty led many to temporarily moderate their internationalist ideologies. Bandung emerged in 1955 from this context, organized by moderate anglophone Asian states seeking to manage regional tensions exacerbated by the Cold War. Their goals were anti-imperial but did not envision a militant bloc. Rather, Bandung sought to encourage decolon-ization while subsuming ideological differences within respect for state borders and diplomatic collaboration in pursuit of common goals.[69] The Third World that the Bandung organizers envisioned was neutralist; states retained maximum flexibility to pursue national interests. As Michele Louro notes in her perceptive study of Nehru, this approach was "distinct

[67] Makalani, *In the Cause of Freedom*, 42–43, 76–82; Brent Hayes Edwards, *The Practice of Diaspora: Literature, Translation, and the Rise of Black Internationalism* (Cambridge, MA: Harvard University Press, 2003), chapter 5.
[68] Adi, *Pan-Africanism*, 125.
[69] See Amitav Acharya and Seng Tan, "The Normative Relevance of the Bandung Conference for Contemporary Asian and International World Order," in Tan and Acharya, eds., *Bandung Revisited*, 1–14.

if not anathema to interwar anti-imperialism."[70] In some ways, it recalled late nineteenth-century attempts to claim status *within* the extant international system, a notion that seemed plausible given the proliferation of nation-states and their supposed equality within global institutions such as the UN.

The state-based reformism quickly proved insufficient. Postcolonial governments – moderate and radical, regionally powerful and marginalized – had varied interests and concerns. Attendees at Bandung were unable even to agree on a common definition of imperialism, though all opposed it. India was a regional power that used neutralism to its advantage, but vague promises for coordination offered little to weaker states burdened with unwanted linkages to former metropoles and minimal leverage. Western interventions still ran roughshod over economic and political sovereignty, as evidenced by the Iran coup and the Suez and Congo crises. Radical leaders such as Indonesia's Sukarno and Egypt's Gamal Abdel Nasser argued aggressive action was needed to root out Northern advantages baked into the international system. This approach contrasted sharply with Nehru's Panchsheel ideal of peaceful coexistence through mutual respect, which augured for a passive non-alignment in line with Bandung's final communique but struggled to respond to events like Suez.[71]

The radical shift led directly to Tricontinentalism. The AAPSO meetings in the 1950s reflected this inclination, incorporating nationalist organizations and flirting with expanded communist alliances. The lack of Third World consensus scuttled attempts to organize an inclusive Bandung II, but the dream of speaking with one voice continued even as ideological lines developed.[72] The formation of the NAM must be understood in this context. It was not a singular movement but a forum where diverging strands of anti-imperialism competed. Nasser hoped it would cement his leadership while Nehru wanted to restrain the radicalization of the Afro-Asian movement.[73] Yet by 1964, militancy was winning out. At that year's NAM conference, Sukarno joined with Nasser, Kwame Nkrumah, and others to champion an active struggle against imperialism. Peaceful coexistence, Sukarno argued, would only emerge from "a

[70] Louro, *Comrades*, 268; Munro, *The Anticolonial Front*, 247, 273–275.
[71] Cindy Ewing, "The Colombo Powers: Crafting Diplomacy in the Third World and Launching Afro-Asia at Bandung," *Cold War History* 19:1 (2019), 17–19.
[72] See chapters by Friedman and Byrne.
[73] Lorenz M. Lüthi, *Cold Wars: Asia, the Middle East, Europe* (New York: Cambridge University Press, 2020), 291.

balance of forces" in which "imperialist States" confronted a Third World with "equal strength we can obtain only through solidarity."[74] These individuals gradually lost power in coming years, but there was a clear shift occurring. The first generation of statesman leaders began to give way to the militant, socialist cadre of Guevara, Castro, Fanon, Cabral, Mehdi Ben Barka, Le Duan, and Yasser Arafat well before the Havana Conference.

EXTENT AND LIMITS OF THE TRICONTINENTAL ERA

In some ways, Tricontinentalism was an attempt to revisit interwar radicalism using the power of independent nation-states. While early radicals flirted with alternative political formations – notably Nasser's UAR and Nkrumah's Pan-African dreams for West Africa – Tricontinental adherents pragmatically accepted the nation-state as the primary mover of international affairs. But they also understood the limits of Southern sovereignty, which made Bandung reformism insufficient. The US-supported coups in Ghana and Indonesia illustrated both the necessity of militant policies and dangers of pursuing them alone. Tricontinental solidarity promised to protect vulnerable revisionist states by imagining new challenges to Northern hegemony that used the full array of diplomatic, military, and economic resources available to postcolonial nations.[75] Armed revolutions grabbed headlines, but they were one tool in the larger anti-imperial arsenal. Specific initiatives, such as the Cuban attempt to change international law on mercenaries that Eric Covey examines in Chapter 11, were sometimes too ideologically specific to gain widespread support. But their articulation at the international level influenced the tenor of Third World politics and helped legitimize ambitious reimaginings of the international system that struggled to gain traction both before and after the Tricontinental era.

---

[74] Sukarno, "Address to the Second Meeting of the Cairo Conference of Heads of States of the Non-Aligned Movement, October 6, 1964," in Ministry of National Guidance, *Conference of Heads of State and Governments of Non-Aligned Countries* (Cairo: National Publication House, 1964), 30. Sukarno and Nkrumah increasingly aligned with nascent Tricontinentalism before their leftward drifts helped invite their ousters. Though Egypt sent a delegation to Havana and championed anti-imperialism, Nasser's regional ambitions strained relations with revolutionary Iraq and his communist crackdowns further weakened ties to Tricontinentalists.
[75] See chapters by Hernandez and Hosek, and Covey.

Therefore, it may be useful to consider the programs related to the New International Economic Order (NIEO) as a product of this era, if not directly of Tricontinentalism. While emphasis on UN negotiations and incrementalism implies connections to Bandung, the program's attempts to challenge Northern hegemony by advocating global socialism reflected Tricontinental priorities and offered a revolutionary challenge to the international order.[76] That advocates believed such a project was possible owed much to the politics of the time. The radical shift in the Third World inspired ambitious agendas while the proliferation of armed revolts made confrontational diplomacy seem tame by comparison. Tricontinental advocates and sympathizers – notably Algeria – acted as catalysts for the NIEO in Southern dominated forums like the 1964 UN Conference on Trade and Development (UNCTAD) that launched the G-77. At the same time, revolutionary states such as Iraq and Libya guided OPEC toward more aggressive negotiations, galvanizing calls for resource sovereignty at the center of the NIEO model. While Jeffrey James Byrne argues in Chapter 6 that the Algerian drift from Cuba signaled the decline of Tricontinentalism, it may be more accurate to describe a divergence of tactics, at least at first. Algeria continued to support armed revolutions for anti-colonial African groups (and famously sheltered Black Panthers into the 1970s) but increasingly emphasized the pursuit of radical programs via diplomatic and economic means. Yet the intellectual connection between these two strategies remained. Head of state Houari Boumédiène conceptualized the nation's international development strategy as "an extension of the struggle for national liberation" and implied that assertive economic proposals were preferrable alternatives to violent means of undoing structural inequalities.[77]

The relationship between these economic proposals, Tricontinental momentum, and the *threat* of militancy partially explains why such initiatives gained broad support. Revolutionary states embraced policies such as resource nationalization, and the popularity of radical leftist ideologies during this period encouraged moderate states to follow suit. As Giuliano Garavini notes in his detailed study of OPEC, the Venezuelan government

---

[76] See Nils Gilman's overview of NIEO priorities in his introduction to a great special issue on the topic. Gilman, "The New International Economic Order: A Reintroduction," *Humanity* 6:1 (Spring 2015): 2.

[77] Boumédiène argued acceptance of resource sovereignty and the NIEO projects was necessary "if we wish to avert the tragic possibility that this problem might one day become a source of uncontrollable conflagration." Houari Boumédiène, "The Problems of Third World Development," *The Black Scholar* 6:8 (May 1975): 2–3.

adopted radical economic policies in response to similar moves by Latin American socialist states such as Chile and pressure from "left-wing opposition that engaged in guerrilla tactics and widespread social unrest [fueled by students and workers]."[78] Many Southern governments adopted policies once deemed overly provocative or even impossible in part to undermine the political attraction of leftism or revolution. And similar considerations may help explain why a surprising number of Westerners believed these ambitious economic programs might succeed and a handful of mainly European politicians entertained negotiations, a reality Nils Gilman finds even more remarkable than the NIEO itself.[79] Figures like Willy Brandt believed that only by addressing the global economic divide could world leaders mitigate the brewing revolts that threatened to engulf both North and South, many of which reflected Tricontinental motivations.[80] By approaching Third World organizations from the NAM to UNCTAD as forums where anti-imperial ideas were debated and often produced compromise policies, we can see the gravitational effects of Tricontinentalism during this era. Relatively few Southern states officially adopted the full breadth of the militant worldview, but the appeal of radical anti-imperialism encouraged postcolonial leaders to imagine ambitious challenges to the international system and compelled reluctant governments to go along for the ride.

Tricontinentalism, though, had limitations. With few formal institutions, solidarity depended on flexible ad hoc alliances between states and transnational groups whose bold ambitions wrestled with insecurity, economic disadvantages, and the need for prudence. The broad coalitions required to mitigate these weaknesses always faced the threat of free-riding and defections as states constantly reassessed their best interests. Moreover, calls for revolution competed with moderate visions of South-South cooperation championed by states ranging from China-wary India and Africa's Monrovia Group to US clients such as Iran and South Vietnam, which remained dependent on Western aid even as they

---

[78] Garavini, *The Rise and Fall of OPEC*, 185.

[79] Gilman, "The New International Economic Order," 1. For Western support among anti-imperial radicals and liberals, see Paul Adler, "'The Basis of a New Internationalism?': The Institute for Policy Studies and North-South Politics from the NIEO to Neoliberalism," *Diplomatic History* 41:4 (September 2017): 665–693.

[80] Concern with instability permeates Brandt's introduction to his 1980 report. He references "dangerous tensions" between North and South "complicating East-West antagonism" as important factors forcing the world to confront the stark choice of "Destruction or Development?" Willy Brandt, "A Plea for Change: Peace, Justice, Jobs," in *North-South: A Programme for Survival* (London: Pan Books, 1980), 9, 13, 15.

explored new coalitions to promote beneficial trade relations and development programs. Dominant within Third World circles beginning in the 1960s, arguably climaxing with the victory of North Vietnam and leftist African revolutions in the 1970s, Tricontinentalism had lost momentum by the time Cuba gained the chairmanship of the NAM in 1979. China and major oil producers gained sufficient power to pursue their national interests without the need for Third World solidarity. Less fortunate states hit hard by the economic downturn of the 1970s drifted from domestic socialism and internationalist goals as they sought austere loans from Western governments and institutions.

Tricontinentalism also suffered from internal weaknesses. Anti-imperial solidarity helped provide states such as Cuba and Vietnam with a national purpose – a unifying myth or what Partha Chatterjee identifies as a sense of community – that united diverse classes, ethnicities, and constituencies within locally constituted but globally relevant struggles.[81] It provided a defense not just against foreign threats but against anti-revolutionary factions at home.[82] Yet this practice had downsides, especially after transitioning to the postcolonial state. Leaders used revolutionary goals and militant mindsets to justify anti-democratic practices, economic disruption, centralization of power, and the crushing of dissent. The ability to contextualize internal challenges internationally allowed officials to summarily dismiss criticism, downplaying setbacks as by-products of foreign meddling or justifying domestic suffering as necessary to achieve bigger objectives. Allied governments expressed objections quietly, hesitant to critique partners in struggle. Western policies that isolated and attacked leftist states – especially in the 1980s – reinforced these tendencies, discouraging the transition from revolutionary conflict to revolutionary development. Tricontinentalism thus became a double-edged sword, legitimizing nationalist revolts but potentially weakening accountability after victory. This dissonance between stated ambitions and realities ultimately blunted revolutionary zeal. As a result, state proponents of Tricontinentalism dwindled, even as its radical vision

---

[81] Chatterjee argues the transition to the modern postcolonial state and pursuit of progress within the global capitalist system interrupted these community narratives. Partha Chatterjee, *The Nation and Its Fragments* (Princeton: Princeton University Press, 1993), 237–238.

[82] See chapters by Asselin, Irwin, Parrott, Covey, and Byrne. See also Brown, *Cuba's Revolutionary World*; Brazinsky, *Winning the Third World*; and Anna Clayfield, *The Guerrilla Legacy of the Cuban Revolution* (Gainesville: University Press of Florida, 2019).

of anti-imperialism took root in academic discourses and continues to inform contemporary movements.

What then replaced Tricontinentalism at the forefront of the Anti-Imperial Project? In Chapter 3, Paul Thomas Chamberlin considers one possibility by looking at the changing politics of the Middle East. The more controversial elements of Tricontinentalism – its ideological litmus tests and flirtation with anti-Western identarian politics – provided fertile ground for the rise of Hamas and the Ayatollah Khomeini. Their sectarian platforms called into question the efficacy and legitimacy of secular leftist groups like the PLO while drawing on historic elements of the Anti-imperial Project. Khomeini defined a fundamentalist Islamist revolution as the only way to purify Iran of the damaging modern "isms" proffered by both the United States and Soviet Union. Situating Iran within the broader struggle waged by many non-Muslim states of the Third World, he argued "Islam ... is the supporter of all oppressed people of the world."[83] While Khomeini and others adapted rhetoric, tropes, and tactics from Tricontinentalism, they definitively broke with the secular worldview and communist-aligned socialism to champion a network of Islamist radicals that eventually spread beyond the Middle East to Asia and Africa.[84]

Byrne offers another possibility in Chapter 6 with his reference to the rise of anti-imperial "negotiators armed with briefcases and professional degrees." Revolutionary states increasingly emphasized the use of diplomatic and economic suasion to change the balance of relationships with the Global North. Yet when certain resources and markets proved more vital than others, many countries quietly abandoned grand Third World projects in favor of individual development. China and oil-rich states found success combining private enterprise with the centralized, targeted investment, many emerging as regional powers. Prashad has called this trend "neoliberalism with southern characteristics," but in so characterizing it he downplays the long history of Southerners redeploying Northern ideas to challenge global inequities.[85] While self-serving, states such as China, Brazil, and even Nigeria position themselves as alternatives

---

[83] Ruhollah Khomeini, "We Shall Confront the World with Our Ideology," *Middle East Report* 88 (June 1988).

[84] Key influences on the Iranian Revolution drew from Tricontinentalism. Jalal Ale Ahmad promoted a Marxian "angry third worldism," and Ali Shariati married "Shia Islam and Marxist method." Ali M. Ansari, *The Politics of Nationalism in Modern Iran* (New York: Cambridge University Press, 2012), 186–189.

[85] Prashad, *Poorer Nations*, 10, 166–180.

to traditional Euro-American dominance trying to bend the existing system to the advantage of historically exploited states. Admittedly, they have done so without grand, egalitarian projects like the NIEO, opting instead to claim the roles of economic drivers and models for Southern development exemplified by the BRIC(S) group (Brazil, Russia, India, China, and South Africa). Joint projects like the New Development Bank hint at potential alternatives to Western institutions but still generally operate within the extant system. This – along with accusations of paternalism and imperialism leveled at China by countries like Zambia – recalls earlier reformist anti-imperialisms, though recent Chinese flirtations with an autocratic anti-US alliance hint that more assertive challenges may be coming. These examples show that the Anti-Imperial Project has consistently sought to reshape the world infrastructure, but the "radical potential" – as one group of scholars laments – has varied depending on the dominant trends motivating politics in the Global South at any given moment.[86]

The broad overview elicits a few final reflections on the Anti-Imperial Project and Tricontinentalism's place within it. First, though it is impossible to talk of a singular anti-imperial movement, consistent elements informed various intersecting ideas that collectively tried to erase the gap between North and South. These include the celebration of Southern cultures as equal or superior to Western civilization, the search for sovereignty, greater global economic equality, and the belief that some level of transnational coordination was needed to combat global Euro-American imperialism. Second, certain approaches became prominent during specific eras in ways that tended to produce a kind of gravity, which influenced the forms and ambitions of various initiatives. The outline above hints at a cyclical toggling between moderation and radicalism. Groups and states sought to use access to new forms of power – education, political sovereignty, or economic resources – to reform the system, only for marginalized groups to adopt radical solutions as North-South inequalities proved stubbornly persistent. Radical turns helped wrest concessions from the North, starting the cycle again. Third, pan-projects gave way to increasingly inclusive visions of Southern solidarity that sought an independent path separate from but informed by the modernizing ideologies of the Cold War. The creation of institutions such as the NAM and the G-77 represented the pinnacle of this unifying impulse, but

---

[86] Pamila Gupta, Christopher J. Lee, Marissa J. Moorman, and Sandhya Shukla, "Editor's Introduction," *Radical History Review* 131 (May 2018): 2.

the nature of the Anti-Imperial Project made speaking with a single voice difficult. The Bandung vision could not deliver effective unanimity, but the ideological cohesion envisioned by Tricontinentalism struggled to obtain and sustain wide support. The elusive dream of uniting behind a singular movement succumbed to the sheer diversity of the Global South and what Sukarno called "an age of division and diverging trends."[87]

Finally, my attempt to define Tricontinentalism's place within the long durée of anti-imperialism tentatively offers a historical vocabulary to discuss Southern politics. The major ideological alternatives described in this section were unique, competing iterations that collectively constituted the *Anti-Imperial Project*, which spanned the last century and continues to inform contemporary debates. The term *Third World* or *Third World Project* is one part of this longer history, collectively describing the countries and ideologies that tried to use the specific power dynamics of the Cold War to advance calls for self-determination and sovereignty within the Global South. This did not preclude collaboration with one or other bloc but positioned the goals of Southern anti-imperialism as distinct from both Western and Eastern uses of the term. While scholars have proposed the *Global South* as describing a specific set of politics, a somewhat constrained definition may be useful within historical circles.[88] I and many authors in this volume use it as geopolitical shorthand for Asia, Africa, and Latin America with attention to their diasporic extensions, which shared historic experiences of colonialism and empire, social marginalization, economic disparity, and resistance. The Global North constitutes the wealthier, industrial regions concentrated in Europe and North America that championed various universal modernizing ideologies with imperial and/or hegemonic overtones. As in the South, these ideas competed, especially during the Cold War's East-West conflict. This geopolitical use captures the common experiences that promoted collaboration across continents and also recognizes the spectrum of ideologies present in both North and South. While far from definitive, this terminology provides some clarity in discussing broad anti-imperial impulses and their relationship to specific historical worldviews, strategies, and programs.

---

[87] Sukarno, "Address to the Cairo Conference," 23.

[88] For an exploration of the Global South term and its evolving usage in historical, literary, and anthropological studies, see Gupta et al. "Editors Introduction" and the articles in *Radical History Review* 131; also footnote 38 and Mahler, *From the Tricontinental to the Global South*, 244–245.

The Tricontinental Revolution explores elements of the ideas above by examining the international affairs of a wide variety of actors. Part I, "Chronologies of Third Worldism" frames the origins, rise, and challenges of Tricontinentalism with a trio of chapters. They situate the Havana conference as a revisitation of interwar solidarities that responded to key events of the 1950s and 1960s, but which ultimately faced powerful alternatives to secular revolution. Part II, "A Global Worldview," explores Tricontinentalism beyond Latin America with attention to North Vietnam, South Africa, and Algeria. These chapters investigate how individual revolutions conceptualized international affairs, as well as the benefits and limitations of radical solidarity politics. Part III, "Superpower Responses to Tricontinentalism," delves deeper into the ways the superpowers received attempts to organize a radical Third World, detailing both Western hostility to the project and the constraints placed upon it by the Sino-Soviet conflict. Part IV, "Frustrated Visions," considers the ambitious visions for the international system held by Tricontinental advocates, ranging from Amílcar Cabral's attempts to bridge the North-South divide to a rethinking of the role of mercenaries in international law. Disappointments emerged not just from the hostile reaction of superpowers but also from the inconsistencies and tensions that existed within the social and political programs of Tricontinentalism.

PART I

CHRONOLOGIES OF THIRD WORLDISM

I

Global Solidarity before the Tricontinental Conference

Latin America and the League against Imperialism

Anne Garland Mahler

More than a conference or an alliance, the Organization of Solidarity with the Peoples of Africa, Asia, and Latin America (Organización de Solidaridad con los Pueblos de Africa, Asia y América Latina or OSPAAAL) should be understood as an engine of radical cultural production that – for over four decades and in multiple languages – shaped and distributed a shared worldview of Tricontinentalism among a transnational, political community.[1] In *From the Tricontinental to the Global South: Race, Radicalism, and Transnational Solidarity* (2018), I use "Tricontinentalism" to refer to a Cold War "political discourse and ideology" containing "a deterritorialized vision of imperial power and a recognition of imperialism and racial oppression as interlinked."[2]

---

[1] Although past its prime, until its closure in June 2019, the OSPAAAL continued to produce some of the political ephemera, detailed later in this essay, for which it became known.

[2] Anne Garland Mahler, *From the Tricontinental to the Global South: Race, Radicalism, and Transnational Solidarity* (Durham: Duke University Press, 2018), 3. Throughout this essay, I use the OSPAAAL and the "Tricontinental alliance" to refer to the Organization of Solidarity with the Peoples of Africa, Asia and Latin America, formed at the 1966 Tricontinental Conference. With "Tricontinentalism," I refer to a broader ideology, discourse, and aesthetics that is more expansive than the propaganda of the OSPAAAL itself. For a more extensive definition of Tricontinentalism, see the introduction and first chapter in Mahler, *From the Tricontinental to the Global South*. There, I draw from conceptualizations of Tricontinentalism by John A. Gronbeck-Tedesco, *Cuba, the United States, and Cultures of the Transnational Left, 1930–75* (New York: Cambridge University Press, 2015); Thea Pitman and Andy Stafford, "Introduction: Transatlanticism and Tricontinentalism," *Journal of Transatlantic Studies* 7:3 (2009): 197–207; Vijay Prashad, *The Darker Nations: A People's History of the Third World* (New York: The New Press, 2007); Besenia Rodriguez, "Beyond Nation: The Formation of a Tricontinental Discourse" (PhD diss., Yale University, 2006); Sarah Seidman, "Venceremos Means We Shall Overcome: The African American Freedom

This discourse, which circulated through the OSPAAAL's cultural production and within related radical movements around the globe, intentionally avoided framing its global, political subjectivity through the language of class struggle. Rather, it employed "a racial signifier of color" to refer to "a broadly conceived transracial political collectivity" organized around a shared ideological position of Tricontinentalism.[3] The OSPAAAL's conception of empire and resistance largely anticipated contemporary theories of racial capitalism, and its ideology of Tricontinentalism continues to reverberate within the contemporary Left.

Whereas *From the Tricontinental to the Global South* provides background for the emergence of Tricontinentalism, including the formation and inner workings of the OSPAAAL, the bulk of that study focuses on the period from the late 1960s to the present day. Building on this work, this chapter seeks to better define the ideological foundations for the OSPAAAL, framing it within the longer historical arc of the interwar League Against Imperialism and for National Independence (LAI) and arguing that it especially recovered core ideological tenets of the LAI's understudied Americas section, the Anti-Imperialist League of the Americas (LADLA).[4]

These two Latin America-based movements – the LADLA of the 1920s–30s and the OSPAAAL that began in the 1960s – arose out of distinct historical contexts, and this essay does not seek to draw a direct lineage in terms of the political activists involved in the two organizations. However, I trace five key ideological tendencies that they had in common in order to argue that although the OSPAAAL consistently rooted its history in the 1955 Asian-African Bandung Conference, it actually drew more closely from the historical memory of the LADLA.[5]

Struggle and the Cuban Revolution, 1959–79" (PhD diss., Brown University, 2013); and Robert J. C. Young, *Postcolonialism: An Historical Introduction* (Oxford: Blackwell, 2001).

[3] Mahler, *From the Tricontinental to the Global South*, 3, 17.

[4] The LADLA was established in 1925, prior to the 1927 founding of the LAI when it was then named as the LAI's Central Organizing Bureau in Latin America. I describe the LADLA as the LAI's "Americas" section because the LADLA was established as a hemispheric organization and maintained chapters in the United States.

[5] According to the Tricontinental's International Preparatory Committee, for example, the OSPAAAL originated at the 1955 Asian-African Bandung Conference. In fact, the OSPAAAL represented an extension of the Afro-Asian Peoples' Solidarity Organization (AAPSO) into the Americas. International Preparatory Committee of the First Solidarity Conference of the Peoples of Africa, Asia and Latin America and the Cuban National Committee, " Background of Tricontinental Conference to Be Held in Havana," *Towards the First Tricontinental Conference* 1 (October 15, 1965): 3.

FIGURE 1.1 Tricontinentalism sought to legitimize revolutions by linking them to powerful cultural symbols and histories of local resistance in the Global South. This image is one of a trio linking contemporary weapons of war to iconography indigenous to each continent (as viewed from Cuba). OSPAAAL, Jesus Forjans, 1969. Offset, 53x33 cm. Image courtesy Lincoln Cushing / Docs Populi.

The LADLA, which eventually included eleven chapters throughout the United States and Latin America, was created in 1925 in
Mexico City. It brought together urban trade unions, agrarian organizations, and cultural and artistic groups across the two continents in
a collaborative effort against US and European commercial and military expansion. Among its core leadership were several Cuban activists, most notably Julio Antonio Mella, living in exile in Mexico
City.[6] Within two years of the LADLA's founding, its members joined
with 174 delegates, "representing thirty-one states, colonies, or
regions" to form the LAI at the Congress against Colonial
Oppression and Imperialism and for National Independence, held in
Brussels from February 10 to 15, 1927.[7] This conference, organized
by German communist Willi Münzenberg with limited financial support from the Comintern, focused primarily on the anti-imperialist
struggle in China, India, and Mexico. However, delegates covered
a broad range of issues during the five days of speeches.[8] There,
LADLA organizers interacted with anti-colonial leaders from around
the world, such as India's Jawaharlal Nehru and Senegal's Lamine
Senghor. In Brussels, the LAI's Executive Committee resolved that the
LADLA's continental organizing committee, based in Mexico City,
would become the LAI's "Central Organizing Bureau for Latin
America."[9]

In rooting the OSPAAAL in the history of the LAI and in its Americas
section (LADLA), I seek to correct a number of missteps in extant
scholarship on both the OSPAAAL and the LAI. In both cases, problems arise from treating the 1955 Asian-African Bandung Conference as
either the opening or the closing of a twentieth-century story of anti-

---

[6] For background on the LADLA, see Daniel Kersffeld, *Contra el imperio: Historia de la Liga Antimperialista de las Américas* (Mexico: siglo xxi editores, 2012).
[7] Michele Louro, Carolien Stolte, Heather Streets-Salter, and Sana Tannoury-Karam, eds., *The League Against Imperialism: Lives and Afterlives* (Leiden: Leiden University Press, 2020), 17.
[8] For studies of the 1927 Brussels Congress, see Michele Louro, *Comrades against Imperialism: Nehru, India, and Interwar Internationalism* (Cambridge: Cambridge University Press, 2018); Louro et al., eds., *The League Against Imperialism*; Fredrik Petersson, *Willi Münzenberg, the League Against Imperialism, and the Comintern, 1925–33* (Lewiston: The Edwin Mellen Press, 2014); and Holger Weiss, *Framing a Radical African Atlantic: African American Agency, West African Intellectuals, and the International Trade Union Committee of Negro Workers* (Leiden: BRILL, 2013).
[9] LADLA, "Última Resolución del Comité Internacional Ejecutivo sobre la América Latina," *El Libertador* 2:13 (August 1927): 12.

imperialist internationalism. For instance, scholarship on the Tricontinental tends to frame its emergence as the first time that Latin American anti-imperialist movements entered into a global solidarity movement with a longer history in Afro-Asian anti-colonialisms.[10] The prevailing narrative positions the 1955 Asian-African Bandung Conference as the origin of both the Non-Aligned Movement and the more radical and Soviet-aligned Afro-Asian People's Solidarity Organization (AAPSO). The formation of the OSPAAAL in 1966 grew out of Cuba's requests to join the AAPSO beginning in 1961, uniting Latin American anti-imperialist movements with prior Afro-Asian formations.[11]

While this accounting from 1955 to 1966 is indeed accurate, beginning the OSPAAAL's story with the 1955 Bandung Conference elides the much longer history of Latin American engagement with Afro-Asian anti-colonialisms through the LAI in the interwar years. Similarly, although the 1927 Brussels Congress, which founded the LAI, is widely viewed as a significant precursor to the Bandung Conference, extant scholarship on the Brussels Congress and the LAI tends to neglect the presence and contributions of Latin American movements there.[12] The scholarship of Michael Goebel and Daniel Kersffeld, who have each focused on Latin Americans' participation at the Brussels Congress, is an important exception to this tendency.[13] However, generally, the LAI, as the precursor to the Bandung Conference, is most often understood in relation to Afro-Asian networks, reifying the false impression that the Tricontinental Conference represents the first entry of Latin American movements onto a global stage.

---

[10] See, for example, Young, *Postcolonialism*, 192; Robert J. C. Young, "Postcolonialism: From Bandung to the Tricontinental," *Historein* 5 (2005): 17.

[11] Here, I draw from the historiography provided in Mahler, *From the Tricontinental to the Global South*, 73–78.

[12] For works that frame the LAI as the precursor to Bandung see Christopher J. Lee, *Making a World after Empire: The Bandung Moment and Its Political Afterlives* (Athens: Ohio University Press, 2010); Prashad, *The Darker Nations*; Weiss, *Framing a Radical African Atlantic*, 81.

[13] Michael Goebel, *Anti-Imperial Metropolis: Interwar Paris and the Seeds of Third World Internationalism* (Cambridge: Cambridge University Press, 2015); Michael Goebel, "Forging a Proto-Third World? Latin America and the League Against Imperialism," in Louro et al., eds., *The League Against Imperialism*, 53–78; Kersffeld, *Contra el imperio*. By including Goebel's essay as its first chapter, *The League Against Imperialism: Lives and Afterlives* makes an important correction to this general trend.

These problems lie not only with scholarship on the OSPAAAL since scholarship on the LAI tends to characterize the Bandung meeting as the endpoint of the LAI's anti-imperialist internationalist vision from the interwar period, thus obscuring its connections to the later formation of the OSPAAAL. For example, Michele Louro's excellent study, *Comrades against Imperialism: Nehru, India, and Interwar Internationalism* (2018), argues that "the Bandung Conference must be seen as a closure" to the LAI's project in that "it marked the triumph of the nation-state and interstate relations in the arena of Afro-Asian politics, and it stood in contradistinction to the anti-imperialist internationalism of the interwar years."[14] While the 1955 Bandung Conference – with its focus on representatives of nation-states – was indeed "distinct if not anathema to interwar anti-imperialism," ending the story in 1955 does not provide a complete portrait of the legacy of internationalisms begun in the interwar period.[15] Rather, the formation of the OSPAAAL recovered the LAI's vision in significant ways, making it an ideological heir to the Afro-Asian-Latin American networks forged through the LAI. Specifically, the OSPAAAL recovered core contributions of the Latin American activists involved in this interwar, global organization through their participation in the LADLA.[16]

The LADLA and the later OSPAAAL would share, I argue, five key ideological tendencies. First, both organizations advanced a global theory of imperial power in which resistant movements developed regional and hemispheric networks with the goal of bridging those regional connections to a broader, worldwide movement. Second, both sought to create a single theory of empire and resistance that would integrate histories of European colonization with twentieth-century patterns of economic domination through multinational monopolies and finance capital. Third, in constructing a political community across national and linguistic lines,

---

[14] Louro, *Comrades against Imperialism*, 16, 258.   [15] Ibid., 258.

[16] Goebel makes a similar argument, arguing that "[i]f there was an effort to imagine Latin America as a part of a Third World *avant la lettre* prior to revolutionary Cuba's official tricontinentalism of the 1960s, surely it was at the LAI's inaugural conference in February 1927." Goebel, "Forging a Proto-Third World?" 70. However, he focuses primarily on the Latin Americans present at the Brussels Congress, who represented a range of differing and conflictual ideological perspectives, and of which LADLA representatives were only a portion. In examining the ideological roots of Tricontinentalism, I would argue that we should look specifically to the LADLA, rather than to the various Latin Americans invited to the Brussels Congress.

both movements exhibited ideological openness and flexibility, incorporating diverse constituencies within a broad anti-imperial solidarity. Though both organizations are often understood as Soviet-backed communist movements, the reality was more complicated. Fourth, while both supported nationalist independence movements, they viewed the success of these movements as wholly dependent on structures of mutual support provided by internationalism. Finally, both took a stance of explicit anti-racism and ultimately intended to unite a global anti-capitalist movement with racial justice struggles in the Americas and around the globe.

Despite the similarities of the political projects of the LADLA and the OSPAAAL, they exhibited a major difference in that the LADLA, in its early years, demonstrated significantly less commitment to Black struggles and was more focused on organizing with Indigenous communities. After the 1927 Brussels Congress, where LADLA members interacted with African American activists and with anti-colonial movements from Africa and Asia, these encounters influenced a shift in the LADLA's focus to issues facing Black and immigrant workers. While the OSPAAAL focused on Black struggles from its inception, it did so largely with respect to these struggles in the United States and South Africa, repeating a tendency of its predecessor to elide the problems of anti-Black racism in Latin America.

In what follows, I trace this longer arc of Latin American involvement in Afro-Asianism. Afro-Asianism influenced Latin American members of the LADLA, who especially identified with the agrarian focus of the Chinese communist movement. However, Latin Americans also brought their own ideas to the 1927 Brussels Congress. Specifically, Latin Americans brought direct experience with US imperialism and a nuanced understanding of how this form of foreign domination overlapped with and differed from the region's prior encounters with European colonialism under the Spanish and British empires. As the US imperial project expanded around the globe over the coming decades, such an integrated theory of empire would form the basis for the later emergence of the OSPAAAL and for the central role that Latin Americans would play in it.

THE LADLA AND INTERWAR INTERNATIONALISM

It is not coincidental that both the LADLA and the OSPAAAL – with their transnational understanding of imperial power that linked histories of European colonization with a more contemporary form of global

capitalism – would emerge out of Latin America. While former Spanish
colonies in the Americas had mostly secured independence by the end of
the nineteenth century, independence did not eliminate the socioeconomic
and racial hierarchies of these former colonial societies. This fact motivated the armed struggles of the Mexican Revolution, which preceded the
Russian Revolution by almost a decade. Formal independence did not
eradicate foreign intervention either as British finance continued to dominate in the region throughout the nineteenth century. With the US intervention into the Cuban War of Independence in 1898 and the repeated US
occupations of Caribbean and Latin American countries in the early
twentieth century, the United States would effectively introduce a new
imperial project for the American hemisphere. In their "Resolutions on
Latin America," Latin Americans who attended the 1927 Brussels
Congress wrote that "British imperialism is progressively ceding to
Yankee imperialism."[17] The United States, they explained, uses
a "politics of penetration," obtaining "the most important sources of
primary materials and impeding the economic development of Latin
American nations."[18] In contrast to prior European forms of colonial
expansion, which historically relied on the occupation of territory and
the installation of a colonial ruling bureaucracy, the US imperial project
was more focused on economic control than direct territorial sovereignty.
This post-1898 model of US intervention in the Americas inspired
Vladimir Lenin's theorization of a new form of imperialism, what he
called the "highest stage of capitalism," in which multinational monopolies, through the cooperation of big banks and with backing by military
power, eventually dominate the global market.[19]

   Lenin's notion of imperialism appealed to many interwar Latin
American radical thinkers, who theorized points of similarity between
prior experiences of colonization and US economic domination. It played
an important role in the establishment of the LADLA in Mexico City in
1925, which primarily sought to counter US and European commercial
and military expansion in Latin America. The LADLA emerged as the
Comintern was developing parallel strategies both on Latin America and

---

[17] "El imperialismo inglés retrocede progresivamente ante el imperialismo yanqui,"
Mahler's translation. LADLA, "Las resoluciones sobre América Latina," *El Libertador*
2:12 (June 1927): 10.
[18] "política de penetración"; "las más importantes fuentes de materias primas e impidiendo
el desarrollo económico de las naciones latinoamericanas," Mahler's translation. Ibid.
[19] Vladimir Lenin, *Imperialism: The Highest Stage of Capitalism* (London: Penguin, 2010
[1917]).

on Black labor in the Americas more broadly. In this vein, it aimed to form a hemispheric, multiracial alliance that united Latin American workers with those in the United States.

The LADLA was conceived as a "mass organization" based on the Comintern's united-front approach of the 1920s, and it sought to unite a broad range of social classes and leftist ideologies behind a position of anti-imperialism.[20] Eventually developing branches in several countries throughout the hemisphere, the LADLA's membership relied on communist networks already in place in Latin America but intentionally avoided direct overlap with local communist parties, developing a broader collectivity of artists, intellectuals, noncommunist members of trade unions and nationalist organizations. Its headquarters in Mexico City included well-known politically conscious artists and intellectuals of the moment, such as Mexican muralists Diego Rivera, Xavier Guerrero, and David Siqueiros; US activists Bertram and Ella Wolfe; exiled Cuban political leader Julio Antonio Mella; and Italian-American photographer Tina Modotti.[21] It was started with the help of Scottish-born union organizer in Chicago, Jack Johnstone, who was sent to Mexico City for this purpose by the US Workers Party in 1924.[22] By 1926, its secretariat included multinational representation from each of its various national sectors.[23] In its early years, the Mexican labor leader Úrsulo Galván Reyes served as director of the LADLA's periodical, *El Libertador*, with Mexican Nahua

---

[20] For a detailed discussion of how the LADLA conceived its relationship to communist parties – wherein the communist party had representation in the league but did not control it – see the transcript from the dialogue on the Leagues Against Imperialism at the First Latin American Communist Conference in Buenos Aires in June 1929. I draw the phrase "organizaciones de masas" from that discussion. Communist International, South American Secretariat, *El movimiento revolucionario latinoamericano: Versiones de la Primera Conferencia Comunista Latinoamericana Junio de 1929* (Buenos Aires: S.S. A. de la I.C., 1929), 320–330.

[21] For a longer list of the LADLA's organizing leadership, see Ricardo Melgar Bao, "The Anti-Imperialist League of the Americas between the East and Latin America," trans. Mariana Ortega Breña, *Latin American Perspectives* 35:2 (March 2008): 9–24; Lazar Jefeits and Victor Jefeits, *América Latina en la Internacional Comunista, 1919–1943, Diccionario biográfico* (Santiago: Ariadna Ediciones, 2015); Kersffeld, *Contra el imperio*.

[22] Kersffeld, *Contra el imperio*, 48; Later, in 1928, Johnstone was sent to India as the LAI representative. Louro, *Comrades against Imperialism*, 129.

[23] Kersffeld, *Contra el imperio*, 61. By 1928, it had expanded to include twelve sections: Argentina, Colombia, Cuba, Ecuador, Honduras, Mexico, Peru, Puerto Rico, El Salvador, Dominican Republic, Uruguay, and the United States. Bao, "The Anti-Imperialist League of the Americas between the East and Latin America," 18.

artist Xavier Guerrero serving as administrator and U.S. activist Bertram Wolfe as editor.[24]

The first issue (March 1925) of El Libertador explains the creation of the organization as the necessary response to the expanding economic and military domination of the United States over Cuba, Panama, Haiti, Dominican Republic, and Mexico. To counter this expansion, El Libertador states, Latin American workers must ally with US workers to form "a single anti-imperialist continental movement," which could then "eventually perhaps save Europe, Asia, and Africa as well."[25] In other words, the LADLA began with a hemispheric vision, but this hemispheric project was intended, from its inception, to build outward toward a global one.[26] The writers of El Libertador asserted that while the publication would focus primarily on the American hemisphere, it would report on movements around the world. As explained in El Libertador, for petroleum workers in a place like Tampico, Mexico, for example, it would be imperative to "seek out alliances with petroleum workers from Europe, Asia, and South America, since the capital of Standard and Royal Dutch Shell is international."[27] A strike against these companies, El Libertador asserted, "in order to be effective, must become international."[28] In this way, connecting workers' movements in Latin America with internationalist labor structures already in existence, especially the Red International of Labor Unions, was one of the LADLA's core goals.

The LADLA expanded on this global vision through the organization's participation in the 1927 Brussels Congress. In a July 1927 article published shortly after the Brussels Congress in América Libre: Revista

[24] LADLA, El Libertador 1:2 (May 1925): 7. In February 1926, Enrique Flores became director. Venezuelan activist Salvador de la Plaza replaced Guerrero as administrator in April 1926, eventually taking on the directorship as well. Then in August 1927, Diego Rivera became director with Venezuelan Gustavo Machado serving as administrator.

[25] "un solo movimiento anti-imperialista continental"; "llegar tal vez a salvar a Europa, Asia, y África también," Mahler's translation. LADLA, "El peligro; las posibilidades, el propósito," El Libertador 1:1 (March 1925): 1.

[26] It should be noted that this hemispheric stance constituted an explicit rejection of the interwar, regionalist discourses of hispanoamericanismo and latinité.

[27] "hay que buscar también alianzas con los obreros petroleros de Europa y Asia y de la América del Sur, puesto que el capital de la Standard y la Royal Dutch Shell es internacional," Mahler's translation. LADLA, "Los obreros de Tampico llevan la delantera en la lucha con el capital petrolero," El Libertador 1:2 (May 1925): 6. The author of this article is not listed; however, it was likely written by the publication's director, Úrsulo Galván Reyes, since much of his labor organizing took place within the petroleum industry in Tampico.

[28] "para ser efectiva, tiene que hacerse internacional," Mahler's translation. Ibid., 6.

Revolucionaria Americana (Free America: American Revolutionary Magazine), a publication affiliated with the LADLA's Cuban section, Diego Rivera acknowledged strong anti-US sentiment among Latin American workers. He argued that a semi-capitalist relationship existed between US and Mexican labor in which Mexican workers extracted primary materials for manufacture by US workers.[29] Within US-owned multinational companies, he explained, an increase in salary for US employees directly translated as depressed salaries in Mexico. Rivera argued that this dynamic could be found in all industrial countries and compared it to the relationship between British and Indian labor. Importantly, in identifying these divisions, he did not mobilize an attack against all US citizens, but rather insisted on the importance of fomenting a greater class consciousness that would transcend the US-Mexico border.

Because of the LADLA's efforts to bridge national, geographic, and linguistic divisions, it maintained an ideological openness to any group that viewed itself as anti-imperialist. The second issue of *El Libertador* (May 1925) explained that the LADLA included "unions; farmworker and Indigenous leagues; political parties of workers and farmers that fight against capitalism and imperialism; student, cultural, and intellectual groups that have participated or shown their desire to participate in our struggle; anti-imperialist revolutionary juntas – like that in Santo Domingo and Venezuela," among others.[30] In this sense, although it was largely funded through the Comintern, it was intended as a "mass organization," conceived within an ideological fluidity that sought to address the practical realities of the region and to unify a broad swath of the Left under a banner of anti-imperialism. It aimed to balance inter-nationalist and nationalist positions by arguing that national independence for "oppressed, colonial, and semi-colonial peoples" could be achieved only through the mutual support provided by internationalism.[31] In other words, self-determination could not be

---

[29] Diego Rivera, "La unión proletaria continental," *América Libre* 1:4 (July 1927): 7.

[30] "sindicatos; ligas campesinas e indígenas; partidos políticos obreros y campesinos que luchen contra el capitalismo y el imperialismo; agrupaciones estudiantes, culturales, e intelectuales que hayan participado o manifestado su deseo de participar en nuestra lucha; juntas revolucionarias anti-imperialistas como la de Santo Domingo y la de Venezuela," Mahler's translation. LADLA, "Un Congreso Anti-Imperialista Continental," *El Libertador* 1:2 (May 1925): 3.

[31] "pueblos oprimidos, coloniales, y semi-coloniales," Mahler's translation. LADLA, "El frente único de la lucha por la emancipación de los pueblos oprimidos," *El Libertador* 2:12 (June 1927): 9.

obtained fully by any one of these communities until it had been obtained by all.

The 1927 formation of the larger umbrella organization, the LAI, would reflect similar ideological fluidity, accommodating nationalist and noncommunist movements from the colonies and often resisting oversight and pressure from Moscow. This flexible and open stance was consistent with the Comintern's united-front approach of the 1920s, seeking to ally with "bourgeois nationalist movements in the colonies as a means to encourage anti-imperialist revolution first, and class revolution later," bringing together "socialists, communists, trade unionists, civil liberties reformers, pacifists, Pan-Africanists, and anticolonial nationalists."[32] For the internationalists from the colonies who participated in the LAI, a commitment to such fluid solidarities with one another would endure, in some cases, beyond the Comintern's 1928 decision to abandon alliances with nationalists.[33]

In addition to the LADLA's hemispheric vision that frequently opened onto a global one and in addition to its ideological openness, the LADLA maintained an explicit stance of anti-racism rooted in the belief that agrarian laborers formed the base of the anti-imperialist struggle. In its early years, the LADLA was especially concerned with allying with Indigenous populations within rural regions most impacted by extractive industries. Such a concern is clearly expressed, for example, in the article "The Indian as the Base of the Anti-Imperialist Struggle" ("El indio como base de la lucha anti-imperialista"), written by Bertram Wolfe and published in the July 1925 issue of *El Libertador*. In this essay, Wolfe, who was living in Mexico City at the time, argued that until Indigenous communities "enter into the struggle, the anti-imperialist movement is condemned to remain a mere literary tendency among intellectuals, a sterile struggle of pamphlets and books denouncing Yankee imperialism in the name of the 'Spanish race,' which does not constitute the race that numerically predominates in the countries most subjected to said imperialism."[34] The very reason that US

---

[32] Louro, *Comrades against Imperialism*, 8, 22. For more on the LAI's ideological diversity, especially in its first few years, see Louro et al., eds., *The League Against Imperialism*.

[33] Louro's *Comrades against Imperialism* traces these lasting solidarities in the case of Jawaharlal Nehru.

[34] "Hasta que entren en la lucha, el movimiento anti-imperialista está condenado a quedar como una mera tendencia literaria de intelectuales, una lucha estéril de folletos y de libros denunciando el imperialismo yanqui en nombre de la 'raza española' que no constituye la raza que predomina numéricamente en los países más sometidos a dicho imperialismo,"

domination was so pervasive in Mexico and Central America, Wolfe maintained, was precisely because of the oppression of Indigenous workers by a domestic white and mestizo oligarchy. Wolfe called for the LADLA to reach out to Indigenous leaders, who could use their linguistic and cultural expertise to organize Indigenous anti-imperialist leagues among agrarian workers.

Despite its commitment to anti-racist politics, the LADLA's vision for a multiracial community was primarily focused on the radicalization of Indigenous, mestizo, and white industrial and farm workers, and in its early years, it was generally silent on problems facing Black communities.[35] This silence is notable not only because of the development of the Negro Question in Comintern strategy at this time but also because the majority of the workers in US-owned companies in the Caribbean sugar-producing region, in the Panama Canal zone, and in the banana industry in Central America were Black. Some of these Black workers were national citizens of the countries in which they worked, but many of them were West Indian and Haitian migrant workers brought in as inexpensive labor by US companies like United Fruit.[36]

Through the interventions of the Committee on the Negro Question at the 1927 Brussels Congress, however, the LADLA would eventually expand its vision to think more deeply about Black labor in the Americas. Although issues facing Black communities were not at the forefront of the Brussels Congress, the meeting played an important role in putting Black African activists – such as Lamine Senghor and James A. La Guma – in contact with Black Americans such as Richard B. Moore. This exchange in Brussels resulted in the production of "The Common Resolution on the Negro Question." Minkah Makalani has characterized the Brussels Congress and the establishment of the LAI as playing a significant role in the history of twentieth-century Black internationalism, writing that "black Communists believed they had a venue where they could pursue the internationalist politics that continued to elude

---

Mahler's translation. Bertram D. Wolfe (Audifaz), "El indio como base de la lucha anti-imperialista," *El Libertador* 1:4 (July 1925): 3. Here, Wolfe references the LADLA's explicit opposition to regionalist anti-imperialisms expressed through cultural *hispanoamericanismo*. The LADLA also notably opposed the assimilationist expressions of *indoamericanismo* practiced by counterparts like José Vasconcelos.

[35] "Trata de organizar 'todas las fuerzas' anti-imperialistas de la América Latina ... de despertar a las masas somnolientas de obreros y campesinos, de indígenas y mestizos y blancos." LADLA, "El peligro; las posibilidades; el propósito," 2.

[36] César J. Ayala, *American Sugar Kingdom: The Plantation Economy of the Spanish Caribbean, 1898–1934* (Chapel Hill: University of North Carolina Press, 1999).

them even within the international communist movement."[37] The LAI's more flexible program and its efforts to minimize Comintern control allowed the LAI to become a space for Black internationalist organizing that attracted Black radicals from a range of leftist ideologies.[38]

The speeches and resolution by the Committee on the Negro Question made an impact on the LADLA. Two members of the Committee on the Negro Question, including Moore, signed onto the Congress's "Resolutions on Latin America." These resolutions were written by Latin American representatives in Brussels who were not exclusively LADLA members. However, the resolutions, which were reprinted in the June 1927 issue of *El Libertador*, largely repeated the LADLA's platform in framing Indigenous communities as disproportionately experiencing the violence of imperialist extractive industries. Yet in a way different from previous iterations of this position, the resolution argued that "[i]mperialist penetration in these countries has exacerbated the inequality faced by Indigenous and Black peoples, because of the concentration of land, since Black and Indigenous people constitute the vast majority of the agrarian population."[39] Through this resolution, the LADLA would redefine its program moving forward to include anti-Black racism as a central part of the imperialist extractive economy, identifying both Indigenous and Black communities as key to the worldwide anti-imperialist struggle. Moreover, whereas LADLA had always identified US workers as potential allies, this resolution recognized that "the oppressed races are also our allies with the United States itself."[40] By framing Black and Indigenous agrarian labor as the base of anti-imperialism, the LADLA would take a further-reaching stance of anti-racism than the Comintern, which sought to incorporate (but not necessarily center) these workers into a struggle of primarily industrial labor and which argued that racial inequities could be resolved through class struggle.

Alongside the "Resolutions on Latin America," *El Libertador* also printed "The Common Resolution on the Negro Question," accompanied

[37] Minkah Makalani, *In the Cause of Freedom: Radical Black Internationalism from Harlem to London, 1917–1939* (Chapel Hill: University of North Carolina Press, 2011), 134.

[38] Ibid., 137–138.

[39] "La penetración imperialista en estos países ha agudizado el problema indígena y el de los negros, por la concentración de la tierra, ya que los negros y los indios constituyen la inmensa mayoría de la población agraria." Mahler's translation. LADLA, "Las resoluciones sobre América Latina," 11.

[40] "las razas oprimidas son también nuestro aliado dentro de los Estados Unidos mismos," ibid.

by a photograph of Senghor delivering his speech at the congress. This document drew connections between Black labor in the United States, Africa, and the francophone and anglophone Caribbeans. However, regarding the hispanophone countries of Latin America, the resolution stated:

In Latin America, except in Cuba, Black people do not suffer the yoke of any special oppression. In Panama, the yankee intervention has transplanted the United States' barbaric customs against Black people, and this is the same origin of social inequalities in Cuba. Social and political equality, as well as the cordial relations between different races in other countries in Latin America, prove that no natural antagonism exists between them.[41]

This statement, printed originally in Spanish in *El Libertador*, represents a slightly revised version of the conference document in English. In this Spanish version, the LADLA editors offered Cuba and Panama as exceptions to the resolution's general claim about Latin America.[42] Although the LADLA's version at least recognized the existence of anti-Black oppression in Latin America, it claimed that it appeared only in Cuba and in Panama, where it was attributed to US influence, suggesting that other Latin American countries with Black native or Black migrant populations lacked such discrimination. This idealized and false understanding of race relations in Spanish-speaking Latin America reflects the LADLA's nascent theorizing on this issue at this point as well as the absence of Spanish-speaking Black Latin American delegates in Brussels. Despite this, the Committee on the Negro Question made a strong impression and raised questions that would be vital for the LADLA moving forward.

---

[41] "En la América Latina, excepto Cuba, los negros no sufren el yugo de ninguna opresión especial. (En Panamá la intervención yanqui ha trasplantado las costumbres bárbaras de los Estados Unidos contra los negros, que es el mismo origen de las desigualdades sociales de Cuba). La igualdad social y política, así como las relaciones cordiales entre las diferentes razas que viven en otros países, prueban que no existe ningún antagonismo natural entre ellas," Mahler's translation. LADLA, "Resolución sobre la raza negra," *El Libertador* 2:12 (June 1927): 14.

[42] The English resolution stated: "In Latin America, Negroes suffer no special oppression. The cordial relations resulting from the social and political equality in the races in these countries prove that there is no inherent antagonism between them." W. Burghardt Turner and Joyce Moore Turner, *Richard B. Moore: Caribbean Militant in Harlem: Collected Writings, 1920–1972* (Bloomington: Indiana University Press, 1988), 146. This claim was not necessarily due to the influence of the Latin American delegates at the congress since the statement was based on a much longer United Negro Improvement Association (UNIA) resolution adopted at its Fifth Annual Convention of the Negro Peoples of the World in August 1926, which contained a very similar claim. Weiss, *Framing a Radical African Atlantic*, 85.

Importantly, "The Common Resolution on the Negro Question" articulated a relationship between imperialism and the ideologies of white supremacism and identified how racism curtailed representation of Black activists in anti-imperialist organizations themselves. This would have an impact on the LADLA, which not only began to recognize how imperialism impacted Black communities throughout the Americas, but also began to incorporate a fight against anti-Black racism as an integral part of its platform.

The relationship between Latin America and the ideas put forth by the Committee on the Negro Question would be advanced especially through the interventions of Afro-Cuban activist and LADLA provisional secretary Sandalio Junco. He would discuss these issues at back-to-back conferences in 1929: the Confederation of Latin American Labor Unions (CSLA) in Montevideo and the First Latin American Communist Conference in Buenos Aires. While the LADLA did not organize either of these events, the continental networks that it had worked to create since 1925 were clearly reflected in the participants. Junco had been living in exile in Mexico City since 1928 along with other Cuban exiles. He led an active political life there, serving as Provisional Secretary of the LADLA and occupying leadership roles in several other closely related organizations, including the Latin American Confederation of Labor and the Association of New Cuban Revolutionary Émigrés.[43] The conferences in Montevideo and Buenos Aires in 1929 were convened by different organizations – the CSLA and the Comintern's South American Secretariat – but they were planned to coincide with one another and included many of the same delegates. At both meetings, the problem of racism within communist and anti-imperialist movements and the strategy of Black self-determination became topics of heated debate. Junco's voice arose as central to these discussions, and he used the conferences to argue that Black labor represented a significant blind spot in the way that many Latin American radicals were conceiving of their project.

At the CSLA conference in Montevideo in May 1929, Junco presented a little known but foundational text of Black internationalism called "The

---

[43] Robert J. Alexander, *Trotskyism in Latin America* (Stanford, CA: Hoover Institution Publications, 1973), 215; American Negro Labor Congress (ANLC), "ANLC Demands Mexico Free Sandalio Junco," *The Liberator* 1:34 (December 7, 1929): 4; ANLC, "Mass Protest Saves Lives of Junco and Other Leaders," *The Liberator* 1:39 (January 11, 1930): 3.

Negro Question and the Proletarian Movement."[44] He called for an outreach campaign to Black American workers and insisted on the need to address anti-Black racism among Latin American workers. Junco argued that Black Americans should be understood as both part of a larger oppressed class and an oppressed racial category and that the exploitation of Black workers could not be resolved solely through class struggle. He disagreed with many of the participants' strict differentiation between Black and Indigenous experiences – directly challenging the Peruvian intellectual José Carlos Mariátegui on this point – and compared the racialization of Black Latin Americans with the more familiar examples of Indigenous peoples, US African Americans, and Haitian and West Indian migrant workers. In a specific example, he compared violent US segregation and inferior working conditions previously described by Black Pittsburgh miner and conference participant Isaiah Hawkins to his home country Cuba, claiming that the post-independence Cuban republic had not followed through on its own promises to Black Cubans and pointing specifically to ongoing racial discrimination in hiring practices. The US and Cuban cases, he argued, were indicative of the inequities faced by Black workers throughout the continent and were especially dire for Black migrant workers employed by US-owned companies in the Caribbean and Latin America.

Junco's interventions made their way into the work of various leftist organizations in Latin America in subsequent years, especially the Comintern's Caribbean Bureau and within the Cuban section of the LADLA and its publication, *Masas* (1934–35).[45] Although the Soviet Union began to backpedal on its commitment to Black liberation and anti-imperialism as it allied with colonial powers against the fascist threat leading up to World War II, these debates would have a much longer life. Specifically, Junco's insistence on the importance of the Black freedom struggle would become central to another anti-imperialist movement a few decades later, the OSPAAAL.

The LADLA ceased all operations by 1935, two years before the closure of the umbrella organization, the LAI. Michele Louro has argued

---

[44] For a transcript of Junco's speech, see CSLA, *Bajo la Bandera*, 160–175. For more on Junco's speech and its context, see Anne Garland Mahler, "The Red and the Black in Latin America: Sandalio Junco and the 'Negro Question' from an Afro-Latin American Perspective," *American Communist History* (Spring 2018): 1–17.

[45] Despite the fact that Junco was expelled from the Cuban Communist Party in 1932 and was no longer affiliated with the Cuban League Against Imperialism, the long-standing influence of his ideas remained.

that the closure of the LAI "marked more than a transition" from anti-imperialism to anti-fascism since "it foreshadowed the demise of a broader internationalist moment," a demise that would be demonstrated by the inter-state focus of the 1955 Bandung Conference.[46] Although Indonesian President Sukarno opened the Bandung Conference "by commemorating the earlier Brussels Congress in 1927 as a pioneering moment for Asian and African solidarity," the Bandung Conference bore little resemblance to the anti-imperialist internationalism of the LAI.[47] The Cold War, Louro writes, "made impossible the 'blending' of communist and non-communist activism, as well as the heterogeneous and flexible solidarities that were easily constructed before World War II."[48] However, the Bandung Conference was not in fact an endpoint to the LAI's vision of internationalism. Rather, this vision continued to resonate during the Cold War through global advocates of Tricontinentalism and the formal institution (OSPAAAL) that sought to define the movement. In the OSPAAAL, we see a recovery of the LAI's "heterogenous and flexible" project, and especially an engagement with the core contributions of Latin American organizers to this interwar project.

THE OSPAAAL AND TRICONTINENTALISM

The January 1966 Tricontinental Conference was announced as "the first time in history that revolutionaries from three continents ... representatives of anti-imperialist organizations from the most distant parts of Africa, Asia, and Latin America" had come together for such a gathering.[49] This characterization reflects the extent to which Bandung's Afro-Asianism had begun to eclipse the longer history of anti-imperialism, obfuscating the history of Latin Americans' involvement in the 1927 Brussels Congress and the LAI. Despite this unrecognized prehistory, the Tricontinental alliance would have significant parallels with its predecessor.

The Tricontinental Conference and the formation of the OSPAAAL, as reported by the Cuban newspaper *Granma*, intended to forge a "strategy

---

[46] Louro, *Comrades against Imperialism*, 259.   [47] Ibid., 267.   [48] Ibid., 268.
[49] U.S. Senate Committee on the Judiciary, "The Tricontinental Conference of African, Asian, and Latin American References Peoples," Staff study prepared for the Subcommittee to Investigate the Administration of the Internal Security Act and Other Internal Security Laws (Washington, DC: U.S. Government Printing Office, 1966), 11.

of the revolutionary movements in their struggle against imperialism, colonialism, and neocolonialism and, especially against Yankee imperialism" and to create "closer military ties and solidarity between the peoples of Asia, Africa, and Latin America, the working class, the progressive forces of the capitalistic countries of Europe and the United States, and the Socialist Camp."[50] Through this goal, the Tricontinental Conference joined together movements from vastly diverse contexts and developed a broad definition of its common enemy of global imperialism, which combined the notions of settler colonialism (faced for example by the Palestinian struggle) and exploitation colonialism (such as in the Portuguese colonies in Africa) with a Leninist theory of imperialism. As Che Guevara declared in his 1967 "Message to the Tricontinental," the OSPAAAL was called to create "two, three ... many Vietnams," a vision akin to Guevara's *foco* theory of guerrilla warfare – where the efforts of small cadres of guerrilla fighters eventually lead to massive insurrection – but on a global scale.[51]

As early as 1959, Castro was already exploring the possibility of overcoming Cuba's growing isolation through relations with the Afro-Asian bloc, sending Guevara, for example, to Cairo in June 1959 to seek the diplomatic support of Egyptian President Gamal Abdel Nasser. Guevara's meeting with Anwar al-Sadat, the Secretary General of the AAPSO, during this visit led to the eventual invitation for Cuba to attend future Afro-Asian conferences.[52] Within two years, a Cuban observer attended the Fourth Session of the Council of Solidarity of the Afro-Asian Peoples, held in Bandung in April 1961, the same month as the Bay of Pigs invasion.[53] There, the Afro-Asian group composed a resolution condemning the US-backed invasion of Cuba.[54] The 1962

---

[50] Ibid., 14.

[51] Che Guevara, *Message to the Tricontinental*, special supplement. *Tricontinental* (April 16, 1967).

[52] Federico Vélez, *Latin American Revolutionaries and the Arab World: From the Suez Canal to the Arab Spring* (Burlington: Ashgate Publishing, 2016), 28–31. The background for the formation of the OSPAAAL in the following pages is drawn from Mahler, *From the Tricontinental to the Global South*, 71–78.

[53] "Political Report Presented by the International Preparatory Committee and Approved by the Conference," in Organization of American States Council, *Report of the Special Committee to Study Resolution II.1 and VII of the Eighth Meeting of Consultation of Ministers of Foreign Affairs on the First Afro-Asian-Latin American Peoples' Solidarity Conference and Its Projections ("Tricontinental Conference of Havana"): New Instrument of Communist Intervention and Aggression* V. 2 (Washington, DC: Pan American Union, 1966), 113.

[54] Prashad, *The Darker Nations*, 554.

ousting of Cuba from the Organization of American States (OAS) exacerbated Cuba's need to seek friends beyond the Americas and to advocate to
officially join the AAPSO, eventually leading to the 1966 Havana
Tricontinental and to the formation of the OSPAAAL.[55]

The AAPSO originated in the First Afro-Asian Peoples' Solidarity
Conference in Cairo in 1957, two years after the 1955 Bandung
Conference. However, the OSPAAAL leadership consistently presented
the OSPAAAL and the AAPSO as having been birthed in the historic
Bandung moment.[56] Despite this claim, there are key differences between
the 1955 Bandung Conference and later AAPSO meetings. Whereas the
Bandung meeting had intentionally excluded the Soviet Union, the
AAPSO included representation from the Soviets and the Chinese and
lacked the same commitment to neutralism that is often attributed to the
Bandung meeting. Similarly, while Bandung was a governmental conference made up of heads of state, the AAPSO included government officials
but also nongovernmental representatives from leftist political parties and
movements.[57] The Tricontinental alliance would generally follow the
structure of the AAPSO, including heads of state as well as representatives
of liberation movements.

Although the OSPAAAL presented itself as the continuation of the
1955 Bandung meeting, the Tricontinental marked a clear shift away
from the development rhetoric, principles of nonviolence, and inter-state
focus associated with Bandung and toward a commitment to global
militant resistance by state and nonstate actors alike. Moreover, as
I have argued elsewhere, "Tricontinentalism represented a shift from
a Bandung-era solidarity, based around postcolonial nation-states and
a former experience of European colonialism, to a more fluid notion of
power and resistance" organized against intersecting colonial and imperial forms.[58] In this way, its internationalism looked much more similar to
the interwar project of the LADLA than to the Bandung vision.
Considering Cuba's close alliance with the Soviet Union and

---

[55] International Preparatory Committee of the First Solidarity Conference of the Peoples of
Africa, Asia and Latin America and the Cuban National Committee, "Agenda Draft," in
Towards the First Tricontinental Conference 1 (October 15, 1965), 4. See OAS, *Report of
the Special Committee* V. 1 for details on the shift from the AASPO to the OSPAAAL.

[56] International Preparatory Committee, "Background of Tricontinental Conference to Be
Held in Havana," 4; "Political Report Presented by the International Preparatory
Committee and Approved by the Conference," 113.

[57] International Preparatory Committee, "Background of Tricontinental Conference to Be
Held in Havana," 3–6.

[58] Mahler, *From the Tricontinental to the Global South*, 23.

announcement in 1961 of the socialist nature of its revolution and considering the profound influence of Marxism on many of the anticolonial and independence struggles represented at the Tricontinental, one might expect that the unity between these diverse movements would be described as a common commitment to communism and international class struggle. However, similar to the LAI's commitment to ideological fluidity, the Tricontinental was not framed in these terms.

This aspect of the Tricontinental was largely due to key disagreements and compromises made in the initial founding of the OSPAAAL. Before merging with Latin American movements to become the OSPAAAL, the AAPSO had strong representation from both the Soviet Union and China, and many of the African and Asian delegates of this organization were closely affiliated with the Soviet-sponsored World Peace Council (WPC).[59] As detailed elsewhere in this volume, the worsening of Sino-Soviet relations caused deep fissures in the organization and, as described by an OAS report, "began to absorb the energies of the meetings and became the principal focus of attention."[60] Planning for the Tricontinental was similarly shaped by Sino-Soviet discord, but in its inclusion of Latin American movements, the Tricontinental presented an opportunity to shift away from the binary power struggle that had characterized the organization thus far.

A proposal for the AAPSO to combine with Latin American leftist movements was initially presented by the Cuban observer at Afro-Asian meetings in 1961 and 1963, but disagreements over the sponsorship of its first conference stalled the conversations. The Soviet Union wanted the conference to be sponsored by the WPC and by Latin American groups affiliated with the WPC under the leadership of one of its vice presidents, Lázaro Cárdenas of Mexico. The Chinese sided, however, with Castro's bid to host the conference. According to an OAS report, because of these disagreements, discussion was eventually transferred from AAPSO council meetings to a secret meeting from which China and the Soviet Union were excluded, held in Cairo in 1964 with Mohamed Yazid of Algeria (who was representing President Ben Bella), Mehdi Ben Barka of Morocco, the Cuban Ambassador to Algeria Jorge Serguera, and the Secretary General of the AAPSO Youssef El Sebai of the United Arab Emirates.[61] There, it was decided to move forward with the Tricontinental

---

[59] OAS, *Report of the Special Committee* V. 1, 4.   [60] Ibid., 5.

[61] Ibid., 12–14. The documentation of a secret meeting is provided by the OAS report written by a special committee assigned to study the Tricontinental Conference. It should be noted, however, that the political report of the Tricontinental's International Preparatory Committee does not discuss any conflict that arose around the proposed conference,

Conference, and at the Fourth AAPSO Solidarity Conference, held in
Winneba, Ghana, in May 1965, Ghanaian President Kwame Nkrumah
presented the formal resolution, as Castro had requested, to hold the
conference in Havana in January 1966 to coincide with the seventh
anniversary of the Cuban Revolution. The International Preparatory
Committee was then composed at Winneba with six representatives
from each continent, with Mehdi Ben Barka operating as Chairman of
the committee until his October 1965 abduction and murder and the
transfer of his chairmanship to Cuban politician Osmany Cienfuegos.[62]

In the first meeting of the Tricontinental's International Preparatory
Committee in Cairo in September 1965, another disagreement arose
between the Soviet Union and China over the composition of the Latin
American delegations. This time, Cuba sided with the Soviets. Cuba
presented a list of pro-Moscow parties and China a list of pro-Chinese
groups. It was eventually agreed that "insofar as possible, there would be
solidarity committees representing all leftist, anti-imperialist and liberation groups in each of the Latin American countries, but under the
direction of the respective communist parties."[63] In practice, this meant
that Latin American communist parties had responsibility for inviting
groups to the Tricontinental Conference but that those groups did not
necessarily have to be communist in affiliation or in ideology. This established a precedent of ideological fluidity within the OSPAAAL that would
be developed much more fully in OSPAAAL cultural production over the
next several decades. Such ideological fluidity represents a significant
recovery of one of the core contributions of the interwar LAI, which
sought to bring together communists, noncommunists, and bourgeois
nationalists in "a collective mobilization against imperialist powers and
capitalist classes."[64]

Chief among the reasons that the OAS would describe the
Tricontinental as "the most dangerous and serious threat" to the inter-
American system that the OAS sought to create was "[i]ts unconcealed
desire to create an effective propaganda impact by rapidly publishing
a great quantity of documents, speeches, and informational material on

stating that the preparatory committee was nominated at the sixth meeting of the Council
of Afro-Asian Solidarity in Algiers and that the meeting held in Cairo in 1964 was simply
a meeting of the nominated members of the preparatory committee. "Political Report
Presented by the International Preparatory Committee and Approved by the Conference,"
115.

[62] OAS, *Report of the Special Committee* V. 1, 15–18.   [63] Ibid., 16.
[64] Louro, *Comrades against Imperialism*, 1.

the event, and widely disseminating these through all available media."[65] In fact, although many smaller meetings and panels of OSPAAAL delegations were held over the next three decades, the entire Tricontinental movement met only once at the 1966 conference.[66] Instead, the OSPAAAL's massive cultural production would become the primary site for communication between its delegations. Through its publications and films, and through the iconic posters for which it is now recognized, the OSPAAAL provided both physical and textual spaces in which diverse political groups came into contact, and its materials shaped and were shaped by the perspectives of the various delegations it represented.

The OSPAAAL had four official arms of propaganda: the *Tricontinental Bulletin* (1966–88, 1995–2019), published monthly in English, Spanish, French, and sometimes Arabic, which provided updates on liberation struggles, interviews, and statements from delegations; radio programs; the posters that were folded up inside of the bulletin; and the ICAIC Latin American Newsreel.[67] Although only these four are mentioned in *Tricontinental Bulletin*, it also produced books and pamphlets, and in August 1967, it began publishing a magazine in English, Spanish, French, and Italian called *Tricontinental* (1967–90, 1995–2019) that included speeches and essays by revolutionaries such as Che Guevara and Amílcar Cabral, as well as interviews and in-depth analyses of the political and economic contexts of each struggle.[68] The Latin American Newsreel, short films made by the Cuban Film Institute (ICAIC),[69] played weekly in Cuban theaters from 1960 to 1990 and were often distributed internationally, engaging themes such as the achievements of the Cuban Revolution and independence struggles in Vietnam and elsewhere.[70]

Through these materials, in a way similar to the LAI and the LADLA, the OSPAAAL articulated its explicit commitment to a struggle against racism. The "General Declaration" of the Tricontinental Conference explicitly identified racial discrimination as a tool of imperialism and

---

[65] OAS, "The First Tricontinental Conference," 68.

[66] The meetings of OSPAAAL delegates are documented throughout *Tricontinental* in the last section of the magazine called "Tricontinental on the March."

[67] OSPAAAL, "Tasks and Objectives of the OSPAAAL," *Tricontinental Bulletin* 37 (April 1969): 44–45.

[68] Ulises Estrada Lescaille and Luis Suárez, *Rebelión tricontinental: Las voces de los condenados de la tierra de África, Asia y América Latina* (New York: Ocean Press, 2006), 2–3.

[69] Instituto Cubano del Arte e Industria Cinematográficos.

[70] Michael Chanan, *BFI Dossier, No. 2: Santiago Álvarez* (London: British Film Institute, 1980), 1.

proclaimed "the complete equality of all men and the duty of the peoples to fight against all manifestations of racism and discrimination."[71] Moving forward, OSPAAAL materials would focus on a struggle specifically against anti-Black racism, spotlighting apartheid South Africa and, especially in its early years, the African American freedom struggle in the US South. Despite consistently pointing to the United States as the quintessential representative of imperialist aggression, from the very beginning, the OSPAAAL identified the cause of African Americans as an integral part of its platform. In the materials published leading up to the 1966 conference, the Tricontinental's International Preparatory Committee defined "support to the negro people of the United States in their struggle for the right to equality and freedom and against all forms of discrimination and racism" as part of the agenda for the upcoming meeting.[72]

Although Robert F. Williams and performer Josephine Baker were the only African Americans listed as official attendees at the Tricontinental Conference, Williams drafted the conference resolution on the "The Rights of Afro-Americans in the United States," along with the Jamaican, Indonesian, and Venezuelan delegates.[73] The full text of this resolution was printed in the August–September 1966 issue of *Tricontinental Bulletin*. A portion of it states:

[A]lthough, geographically Afro-Americans do not form part of Latin America, Africa, or Asia, the special circumstances of the oppression which they suffer, to which they are subjected, and the struggle they are waging, merits special consideration and demands that the Tri-Continental Organization create the necessary mechanisms so that these brothers in the struggle will, in the future, be able to participate in the great battle being fought by the peoples of the three continents.[74]

In this statement, the OSPAAAL does not just express its support for African Americans but also explicitly brings them within the Tricontinental alliance.

This solidarity with the U.S. Black freedom struggle became more pronounced in the years following the Tricontinental Conference, as is clearly evinced by the many articles devoted to it in *Tricontinental Bulletin* as well as the many posters in solidarity with African American people

[71] OSPAAAL, "General Declaration from the Tricontinental," *Tricontinental Bulletin* 1 (April 1966): 20.
[72] International Preparatory Committee, "Agenda Draft," 8.
[73] Seidman, "Venceremos Means We Shall Overcome," 89–91; Rodriguez, "Beyond Nation," 140.
[74] OSPAAAL, "Documents of the First Tricontinental Conference: The Rights of Afro-Americans in the United States," *Tricontinental Bulletin* 5–6 (August–September 1966): 21.

that were folded up inside *Tricontinental*. In these materials, the Tricontinental maintained that African Americans were subject to the very same oppression that the delegations of the three continents were, and thus, not only considered African Americans to belong to the Tricontinental but – because they were said to be fighting within the belly of the beast of the imperialist United States – deemed them particularly representative of its global political subjectivity. In essence, the OSPAAAL framed the Jim Crow South as a microcosm of a worldwide, Tricontinental struggle.

Although the African American struggle continued to feature in OSPAAAL publications throughout the late 1970s and 80s and although the OSPAAAL expressed a commitment to anti-apartheid in South Africa from its very inception, OSPAAAL materials turned their focus from the US South toward southern Africa as Cuba ramped up its involvement in the Angolan Civil War. Whereas initially OSPAAAL materials consistently represented the US South as a microcosm of an expansive global empire characterized by racial capitalism, from the mid-1970s onward, apartheid South Africa became the fulcrum on which Tricontinentalist understandings of power and resistant solidarity cohered. For the next decade, OSPAAAL cultural production shined a spotlight on southern Africa with posters condemning apartheid and declaring solidarity with southern African liberation movements, articles by leaders such as Oliver Tambo of the African National Congress and Namibian politician Sam Nujoma, proclamations calling for the release of Nelson Mandela, analyses of South African military strategy in Angola, and reporting on anti-apartheid organizing around the globe.

Through the OSPAAAL's focus on the struggle for Black freedom in the US South and South Africa, it expanded upon the LAI's "The Common Resolution on the Negro Question."[75] In centering Black liberation struggles, the OSPAAAL diverged from the LADLA's primary focus on Indigenous movements, better incorporating African and African American perspectives to confront the problem of anti-Black racism. In this way, the OSPAAAL could be viewed as belatedly responding to Junco's 1929 interventions on the so-called Negro Question. However, in his 1929 speech, Junco also called for an engagement with the oft-ignored inequalities faced by Black peoples in Latin America. Whereas OSPAAAL materials spotlighted Black struggles in places like the United States and South Africa, these materials exhibit a consistent silence

---

[75] Weiss, *Framing a Radical African Atlantic*, 83.

regarding the conditions of Black peoples in Latin American countries.[76] Indeed, by effectively externalizing anti-Black racism to African and North American contexts, the OSPAAAL repeated a major error of both the LADLA and its umbrella organization, the LAI.

THINKING TRICONTINENTALISM BACKWARDS AND FORWARDS

Tracing the full arc of the OSPAAAL's history and legacy is crucial for understanding the Tricontinental movement. A discussion of Tricontinentalism without the larger framework of its deep roots in interwar internationalism fails to adequately address the way it responded to the accomplishments and missteps of the LAI's interwar project. Placing these two movements together reveals that Latin America had a longer history of radical, global anti-imperialism than is often understood. Though sharing common goals, Tricontinentalism went further in embracing an anti-imperialism that linked anti-capitalism with racial justice, even as its solidarity with Black freedom struggles did not always produce self-reflection about the inequalities of Latin American societies. In the same way that we need to better understand the roots of Tricontinentalism, we must also look beyond the 1966 conference and beyond the immense propaganda of the OSPAAAL itself to comprehend the long-term implications of this political project. In addition to the scholarly importance of such an endeavor, studying the history and contemporary resonances of radical internationalisms, which includes examining the failures of these movements, is a vital baseline for forging global justice movements into the future.

---

[76] The OSPAAAL's silence on Black struggles in Latin America is related, although not identical to the Cuban government's own complicated racial discourse through which it supported Black radical organizing abroad while suppressing it in the domestic realm. Although OSPAAAL materials became a tool for the exercise of Cuba's duplicitous racial politics, the OSPAAAL's discourse was the result of a transnational exchange and was not exactly identical to the discourse of the Cuban state. For more on these complex racial politics, see chapters 3 and 4 in Mahler, *From the Tricontinental to the Global South*.

2

Tricontinentalism

The Construction of Global Political Alliances

Rafael M. Hernández and Jennifer Ruth Hosek

Tricontinentalism expressed a rebel movement within the international system. The rebellion of the South against the North predated the time in which the specter of Marxism or communism spread over the face of the earth. It opposed the structure of North-South domination established with the conquest and colonization of people in Latin America, Asia, and Africa by European powers in the Global North from the sixteenth century onwards. Beginning with the scramble for Africa and continuing through the early twentieth century, European imperialism increasingly took a more modern form, finding increasingly efficient ways to exploit and export natural resources and the fruits of colonial labor. Anticipated by the United States from the time of the Spanish-American War (1898),[1] this new style of imperialism did not require direct political and military domination of the colonial regimes and its associated costs, but instead control of the colonial economies through trade, financial, and techno-logical dependence, and pacts with local establishments. As the colonial countries gained independence through uneven and disconnected political and military struggles in Asia, Africa, and Latin America, the new sover-eign states confronted a world order where uneven economic structures and conditions continued to favor the interests of Euro-American states – what was called then and since neocolonialism.[2]

[1] Louis Perez Jr., *The War of 1898: The United States and Cuba in History and Historiography* (Chapel Hill: University of North Carolina Press, 1998).
[2] Anthony Brewer, *Marxist Theories of Imperialism: A Critical Survey* (London: Routledge and Kegan Paul, 1980).

esta gran humanidad ha dicho:¡basta!
this great humanity has said:"enough"!
cette grande humanité a dit: "assez"!

jornada mundial de solidaridad tricontinental
3-10 enero/1968
international week of tricontinental solidarity
January 3rd to 10th/1968
semaine mondiale de solidarité tricontinentale
janvier 3-10/1968

OSPAAAL

FIGURE 2.1 This image served as the OSPAAAL logo and was projected onto the Hotel Habana Libre during the 1966 Havana conference. OSPAAAL, Artist Unknown, 1968. Offset, 52x31 cm. Image courtesy Lincoln Cushing / Docs Populi.

It was between these first independent states of the colonial world in Asia and Africa – Indonesia, India, Pakistan, Sri Lanka, the United Arab Republic (UAR), and Ghana – where the first attempts to build alliances developed, even beyond their own regions. From the Afro-Asian Conference in Bandung held in Indonesia in 1955 through the constitution of the Movement of Non-Aligned Countries established in 1961, the notion of an international forum responsive to the interests of the Global South emerged around five key principles: mutual respect for territorial integrity and sovereignty; nonaggression; noninterference in internal affairs; equality and mutual benefit; and peaceful coexistence.[3]

In the 1960s, the evolution of this movement would produce a grand strategy aimed at uniting states that had emerged from anti-colonial and national liberation struggles, revolutionary movements, and progressive forces throughout the world. They would oppose the hegemony of the United States and its allies, the exclusionary logic of a bipolar world, and the sectarianism and disagreements that divided the major socialist powers: the Soviet Union and China. This strategy sought to claim the right for states in the Third World to define their own paths of national liberation – the construction of socially just societies and sovereignty – on the edges of these spheres of influence. Broadly defined, this movement sought to create a new space of dialogue as an alternative to the bipolar international system that emerged during the Cold War.

Popular memory of the era has reduced it to a time of idealism and frustrated struggles, utopias and voluntarist projects, insurgent movements and guerrilla war, all overcome by the pragmatic demands of realpolitik.[4] Scholarly history has enshrined many of these attitudes, reproducing ideological stereotypes and political simplifications first generated during the Cold War, which still permeate popular understandings and academic assessments of the period.[5] By this logic, nothing of that period has anything to do with the challenges and problems of today's world, much less with plausible responses to and collaborative ways of

---

[3] First articulated by Jawaharlal Nehru, in 1954. Ministry of External Affairs, Government of India, "Panchsheel": www.mea.gov.in/Uploads/PublicationDocs/191_panchsheel.pdf.
[4] Joseph Tulchin, *Latin America in International Politics: Challenging US Hegemony* (Boulder, CO: Lynne Rienner, 2016).
[5] Gilbert Joseph and Daniela Spenser, eds., *In from the Cold: Latin America's New Encounter with the Cold War* (Durham, NC: Duke University Press, 2008).

confronting them. To reach a more accurate understanding of Tricontinentalism and the broader Third World project, scholars need to more critically explore the specific global and regional contexts in which this movement took place, review the main strategic conceptions of Tricontinentalism, appreciate its vision of alliance politics, and evaluate them within the context in which they evolved.

Tricontinentalism is sometimes perceived as a Marxist-like set of ideological principles and armed liberation agendas. Our essay argues for its multiplicity of aims and strategies. Building on the insights provided by declassified primary material from the OSPAAAL archives in Cuba, this investigation will explore some of the complexities that characterize the Tricontinental movement and the huge task of creating a Third World alliance, independent from Soviet and Chinese hegemonic influences. It will explain some interests and motivations behind these power factors and ideological contradictions, and the role played by Cuba in moderating them, from its leading position in the Tricontinental movement and Havana conference (1966). And, making use of sources from the German Democratic Republic (GDR) and the Federal Republic of Germany (FRG), it will explore a particular and not-yet-investigated set of interactions between the Third World and Second World nations other than the Soviet Union. These negotiations between Germans and Cuba around the Tricontinental also demonstrate the complexity of the Tricontinental movement, a movement that was anything but just responding to the Soviet versus US alignment and singular in its tactics.

COLD WAR, NON-ALIGNED, AND REVOLUTIONARY LOGIC

After World War II, the Cold War divided the planet into geopolitical poles. Gdansk, Budapest, and Rostock were under the Warsaw Pact bloc, while Marseille and Turin – where the two largest Communist parties outside the USSR held sway – fell within the borders of the North Atlantic Treaty Organization (NATO) and the anti-communist bloc. The new left variously emerging around the globe worked to separate itself from this old guard: from the communist heirs of the Comintern attached to Moscow's line; from betting all on electoral-parliamentary systems; and from the order that emerged from the Yalta Conference, which divided the world between the Soviet East and capitalist West.

On the crest of this new heterodox wave, the left wings of almost all the established parties, from the Communists to the Christian Democrats, broke off; a proliferation of new movements of radical inspiration emerged; Marxist thought came into fashion, even in the great universities of the West; new publishers dedicated to its provisioning appeared, disseminating works from Lenin and Trotsky to José Carlos Mariátegui and Che Guevara, Mao Zedong and Amílcar Cabral, Antonio Gramsci and György Lukacs, Frantz Fanon and Mehdi Ben Barka.[6]

In that context, the political challenge posed by the Cuban revolution toward the hegemonic power of the United States can be measured by what Americans call the Cuban Missile Crisis, but which is better known in Cuba as the October Crisis (*La Crisis de Octubre*). The manner in which the superpowers reached a compromise, a verbal agreement between Kennedy and Khrushchev, without any formal treaty that considered Cuba's national security, avoided nuclear war, but left Cuba exposed to a simple US pledge not to invade the island. After the Crisis of October in 1962, Soviet aid remained vital, but the military umbrella provided by the alliance appeared to have weakened. So close to the United States, so far from the European and Asian East, Cuba felt isolated and far from secure. The only socialist state that truly shared its vision of active revolution was the Democratic Republic of Vietnam, a comparable country on the periphery of the bipolar order, which would attract almost all the destructive capacity of the American Empire, and would, unintentionally, become a lightning rod for the island.[7]

It is for this reason that Che Guevara's 1967 urging to "create two, three, many Vietnams"[8] was not a mere war cry in the ears of Cubans, but a strategic requirement for the common cause of the national liberation revolutions on three continents.[9] With the Soviet Union seeking

---

[6] Karen Dubinsky et al., *New World Coming: The Sixties and the Shaping of a Global Consciousness* (Toronto: Between the Lines, 2009).

[7] Rafael Hernández, "Thirty Days: Lessons from the October 1962 Missile Crisis and U.S.-Cuban Relations," in *Papers on Latin America, Institute of Latin American and Iberian Studies* (New York: Columbia University Press, 1991).

[8] Ernesto Guevara, "Mensaje a los pueblos del mundo a través de la Tricontinental," 16 de abril, *revista Tricontinental*, 1967: www.marxists.org/espanol/guevara/04_67 .htm.

[9] As for armed movements, a short list of those that proliferated only in Latin America: FLN and MIR in Venezuela; FARC, EPL, and ELN in Colombia; FAR in Guatemala; Frente Sandinista in Nicaragua; MIR in Perú; ELN in Bolivia; ALN and VPR in Brazil; FPL in El

accommodation with the First World (see Friedman, Chapter 7), it was vital for Asian, African, and Latin American states to collectively confront the power of the United States since no one had the power to do so alone. This message had an impact beyond the Global South. Actors around the globe interpreted Guevara's message both in solidarity and according to their particular circumstances; we discuss the example of West German activists later.

The undeclared, 55-plus year war that the United States continues to wage upon the Revolution isolated the young Cuba within the hemisphere and left it with few opportunities for dialogue. From early on, the ideological and political struggle, often silent but very evident, between the island and the two largest socialist powers separated Cuba, China, and the Soviet Union on the paths of the Revolution and in the building of the new society. Between 1964 and 1970 that geopolitical isolation became critical.[10] From this situation of regional diplomatic isolation, marginalization in the socialist camp, and imminent danger, the heretic Havana found its partners almost exclusively in Latin America and the Caribbean, Africa, and Asia, especially among the revolutionaries.[11]

THE TRICONTINENTAL: AN INSIDE LOOK

Tricontinentalism expressed not only the rebellion of the South against the North but also a confrontation of various and sometimes competing interests within the South. The coincidence of processes of colonial independence with the revolutions in Russia in 1917 and China in 1949, along with the emergence of these states as defiant actors in a world order dominated by the Western powers, led to a new form of dependency within the movement of Southern countries. In search of support, the newly independent states gravitated increasingly toward the international sphere created by the Soviet

Salvador; MIR in Chile; ERP, and FAR and FAP in Argentina. Their principal leaders included Jorge Ricardo Masetti, Douglas Bravo, Fabricio Ojeda, Manuel Marulanda, Fabio Vázquez Castaño, Camilo Torres Restrepo, Carlos Fonseca Amador, Luis Augusto Turcios Lima, Marco Antonio Yon Sosa, Luis de la Puente Uceda, Javier Heraud, Carlos Marighella, Inti and Coco Peredo, Miguel Enríquez, Cayetano Carpio, and Mario Roberto Santucho.

[10] Rafael Hernández, "El año rojo. Política, sociedad y cultura en 1968," *Revista de Estudios Sociales* 33 (August 2009): 44–54.

[11] Piero Gleijeses, *Misiones en conflicto: La Habana, Washington y África, 1959–76* (Havana: Editorial de Ciencias Sociales, 2002).

Union, converted as the USSR had been into a great power following World War II. With China's emergence, and even more so with the discrepancy between China's line and that of the post-Stalin Soviet Union, these two poles of the socialist camp vied for influence in this peripheral South, which was becoming increasingly more central in global geopolitics.

Tricontinentalism channeled the interests of the national liberation movements in the face of this new order of superpower patronage, a system that until then had shaped their struggles along the prevailing bipolar configuration within the South itself. The road to the Havana conference in 1966 marked a turning point in the established Afro-Asian People's Solidarity Organisation (AAPSO, known in Spanish as the Organización de Solidaridad de los Pueblos de Asia y África, or OSPAA), a point at which Southern actors sought to counterbalance competing East-West politics within the movement for liberation and self-determination in Asia, Africa, and Latin America. The Tricontinental Conference crystallized this struggle and defined a concerted institutional order in which the alliance between the weaker players prevailed over the logic of superpower realpolitik in which the Chinese-Soviet pattern was rooted.

Havana was the natural home for this emerging challenge to bipolarity. In the 1960s, Cuba was at the height of its prestige and political and moral authority, especially within the broad anti-imperial movement. While Fidel Castro's charismatic personality and his *guerrillero* image were influential, the country's prominence owed a greater debt to more concrete factors. Cuba had achieved national liberation by its own means and had shown itself capable of defending itself and surviving on the border of the United States, which had supplanted Europe as the center of imperial power in the eyes of many nationalists in the Global South. Cuba was also resisting pressure to align either with China or the Soviet Union, claiming a path between these increasingly vitriolic poles of the socialist world. In so doing, Cuba projected a distinct socialist model and an independent foreign policy, which envisioned a unified anti-imperial left that respected self-determination and sovereignty, especially for small countries.[12]

To understand the Tricontinental Conference is to appreciate this broader set of ambitions, rather than simplifying it as a meeting of

---

[12] Comité Preparatorio de América Latina, *Cartas al CIP de la Conferencia Tricontinental.*

armed conspirators and their sponsors. The conference was part of the movement's arduous process of building political alliances. Whereas intelligence services, governments, and the established media limited themselves to identifying a meeting of subversives, in fact, it was an exercise in diplomatic dialogue between anti-hegemonic and progressive forces from most regions of the world, state and nonstate actors – legal and armed, atheists and believers, socialists, communists and *independentistas*.[13] The question of national liberation that was discussed is a topic far more expansive than insurgency or guerrilla warfare.

The declassified documents of the Tricontinental Conference shed light on this political process and its challenges and map out alignments and their reconfigurations.[14] According to these documents, the project of building an Organization of Solidarity of the Peoples from Africa, Asia and Latin America (Organización de Solidaridad de los Pueblos de Africa, Asia y América Latina, or OSPAAAL) – the permanent institution envisioned by the Tricontinental movement – faced three major challenges.[15]

---

[13] Socialists from legal parties like Salvador Allende (Chile) and Heberto Castillo (Mexico), communists like the Communist Party of Vietnam, independentistas like the Partido Africano para a Independência da Guiné e Cabo Verde (PAIGC) led by Amílcar Cabral.

[14] All the Cuban document references are from the OSPAAAL Archives in Havana, particularly from these six folders. OSPAAAL, Archivo histórico:

1. *Análisis general de la Conferencia Tricontinental.* Enero 1966. Gaveta No. 1, File 1.
2. *Breve Informe sobre la Conferencia Tricontinental.* 1966. Gaveta No. 1, File 1.
3. Comité Preparatorio (CP) de la Conferencia de los Tres continentes (1965). *Llamamiento para la 1ª. Conferencia de los Pueblos de Asia, Africa y América Latina (La Habana, 3–10 de enero, 1966).*
4. Secretariado Permanente OSPAA, El Cairo, 1–2 septiembre. Gaveta No. 1, File No. 1-A.
5. Primera Conferencia de Solidaridad de los Pueblos de Asia, Africa y América Latina (1966). *Credenciales, control de participantes acreditados hasta los días 5 y 10 de enero. Enero.* Gaveta 1, File No. 84.
6. Comité Preparatorio de América Latina (1965). *Cartas al CIP de la Conferencia Tricontinental, El Cairo, 31 de agosto y 1 de septiembre, 1965.* Documentos del CIP. Conferencia Tricontinental. Gaveta 4. File 254-A.

[15] *Análisis general de la Conferencia Tricontinental.* This "Análisis" is a political report about the main issues of the conference, with critical judgments and assessments by top Cuban representatives. It is not signed and is not addressed to a specific person, but it must have been written by the leadership of the Cuban delegation (Osmani Cienfuegos, Manuel Piñeiro, and Raúl Roa García) to Fidel Castro. When a reference to this key document is made, we reproduce its exact words and concepts.

The first was the coordination of an anti-imperial agenda. This agenda encompassed the major themes of Tricontinentalism: in the words of the movement as expressed in the documents: "the fight against imperialism, colonialism, and neo-colonialism"; reaffirmation of a genuine peace agenda; and disarmament and peaceful coexistence for all, not only the great powers. For the Cuban hosts and many other delegations, the most important component of this struggle, one that should supersede all other issues, was unrestricted, multifaceted institutional support for the achievement and defense of national liberation. As explained above, national liberation was much more expansive than armed struggle.[16]

The second challenge was to achieve an organization capable of providing this support through the development of active transnational solidarity. This support would transcend what some documents describe as the style and bureaucratic limitations experienced in AAPSO and other international democratic organizations, such as the World Federation of Democratic Youth. Expressions of alliance between the USSR and the newly independent nations of Asia and Africa had remained more symbolic than effective in solving the specific tasks of the movement.

The third was the Sino-Soviet divergence. Its impact on the movement will be explained in more detail later; generally speaking, it weakened the socialist camp. In regard to the conference, this divergence and the subsequent polar alignment of states and political organizations of all three regions made negotiations more complex. In the lead-up to the Havana Conference, the USSR and China both urged specific organizational and methodological additions to the program that had potential implications for the substance of future debate. For example, the Soviets advocated granting observer status – with the right to speak – to international organizations that they controlled. The Chinese opposed time limits on interventions in the plenary, and its representatives pushed to adopt accords by a two-thirds majority instead of unanimity, part of Beijing's effort to advance more radical positions than state delegations aligned with the Soviet Union might have been willing to consider.[17] That vocal and disciplined minorities could hijack discussions was more of a threat to the event than any that could have been dreamed up by European and North America enemies or the authoritarian regimes in Latin America.

---

[16] *Análisis general de la Conferencia Tricontinental.* These two fundamental concepts of the Non-Aligned movement and the Tricontinental movement, *pacific coexistence* and *national liberation*, were both legitimated as part of the Cuban agenda.

[17] *Análisis general de la Conferencia Tricontinental.*

Most of the discussions at the conference focused on these three problems. But the third was the most pervasive and divisive, even to the point of influencing responses to the first two. Plenary sessions were extended beyond the regulations, taking time and energy from discussions in the commissions where specific and emerging tasks were to be considered, debated, and established. Among the most important of these "burning issues" were those cases that the conference defined as military occupations, such as South Vietnam and the Dominican Republic, both of which had recently become sites of American military intervention.

The Cuban delegation to the International Preparatory Committee (IPC) of the Tricontinental found that the Sino-Soviet split had turned AAPSO into an "arena of confrontation," whose course shifted between two poles according to how the majority of the AAPSO aligned at any given time.[18] For instance, the United Arab Republic (Egypt) under Nasser aligned with the USSR; Pakistan and the Democratic People's Republic of Korea with China. African states, for their part, associated with one or the other according to the situation, and in many cases followed the lead of the National Liberation Movement (NLM) of their region or nation. Other signs of this matrix of contention were expressed by Japan's distrust of supporting armed struggle, the condemnation of the United Nations as an "instrument of imperialism" by China, and the debate over whether Yugoslavia was a legitimate participant.

Despite these contentious issues, several benchmarks were met during preparation for the conference. When consensus on holding the event was reached in the AAPSO secretariat and its organization was started, the number of NLMs exceeded the number of states in the IPC for the first time. The entry of Latin America and the Caribbean, with five NLMs and only one state (Cuba), had changed the representation on the board of directors. Previously, AAPSO's board composition had favored states – nine including the USSR and China over only six NLMs. In the lead-up to the Tricontinental, this predominance of states in the IPC (India, Guinea, Algeria, Tanzania, Indonesia, the UAR, China, and the Soviet Union) ended. The NLMs of the Latin American countries (Venezuela, Mexico, Guatemala, Chile, Uruguay), Cuba, and the remainder of the Committee (South Vietnam, Japan, South Africa, Morocco), constituted a new

---

[18] "La OSPAA se volvió burocrática, inepta e ineficaz para la liberación nacional [AAPSO became bureaucratic, inept, and ineffective for national liberation]." *Análisis general de la Conferencia Tricontinental.*

majority.[19] The NLMs had rather different commitments and were more independent from the influence of governments, although they also experienced alignment pressures from China and the USSR.

Another change in the lead-up to the conference was that the newly admitted Latin American NLMs galvanized the Preparatory Committee to modify the terms upon which national committees were established.[20] This move countered China's motion, which advocated selection from the central communist parties in order to favor pro-Chinese political groups. This background, coupled with other disagreements between Cuba and China, heralded the shocks that would characterize the relationship between this host country and one of the largest delegations at the conference.

The significance of the OSPAAAL project itself assured that part of the agenda would focus on discussing OSPAAAL's constitution, a topic that attracted many to the Organizing Committee. The idea of creating a Tricontinental organization was not an end in itself but, rather, a political instrument to strengthen the NLMs and consolidate a united front against the violence of the United States and its allies in Indochina. Fundamental variants were many and debated. The USSR advocated replacing AAPSO with OSPAAAL. China wanted to retain the AAPSO and create a complementary Organization of Latin American Solidarity (OLAS). The United Arab Republic was willing to adopt OSPAAAL but wanted it headquartered in Cairo. Latin American representatives desired that a new OSPAAAL be based in Havana, with AAPSO remaining independent.

According to the confidential report of the Cuban delegation, its strategy was not defined by any preconceived formula to create the Tricontinental. Havana's main goal was to reach an agreement on building a balanced structure for the new organization without harming the unity of the movement. In their position between the competing Soviet and Chinese factions, Cuban delegates tried to moderate the antagonistic positions of every actor, including themselves: "We did not reject the possibility that the Tricontinental would have its headquarters in Havana, but we did not fight for it at all costs."[21]

The Cuban strategy was to avoid discussing every issue in the plenary, where confrontations became very heated. Instead, they negotiated

[19] *Análisis general de la Conferencia Tricontinental.*
[20] Comité Preparatorio de América Latina, *Cartas al CIP de la Conferencia Tricontinental.*
[21] *Análisis general de la Conferencia Tricontinental.*

bilaterally with key actors of various sizes – large (USSR, China), medium (UAR), and small (African and NLMs) – which had various types of influence, as well as with allies (Democratic Republic of Vietnam, South Vietnam's National Liberation Front, and the Pathet Lao). Following the leadership of their representatives at the conference, the Cubans deployed the flexible diplomacy necessary to win over both pro-Chinese countries like Sukarno's Indonesia and others like Guinea, which depended heavily on Soviet aid. In deploying this bilateral negotiation strategy at different levels, their key method was to demonstrate that they sought consensus above everything else. These examples illustrate the extent to which the seven-year-old Cuban government – under an intense US siege and almost totally isolated in the hemisphere – felt compelled to develop ties with a diversity of ideological and geopolitical actors on four continents and thereby both garner international respect and expand Havana's global influence.

One such issue was the question of armed struggle, which outside observers have emphasized but which was actually discussed only a little within the conference. This inattention may have been because, with a few exceptions, most of the participants had accepted that armed revolt was necessary in certain situations where colonialism and imperialism were defended with violence. Though the Soviet Union and its closest allies expressed a preference for peaceful coexistence, many of the influential – if smaller – nations present had come to power after bloody struggles, as was the case for Algeria, Cuba, and the Democratic Republic of Vietnam. Moreover, many delegations from armed movements that were fighting for national liberation or preparing to do so at the time, such as Venezuela, South Vietnam, Zimbabwe, South Yemen, Palestine, Mozambique, Guinea-Bissau, Laos, Guatemala, and South Africa were attending the conference.

The global geopolitical circumstances also furthered widespread sympathies toward various types of violent resistance. In 1965 alone, the United States had landed troops en masse in South Vietnam, while American forces and their Latin American allies occupied the Dominican Republic. Ongoing revolutions in Mozambique and Angola, supported by the Organization of African Unity (OAU), sought to oust colonial Portugal, which benefited greatly from membership in the North Atlantic Treaty Organization (NATO).[22] As a result, progressive political

---

[22] Horace Campbell, "Imperialism and Anti-imperialism in Africa," *Monthly Review* 67:3 (July–August 2015): 98–113.

and intellectual circles in Europe and the United States did not immediately reject armed nationalists as terrorists or as bellicose, especially in the case of Vietnam. Public figures like Lord Bertrand Russell sent emissaries to Havana to make contact with the national liberation movements and the Cuban government. Within two years of the Tricontinental, the assassination of Che Guevara in Bolivia would further arouse world opinion and produce a wave of admiration for the causes of anti-colonialism and national liberation, extending a political climate that made room for armed revolt as a legitimate strategy for the disenfranchised. Indeed, the 1960s and beyond saw a rise in perceived disenfranchisement in the North as the Cold War initially entrenched hierarchical societal and governmental structures that were perceived as restrictive and objectionable. Activists in the North increasingly looked to the South for inspiration, as role models and as evidence that a new world was possible or even probable. Actors in the North practiced solidarity of deed such as protests, international visits, and fundraising in support of revolution in the South. Many on the left, even those perhaps skeptical of particular national governments in the South felt and acted upon what might be loosely called elective affinities or transnational solidarity.

The differences around armed struggle that arose in conference deliberations did not reflect a general reluctance to acknowledge the legitimacy of this strategy. Rather, some organizations and governments were reticent about excluding other forms of political struggle, namely participation in electoral politics. Many delegations to the conference consisted of individuals who did not advocate guerrilla war, such as the socialists Salvador Allende of Chile, Heberto Castillo from Mexico, the Argentinian John William Cooke, and the former premier of British Guiana Cheddi Jagan, as well as the delegations from Uruguay, Costa Rica, Honduras, and Haiti, to speak only of Latin America and the Caribbean. The image of the conference as comprised solely of violent groups was a caricature broadcast by its enemies,[23] whether by design or through ignorance.

Other central themes that occupied the discussion in the commissions were US imperialism's role in culture, as well as relations with mass organizations such as unions, student, and women's groups that were invited to participate in the conference.[24] The impact of the sessions devoted to economic, political, and cultural topics was felt beyond the

---

[23] For enemies' views: http://pdf.oac.cdlib.org/pdf/hoover/97004.pdf.
[24] *Breve Informe sobre la Conferencia Tricontinental.*

halls of the conference, the tendency to caricature the event notwithstanding.

It must be said that the persistence of these stereotypes and prejudices was not confined to the Western governments, or the far-right wing. In those years and subsequently, Cuban students in Eastern Europe and the USSR had to suffer them on many occasions. The representation of the Tricontinental as an encounter of extremists and romantics, and of Che Guevara as an idealistic adventurer obsessed by war and lacking in profound ideas, was common in Soviet political culture then, even in the universities. Many Eastern Europeans who knew the island recognized that Cubans lived their revolution differently and that in addition to passion and patriotism there was a civic culture full of thought and discussion; however, visitors from Eastern countries, journalists, civil servants, and even artists and writers did not always penetrate beyond the epidermis or understand Cuban society. The negotiations between Cuba and the two Germanies around the Tricontinental variously demonstrate romanticization, solidarity, and national political aims on the part of the Germans. Of interest in their own right, these engagements demonstrate the complexity of the Tricontinental and illustrate attempts by Cuba to move beyond the bipolar world desired by some of the most powerful nations.

THE TRICONTINENTAL AND CUBA THROUGH GERMAN EYES

The ideological and political diversity of the participants and observers was expressed in the range of their perceptions and interpretations of the Tricontinental. The German example is an under-recognized case in point. The socialist GDR, the capitalist FRG, and activist groups in the FRG – the West Berlin anti-authoritarians, for example – each interpreted the conference, Cuba's actions, and their own position relative to their particular interests, aims, and desires. Although they were in different *worlds*, the GDR in the Second World and Cuba in the Third World, each negotiated toward an alliance by highlighting the similarities of their geopolitical circumstances in the polarizing world of the Cold War. Meanwhile, the left-leaning student activists in the First World styled themselves as being in circumstances analogous to those of the Cubans. And left-leaning Germans on both sides of the Wall came together over critiques of neocolonialism and Third World solidarity.

An overview of the relative positionings of the Tricontinental Conference participants shows the complexity of the political enlacements among these three worlds. Since the Tricontinental was, by definition, regional and excluded Europe, North America, and Australia, most participant delegates (full members) came from Asia, Africa-Middle East, and Latin America. As has been pointed out, some of them represented national liberation movements, but many others did not. The delegations from Chile, Argentina, Algeria, Bolivia, Brazil, Costa Rica, Korea, Ecuador, Ghana, and Guadeloupe, for example, represented official state governments or political factions that had yet to adopt ambitions for political insurrection. The AAPSO had also recognized solidarity organizations from the USSR, the People's Republic of China, the Democratic Republic of Vietnam, and even from Japan as full members. Apart from the DRV, they were not related to any national liberation movement. The two largest delegations to the Havana conference came from China (34) and the USSR (40), which added to the political complexity of the Tricontinental fabric; it was well known that the Sino-Soviet divergence was over more than a simple dichotomy of armed struggle versus peaceful coexistence. As for the Second World, seven solidarity organizations attended the conference as observers. With seven representatives, the largest delegation came from the GDR.

Like other Soviet-aligned socialist countries in Europe and the Soviet Union itself, the GDR saw in the Tricontinental Conference and in Cuba an opportunity and a danger, which several key documents show. The meeting on February 15, 1966, of the Politburo of the Central Committee of the GDR's ruling Socialist Unity Party (Sozialistische Einheitspartei Deutschlands, or SED) in Berlin includes an analysis of the conference. The report highlights principled successes of the GDR delegation there. It articulates GDR and socialist state aims of aligning the Tricontinental and Cuba toward the Soviet Union and Marxist-Leninism. It emphasizes the GDR's allegiance to the Soviets by describing the delegation as particularly active in working to meet these goals, for instance by strengthening long-standing relationships and developing new ones. It also asserts that the GDR received extensive recognition from the anti-imperialist movement, for instance State Council Chair Walter Ulbricht's telegram was one of the first read to the attendees and was warmly received.[25]

[25] Folder: SAPMO-BArch DY30/J IV 2/2/1045 Protokoll Nr. 6/66 (Einschätzung Politbüros ZK SED Drei-Kontinente Konferenz 3 10 Jan 1966). The report was written by Comrade Markowski and Comrade Heinz Schmidt, the latter the honorary president of the GDR's Afro-Asian solidarity committee at the time. They had not themselves attended the conference.

A full, polyadic analysis could thoroughly consider GDR relations with the FRG and NATO countries, the USSR, and the Eastern European socialist camp, the Third World and Latin America (as arenas of confrontation with its enemies), and with Cuba; this essay will focus on the Politburo's assessment of the Cuban role in the Tricontinental. The report emphasizes Cuba's socialist bent and its allegiance with the Soviet camp. It states that "having the conference in a socialist country like Cuba gave it an importantly positive impetus." In preparation for the conference, it continued, there was increasing agreement between the Cubans and the USSR, "although the Cubans emphasized the necessity to make tactical concessions so that the Chinese could not achieve their aims [*nicht zum Zuge kommen könnten*]." According to this official report, then, the Cubans collaborated with the Soviets in order to better negotiate Chinese tactics that sought to unduly influence the conference's political objectives and definitions. This perception is consistent with the tensions reported by the Cuban delegation vis-a-vis the Chinese line in the planning and organization of the conference, and particularly in regard to the independent role that Latin America sought toward the new OSPAAAL. In the Tricontinental context, the Cuban government perceived these Chinese policies as an expression of hegemony that put pressure on Third World actors – national liberation movements in Latin America and Africa, as well as socialist countries such as Vietnam and Cuba itself – to align with Beijing, thereby limiting their diplomatic freedom. One stark example is that during this period Mao Zedong was using trade mechanisms – namely aid shipments of rice – to try to force Cuba to join the pro-China communist faction.

The Cuban position was much more complicated than the East-West geopolitical equation, particularly the zero-sum game that largely defined the GDR's situation. After all, the Cuban-Soviet alliance remained on rocky ground as well. Three years after the Missile Crisis of 1962, Cuba did not trust the Soviet Union's political support; it was skeptical that the geostrategic umbrella that protected the GDR and the European socialist camp would provide any protection to Cuba. The following quote from the report about Cuba's actions at the conference merits detailed consideration. Although as we will see further on, Cuban and GDR diplomatic discourse emphasized parallel geopolitical narratives between the island and East Germany, both countries experienced quite different circumstances. These on-the-ground differences help explain why this report assesses the Cuban position in the conference as exceptionalist:

[The Cubans] overemphasized the importance of their so-called own experiences in armed liberation struggle for the entire movement. Upon this they based their claim to lead the movement. They were patronizing to the other delegates and went as far as a break with the SU, to intrigues against representatives of the communist party of Latin American, and to eliding the role of the SU in speeches and in the drafting of documents. The Latin American movement of armed struggle under the leadership of Cuba was deemed as having higher quality than that of the struggle of the African peoples.

The African, Arabic, and Indian delegates were deeply perturbed and angered with the Cuban position and threatened in part to leave the conference early.

The Cuban position threatened the success of the conference, threatened the unity of the anti-imperial movement, and hindered a decisive rejection of the Chinese attempts at obstruction [*Störversuche*].

The document further states that Cuba insisted upon making Havana the seat of the Tricontinental, which also hindered cooperation. It goes beyond the scope of this investigation to determine whether Cuba's or the GDR's reporting on this position and its effects is more accurate; the fact that the GDR decried Cuba's actions in this regard points to tensions between the two. The Cubans' actions are portrayed as an impediment to the cohesion of the event: arrogant, overbearing, and excessively patriotic. The depiction of the Cubans as divisionaries may be interpreted as official GDR discontent about Cuban actions that would move the conference outside of the sphere of influence of the Soviet Union. It demonstrates that the positions of the GDR and Cuba were quite distanced. The GDR considered its present and future to be with the Soviets, while the Cubans considered both the Soviets and the Chinese to be distractions.

As we will see, however, other official documents from the GDR highlight similarities between the Cuban and GDR positionalities. These seeming dichotomies show us that there were many aspects to the GDR's relationship with Cuba. This example of complex relations between the Third World country of Cuba and the Second World country of the GDR also functions as a corrective to the commonly held myth of bipolarity at the conference and beyond. The document to which we now turn suggests that the GDR understood Cuba better than some other Eastern bloc countries due to its own positioning on the West-East border and its assessment of Nazi Germany's and the FRG's actions as imperialist. These situations were not abstract for them. Furthermore, the GDR could leverage these parallels as a means of influencing Cuba, which was its aim at the Tricontinental Conference. Cuba and others were skeptical of the USSR; by winning over Cuba, the GDR could garner favor with the USSR and gain power on the world stage.

A memorandum on a follow-up meeting to the conference on July 20, 1966, between a GDR delegation visiting Havana for the 26th of July commemoration and representatives of the Tricontinental movement's executive committee shows how both sides emphasize parallels between Cuba and the GDR. Each side depicts these similarities as reasons to support closer alliance and cooperation. The Guinean representative and leader of the meeting, Kouyaté, explicitly describes European issues and the German Problem as central to joint concerns. Further, the Cuban representative is reported to have invited the GDR representatives to a July symposium "condemning the war of mass destruction against the Vietnamese, at which the role of 'West German imperialism' would also be exposed." GDR diplomat Dieter Kulitzka highlights the connection in his assessment:

> The Executive Secretariat's unmistakable allusion that our national mission is to be supported to the extent that we take seriously and further the Tricontinental Movement must be seen as noteworthy. Seemingly (and certainly rightly) the struggle against West German imperialism is deemed an effective main point of connection [*Hauptanknüpfungspunkt*] between the Tricontinental Movement and the GDR. Precisely this commonality was also especially emphasized in Comrade Ducke's [representative of the Afro-Asian Solidarity Association] statements.[26]

In the 1960s, left-leaning thinkers commonly labeled the FRG's agenda as imperialist based on its participation in NATO, its bellicose attitude toward the GDR, and its support for US military actions around the world.[27] Both the Cubans and the GDR saw parallels in the "hot" aggression of the United States and the "cold" aggression of the FRG. We have seen that the Tricontinental Conference itself categorized armed and unarmed aggression differently; hence at least some of the emphasis on the similarity should be seen as a means to further ties between these countries on different sides of the North-South division.

The GDR's engagement with the Cubans and the Tricontinental movement also aimed to augment the GDR's importance among the Warsaw Pact countries and the Soviets. The socialist German nation may have

---

[26] Unless otherwise indicated, all the archival material in this section on Germany stems from the following folders: Federal Foreign Office Political Archive MFAA 3231 B40 nr. 100 and B33 nr. 470 and SAPMO—BARCH DY30-IVA2120-63. Here MFAA3231 B40 nr 1—B33 nr 470.

[27] We would like to thank Will Gray for an email discussion (March 21, 2017), in which he also notes that West Germany supplied military aid to several African countries in the 1960s, as well as supplying weapons to Israel.

considered it beneficial to show these Southern players with whom it seemed to have some influence in a politically beneficial light. Kulitzka's report carefully outlines the structure of the Tricontinental and makes its mission clear without highlighting its interest in armed struggle, from which the Soviet Union had distanced itself after the conference. Kulitzka describes Kouyaté's words on this matter, which smooth and diminish the tension without dismissing it:

> The Tricontinental Movement is, just as the socialist countries are, determinedly decided for world peace. Its way to achieve its goal is not by means of a world war, although the way of the Tricontinental Movement is militant [*kämpferische*].

In this statement Kouyaté seeks to mitigate potential objections to militancy through clever formulations. Such phrasing may be tactical vis-à-vis (mistrustful) representatives of socialist nations and, also, expresses contradictions within the Tricontinental movement itself.

While discussions among socialists such as the one described in the documents above make clear that Tricontinentalism did not need to be seen as requiring armed rebellion, the perception of Cuba as a revolutionary state continued to stoke international fears. In the immediate wake of the Tricontinental Conference, many Latin American governments reacted against what they perceived as a potentially violent communist threat in the heart of the Inter-American Treaty of Reciprocal Assistance (commonly known as the Rio Pact or TIAR in Spanish). By January 25, 1966, Peru had called for a special session of the Organization of American States to protest the conference's final resolution, accusing the Soviet Union and Cuba by name. Venezuela was adamant in its complaint. The government of the Dominican Republic barred its delegates from reentry on the charge that while in Havana these participants had stated their aim to hinder voting and to start a new civil war modeled on Vietnam. It is, of course, useful to keep in mind here that most of these Latin American governments were under authoritarian or military control that they sought to maintain against popular support: Argentina (1966–73), Bolivia (1964–66), Brazil (1964–85), Ecuador (1963–66), Paraguay (1954–89), El Salvador (1931–82), Guatemala (1957–66), Honduras (1963–71), Nicaragua (since the 1930s), among others. Moreover, the Dominican Republic was militarily occupied by the Inter-American Peace Force when the conference took place, with no civilian president-elect, but military rule by two generals, one Brazilian and one American. Of course, these military regimes were unhappy with the Tricontinental, even if some would engage with similar politics in the future.

While the GDR was participating in the conference and developments stemming from it in the manner sketched above, the FRG was bound by the Hallstein Doctrine – which meant it could not recognize Cuba because of Cuba's diplomatic relations with the GDR – and by restrictive US policies toward Cuba. Restricted by this Cold War legislation, it watched attentively from the sidelines. Accordingly, archival material from the Federal Republic consists primarily of communiqués from German embassies about the conference. A report dated February 4, 1966, from the German embassy in Montevideo highlights the GDR as an important, and, importantly, more palatable representative in Latin America than the Soviet Union. According to this document, Uruguay had been adamant over its concern about the conference resolution and "the SU's expressed desired role in Latin American armed struggle." Although Uruguay is a "main bridgehead [*Hauptbrückenkopf*]" for the Soviets in Latin America, the report states, Uruguay's signing of the joint protest petition should be a warning for the Soviet Union to avoid an obvious presence in Uruguay. This West German description of the conservative Partido Nacional government in Uruguay as an ally of the Soviets, who were on the other side of the political spectrum, and of the Soviet policy as supporting armed struggle in Latin America reflects a typical Cold War shortsightedness. Moreover, as in the East German examples above, such reporting from the FRG shows that Bonn's main concerns around the Tricontinental Conference were its own German-German affairs and, relatedly, that both Germanies saw the potential for a special relationship between the GDR and Cuba.

Among the FRG populace, interest in Cuba and the Tricontinental also accorded with its own concerns. While left-leaning GDR citizens may have felt that their government did not go far enough in their collaboration with or emulation of Cuba, left-leaning FRG citizens disagreed with the position of their leaders. In some ways the situation in West Germany recalled leftist liberation movements who visited the Tricontinental Conference and, to the chagrin of those formally in power, left energized to unsettle their governments back home. The West Berlin anti-authoritarians are an example of the Northern political groups who were inspired by the Tricontinental and its support of armed violence, perhaps inordinately so. They had no first-hand experience with the pain of such struggle after all. The anti-authoritarians did not attend the conference, but they followed it, the Tricontinental Organization,

AAPSO, OSPAAAL, and the OLAS, as well as many activist and liberation organizations of the Third World, closely. In parallel with Cuba's situation, they saw the relationship between West Berlin and West Germany and West Germany and the United States as neocolonial. After all, the Federal Republic of Germany was being built up as a primary US trade and strategic ally in Europe through the Marshall Plan and the stationing of American and NATO troops in the FRG.[28] Indeed, as Jennifer Ruth Hosek has shown in detail elsewhere, the anti-authoritarians – mostly students, and famously led by Rudi Dutschke – strategized/fantasized about "liberating" West Berlin using the *foco* theory made famous by Che Guevara.[29]

Deeply skeptical of fascist nationalism, these youths were nevertheless inspired by the revolutionary nationalism espoused by the non-aligned movement since the 1950s and articulated at the conference. They identified with what Michael Hardt and Antonio Negri call subaltern nationalism: "whereas the concept of nation promotes stasis and restoration in the hands of the dominant, it is a weapon for change and revolution in the hands of the subordinated."[30] These Northern students and intellectuals embraced subaltern nationalism and sought alignment with Third World groups. The protests that they undertook in Berlin were informed by and in solidarity with Southern struggles. They were inspired by Guevara's 1967 call for multiple Vietnams as they resisted their government's move to the right and crackdown on dissent. Their take on the Tricontinental and the movement it sought to create may have been one that exaggerated its emphasis on armed struggle while also expressing an affective solidarity with the Global South.

More generally, the relationships of leftist activists in the North with liberation struggles in the South may be seen as a solidarity of the type for which conference participants strove translated into a Northern register. These connections are often understood as revolutionary romanticism, perhaps leading, in extreme cases, to domestic terrorism. While attending

---

[28] For example, Nick Thomas, *Protest Movements in 1960s: West Germany, a Social History of Dissent and Democracy* (Oxford: Berg, 2003); William Glenn Gray, *Germany's Cold War: The Global Campaign to Isolate East Germany, 1949–1969* (Chapel Hill: University of North Carolina Press, 2003); Quinn Slobodian, *Foreign Front: Third World Politics in Sixties West Germany* (Durham: Duke University Press, 2012).

[29] Jennifer Ruth Hosek, "'Subaltern Nationalism' and the Anti-Authoritarians," *German Politics and Society* 26:1 (2008): 57–81.

[30] Michael Hardt and Antonio Negri, *Empire* (Cambridge, MA: Harvard University Press, 2000), 60, 105–106.

to this criticism, recent scholarship has been investigating practices of solidarity across North and South that exceed the physical and the cognitive. It explores the political significance of affective relationships – sympathy, empathy – in the absence of international relations between states or organizations and a critical mass of support for political action.[31] While their results will be different and perhaps not immediately massively influential, taking them seriously can enrich understandings of solidarity and its potential for creating change.

Significantly, dismissals of Southern-inspired liberation movements in the Global North have tended to coincide with the end of broad-scale state socialism and a concomitant sense that perhaps socialism itself has failed. In the German case, established left-leaning scholars have been levelling self-criticism since the mid-1980s. As the Soviet bloc became destabilized, many reassessed their interest in and work with Third World issues and found them lacking. A related critique noted that transnational solidarity allowed Northerners to align on the politically emancipatory side of history and escape their guilt about their own national pasts by identifying with the victims and/or translating this guilt into responsibility for neocolonialism. Many of these intellectuals had also moved politically to the right, into the fold of the dominant society. Therefore, in making this self-critique, the now well-established 1960s generation shifted from what had become the "losing" side.[32] In contrast, scholars without direct experience with – and unconvinced of – the state socialisms of the Cold War and yet hoping for something better are investigating the possibilities opened by the limited solidarity of privileged Northerners: for instance, that affective solidarity and identification drove emancipatory political actions of the West Berlin anti-authoritarians; for instance, as Robert J. C. Young argues, that postcolonial theory itself – an influential model of thinking based in non-Western political and cultural production – would seem to have originated at the Tricontinental Conference.[33]

[31] Three contributions to the question of German solidarity with the Third World are Jamie Trnka, *Revolutionary Subjects: German Literatures and the Limits of Aesthetic Solidarity with Latin America* (Berlin: De Gruyter, 2015); Slobodian, *Foreign Front*; and Marike Janzen, *Writing to Change the World: Anna Seghers, Authorship, and International Solidarity in the Twentieth Century* (Rochester, NY: Camden House, 2018).

[32] Jennifer Ruth Hosek, "Interpretations of Third World Solidarity and Contemporary German Nationalism," in *New World Coming: The Sixties and the Shaping of Global Consciousness*, Karen Dubinsky et al., eds. (Toronto: Between the Lines, 2009).

[33] Robert J. C. Young, *Postcolonialism: An Historical Introduction* (Oxford: Blackwell, 2001).

CONCLUSION

Each of the stakeholders in the Tricontinental project had a particular agenda for the conference and for shaping North-South anti-imperialist and Cold War strategies. Cuba was deeply involved before and after the conference in negotiating the tensions and infighting between anti-imperialist and socialist liberation movements and parties, national governments, and the major powers of the Soviet Union, China and, indirectly, the United States. German actors – the GDR, the FRG, and the West Berlin anti-authoritarians – present particularly interesting cases of interaction with Northern actors. German positioning at the borders of the Cold War conflict in Europe led to the two governments being particularly interested in how the conference and GDR relations with Cuba could increase Southern solidarity with the German-German problem and improve their statures on the world stage. The anti-authoritarians exemplify a Northern-based liberation group inspired by Southern anti-imperialist theory and practice. Variously considered dilettantes and dangerous rabble-rousers, their domestic, progressive political actions were fueled by their assessment of the Tricontinental and Cuba. While the conference is often viewed as a South-South attempt to foment revolution, it was far more ambitious and complex in terms of its goals, structures, and membership. Not only did armed revolution constitute just a single goal of Tricontinentalism, but the conference and broader movement centered on uniting global anti-imperial forces. This focus encompassed not just countries of the Global South but also socialist bloc states and sympathizers in Western countries disillusioned by what they saw as unjust foreign policies of their homelands, specifically their approach to the Global South.

This essay has focused on the strategic interpretations and practices of Cuba, one of the main organizers of the conference and key actors in the Tricontinental movement; on the perceptions of the GDR, not a member of the movement, but rather an observer in the Tricontinental framework, and also an actor aligned with the Soviet Union in the East-West bipolar system; and has touched on the strategic interpretations of the FRG, a spectator interested, as was its sibling nation the GDR as well, in the impact of the Tricontinental on the German problem. Additional comparison with a group of activists who avidly read Third World texts in their Northern cities and sought solidarity in emulation may have seemed irrelevant, governed as they were by affect and elective affinity. Consider, however, this comment from Markus Wolf of the GDR's secret service for international affairs upon an official visit to Havana in January 1965, an indication that even the line between affective solidarity and strategic intelligence is neither straightforward nor bound by national borders:

The Cuban comrades have only these words in their mouths, "before the revolution . . .." It's what they have really done, beneath the sun of the tropics. While we, the others, in the grey daily grind, have moved from the rubble of Nazism to socialism in the trucks of the Red Army.[34]

---

[34] Roger Faligot, *Tricontinentale: Quand Che Guevara, Ben Barka, Cabral, Castro et Hô Chi Minh préparaient la révolution mondiale (1964–1968)* (Paris: La Découverte, 2013), 88.

3

The PLO and the Limits of Secular Revolution, 1975–1982

Paul Thomas Chamberlin

Black Saturday began on the morning of December 6, 1975, in Lebanon's seaside capital, Beirut. After months of fighting, the city's residents had become accustomed to violence. But they were unprepared for what came that morning. Enraged over the killing of four of their comrades, Christian militiamen had thrown up barricades along several of Beirut's major highways. Armed men demanded that drivers produce their official identity cards, which marked individuals by religion. Many of those identified as Muslim were dragged from their cars and executed, setting off a wave of panic throughout the city. By 2 p.m., state radio declared the city streets unsafe and warned residents to remain inside. Cars careened through dangerous neighborhoods, pulling violent U-turns and dodging potentially deadly roadblocks. Meanwhile, reports of summary executions spread through the capital. Sporadic gunfire and grenade explosions echoed against the concrete and glass sides of Beirut's high-rises. Some estimates placed the number of massacred Muslims at higher than 300. Muslim militias responded by launching an assault on three of the city's largest hotels – the St. George, Phoenicia, and Holiday Inn – which lay under the control of Christian forces. The fighting set off a wave of sectarian cleansing punctuated by more massacres in the coming weeks as Lebanon descended deeper into a dystopia of ethno-religious warfare.[1]

---

[1] David Hirst, *Beware of Small States* (New York: Nation Books, 2010), 111; James Markham, "Panic Grips Beirut Amid New Killings and Kidnappings," *New York Times*, December 7, 1975.

The sectarian violence raging in Lebanon confounded observers around the world. That quarreling religious communities inside a prosperous, modern state could fall into a vicious civil war flew in the face of prevailing Cold War logic. It was assumed that late twentieth-century wars were fought over political ideology, not religious faith. And 1975 should have been a banner year for the secular revolutionaries, who had long championed the vision of a Third World united in the face of world imperialism. Progressive forces around the world that supported the cause of Palestinian liberation (Figure 3.1) began the year rejoicing in the news Yasser Arafat – leader of the secular Palestine Liberation Organization – had delivered a triumphal speech on the floor of the United Nations (UN) General Assembly to thundering applause only weeks earlier. In January, North Vietnamese forces launched a military campaign that would bring them final victory in April with the Fall of Saigon. That same month, Cambodian communists seized control of Phnom Penh, creating the new socialist state of Democratic Kampuchea. In June and November, Mozambique and Angola gained independence from Portugal, driving the final nail into the coffin of the Portuguese empire and ending an era of European imperialism that had lasted some 500 years. The year 1975, then, marked the high tide of a movement of secular left-wing forces sweeping through the Third World. But even as the revolutionaries celebrated, events such as Black Saturday suggested that that revolutionary tide had begun to recede.

Between 1975 and 1979, secular revolutionaries around the postcolonial world suffered a series of devastating blows as an array of forces aligned against them. Geopolitical transformations in the Cold War, the increasingly acrimonious Sino-Soviet split, and the emergence of a new set of religious revolutionaries combined to slow the series of left-wing victories and open the door to a resurgence of ethnic and religious conflict around the developing world. By the end of the decade, left-wing forces found themselves embattled and the world they had sought to create in turmoil. Although this process was not confined to the Middle East, the region provided perhaps the clearest indications of the shift away from secular-progressive forms of revolutionary activity and toward ethno-sectarian models.[2] These changes were driven not only by the failures of

---

[2] For more on this process see Gilles Kepel, *Jihad* (Cambridge, MA: Harvard University Press, 2000); and Nader Hashemi and Danny Postel, eds., *Sectarianization: Mapping the New Politics of the Middle East* (New York: Oxford University Press, 2017).

FIGURE 3.1 Support for Palestine emerged in the late 1960s as a key element of the Tricontinental movement, providing a shibboleth of revolutionary solidarity that stretched beyond the Arabian Peninsula and North Africa. In Europe and the Americas in particular, solidarity with Palestine helped differentiate the New Left from the old. OSPAAAL, Faustino Perez, 1968. Offset, 54x33 cm. Image courtesy Lincoln Cushing / Docs Populi.

secular postcolonial states to deliver on a range of programs but also by the deliberate policies of anti-Soviet governments in Washington, Beijing, Cairo, Islamabad, and Riyadh; the emergence of dynamic new political actors who sought to use ethnic and sectarian politics as a vehicle in their efforts to seize official power; and the disintegration of global communist solidarity. These three forces would combine to transform the face of revolutionary politics in the late Cold War and the coming twenty-first century.

Several factors have served to obscure these dynamics in traditional studies of the period. The most basic of these is the artificial scholarly separation between East Asian and West Asian history. For generations, historians in Europe and the United States have tended to cordon off East Asia from the Middle East. However, recent scholarship has begun to transcend these boundaries as global and international historians have sought to trace the connections between regions previously treated as distinct. A second factor came as the result of conventional Cold War historiography, which tended to impose an East versus West binary upon the international politics of the post-1945 era. This binary, in turn, obscured the deep fractures within the communist world, which, by the late 1970s, were in many ways even more acrimonious than the rivalry between Washington and Moscow.[3] Third, the nature of the anti-Soviet coalition between Washington, Beijing, Islamabad, Riyadh, and Cairo was largely covert. The cooperation between these regimes in theaters such as the Soviet-Afghan War was rarely well-publicized. A fourth factor in obscuring these dynamics lay in the difficulties that many US leaders had in recognizing the rising power of ethno-sectarian revolution. Mired in a Cold War mindset, officials in the Carter and Reagan administrations frequently underestimated the impact of these new forces.[4] Indeed, even Zbigniew Brzezinski's much discussed 1978 warning of an "Arc of Crisis" focused on the threat that Soviet forces would capitalize on the upheavals in the postcolonial world rather than the threat posed by the revolutionary forces themselves:

---

[3] See Lorenz M. Lüthi, *The Sino-Soviet Split: Cold War in the Communist World* (Princeton: Princeton University Press, 2008); Jeremy Friedman, *Shadow Cold War: The Sino-Soviet Competition for the Third World* (Chapel Hill: University of North Carolina Press, 2015).

[4] See Nathan Citino, *Envisioning the Arab Future: Modernization in U.S.-Arab Relations, 1945–1967* (New York: Cambridge University Press, 2017).

"An arc of crisis stretches along the shores of the Indian Ocean, with fragile social and political structures in a region of vital importance to us threatened with fragmentation," Brzezinski posited. "The resulting political chaos could well be filled by elements hostile to our values and sympathetic to our adversaries."[5] For all these reasons, the late Cold War transformation of revolutionary politics has flown under the scholarly radar. Only in the twenty-first century has it become clear that events such as the 1979 revolution in Iran were neither a communist foil nor were they some sort of aberration – rather, they helped to announce the rise of a new revolutionary politics in the postcolonial world that would eclipse the secular progressive movements of the 1960s.

THE UNRAVELING OF COSMOPOLITAN REVOLUTION

No force was more disruptive to the spirit of cosmopolitan revolution than the growing rift between Moscow and Beijing. By the mid-1970s, that cleavage hit the developing world with full force. While Soviet and Chinese leaders hurled insults at one another and their troops patrolled the border along the Ussuri River, left-wing parties in the Third World were left to choose between the two communist powers. Meanwhile, China itself had emerged from the depths of the Cultural Revolution. With the death of Mao Zedong in 1976, a new faction rose to power in Beijing led by Deng Xiaoping. Deng launched a sweeping campaign of reforms that transformed the PRC's financial system into a de facto market economy under the control of a nominally communist government. Combined with Beijing's antagonism toward Moscow and its Cold War tilt toward Washington, these transformations shocked left-wing forces around the world, who had looked to China as a model for applying Marxist thought in Third World agrarian societies.

The second great defection of the 1970s came from Cairo. Under Gamal Abdel Nasser, Egypt had carried the flag of Arab revolution and had hosted the largest Soviet military deployment in the developing world. But following Egypt's crushing defeat in the Arab-Israeli War of June 1967, Yasser Arafat and the Palestine Liberation Organization emerged as the new vanguard. Nasser's successor, Anwar al-Sadat, was determined to change course. Nasser's progressive, pan-Arabist policies

---

[5] "Iran: The Cresecent of Crisis," *Time Magazine*, January 15, 1979.

had not delivered the desired gains at home or abroad. Egyptian economic development remained sluggish and Israel's victory in 1967 exposed Cairo's weakness in regional affairs. Likewise, Egypt's failed United Arab Republic with Syria revealed the limitations of the pan-Arab experiment, while the bloody intervention in Yemen proved to be far more trouble than it was worth. If Nasser's policies had failed, perhaps a different approach might work. Over the course of the 1970s, Sadat would begin to open Egypt's economy to market mechanisms and Western investment, seek to reintegrate the Muslim Brotherhood into domestic politics, stage a formal break with the Soviet Union in order to partner with Washington, and forge a peace with Israel.[6]

But most immediately, Sadat needed to focus on regaining Egyptian territory lost to Israel in 1967. After launching a surprise attack on Israeli military forces in the occupied Sinai in October 1973, Sadat managed to force a new round of negotiations in the Arab-Israeli peace process. In 1975, Sadat signed the Sinai Interim Agreement, which effectively returned the peninsula to Egyptian control in exchange for a de facto strategic alliance between Egypt, the United States, and Israel. For all intents and purposes, Egypt had switched sides in the Cold War, dealing yet another blow to the global cause of left-wing revolution.

Meanwhile, at the far southeastern corner of Asia, any lingering doubts about the solidarity of the global Marxist project were destroyed in 1979 when two of the most celebrated revolutionary states in East Asia – China and Vietnam – went to war against one another. Following the retreat of American forces from Saigon in 1975, tensions had grown between the erstwhile communist allies in Cambodia and Hanoi, due in part to the Cambodian regime's suspicion of North Vietnamese regional ambitions. After years of clashes in border areas, a unified Vietnam under Le Duan – passively supported by the Soviet Union – finally invaded the country, now known as Democratic Kampuchea. China responded to the invasion of its Cambodian ally by launching its own short-lived incursion into Vietnam, plunging the region into conflict. Four of communism's greatest twentieth-century revolutionary states – the Soviet Union, China, Vietnam, and Cambodia – had fallen into fratricidal war.

Thus, while the 1970s marked the high point of the secular revolutionary project in the global arena, they also saw that project fall into decline.

---

[6] For more see Paul Thomas Chamberlin, "A World Restored: Religion, Counterrevolution, and the Search for Order in the Middle East," *Diplomatic History* 32:3 (June 2008): 441–469.

Nowhere would these changes be more pronounced than in the Middle East. Between 1975 and 1982, conflicts in Lebanon, Iran, Saudi Arabia, and Afghanistan fundamentally transformed the geostrategic landscape of the Middle East, marginalizing secular revolutionaries and presenting new opportunities to sectarian fighters.

THE WINDS OF CHANGE IN THE MIDDLE EAST

Among the earliest harbingers of this new stage of violence was the beginning of the Lebanese Civil War in 1975. Lebanon sat at the intersection of many forces in the Middle East. The small republic's confessional system aimed to integrate Christian, Sunni, Shia, and Druze minorities into a fixed sociopolitical system. The nation's capital, Beirut, was a financial, cultural, and political gateway between the West and the Arab world. It was also a city filled with Cold Warriors: KGB, Mossad, and PLO agents prowled its streets, and the US embassy and CIA stations were among the largest in the Middle East. That this city of modern highrises and luxury hotels could become a battleground filled with sectarian militias who massacred thousands of civilians hinted at the massive changes underway.

Three years later, one of the greatest bastions of American power in the Middle East began to collapse. The sharp rise in the price of petroleum over the 1970s dramatically expanded the influence of conservative, oil-rich states with expanding ties to the United States, most notably Saudi Arabia and Iran. Gone was the Nasserite progressive vision of a secular, anti-colonial Arabic world strategically positioned between the Cold War superpowers. While Riyadh launched sweeping initiatives to set up Islamic charities and Wahhabi-influenced madrasas throughout the region, Tehran worked to modernize its military forces, buying up state-of-the-art military equipment from the United States as a way of solidifying both domestic stability and regional influence. But the flood in petrodollars sparked sharp inflation in the Iranian economy that combined with festering resentments against the Shah's repressive state to unleash a mounting rebellion in Iran. Over the course of 1978 and 1979, increasing numbers of Iranians took to the streets in protest against the Shah. Though the revolution initially comprised a broad base of Iranians, religious clerics and their followers soon began pushing aside secular left-wing groups with the unintentional assistance of the Shah. Spearheaded by the SAVAK – a massive secret police organization trained by the American CIA and the Israeli Mossad – official repression eliminated all bases of power outside the region save the top religious establishment. Once the Shah's hold on power began to slip, Iran's Shia clergy represented the most organized force in Iranian society. The exiled cleric Ayatollah Khomeini, long a violent critic of the regime, emerged as the voice of this movement by defining an Islamic internationalism that rejected both Western capitalism and Soviet Communism as equally corrupt, dangerous, and morally bankrupt. The revolution's theocratic turn shocked outside observers who had become accustomed to see Marxist thought rather than religious faith as the hallmark of the twentieth-century revolutionary. The Shah fled the country in January 1979, paving the way for the Ayatollah Khomeini's triumphal return in February, and removing one of Washington's staunchest allies in the region.[7]

Although the drama in Tehran marked the clearest indication that the locus of revolutionary power had shifted from secular radicals to religious leaders, it was far from the only one. The Sunni world fostered its own cadre of religious revolutionaries as well. In November 1979, a group of religious extremists anticipating the end of days seized the Grand Mosque in Mecca. Over the next two weeks, the rebels fought off a series of ferocious assaults by government forces. When the smoke cleared, nearly 300 pilgrims, soldiers, and rebels lay dead. The following January, Saudi officials beheaded 63 of the captured insurgents in public squares across the country. But the larger impact was to lead the Saudi government to grant greater power to religious authorities and to tighten religious restrictions throughout the country. Riyadh managed to maintain control of the state and continue its drift toward an American alliance that many revolutionaries deemed unacceptable by canalizing and co-opting the religious fervor that was overtaking the region.

Such revolution was not limited to American allies. Three weeks after Saudi forces regained control of the Grand Mosque, the Soviet Union launched a massive military intervention in Afghanistan to defend the Marxist regime in Kabul against Islamic rebels. Although officials in Washington worried that the intervention was the first step in a larger offensive aimed at the Persian Gulf, the Soviet move was driven by deep anxieties in Moscow. Soviet leaders worried that Kabul might choose to align with the United States and thus transform Afghanistan into a base for American missiles along the Soviet Union's southern frontier. Others in the Kremlin worried that the Islamic revolution in neighboring Iran

---

[7] For more on the Iranian revolution, see Said Arjomand, *The Turban for the Crown* (New York: Oxford University Press, 1989).

coupled with the rise in Islamic militancy in Afghanistan could spill across the border, infecting the millions of Muslims living inside the Soviet Central Asian republics. Fueled by these concerns, a reluctant Soviet leadership chose to send their forces into Afghanistan to save the failing regime in Kabul.[8] In a war that lasted more than nine years, Soviet troops battled Afghan guerrillas across thousands of miles of rugged territory.

Throughout the conflict, US, Pakistani, and Saudi intelligence services shipped large stores of weapons to the Afghan rebels. Pakistani agents ensured that the largest shipments went to Islamic fundamentalist groups aligned with Islamabad. The ideological and religious connotations of the struggle against infidel invaders from the Soviet Union – which had long suppressed its Muslim minorities and discouraged religious practice – contributed to the evolution of a revolutionary Islamic solidarity. Prioritizing Cold War security interests over its unease with radical Islamists, US and Saudi agents helped establish a network of volunteers in the Arab world, many of whom journeyed to Afghanistan to participate in the jihad. By the end of the war, pro-Pakistani religious warriors supported by radical Arab volunteers commanded the most formidable rebel forces inside Afghanistan. In this way, the Soviet-Afghan War became the fountainhead for what would become a globalized jihadist movement in the closing years of the twentieth century and the first decades of the twenty-first century.

The year 1979 marked a pivotal conjuncture in Middle Eastern political history. Though direct linkages between the Camp David Accords, the Grand Mosque siege, the Iranian Revolution, and the Soviet intervention in Afghanistan remain largely elusive, historians now recognize the end of the 1970s as a watershed in the region.[9] From a global perspective, 1979 represented an even larger shift. For the next decade, brutal wars raged in Afghanistan, Lebanon, and along the Iran-Iraq border. While East Asia had been the deadliest region in the preceding three decades, the Greater Middle East became the most violent part of the world after 1979. Thus, this critical juncture at the end of the 1970s and the beginning of the 1980s witnessed the convergence of three, global historical transformations. The Greater Middle East became the most violent region in the world, the path of postcolonial revolution

[8] For more see Artemy Kalinovsky, *A Long Goodbye* (Cambridge, MA: Harvard University Press, 2011).
[9] See for instance David Lesch, *1979: The Year that Shaped the Modern Middle East* (Boulder, CO: Westview Press, 2001).

turned away from Marxism and toward ethno-religious avenues, and the Cold War came to an end. This was no coincidence. Rather, the same forces that led to the end of the contest between the United States and the Soviet Union brought war to battlefields across the Middle East and paved the way for the onset of a new set of revolutionary dislocations in the postcolonial world.[10]

The developments in the Middle East in the 1970s and 1980s helped transform the Third World revolutionary project from one focused on Marxism to one increasingly focused on ethnic and religious identity. It is worth noting, moreover, that this process cut across religious groups. Christian forces in Lebanon; Iranian Shia; Saudi, Pakistani, and Afghan Sunnis; and Jewish radicals in Israel all answered the call of holy war. The transnational nature of these changes and their occurrence at the same time as major transformations in the Cold War international system defies purely local explanations.

THE PALESTINIAN BELLWETHER

The PLO's case maps neatly onto these transitions. The PLO emerged, in its authentically Palestinian form, out of the zeitgeist of the global 1960s. Like many in the Arab world, Palestinian leaders had looked to Nasser and Pan-Arabism in the decade between 1956 and 1966. Arab unity and state-based development under the leadership of the most powerful government in the Arab world appeared as the most promising means of national salvation. The PLO itself was created by the Egyptian government in 1964 in a bid to bind the power of Palestinian nationalism to Nasser's regime. But the humiliation of the 1967 war crushed the allure of pan-Arabism and opened the door for new leaders such as Yasir Arafat and George Habash who would wrest control of the Palestinian nationalist movement from Egypt in the months after the 1967 war.[11]

While Cairo had been humbled, the exploits of another revolutionary capital enthralled the postcolonial world. Waging a desperate liberation war against the greatest superpower on earth, Hanoi and its legions of soldiers and guerrilla fighters were in the process of pulling off the greatest military upset of the Cold War. In January 1968, Vietnamese communist

[10] See Paul Thomas Chamberlin, *The Cold War's Killing Fields* (New York: HarperCollins, 2018).
[11] Paul Thomas Chamberlin, *The Global Offensive* (New York: Oxford University Press, 2012).

fighters launched the Tet Offensive, which would come to be seen as the decisive turning point in America's Vietnam War. Though their ranks were devastated, the Vietnamese guerrillas achieved a political and psychological victory that reverberated across the globe. Two months later, Palestinian guerrillas snatched their own victory from the jaws of military defeat at the Battle of al-Karamah in Jordan. There, Arafat's Fatah chose to stand and fight against a superior column of Israeli forces. Arafat's men suffered heavy casualties, but their actions provided grist for Fatah's propaganda mills. In the following weeks, a flood of volunteers rushed to join the Palestinian liberation movement and Arafat emerged as the new face of the revolution in the Middle East.[12]

Electrified by the myth of the heroic national liberation fighter, Palestinian cadres heralded Chinese, Vietnamese, Cuban, and Algerian guerrillas as comrades in what Yasir Arafat dubbed "the struggle against oppression everywhere." Palestinian groups used the teachings of Mao and Che Guevara and the lessons of the Algerian war to devise their own set of tactics in their liberation war against Israel. PLO leaders also devised a new set of international strategies targeting international transportation networks and global organizations that they, and others, understood to be a significant contribution to the playbook on revolutionary war.[13]

Although Islamic revolutionaries would adopt the group's strategies in the 1980s, the PLO remained ardently secular. Clothed in the guise of Third World liberation warriors, Palestinian fighters achieved startling gains in the late 1960s and early 1970s. This was the heyday of the secular Third World guerrilla. Havana's Tricontinentalism, Algiers' status as the Mecca of revolution, and Hanoi's fight on the frontlines against neo-imperialism – not to mention the animated youth movements in the United States and Western Europe – all fueled the sense that a worldwide revolution was underway. For these groups, secular liberation appeared as the most viable vehicle for achieving revolutionary success. Third World solidarity paid impressive dividends to the PLO. Riding a wave of popular support in forums such as the United Nations and the Conference of Non-Aligned States, PLO representatives swept onto the international stage in 1973 and 1974. Arafat's dramatic address to the UN General Assembly in late 1974 marked the culmination of this global diplomatic offensive. In the space of seven years, the PLO had managed to gain international recognition as the sole legitimate representative of the Palestinian people, to return the Palestine question to the

[12] Ibid.   [13] Ibid., 22.

center of the world stage, and to establish itself as a seemingly permanent fixture in the politics of the Arab-Israeli dispute.[14]

But 1975 marked a troubling turning point for these revolutionary forces as well as for the PLO. The start of the Lebanese Civil War, which witnessed an attack on a busload of Palestinians by Christian militiamen, heralded the dawn of a challenging new era for the organization. Palestinian leaders initially tried to stay out of these internal clashes. Although the presence of the PLO in Lebanon had played a key role in pushing the nation over the brink into civil war, the PLO recognized that a messy war against Lebanese militias would merely drain energy and resources from the real struggle against Israel. But despite their efforts, the Palestinians found themselves pulled into the fray. As the war dragged on, the PLO was forced to commit forces to fighting fellow Arabs in defense of refugee camps in Beirut. In short order, the camps became fortified bases in a war marked by ethnic and religious massacres.

Although the war's initial alignments broke down roughly into a struggle between left-wing Muslim and Druze forces and conservative Christian militias, a string of victories by the PLO and its allies in late 1975 and early 1976 prompted a Syrian intervention to restore the status quo. Hafiz al-Assad's regime in Damascus feared that a PLO victory would destabilize Lebanon – a development that would dramatically compromise Syrian security – and recognized an opportunity to expand Syria's influence in the Levant. Coupled with Sadat's defection after the 1973 war, Assad's intervention against the PLO and its left-wing allies in Lebanon dealt yet another blow to any hopes of progressive Arab solidarity.[15]

Likewise, the Sino-Soviet split and the Sino-Vietnamese War complicated the situation in the Middle East just as the 1979 Egypt-Israeli Peace Treaty was being finalized. In the years following Sadat's 1972 expulsion of Soviet advisors from Egypt, relations between Cairo and Beijing had improved. Chinese leaders had picked up some of the Kremlin's commitments as an important outside supporter of the regime in Cairo. Beijing recognized the Middle East as an arena in its rivalry with Moscow. As such, Chinese leaders worried about any potential Soviet moves in the region, a stance that ultimately undermined the cause of secular left-wing revolutionary activity in the Arab-Israeli conflict. As Chinese Foreign

---

[14] Ibid.
[15] On the Syrian intervention see Patrick Seale, *Asad: The Struggle for the Middle East* (Berkeley: University of California Press, 1989).

Minister Huang Hua argued in April 1979, the "main foe of Arab unity and peace in the Middle East was not Israel but the Soviet Union."[16] Beijing thus recognized the Egyptian-Israeli Peace Treaty as a potential wedge against Moscow's influence in the Middle East. Nevertheless, the Arab opposition to the treaty and Sadat's increased isolation in the region created a precarious situation for Beijing.

Furthermore, Chinese leaders had no intention of letting their support for the PLO complicate their relationship with Egypt and their larger goal of diminishing Moscow's role in the region. Warmer relations between the PLO and the Kremlin served to further diminish Beijing's sympathies for the Palestinians. The result, British officials noted in 1979, "has naturally led the Chinese to pull their punches in support of the PLO."[17] The public support from some PLO members for Vietnam during the Sino-Vietnamese War represented yet another blow to relations between Beijing and Palestinian leaders.[18]

THE NEW FACE OF REVOLUTION

Thus, by the early 1980s, the glory days of revolution seemed very far away. The 1982 Israeli invasion, which aimed to reinstall a pro-Western Christian government in Beirut and eradicate the PLO, marked a climax to the civil war in Lebanon. Palestinian fighters found themselves besieged in Beirut, dodging Israeli artillery shells along with the city's civilian population. The agreements that ended the siege forced the PLO's evacuation to Tunisia, some 1,500 miles from Palestine. Removed from the frontlines of the struggle against Israel, the organization fell into crisis. The horrific massacres of Palestinian civilians at the Sabra and Shatila refugee camps by Christian militiamen under the protection of Israeli soldiers followed. So too did the US intervention in Lebanon and the Marine Barracks Bombing by the Shia guerrilla group Islamic Jihad. The PLO's expulsion from Beirut did little to quell the tides of war in Lebanon. If the first half of the civil war had revolved around the PLO's presence, the second half would focus largely on the rise of the Lebanese Shia, and

[16] Huang Hua quote: K. Sullivan, "China and the Middle East," April 30, 1979, British Embassy – Peking, FCO 93/2211, National Archives, United Kingdom (henceforth UKNA), *Archives Direct.*
[17] T. J. B. George, "China and Israeli/Egyptian Relations," April 23, 1979; British Embassy – Peking, FCO 93/2211, UKNA, *Archives Direct.*
[18] Draft Brief, "China and the Arab Israeli Dispute," Confidential, Undated, FCO 93/2211, UKNA, *Archives Direct.*

Hezbollah. The PLO's exit in 1982 served as a fitting symbol for the decline of the secular revolutionary and the rise of ethno-religious violence in the developing world.[19]

The PLO's evacuation to the shores of the western Mediterranean removed the leading force in secular Palestinian politics from the primary theater of the Israel-Palestine struggle. But Arafat's banishment did nothing to quash the grassroots force of Palestinian nationalism. As the Israeli occupation dragged on, the frustration of ordinary Palestinians broke out in a popular uprising in 1987. The so-called Intifada caught Arafat and the PLO off guard. Here were everyday Palestinians living in the West Bank and Gaza rising up in their own, predominately non-violent protest against the Israeli authorities. While Arafat scrambled to reassert leadership over the uprising, factions within the Palestinian Muslim Brotherhood inside the Occupied Territories formed a new resistance organization, Hamas, which eschewed the PLO's secular ideology at the same time as it embraced the organization's tactics of guerrilla war. Finding the path to secular liberation blocked, many of the Palestinians living in the West Bank and Gaza were ready to embrace this new political movement and its promise of Islamic liberation. In the coming decades, Hamas would emerge as a powerful challenger to the mantle of Palestinian leadership.[20]

CONCLUSION

The PLO's case thus serves as a microcosm of the complex set of changes taking place during the late Cold War centered on the demise of the secular liberation movement typified by the participants of the Tricontinental movement and the rise of a trend toward ethnic and religious violence. This transition was not purely a product of a resurgence of local traditionalism and fundamentalism. Rather, this phenomenon was born at the intersection of local dynamics and global changes taking place across the Cold War world. The East-West struggle led both Washington and Moscow to bankroll a system of highly militarized states around the developing world. These states relied on foreign aid and bloated militaries rather than popular support.

---

[19] See Hirst, *Beware of Small States.*
[20] See for instance Yezid Sayigh, *Armed Struggle and the Search for State* (New York: Oxford University Press, 1998).

Meanwhile, Washington's containment strategies, which included everything from financial and military aid to right-wing states to covert operations and full-scale military interventions, crippled secular revolutionary movements around the Third World. Likewise, right-wing regimes in Africa, Asia, Latin American, and the Middle East built their own networks aimed at combating the tide of left-wing movements around the world. Just as damaging, however, was the unraveling of global communist solidarity with the Sino-Soviet split and the Sino-Vietnamese War. Although the Third World aid networks linking PLO fighters to Hanoi, Beijing, Algiers, and Havana had been broad, they were seldom deep. The most common form of assistance came in the symbolic realm. Postcolonial revolutionaries could employ Mao's writings or the Vietnamese example to mobilize their own cadres and explain their struggle to the wider world. These efforts generated wide support among progressive forces around the globe. More often than not, these symbolic identifications led to diplomatic support from revolutionary states in international forums such as the UN General Assembly and the Conference of Non-Aligned States. But by the 1970s, the value of such rhetorical support was on the decline. The Sino-Soviet split and the Third Indochina War gutted the symbolic allure and diplomatic weight of Third World communist solidarity.

Furthermore, neither symbolic identification nor diplomatic support typically demanded significant resources. Rhetoric rarely translated to extensive material aid and could not make up for the loss of the concrete assistance provided by more invested local actors if they – like Egypt – switched political courses. Once revolutionary states such as China, Vietnam, and Algeria were called upon to put their money where their mouths were, so to speak, dynamics changed. Indeed, financial and military aid networks among revolutionary states and movements were not nearly as extensive as symbolic and diplomatic connections. Beijing and Algeria operated a number of guerrilla training camps in the 1960s, which served as important nodes in these global revolutionary networks. The PLO would set up their own camps in the 1970s where they famously hosted members of the German Baader–Meinhof Gang among others. But by the 1980s, the world's largest complex of guerrilla training camps was being funded by the US and Saudi governments in Pakistan. These camps focused not on training secular left-wing revolutionaries but on building legions of anti-Soviet Mujahideen, many of whom were inspired by calls to holy war. A similar story emerges when one turns to look at military aid. The PRC had served as an important patron of revolutionary movements in the 1950s and 1960s, as the ubiquity of Chinese-made Kalashnikovs among postcolonial liberation fighters indicated. And these small arms were potent weapons in the hands of the committed guerrilla revolutionaries of the long 1960s. But over the 1970s, as China and the United States achieved rapprochement, Chinese leaders focused their energies elsewhere. By the 1980s, Beijing, Washington, Islamabad, and Riyadh were directing large numbers of weapons into the hands of the Afghan Mujahideen.[21]

It could also be argued that Third World revolutionary solidarity became, in some sense, a victim of its own success. Once in power, victorious revolutionaries in Havana, Beijing, Hanoi, Algiers, and Phnom Penh, among other capitals, faced the challenge of building new governments. The burdens of governance often quenched the fires of revolution as they transformed guerrillas into bureaucrats. In this way, after achieving success, many revolutionary governments recognized that their interests diverged from their former revolutionary comrades. Beijing's recognition in the mid-to-late 1960s that Moscow – not Washington – represented the greatest threat to Chinese national security serves as a key example of this dynamic.[22]

Thus, by the end of the 1970s, the always slapdash alliance of postcolonial revolutionary forces had lost much of its symbolic luster, been deprived of some of its key state sponsors, and been outclassed by the new US-Saudi-Pakistani syndicate that was intent on mounting a jihad against the Soviet Army in Afghanistan. Khomeini's triumph in Tehran may have driven the final nail into the coffin of Third World revolutionary solidarity as a dynamic force in world affairs. Not only did the forces of sectarian revolution appear more energized, but their patrons proved more generous than their secular counterparts. In this way, Washington and Riyadh provided the largest financial contributions to revolutionary forces in the 1980s under the auspices of its clandestine aid program to the Mujahideen.

It should come as no surprise, then, that the revolutionary forces of the late Cold War increasingly turned away from secular visions of liberation and toward ethnic and religious ideologies. But as the Afghan, Lebanese, Iranian, Iraqi, and Palestinian cases show, these ostensibly local transformations were fueled by infusions of aid from the superpowers and by transnational flows of ideas and soldiers. Thus, though they were born

[21] For a fuller discussion of these transitions, see Chamberlin, *Cold War's Killing Field*.
[22] See Odd Arne Westad, *Restless Empire* (New York: Basic Books, 2012), 360–362.

from local circumstances, these changes were firmly embedded in the global currents of the Cold War international system. It was no coincidence, then, that the resurgence of ethno-religious warfare in the Middle East and the wider Third World took place on the heels of the Sino-Soviet split, the Sino-Vietnamese War, Egypt's break with the Soviet Union, and the Deng Xiaoping's rise to power. By 1979, Moscow was fighting a bloody intervention in postcolonial Afghanistan; Vietnamese, Cambodian, and Chinese soldiers were in open war with one another; Beijing was leaning toward Washington and beginning a series of market reforms; and Egypt had forged a de facto alliance with Israel and the United States. The unraveling of the Third World communist project foreshadowed the end of the Cold War and the collapse of the Soviet state. The rise of ethno-religious conflict in the Middle East must ultimately be understood as a crucial dimension of the story of the end of the Cold War. Likewise, the end of the Cold War and the demise of the global communist bloc should be seen as a crucial component of the resurgence of ethno-religious conflict in the Middle East and elsewhere.

PART II

A GLOBAL WORLDVIEW

4

Fueling the World Revolution

Vietnamese Communist Internationalism, 1954–1975

Pierre Asselin

The Cold War divided the world into two implacable blocs and made the situation in Vietnam after 1954 a major expression of that implacability. Recognizing that fact, leaders of the Democratic Republic of Vietnam (DRV) in Hanoi convinced themselves that success in their revolution could tip the worldwide balance of power in favor of the socialist bloc and national liberation movements throughout the decolonizing world. This conviction, combined with the fact that they had to conduct their struggle for national liberation and reunification from a position of relative military weakness, made those leaders accomplished practitioners of international politics. So, too, did the totality of their commitment to Marxism-Leninism and thus to anti-imperialism and anti-Americanism.

This chapter addresses Vietnamese communist internationalism in the period from 1954 to 1975. It considers Hanoi's self-appointed mission to advance the causes of socialism, national liberation, and anti-imperialism worldwide as it struggled to reunify Vietnam under its aegis. It demonstrates that even at the height of the war against the United States, DRV leaders never thought strictly in terms of the national interest. Obsessed as they were with the liberation and reunification of their country, they were also committed to the wider causes of socialism, "world revolution," and *"tiers-mondisme"* (Third Worldism). While Hanoi did not share the commitment to non-alignment that sometimes animated Third Worldism, it applauded and encouraged calls for unity among decolonized and decolonizing states, for both ideological and practical reasons (Figure 4.1). During the second half of the 1950s, it endorsed the peaceful "spirit of Bandung" promoted by

FIGURE 4.1 A secondary theme of OSPAAAL imagery was the political value of solidarity. Rising identification with North Vietnam and revolutionary movements went hand in hand with hostility to US interventions in the Global South. OSPAAAL, Olivio Martinez, 1972. Offset, 54x33 cm. Image courtesy Lincoln Cushing / Docs Populi.

the first generation of Third World states and leaders. The following decade, it fervently supported the second generation of states and leaders embracing a more radical, even militant, revolutionary vision inspired by the triumph of the Cuban and Algerian revolutions and the overseas travails of Ernesto "Che" Guevara.

To be sure, the Cold War, to say nothing of the Sino-Soviet dispute, created myriad challenges for Hanoi. But the contemporaneous process of decolonization in the Third World also created opportunities it sought to exploit to enhance its legitimacy and elevate its image world-wide, meet its core goals in Vietnam, and advance its vision of human progress.

THE DRV AND THE INTERNATIONAL COMMUNITY, 1954–63

Vietnamese communist leaders learned to appreciate the merits of actively engaging the international community during their war against France – the Indochina War (1946–54). During the Party's Second Congress of February 1951, held after a crushing defeat suffered by Vietminh forces at Vinh Yen outside Hanoi, the leadership stressed the imperative to sustain the war against France until complete victory. To meet that end in light of the difficult situation confronting their forces, Party leaders mandated better mass organization and mobilization efforts at home, on the one hand, and resort to "people's diplomacy" (*ngoai giao nhan dan*) – namely, exploitation and manipulation of anti-war and anti-colonial/imperialist sentiments – abroad, on the other. The DRV would henceforth endeavor to "maintain friendly relations with any government that respects the sovereignty of Vietnam" and "establish diplomatic relations with countries on the principle of freedom, equality and mutual benefit."[1]

Starting that year, the international community figured prominently in the strategic calculations of the leadership. The so-called diplomacy struggle became a cornerstone of the ideology and national liberation strategy espoused by Ho Chi Minh and the rest of the Party leadership. "International unity and cooperation are necessary conditions for the

---

[1] "Chinh cuong Dang Lao dong Viet Nam (2–1951)" [Program of the Vietnamese Workers' Party, February 1951], in Dang Cong san Viet Nam, *Van kien Dang – Toan tap – Tap 12: 1951* [Party Documents – Collected Works – Volume 12: 1951] (Hanoi: Nha xuat ban Chinh tri quoc gia, 2001), 441.

triumph of the national liberation revolution," they surmised, contributing as it did to "development of the new regime, the socialist
regime."[2] In order to serve the goals of that struggle, Ho and the
leadership publicly downplayed their embrace of Marxism-Leninism
and links to Beijing and Moscow, professing instead a commitment to
nationalism and patriotism, and to national liberation across the Third
World. The approach was self-serving, to be sure. At the same time,
there was a clear affinity between the struggle led by Vietnam's communist party and that waged by revolutionary nationalist leaders
across the colonial and semi-colonial world. Most obviously, both
struggles accentuated anti-imperialism.

In July 1954, the DRV government entered into the Geneva accords
with France. The accords provided for a ceasefire; the regrouping of
Vietminh forces above the seventeenth parallel and of forces loyal to
France below that demarcation line; the free movement of civilians
between the two zones for a period of 300 days; the return of prisoners
of war; guarantees against the introduction of new foreign forces in
Vietnam; and a plebiscite on national reunification within two years.
Until then, the northern zone would be under the authority of the DRV
regime and the southern zone under the jurisdiction of France and its local
clients.

Ho Chi Minh and the Party leadership accepted the Geneva accords
because they thought they were the best they could get under the
circumstances and that they might be workable. That is, they believed
the accords would not only end the eight-year-long Indochina War but
also might bring about the peaceful reunification of Vietnam under
their governance. The accords were far from perfect. Their terms, Ho
and other leaders felt, could have been more generous. Still, they were
satisfied because at a minimum the accords guaranteed that the United
States would not intervene militarily in Indochina – in the near future,
at least. Earlier that year, the Party, now called the Vietnamese
Workers's Party (VWP), had decreed that the United States constituted
the "foremost enemy" of the Vietnamese revolution. By its rationale,
the French would never have managed to sustain their war in
Indochina for as long as they did without American backing.
Washington had enabled Paris since 1950, in the wake of the

---

[2] Hoang Duc Thinh, *Duong loi tranh thu su giup do quoc te cua Dang, 1965–1975* [The
Party's Policy to Enlist International Aid, 1965–1975] (Hanoi: Nha xuat ban Chinh tri
quoc gia, 2015), 8.

recognition of the DRV by the People's Republic of China (PRC) and the rest of the socialist camp. American "imperialists" had not only supported French "colonialists" materially and politically from that moment onward but in fact manipulated Paris into staying the course in a war that served Washington's interests more than France's own. The Americans had essentially used the French as proxies to neutralize the Vietnamese revolution and contain the national liberation cause in Southeast Asia because it threatened their own designs and ambitions in the region.

When Paris decided to negotiate the terms of its extrication from Indochina with DRV representatives in Geneva beginning in May 1954, just as the Battle of Dien Bien Phu ended, Washington turned to a new proxy, as Hanoi saw it, to do American bidding: Ngo Dinh Diem. Thanks to US patronage, in June 1954 Diem became prime minister of the State of Vietnam, the "puppet" state set up by the French under Emperor Bao Dai in 1949 to enhance the legitimacy of their struggle against the DRV-led Vietminh. Though his authority was initially tenuous at best, Diem – a staunch anti-communist with respectable nationalist credentials – became in time a major impediment to the realization of communist objectives in Indochina.

No sooner had it signed the Geneva accords with France than Ho's government recognized the difficulties it would face in trying to implement them. While Paris seemed prepared to honor their terms, Washington, and Diem in particular, would not even endorse the Final Declaration of the Geneva Conference confirming the accords' legitimacy. With acquiescence in the Geneva formula from neither Washington nor Saigon, the chances that Vietnam would ever be peacefully reunified under communist governance were slim.

To improve its prospects in the face of a highly problematic situation, Ho's government turned to diplomacy, as it had in 1951 to offset the consequences of the Vietminh defeat at Vinh Yen. It mounted a major propaganda campaign emphasizing the merits of its cause, the legitimacy of the DRV, as well as its commitment to the peaceful reunification of Vietnam, and denouncing the "crimes" and nefarious intentions of Washington and its local "reactionary" allies. The central purpose of this exercise in people's diplomacy was to draw international attention to the situation in Vietnam and, most critically, prompt other governments and influential organizations to see circumstances there as Ho's regime saw them. Winning over world opinion – gaining wider public sympathy – would not only help muster political and moral support for the DRV's cause; it would also make it more difficult for Washington and Saigon to violate the letter and spirit of the Geneva accords. That is, diplomatic isolation would make the revolution's enemies hesitate to further subvert peace in Indochina. At a minimum, it would make Washington think twice before intervening militarily, a prospect Ho himself feared to the extreme and hoped to preclude at all costs. Favorable, supportive world opinion would serve as a hedge against US intervention and improve DRV prospects for success in the new context. Ho's government effectively used diplomacy to advance its own interests at the expense of its enemies.

To meet the ends of this latest diplomatic campaign, DRV leaders and pertinent organs attuned themselves to international affairs and made concerted efforts to engage other governments, particularly nationalist regimes in the Third World and "progressive" movements and organizations in the First. Consistent with the decree endorsed during the 1951 Party Congress, they legitimated their state's existence above the seventeenth parallel after July 1954 by seeking formal diplomatic recognition from other governments and promptly recognizing newly independent countries when suitable. As previously noted, in 1950 the DRV had obtained recognition from the PRC, the Soviet Union, Poland, Czechoslovakia, East Germany, Hungary, Bulgaria, Albania, Romania, and North Korea. In 1954, Mongolia followed suit. That same year India, a vanguard of the Non-Aligned Movement, became the first noncommunist country to open a diplomatic mission in North Vietnam, and Prime Minister Jawaharlal Nehru visited the DRV in October. France, the United Kingdom, and Canada each had diplomatic representation in the North by then, but largely to meet their various obligations under the terms of the Geneva accords.[3]

A socialist state and avowed member of that camp after 1954, the DRV publicly downplayed its ties to communism and sought to insinuate itself into other circles to gain wider legitimacy and support for its agenda. To the same end, it tried to keep under wraps the transformation of the North

---

[3] It was not until 1969 that a Western state, Sweden, granted full recognition to the DRV. Senegal (1969), Ceylon (1970), Switzerland (1971), India, Chile, and Pakistan (1972) followed suit. By the time the Vietnam War ended, forty-nine countries had established formal diplomatic ties with the DRV. See Vien su hoc, *Viet Nam: Nhung su kien lich su, 1945–1975* [Vietnam: Historical Events, 1945–1975] (Hanoi: Nha xuat ban Giao duc, 2006), 145.

Vietnamese economy and society along socialist lines, in full swing at the time. Instead, it leveraged its status as a semi-colonial state and victim of French and now American imperialism to gain political and moral support from revolutionary leaders, movements, and government across the Third World, otherwise wary of strict communism with its emphasis on class struggle at the expense of national unity. To such strategic aims, labor, student, and women's unions from the DRV regularly participated in international conventions. Those forums provided "an indispensable format for enabling successful diplomacy" while providing opportunities to network with other states and affirm DRV sovereignty.[4] Representatives from the DRV attended meetings of the World Peace Council (WPC), Moscow's answer to what Soviet leaders perceived was a United Nations Organization stacked against them. Formed in 1950, the WPC acquired a measure of international legitimacy over time through its promotion of peaceful coexistence, sovereignty, nuclear disarmament, and decolonization. Unlike the United Nations, its members were not states but progressive individuals and action groups, including associations and unions representing women, students, writers, journalists, and scientists. Jean-Paul Sartre participated in the WPC's congress of 1952. Other notable individuals who attended WPC-sponsored meetings or otherwise supported its activities included Pablo Picasso, W. E. B. DuBois, Paul Robeson, Louis Aragon, Diego Rivera, and Pablo Neruda.[5] That made the WPC an ideal target for the DRV's people's diplomacy.

In 1955, Ho's government participated in the Asian-African Conference in Bandung. This international conference offered DRV representatives a unique opportunity to meet, discuss, and fraternize with leaders and diplomats from dozens of countries outside the socialist camp sharing experiences of colonialism and embracing, to varying degrees, independent Third World nationalism. Bandung facilitated the forging of ties with other Third World governments, culminating in the exchange of diplomatic missions, among other undertakings. Indonesia, the host country, established formal diplomatic relations with the DRV

---

[4] Christopher J. Lee, "The Rise of Third World Diplomacy: Success and Its Meaning at the 1955 Asian-African Conference in Bandung, Indonesia," in Robert Hutchings and Jeremi Suri, eds., *Foreign Policy Breakthroughs: Cases in Successful Diplomacy* (New York: Oxford University Press, 2015), 49.

[5] On the WPC see United States Department of State, "The World Peace Council's 'Peace Assemblies'," in Foreign Affairs Note, May 1983: http://insidethecoldwar.org/sites/defau lt/files/documents/Department%20of%20State%20Note%20World%20Peace%20Coun cil's%20Peace%20Assemblies%20May%201983.pdf.

immediately after the conference. Burma opened a diplomatic mission in Hanoi, as had India, as previously noted. Essentially, Bandung allowed the DRV to build networks with other Third World governments while affirming its legitimacy and Vietnam's sovereignty. Beyond that, the conference, spurred in large part by mounting Cold War tensions in Southeast Asia and in Indochina specifically, provided a stage for mustering political and moral support for Hanoi's national liberation and reunification struggle. For years thereafter, that is, until Vietnamese communist leaders shifted to a more militant approach to address the situation in South Vietnam, Hanoi promoted and extolled the virtues of the "Bandung Spirit" because it served the goals of its diplomatic struggle and remained consistent with its own domestic imperatives.

Bandung played a seminal role in bringing about the Afro-Asian People's Solidarity Organization (AAPSO), created in Cairo in 1957; the Non-Aligned Movement, formally established in Belgrade in 1961; and the Afro-Asian Latin American People's Solidarity Organization, formed in Havana in 1966. Individually and collectively, these organizations promoted "a political consciousness against Western norms and power" that persisted and grew as more countries in Asia and Africa secured independence.[6] As increasing numbers of Third World states joined the United Nations, the Non-Aligned Movement in particular came to "have a great voice on the world stage, making great changes on the international chessboard, becoming a force that both socialist and imperialist countries wished to fight for," according to a semi-official Vietnamese account.[7] The DRV's involvement in that and other such movements supported the aims of its public diplomacy as well as its efforts to shame the United States into curbing its interference in Vietnamese affairs. It also suggested that the DRV regime was more nationalist than it was communist, beholden more to the Third World than to Moscow or Beijing. Hanoi's Third World activism enhanced its image across the noncommunist world and invested the Party with a degree of autonomy without alienating its socialist allies.

DRV authorities, ensconced in Hanoi after completion of the French withdrawal from the city in October 1954, gradually became loud and recognizable voices advocating on behalf of "oppressed" masses everywhere. At first, the latter meant those suffering under the yoke of colonialism and neo-imperialism in the Third World. In time, it also included

---

[6] Lee, "Rise of Third World Diplomacy," 54.
[7] Hoang Duc Thinh, *Duong loi tranh thu su giup do*, 19.

victims of capitalist greed generally defined, including the poor and marginalized communities in the First World. Audiences worldwide were receptive to the authorities' message. The Indochina War, and especially the DRV victory at Dien Bien Phu, had sounded the death knell for France's overseas empire. Events in Vietnam galvanized revolutionaries in Algeria and across the rest of the Third World including, in time, the Middle East, sub-Saharan Africa, and Latin America.[8] Thus, the more the DRV publicized others' causes and developed ties to them, the more those others felt sympathy for its efforts to complete the "liberation" of Vietnam. The DRV's backing of Algerian independence, sub-Saharan African decolonization, and the African National Congress (ANC)'s anti-apartheid struggle in South Africa were especially important in that respect.[9] Identifying with national liberation movements solidified the bond between the DRV and other Third World governments supportive of causes championing self-determination and anti-imperialism.[10]

Hanoi's diplomacy facilitated manipulation of public perceptions of its purposes and policies and enabled communist policymakers to cultivate a favorable, broad-based, global political awareness and understanding of their aspirations. In 1958, VWP theoretician Truong Chinh elaborated on the DRV's international obligations even as it endeavored to build socialism above the seventeenth parallel and bring about "liberation" in the South. Hanoi, he observed, must oppose "all war kindling schemes of the imperialist aggressors and their agents," strengthen "friendly solidarity and the fraternal cooperation with the USSR, China, and [other] people's democracies," and "support national liberation movements in the world" and the ongoing one in Algeria in particular.[11] A year later, the VWP Central Committee noted that "the problem of achieving the unification of our country, the achievement of independence and democracy in all of our country" was not only "the problem of the struggle between our nation against the American imperialists and their puppets," but also "the

[8] Odd Arne Westad, *The Global Cold War: Third World Interventions and the Making of Our Time* (New York: Cambridge University Press, 2005), 190–192.

[9] See Merle Pribbenow, "Vietnam Covertly Supplied Weapons to Revolutionaries in Algeria and Latin America" Cold War International History Project e-Dossier No. 25, 2 November 2011: www.wilsoncenter.org/publication/vietnam-covertly-supplied-weapons-to-revolutionaries-algeria-and-latin-america.

[10] Vo Kim Cuong, *Viet Nam va chau Phi trong su nghiep dau tranh giai phong dan toc* [Vietnam and Africa in the Struggle for National Liberation] (Hanoi: Nha xuat ban Chinh tri quoc gia, 2004), 182–188.

[11] Quoted in Nguyen Thanh, *Bac Ho voi Chau Phi* [Uncle Ho and Africa] (Hanoi: Nha xuat ban Ly luan Chinh tri, 2005), 200.

problem of the struggle" between the progressive camp and the imperialist camp. The "victory of the Vietnamese Revolution," the Committee concluded, would have "an enthusiastic effect" not only on the rest of the communist world but also "on the movement of popular liberation in Asia, Africa, [and] Latin America" to the point of precipitating "the disintegration of colonialism throughout the world." Fundamentally, the Vietnamese revolution was "part of the world revolution."[12] The triumph of the Cuban revolution in January that same year marked, in the eyes of Vietnamese communist leaders, "the expansion of the scope of socialism on three continents" as well as a major defeat for imperialism and solidified their commitment to internationalism.[13]

Through 1959 and the early 1960s, the DRV quietly asserted itself as a member of the socialist camp as it expanded its ties to the non-aligned and national liberation movements. Following the onset of the Sino-Soviet dispute in the late 1950s, Hanoi played a leading role in the effort to reconcile the two communist giants. Though that effort failed to end the dispute, the Vietnamese gained a great deal of respect from both Moscow and Beijing as well as from the rest of the socialist camp for attempting to mitigate the dispute despite being one of that camp's youngest – and smallest – members and embroiled at the time in a serious conflict of its own. All the while, the DRV sustained its engagement with the Third World, effectively seeking to define itself as a postcolonial state, aggressively advocating for the end of colonial rule in Africa and promptly recognizing states on that continent after they gained independence. It established diplomatic relations with Guinea (1958), Mali (1960), Morocco (1961), the Democratic Republic of Congo (1961), Egypt (1963), the Republic of Congo (1964), Tanzania (1965), Mauritania (1965), and Ghana (1965). The DRV was among the first governments to recognize the new Algerian state in 1962, a logical move considering Hanoi had extended material, political, and moral support to revolutionaries there during their war against France.[14] "Despite the fact that the

---

[12] "Nghi quyet Hoi nghi Trung uong lan thu 15 (mo rong): Ve tang cuong doan ket, kien quyet dau tranh giu vung hoa binh, thuc hien thong nhat nuoc nha" [Resolution of the 15th Plenum (expanded): On Increasing Unity and Determination to Struggle to Preserve Peace and Achieve Unification of the State], in Dang Cong san Viet Nam, *Van kien Dang – Toan tap – Tap 20: 1959* [Party Documents – Collected Works – Volume 20: 1959] (Hanoi: Nha xuat ban Chinh tri quoc gia, 2002) [hereafter *VKD: 1959*], 66–67.

[13] Hoang Duc Thinh, *Duonh loi tranh tu su giup do*, 18.

[14] After 1954, Hanoi dispatched military instructors to Egypt to train insurgents to fight in the Algerian war of independence.

country was divided and invaded by the United States," historian Vu Duong Ninh has written, "Vietnam remained trusted by many countries in the struggle against colonialism and imperialism," and could thus "contribute significantly to national liberation movements across the world."[15] As an act of policy, each year on the day marking the anniversary of the independence of a Third World country, Ho Chi Minh sent the head of that state a telegram wishing continued peace and prosperity on behalf of "the people of Vietnam and the Government of the Democratic Republic of Vietnam." The gesture was effortless, to be sure, but did not go unnoticed and unappreciated by the recipients of those telegrams.[16]

This tendency to associate with and engage international and transnational movements became a hallmark of DRV diplomacy and a defining aspect of its revolutionary strategy and ideology. In May 1963, for example, a meeting of African states in the Ethiopian capital of Addis Ababa concluded with the formation of the Organization of African Unity, joined by thirty-two governments. According to an editorial in *Nhan dan*, the VWP mouthpiece, the conference "highlighted the humiliating defeat of and the end of the road for colonialism," on the one hand, and "the great victory of the national liberation revolution," on the other. "Our southern [Vietnamese] compatriots involved in a difficult and heroic struggle against the US- Diem clique are very excited about the outcome of this conference, and see the success of the African people as their own success," the editorial concluded.[17] There was a logic to such support. Pan-Africanism, Pan-Asianism, and communist internationalism, among other movements, shared a common ideological aversion to neo-imperialism and Western capitalism. Each also sought to empower historically marginalized constituencies, to give a voice to the voiceless, and to emancipate the oppressed. More practically, these movements allowed states such as the DRV to "place their political aspirations in identity-based communities that extended beyond the formal boundaries of nation-states," historian Christopher Lee has noted. That achievement facilitated the pursuit of their most fundamental political goals. "Frequently guided by an ambitious intellectual leadership," Lee writes, "these transnational endeavors sought to collect and stand for the hopes

---

[15] Vu Duong Ninh, *Lich su quan he doi ngoai Viet Nam, 1940–2010* [History of Vietnamese Foreign Relations, 1940–2010] (Hanoi: Nha xuat ban Chinh tri quoc gia, 2015), 166.
[16] Nguyen Thanh, *Bac Ho va Chau Phi*, 185.
[17] *Nhan dan* [The Nation], May 26, 1963. See also Nguyen Thanh, *Bac Ho va Chau Phi*, 222–223.

of broadly defined social groups that faced political restrictions locally and globally."[18]

VIETNAMESE COMMUNIST INTERNATIONALISM, 1964–75

Through the late 1950s and early 1960s, Hanoi regularly asserted publicly its commitment to the "world revolutionary process"; however, its words were slow to translate into direct action. It provided troop and material support to the nascent insurgency in South Vietnam but in cautious, deniable ways. Ho was adamant about avoiding the resumption of "big war" in Indochina and thus giving Washington no pretext to intervene militarily in Vietnam. During this early period, the DRV leadership felt it was best to wait on events in the South and focus on building the socialist economy in the North.

That all changed in 1963–64. Convinced by the domestic and international situation that imperialism and capitalism were on the defensive worldwide, increasing numbers of VWP members, including members of the Politburo, demanded that Hanoi seize this "opportune moment" and adopt a more "forward" strategy in the South. If the DRV was ever to become a "vanguard" for national liberation movements across the Third World, these galvanized Party members believed, then it had to get over its fear of provoking US intervention and act decisively in the South.

That attitude was both cause and consequence of the growing influence in Hanoi of a hard-line, radical clique obsessed with moving to direct action to confront imperialism and reactionary capitalism in Indochina. Emboldened by circumstances, members of that clique proceeded to seize the reins of power from Ho and other moderates in a bloodless palace coup during the Ninth Plenum of the VWP Central Committee of December 1963. Whereas Ho and his associates had conducted their foreign policy largely based on pragmatic considerations, seeking to avoid confrontation with the United States, the men who controlled decision-making in the aftermath of the Plenum were committed ideologues with strong internationalist proclivities who were hell-bent on leaving their mark on the world. The interests of the wider socialist world and of "oppressed masses" in the rest of Asia, Africa, and Latin America were as important to them as the liberation and reunification of their own nation.[19]

---

[18] Lee, "Rise of Third World Diplomacy," 53.
[19] See "Nghi quyet cua Hoi nghi lan thu chin Ban Chap hanh Trung uong Dang Lao dong Viet Nam: Ve tinh hinh the gio va nhiem vu quoc te cua Dang ta, thang 12 nam 1963" [Resolution of the Ninth Plenum of the Central Committee of the Vietnamese Workers' Party: On the

Le Duan, the brains behind the coup who replaced Ho as paramount leader, personified this new consensus. From the moment Ho acquiesced in the Geneva accords, Le Duan maintained that was a mistake, that Saigon and especially Washington would never honor the terms of those accords, and that only war could solve the Party's predicaments in Indochina. Vindicated by circumstances, Le Duan would shape DRV foreign policy on the basis of rigid ideological considerations starting in 1964. As he and his chief lieutenants were fond of Chinese revolutionary prescriptions, they became strong proponents of revolutionary militancy in South Vietnam for the sake of socialist solidarity and in the name of proletarian internationalism. Those lieutenants included VWP Organization Committee head Le Duc Tho, PAVN General Nguyen Chi Thanh, and DRV Deputy Prime Minister Pham Hung. All were members of the Politburo. As southern veterans of the Indochina War and hardened revolutionaries, they firmly believed in the merits of Marxism-Leninism – its Maoist Chinese variant to be specific – as a blueprint for revolutionary success. Inspired by the Russian, Chinese, and Cuban examples, they sought nothing less than total victory over their enemies to augur a new era in their nation's – and the world's – history.[20]

For Hanoi's new sheriffs, the Vietnamese revolution constituted more than a component in a global movement opposing the United States and capitalist imperialism: it was a potential model for all others similarly engaged in national liberation struggles, much as their allies in Moscow, Beijing, and Havana were for them. The VWP, according to Le Duc Tho, was a "vanguard unit of the working class and capable of leading the revolution throughout the country to complete victory, thereby making worthwhile contributions to the revolutionary cause of the working class and the laboring people throughout the world."[21] Tho, like Le Duan,

World Situation and the International Tasks of Our Party, December 1963], in Dang Cong san Viet Nam, *Van kien Dang – Toan tap, Tap 24: 1963* [Party Documents – Collected Works – Volume 24: 1963] (Hanoi: Nha xuat ban Chinh tri quoc gia, 2003), 716–800. For an English version of this document, see Le Duan, *Some Questions Concerning the International Tasks of Our Party: Speech at the Ninth Plenum of the Third Central Committee of the Viet Nam Workers's Party* (Peking: Foreign Language Press, 1964).

[20] See Pierre Asselin, *Hanoi's Road to the Vietnam War, 1954–1965* (Berkeley: University of California Press, 2013), 169–173.

[21] Le Duc Tho, "Let Us Strengthen the Ideological Struggle to Consolidate the Party," in *Tuyen huan* (March 1964), reproduced in "Let Us Strengthen the Ideological Struggle to Consolidate the Party," April 1964, Folder 03, Box 25, Douglas Pike Collection: Unit 06 – Democratic Republic of Vietnam, The Vietnam Center and Archive, Texas Tech University, 26.

believed that defeating the Americans and their lackeys was necessary not only to achieve Vietnamese liberation and reunification, but also to protect and advance the cause of all "peace-loving" peoples. Hanoi's war against the United States and its reactionary allies in Saigon was "a part of the world revolution," waged in "the cause of revolutionary forces worldwide."[22] Under Le Duan's regime, the diplomatic campaign initiated in 1954 to enlist foreign support for the DRV and the Vietnamese revolution developed into an ideologically driven mission to spearhead the struggle against imperialism and reactionary tendencies across the globe.

Though they remained devoted Marxist-Leninists at heart, Le Duan and his chief lieutenants publicly proffered their commitment to nationalism and anti-imperialism because it suited their purposes, especially as they concerned the DRV's diplomatic endeavors. Relative to the previous regime under Ho, Le Duan's was significantly more dogmatic and doctrinaire. Unlike Ho, whose hard-line comrades within the Party always questioned his commitment to Marxism-Leninism and deemed him too much of a nationalist, Le Duan's communist and internationalist credentials were impeccable.[23] That is, whereas Ho had had a nasty habit of prioritizing national unity over class struggle, Le Duan always knew to subsume the former under the latter. Here was a true believer in the infallibility of communism and the purposive nature of History. Here was also an individual who considered nationalism a mere tool, a means, to the achievement of national liberation under the Party's own brand of governance, and not an actual motive force of or genuine raison d'être for the Vietnamese revolution.

The onset of the American War in spring 1965 solidified the resolve of Le Duan and other DRV leaders to make their revolution a vanguard for Third World liberation movements. As their country became a crucible and violent expression of the global Cold War, the Vietnamese revolution gained widespread notoriety. According to political scientist Tuong Vu, DRV leaders embraced their situation because it "vindicated their beliefs about the fundamental cleavage in international politics between

---

[22] *Tim hieu lich su Dang Cong san Viet Nam qua cac Dai hoi va Hoi nghi Truong uong, 1930–2002* [Understanding the History of the Communist Party of Vietnam through Its Congresses and Plenums, 1930–2002] (Hanoi: Nha xuat ban Lao dong, 2003), 422; Stein Tønnesson, "Tracking Multi-Directional Dominoes," in Odd Arne Westad et al., eds., *77 Conversations Between Chinese and Foreign Leaders on the Wars in Indochina, 1964–1977* (Washington, DC: Cold War International History Project Working Paper No. 22, 1998), 33–34.

[23] See Sophie Quinn-Judge, *Ho Chi Minh: The Missing Years 1919–1941* (Berkeley: University of California Press, 2003).

capitalism and communism, between revolutionaries and counterrevolutionaries." Beyond that, it "allowed them to proudly display their revolutionary credentials" as well as to work on "realizing their radical ambitions."[24] As an expression of the Cold War, the American War was welcomed by radical leaders of the Vietnamese communist movement and Le Duan in particular. By one account, following the onset of the American War, Le Duan became "intoxicated" with the prospect of "winning *everything*" on every front.[25]

DRV leaders marketed their "anti-American resistance" as a "just struggle" and manifestation of the global fight against imperialism for "peace and justice." On one side of the struggle, as Le Duan put it in a characteristic formulation, was "the most stubborn aggressive imperialism with the most powerful economic and military potential"; on the other were "the forces of national independence, democracy and socialism of which the Vietnamese people are the shock force in the region."[26] Sustaining the fight against the United States was the "moral obligation" of the Vietnamese on behalf of the national liberation movement and of oppressed masses everywhere, Hanoi stressed in both its domestic and foreign propaganda. Bringing about Vietnamese reunification under communist aegis was, for its part, the DRV's and the VWP's duty on behalf of "the international Communist movement" and in "the spirit of proletarian internationalism."[27]

Devout Marxist-Leninists as they were, Le Duan and other Vietnamese communist leaders cleverly downplayed ideology and their communist credentials in propaganda and other forms of engagement targeting nonsocialist states. Their travails against the United States and its southern "puppets" were, they affirmed, purely nationalist endeavors. The Vietnamese were heirs to a long, glorious, and heroic tradition of resistance to foreign aggression, their propaganda claimed, and the fight against the United States was but a continuation of that tradition.[28] The Vietnamese resistance maintained close ties with the Soviet Union and China, Hanoi

[24] Tuong Vu, *Vietnam's Communist Revolution: The Power and Limits of Ideology* (New York: Cambridge University Press, 2017), 92.

[25] Robert S. McNamara, James Blight, and Robert Brigham, *Argument without End: In Search of Answers to the Vietnam Tragedy* (New York: Public Affairs, 1999), 183. Emphasis is in the original.

[26] Le Duan, "Forward to the Future" in Le Duan, *Selected Writings* (Hanoi: Foreign Languages Publishing House, 1977), 529.

[27] Quoted in Tuong Vu, *Vietnam's Communist Revolution*, 95.

[28] On this theme see Patricia M. Pelley, *Postcolonial Vietnam: New Histories of the National Past* (Durham, NC: Duke University Press, 2002).

acknowledged, but that was only because circumstances warranted such ties. Everyone engaged in the struggle against American "imperialists," from top decision maker to common foot soldier, was a nationalist at heart whose sole aspiration was to live to see the day when the nation was fully "liberated" from the clutches of foreign "invaders" and their "reactionary," treacherous local clients. All else was inconsequential.

In repeating that line and marketing their war against the United States on such terms, Le Duan's regime sought not only to win over world opinion but also to encourage other "oppressed masses" to take up arms and fight, to demonstrate that seemingly minor actors could play important roles in the Cold War and contribute to the world revolution and the demise of imperialism. Its conscious effort to inspire others to fight imperialism even as it attempted to rally them in support of its cause bore dividends. Its "determined stance in the face of American technological might," historian Michael Latham has written, "became an appealing symbol of determined resistance and the power of popular revolutionary war."[29]

Following American intervention, Hanoi developed intimate ties with numerous foreign governments and movements, in the socialist world and beyond, which provided much-needed political, moral, and material support. China, the Soviet Union, and other communist states supplied indispensable military hardware and other aid. Limited in their ability to provide such assistance, Third World governments aided Hanoi by heralding its troops and southern insurgents belonging to the National Front for the Liberation of Southern Vietnam (NLF, or Viet Cong, in Western parlance) as heroes fighting for the cause of national liberation worldwide. Such rhetorical and moral support proved instrumental in publicizing the "just struggle" of the Vietnamese and increasing the pressure on American policymakers to desist in Indochina. Even as the United States subjected the North to sustained bombings, foreign delegations – including many from the United States – visited the DRV and, while there or upon their return home, publicly expressed their support and admiration for the resistance of the "brave" Vietnamese. They also widely and openly condemned the American military intervention and the bombing of "innocent civilians" in the North, fueling anti-war sentiment across the world and in the United States.[30]

---

[29] Michael E. Latham, "The Cold War in the Third World, 1963–1975," in Melvyn P. Leffler and Odd Arne Westad, eds., *The Cambridge History of the Cold War – Volume II: Crises and Détente* (New York: Cambridge University Press, 2010), 276.
[30] See Judy Tzu-Chun Wu, *Radicals on the Road: Internationalism, Orientalism, and Feminism during the Vietnam Era* (Ithaca: Cornell University Press, 2013) and James

The importance of Vietnam to this global revolutionary movement was impossible to miss in January 1966, when Fidel Castro hosted the Tricontinental Conference in Havana to promote national liberation and communism in Asia, Africa, and Latin America. Some 600 participants representing more than eighty sovereign governments, national liberation movements, and other organizations attended the thirteen-day event, but Vietnam and its struggle against American militarism occupied a prominent place in deliberations. In a stirring "message to the Tricontinental," Che Guevara, an architect of the Cuban revolution and world's most famous itinerant revolutionary, noted that "every people that liberates itself is a step in the battle for the liberation of one's own people." Vietnam, he said, "teaches us this with its permanent lesson in heroism, its tragic daily lesson of struggle and death in order to gain the final victory." In that country, "the soldiers of imperialism encounter the discomforts of those who, accustomed to the standard of living that the United States boasts, have to confront a hostile land; the insecurity of those who cannot move without feeling that they are stepping on enemy territory; death for those who go outside of fortified compounds; the permanent hostility of the entire population." "How close and bright would the future appear," Che famously concluded, "if two, three, many Vietnams flowered on the face of the globe, with their quota of death and their immense tragedies, with their daily heroism, with their repeated blows against imperialism, forcing it to disperse its forces under the lash of the growing hatred of the peoples of the world!"[31]

The meeting in Havana spawned the Organization of Solidarity with the Peoples of Africa, Asia, and Latin America (commonly known by its Spanish acronym OSPAAAL), which staunchly supported Hanoi and the NLF's anti-American war. Che's message, published a year later under the title "Create Two, Three ... Many Vietnams, That Is the Watchword," became a rallying cry for revolutionary organizations and movements all around the world, increasing Vietnam's international profile and the notoriety of its anti-American resistance. Even French President Charles de Gaulle jumped on that bandwagon through a much-publicized speech in Phnom Penh, the Cambodian capital, in September 1966. Attempting to curry favor with former French colonies largely sympathetic to Hanoi, he condemned US

W. Clinton, *The Loyal Opposition: Americans in North Vietnam, 1965–1972* (Niwot: University Press of Colorado, 1995).

[31] Reproduced in David Deutschmann, ed., *Che Guevara Reader: Writings on Politics & Revolution* (Melbourne: Ocean Press, 2003), 360–362.

military intervention in Southeast Asia and called for Washington to end the war at once. In doing so, de Gaulle also reaffirmed his intent to distance his government from the United States, a desire most blatantly expressed through his decision to dramatically curtail French involvement in the North Atlantic Treaty Organization (NATO) earlier that year.[32]

Through propaganda and manipulation of foreign journalists, dignitaries, and other personalities, the DRV molded world opinion to suit the interests of its armed struggle. Thanks to Hanoi's own fastidiousness and to the loud voices of its allies and friends, media outlets from across the world closely followed the situation in Vietnam, paying particular attention to the activities and behavior of American forces. The International War Crimes Tribunal, also known as the Russell Tribunal after its founder – the philosopher and delegate to the Tricontinental Conference, Bertrand Russell – proved meaningful in that respect. Its ideologically motivated investigation into the nature of the American war in Indochina found the United States guilty of genocide against the region's peoples. For good measure, Hanoi created a special government agency, the American War Crimes Investigative Commission, tasked with compiling numbers and producing detailed, though quite exaggerated, reports on "illegal," "immoral," and "criminal" American activities in Vietnam. As developments in Vietnam or related to the war there regularly made front-page news everywhere, audiences around the world became captivated by the conflict. DRV authorities made sure those reports found their way into the hands of anti-war activists and leaders, including members of the Russell Tribunal.

This ostensible globalization of the Vietnamese revolution dramatically increased Hanoi's stakes in the Vietnam War. Just as success stood to rouse others struggling against reactionary enemies, defeat might spell the doom of the world revolution and deject national liberation fighters across the Third World. But Le Duan and his chief lieutenants would not be deterred. That is, the small size of their country, its low level of economic development, and the daunting political challenges it faced did not preclude them from accomplishing remarkable feats and meeting their obligations to the international community. Egypt, Yugoslavia, Albania, Algeria, and, most notably, Cuba had each demonstrated that small states were capable of impacting the world, influencing the international system, and transcending or otherwise challenging Cold War bipolarity.[33]

---

[32] Pierre Journoud, *De Gaulle et le Vietnam* (Paris: Tallandier, 2011), 244–245.

[33] On the impact of such states on the Cold War international system see Jeffrey James Byrne, *Mecca of Revolution: Algeria, Decolonization, and the Third World Order* (New York:

Hanoi's stubborn refusal to abandon its goals following the onset of the American War, its resilience, and even the mere fact that it and the NLF were not losing badly challenged conventional thinking on American military might and the merits of guerrilla warfare. Despite their techno-logical superiority and abundant wealth, the Americans were incapable of defeating Vietnam's "peasant armies" and halting their march to inde-pendence. The Vietminh and Algeria's own NLF deserved praise and respect for defeating the French in their respective anti-colonial struggles after World War II; but Hanoi's willingness to take on the United States in the Vietnam War and its successes were nothing short of remarkable.

Le Duan sought to deal the United States a coup de grâce with the Tet Offensive of January 1968. Consisting of surprise, concerted attacks on all major southern cities and towns, the campaign aimed to precipitate a general uprising of the southern masses demanding the withdrawal of American forces and abdication of the regime in Saigon. Le Duan had long hoped for such an uprising in the South, which he thought would leave Washington no choice but to abandon Vietnam unconditionally.[34] As it turned out, internationalist concerns also figured prominently in his cal-culations. Le Duan confided in his Chinese counterparts that his regime accepted the possibility of "enormous bloodletting" to achieve total vic-tory over the Saigon regime and the Americans because that would not only contain American neo-imperialism in Indochina but inspire other peoples in Asia, Africa, and Latin America to free themselves from the oppression induced by Western capitalism.[35] "We have to establish a world front that will be built first by some core countries and later enlarged to include African and Latin American countries," Le Duan told Chinese Premier Zhou Enlai.[36]

The Tet Offensive and follow-up campaigns produced none of the results expected by Hanoi leaders. They were, in fact, a complete disaster, costing the lives of more than 40,000 North Vietnamese and Viet Cong combatants.[37] However, support for the war in the United States had

---

Oxford University Press, 2016) and Piero Gleijeses, *Conflicting Missions: Havana, Washington, and Africa, 1959–1976* (Chapel Hill: University of North Carolina Press, 2003).

[34] William J. Duiker, "Victory by Other Means: The Foreign Policy of the Democratic Republic of Vietnam," in Marc Jason Gilbert, ed., *Why the North Won the Vietnam War* (New York: Palgrave MacMillan, 2002), 67.

[35] See Stein Tønnesson, "Tracking Multi-Directional Dominoes," 33–34.

[36] Quoted ibid., 35.

[37] On casualties suffered by communist forces see Tran Van Tra, "Tet: The 1968 General Offensive and General Uprising," in Jayne S. Werner and Luu Doan Huynh, eds., *The*

begun to fray, and images of American forces seemingly on the defensive only served to encourage emerging doubts. By March, events in Vietnam led Lyndon Johnson to withdraw from the presidential election and set in motion a series of highly public protests that would divide the United States and further erode popular will to continue the war in Southeast Asia. Hanoi snatched victory from the jaws of defeat. That is, what looked to be a severe setback for its cause became a major triumph. That triumph was a testament to the effectiveness of Hanoi's diplomatic struggle, a fruit of its longstanding commitment to cultivating harmonious relations with noncommunist state and nonstate actors and exploiting anti-war sentiment in the West, including the United States.

In the aftermath of the offensive, in April, Hanoi opened peace talks with Washington. Despite what the gesture suggested, Vietnamese communist policymakers did not intend to negotiate seriously. Committed as ever to military victory, they used the talks merely to pander to world opinion, as well as to probe the intentions of American decision makers. Losses suffered by communist forces in the Tet campaign had been heavy, Le Duan recognized, but achieving unmitigated triumph over the United States remained essential to win "everything" in Vietnam, on the one hand, and contribute to the eradication of capitalism around the world, on the other. As long as capitalism existed, Hanoi's thinking went, peace in Vietnam and elsewhere would be threatened and "peace-loving" peoples would never be truly safe. Just as the Soviet Union's victory in the "Great Patriotic War against Fascist Aggression" had contributed to the demise of fascism as a viable political ideology, Vietnam's victory over the United States would herald the demise of capitalism.[38] By official VWP account, American policymakers were "neo-fascists" bent since 1954 on depriving the Vietnamese people of peace and freedom by keeping the country divided.[39] In defeating the United States, Hanoi would discredit the ideology Washington held so dear. It would also by extension

Vietnam War: Vietnamese and American Perspectives (Armonk, NY: M.E. Sharpe, 1993), 37–65; Van Tien Dung, *Buoc ngoat lon cua cuoc khang chien chong My* [The Great Turning Point of the Anti-American War] (Hanoi: Nha xuat ban Su that, 1989), 183–234; and Ronald H. Spector, *After Tet: The Bloodiest Year in Vietnam* (New York: Free Press, 1993).

[38] Quoted in S. Ivanshin and I. Osotov, "Vietnam: A Victory of Historic Significance" in *Vietnam: Internationalism in Action* (Moscow: Novosti Press Agency Publishing House, 1973), 17.

[39] *American Imperialism's Intervention in Vietnam* (Hanoi: Foreign Languages Publishing House, 1955), 17–18.

demonstrate the superiority of socialism and of socialist modernity over the capitalist, bourgeois reactionary system.

Moreover, sustaining the war effort until the United States was defeated would vindicate the forward strategy embraced by the VWP leadership since 1964 and, more broadly, the policy of active, aggressive struggle favored by orthodox Marxist-Leninists. Most overtly championed by Mao and other "radicals" in Beijing, that policy had run contrary to the policy of peaceful coexistence and peaceful resolution of East-West disputes sanctioned by Soviet Premier Nikita Khrushchev during the 20th Congress of the Communist Party of the Soviet Union (CPSU) in 1956. American actions during the Chinese Civil War and then the Korean War reinforced Beijing's view that defiance was the only realistic way of dealing with the United States. "War is the highest form of struggle for resolving contradictions," Mao said, and starting in 1962 Beijing actively encouraged Hanoi to stand firm against American provocations, prepare to fight, and forego a diplomatic solution, as Moscow advocated.[40] By continuing the war effort, the Vietnamese could demonstrate their commitment to national liberation and avoid the mistakes made by their foreign comrades over Korea in 1953, when Pyongyang and Beijing had accepted a ceasefire and consented to the continued, permanent division of the peninsula. Victory in Vietnam could show the Third World that complete liberation by force of arms was not impossible and that it could be achieved even when the Americans themselves stood in the way. Besides, a determined stance against American imperialism in the aftermath of the Tet Offensive would restore revolutionary momentum and facilitate continued mobilization of public opinion at home and abroad.

Le Duan and other core leaders made no secret of their contempt for the Soviet "revisionist" line advocating negotiated solutions to East-West conflicts, and of their partiality to Chinese revolutionary prescriptions. Moscow resented Hanoi's insubordination, its assertion of an independent and defiant policy more in line with China's own stance in the global Cold War, affirmed by its decision to forego a diplomatic solution and rely on armed struggle to bring about national reunification. Soviet leaders inferred from that decision that Hanoi had aligned itself with Beijing in the Sino-Soviet dispute then wreaking havoc in the socialist camp. Though they refused to take a public stance in the Sino-Soviet split, DRV decision makers subscribed to Chinese revolutionary theses because they genuinely believed they constituted the best way of meeting core strategic objectives,

---

[40] *Quotations from Chairman Mao Tse-Tung* (New York: Bantam Books, 1968), 32.

domestically and internationally. Besides, the Vietnamese had their own ideas on the merits of revolutionary violence. "Only through the use of revolutionary violence of the masses to break the counter-revolutionary violence of the exploitative governing classes is it possible to conquer power for the people and to build a new society," VWP theoretician Truong Chinh advised.[41] Violent revolution was the "only just path" to victory, just as using violence against class enemies represented a "universal law."[42] In continuing to pursue final triumph over the United States, Hanoi demonstrated that violent struggle was most suitable given its own circumstances at the time and silenced detractors of its strategy.

Thus, through the post-1968 period, Hanoi steadfastly adhered to its revolutionary strategy predicated on armed struggle and defeat of the American "imperialists" despite what its participation in peace talks suggested. Over the next seven years, Le Duan and his regime met the bulk of their objectives, domestically and internationally. They defeated the United States and its allies and reunified Vietnam under their governance. That success roused Third World revolutionaries, particularly in sub-Saharan Africa and Latin America. The culmination of wars for national liberation in Angola and Mozambique in the mid-1970s – just as Saigon fell to communist-led armies – and the support proffered to rebels there by the Soviet Union and Cuba, among others, were to no insignificant degree prompted by the triumph of the Vietnamese revolution and attendant American retrenchment from the Third World. In Latin America, leftist insurgents emboldened by events in Indochina and benefiting from Vietnamese moral and – in at least one instance – material support found new life and made meaningful gains in their struggles against right-wing dictatorships beholden to Washington.[43] The Palestine Liberation Organization (PLO) drew both lessons and strength from the experiences of the Vietnamese, and in fact came to see itself as closely intertwined with them in a common struggle against Western imperialism.[44]

---

[41] Truong Chinh, *Écrits, 1946–1975* [Selected Writings, 1946–1975] (Hanoi: Éditions en langues étrangères, 1977), 642.

[42] Ibid., 644.

[43] Merle Pribbenow, "Vietnam Covertly Supplied Weapons to Revolutionaries in Algeria and Latin America."

[44] Paul Thomas Chamberlin, *The Global Offensive: The United States, the Palestine Liberation Organization, and the Making of the Post-Cold War Order* (New York: Oxford University Press, 2012), 14–32.

Hanoi's anti-American resistance even had major ramifications in the West, where it produced great tumult. It contributed to a growing malaise there, variously dividing populations, driving a wedge between people and their governments, exacerbating socioeconomic tensions. It prompted mass protest movements from Paris to Chicago and facilitated the advent of anti-establishment radical organizations from West Germany to Canada. Most notably, the Vietnam War contributed to the emergence of a vigorous and raucous countercultural movement that seriously challenged and contested traditional sources of authority and, in some countries, brought about the collapse of governments or, at a minimum, a reassessment of the parameters governing executive power. According to historian Jeremi Suri, the countercultural movement was so disruptive in the West that it encouraged constructive engagement of the Eastern bloc by its leaders. Détente between the Soviet Union and the United States, rapprochement between Beijing and Washington, and *Ostpolitik* in Europe were each to varying degrees prompted by domestic challenges facing Western governments. Ultimately, East-West détente did not just reduce Cold War tensions; it indirectly helped build momentum in the Third World for national liberation causes.[45]

In the eyes of its most ardent critics, the American war in Vietnam epitomized all that was wrong with the West: the disconnect between rulers and ruled, the disregard for the rights of others, the greed of capitalist entrepreneurs, and the abuse of power by government leaders. How else to account for the decision of American and other leaders to send so many young men halfway around the world to contain a "peasant insurgency," to stand in the way of "good" and "valiant" "freedom fighters" merely seeking their country's reunification and independence? To many critics, the refusal of Western leaders to do more to curtail the war in Vietnam was symptomatic of a growing generational gap, of the widely contrasting values of young people with those who had authority over them, the "over 30" generation. Opposing the war was for estranged youths a way to manifest their frustration with the status quo. It served as a vehicle to articulate myriad grievances and show that the existing system was not working, at least for them and other "oppressed" demographics at home and abroad. In time, opposition to the war, to the governments that abetted it, and to Western sources of authority broadly defined served as a rallying point for activists supporting a broad range of reformist and

---

[45] See Jeremi Suri, *Power and Protest: Global Revolution and the Rise of Détente* (Cambridge: Harvard University Press, 2005).

radical causes. It even facilitated the creation of transnational terrorist networks that brought together French-Canadian separatists, African American extremists, German radicals, Italian paramilitaries, Japanese communist militants, and Palestinian nationalists. While the Vietnam War was not the main reason these elements came together, it galvanized them like no other outside event.

CONCLUSION

Historian Huynh Kim Khanh maintained in an influential work that from its onset the Vietnamese revolution was both "a national liberation movement, governed by traditional Vietnamese patriotism" and "an affiliate of the international Communist movement, profoundly affected by the vicissitudes of the Comintern."[46] To be sure, the Vietnamese revolution was never just a movement for national emancipation conducted under the auspices of dedicated rebels who were nationalists, first and foremost. Whether of moderate or hard-line persuasion, those rebels and particularly their leaders proved to be devout Marxist-Leninists and dedicated internationalists committed to class struggle and world revolution, just as they were to national liberation.

The internationalism espoused by Hanoi's communist leaders was imbued with a clear ideological hue emphasizing the necessity of a socialist revolution to successfully resist and overcome American capitalist imperialism. In hindsight, a syncretic adaptation of Marxism-Leninism conditioned the thinking and behavior of Hanoi decision makers in the period 1954–75. That adaptation mixed a concern, an obsession really, with national liberation and Vietnamese reunification under communist aegis, on the one hand, with an aspiration to inspire and act as a vanguard for revolutionary movements across the Third World, on the other. According to Tuong Vu, the struggle waged by Hanoi after 1954 was "at heart, a communist revolution." Leaders there were internationalists "no less than their comrades in the Soviet Union and China." For Le Duan and his acolytes, "a successful proletarian revolution in Vietnam was a step forward for world revolution, which was to occur country by country, region by region."[47]

---

[46] Huynh Kim Khanh, *Vietnamese Communism, 1925–1945* (Ithaca: Cornell University Press, 1982), 99.
[47] Tuong Vu, *Vietnam's Communist Revolution*, 7.

Hanoi's leaders behaved as patriotic internationalists during the period from 1954 to 1975. They were not communists in the classical sense; nor were they mere nationalists, as is often assumed by American historians of the Vietnam War. They sought to co-opt all ethnic groups, not just ethnic Vietnamese, for the sake of freeing and reunifying their country. That made them patriots. They also cared deeply about the fate of revolutionary and other progressive movements elsewhere. In fact, they considered it their duty to contribute to the global revolutionary process, to the final triumph of communism, by rousing opponents of capitalism, imperialism, and neocolonialism everywhere. And that made them internationalists. Thus, as Vietnamese communist authorities committed themselves to defeating their enemies in Vietnam to preserve their country's territorial integrity and secure its complete sovereignty, they sought to contribute to the worldwide struggle against imperialism and capitalism with a view to becoming a model, an exemplar, of the possibilities of national liberation and socialist as well as Third World solidarity. National liberation was for them, and for Le Duan in particular, a means to even greater, nobler ends: liberation of all oppressed masses, social advancement of the underprivileged, and the demise of imperialism and global capitalism. And in that respect, Vietnam's revolutionary struggle shared an affinity with the Third World and the ideology of *tiers-mondisme* informing the decision-making of its more prominent leaders.

The pursuit of class struggle, a hallmark of committed Marxist-Leninist parties, was as central in Hanoi's strategic thinking as southern liberation itself. However, the DRV knew better than to publicly mention or discuss that aspect of their revolutionary agenda because they understood it would alienate actual and potential supporters of their struggle outside the socialist camp, and in the Third and Western worlds, especially. In the immediate aftermath of the Geneva accords and partition of the country into two distinct regrouping zones, Vietnamese communist leaders set out to complete the land reform program they had initiated during the last year of the war against France and, shortly thereafter, nationalized industry and collectivized agriculture. Class struggle mattered to them, as it did to devout communists everywhere. And it is that commitment to class struggle, reaffirmed after the fall of Saigon through efforts to transform southern society and its economy along socialist lines, that set the DRV apart from non-aligned Third World states and faithful adherents to *tiers-mondisme*. While one could argue that the synthesis of Marxism-Leninism with *tiers-mondisme* effectively constituted Maoism (stressing anti-imperialism, the centrality of peasants in revolutionary processes, small-scale industry, rural collectivization, and permanent revolution), the syncretic ideology espoused by the Vietnamese in the post-1954 period proved far more complex. Most notably, that ideology comprised a diplomatic, internationalist component entirely absent from Maoism.

Noncommunist Third World states and sympathetic Western constituencies proved useful if not indispensable allies in Hanoi's fight against a common enemy (imperialism) in pursuit of a common goal (liberation) to a singular end (communism). Le Duan believed that his people, having gained international notoriety for their contributions to decolonization through their war against France and their dramatic triumph at Dien Bien Phu, were in an ideal position to lead the charge against American imperialism, and inspire others to do the same. It was arguably Le Duan's greatest aspiration to make all of this culminate on his watch.

In hindsight, DRV leaders supported the Third Worldist project only to the extent that it served their own purposes and its adherents supported their war effort against the United States. Between 1954 and 1975 they variously identified publicly as nationalists, non-aligned, supporters of national liberation, members of the Afro-Asian bloc, and neutralists. Ultimately, they only consistently and genuinely embraced Marxism-Leninism as they understood and defined that ideology. They respected other Third World regimes and movements, to be sure, but not to the extent they did those similarly committed to socialist transformation and unity, such as Cuba. In Hanoi's own understanding, "true" Third World states, that is, genuine believers in the merits and full potential of *tiers-mondisme*, were those that looked to Marxism-Leninism as a blueprint for achieving complete liberation, economic development, political stability, and social harmony. As a militantly anti-imperial and avowedly Marxist state, the DRV positioned itself perfectly to shape and inspire the Tricontinental movement.

DRV leaders deserve credit for meeting their goals at home and abroad. They succeeded not only in reunifying their country under their own governance, but also in inspiring and emboldening "progressive" movements and individuals elsewhere. Their war against the United States profoundly impacted the Cold War system and left an indelible mark on the world. It did not herald the end of capitalism, but it did electrify national liberation fighters in the Third World. Clearly, that all came at a cost, an exorbitant cost, which the Vietnamese masses, not the men in Hanoi, assumed.

5

Through the Looking Glass

African National Congress and the Tricontinental Revolution, 1960–1975

Ryan Irwin

A near cloudless morning greeted Abdulrahim Farah as he stepped onto the tarmac of the Lusaka International airport on August 17, 1969. The fifty-year-old Somali diplomat was only months into his tenure as the chairman of the UN Special Committee on Apartheid. He had left New York in the midst of an intense summer heat wave and the city behind him – like most of America in 1969 – was simmering with tension. Surrounded now by an entourage of UN diplomats, Farah probably relished the change of scenery. Zambian soil must have been a welcome reprieve from his life as an expatriate in urban America.[1]

However, turmoil was hard to escape in 1969. The Apartheid Committee Farah presided over had been established at the height of the so-called postcolonial moment, shorthand for the period when decolonization changed Africa's political map between 1957 and 1963. The Committee had been the centerpiece of a set of initiatives that sought to use the United Nations to end white supremacy in Southern Africa, but those heady days were gone. Farah had journeyed to Zambia because he hoped to reach out to the liberation movements living there, many of which questioned the UN's usefulness in the anti-apartheid fight, and to repair the bonds that once linked African people through Pan-Africanism.

---

[1] Itinerary, Apartheid Committee's Trip to Lusaka and Dar-es-Salaam, box 17, E. S. Reddy Collection, Yale University Manuscripts and Archives (YUMA); depiction stems from author's discussions with Enuga Reddy, who served as Secretary of the Committee.

FIGURE 5.1 Tricontinental movements won support by combining political and social revolution, which often promoted the liberation of women alongside national independence. This image also attests to the global movement of iconography via Tricontinental networks. The Cuban artist Lazaro Abreu adapted this poster from an Emory Douglas illustration in *The Black Panther* depicting African revolutions. The combination of woman, gun, and baby appeared in Asian and African revolutionary imagery, which proved popular with young leftists in Europe and the United States. Lazaro Abreu after original by Emory Douglas, 1968. Screen print, 52x33 cm. Image courtesy Lincoln Cushing / Docs Populi.

Things did not go well. During the Committee's initial round of discussions, the African National Congress (ANC) requested that Farah and his associates stop seeking publicity for themselves and "humbly suggest[ed]" that these self-serving vacations had outlived their utility. "In our view it would be less expensive ... if the United Nations invited, at its expense, delegations from genuine liberation movements to attend meetings ... and assist in discussions and decisions." Heralded once as the anvil that would destroy apartheid, the United Nations – and specifically the Apartheid Committee – was now portrayed as useless. In another meeting, an activist argued that "concrete evidence" proved that the United Nations was "a tool of the imperialist powers, particularly the United States," while a third freedom fighter said that the "time for the verbal, the constitutional, was passed." The only way forward now "was to face the enemy with a gun."[2]

Members of Farah's party were taken aback. They saw themselves at the vanguard of the revolution against racial discrimination, and they were being told they were part of the problem. A few UN delegates accused the activists of being ignorant about "the workings of the United Nations." However, Farah responded to the criticism directly. If the ANC wanted violence, it had to recognize that "nobody would pay any attention" until its members were "killed and maimed." Ultimately, repudiating the Apartheid Committee was an act of self-isolation. Unless there "were more Sharpevilles" – a reference to a massacre outside Johannesburg in 1960 – "there would be indifference."[3]

What explains the hostility Farah faced in 1969? Arguably, the antiapartheid movement was the most prominent social cause of the twentieth century; it lasted decades and drew support from people in the Americas, Europe, Asia, Australia, and Africa. But Farah's experience

---

[2] Recommendation Submitted by the African National Congress of South Africa to the Meeting of the Special Sub-Committee on Apartheid held in Lusaka on August 18, 1969, box 17, E. S. Reddy Collection, YUMA; Minutes of the Meeting of the Sub-Committee of the Special Committee on Apartheid with Representatives of the Zimbabwe African National Union in Lusaka, August 19, 1969, box 27, E. S. Reddy Collection, YUMA; Minutes of the meeting of the Sub-Committee of the Special Committee on Apartheid with representatives of the African National Congress of South Africa in Lusaka, August 18, 1969, box 27, E. S. Reddy Collection, YUMA; Minutes of the Meeting of the Sub-Committee of the Special Committee on Apartheid with Representatives of the South West Africa People's Organization in Dar es Salaam, August 21, 1969, box 27, E. S. Reddy Collection, YUMA.

[3] Meeting with A.N.C. in Lusaka, August 18, 1969, Pan Africanist Congress, 1969, box 17, E. S. Reddy Collection, YUMA.

reminds us that apartheid's critics quarreled often and with considerable fervor. The anti-apartheid movement's resilience, and eventually its ubiquity, stemmed from this fractiousness. Farah and the ANC disagreed about tactics, specifically the utility of special committees, and they articulated opposing conclusions about the United Nations' usefulness in the worldwide decolonization movement. But both sides wanted legitimacy, and their boisterous fight, while not a zero-sum contest, made the apartheid issue harder to ignore during the second half of the twentieth century. Even as apartheid's critics unanimously blasted the vagaries of white minority rule, they maneuvered among the subtle differences between solidarity and self-interest.

Historians of South Africa have largely ignored this tension. Astute monographs by Gail Gerhart and Tom Lodge consider rifts among anti-apartheid activists, but their books focus on black power and racial pluralism.[4] Although Stephen Ellis and Paul Landau offer an alternative framework, their work overdramatizes Moscow's control of the ANC.[5] Hilda Berstein, Hugh Macmillan, and Scott Couper provide soberer accounts, lingering on the disagreements between the ANC's various headquarters and the generational differences among its leaders, and Arianna Lissoni and Saul Dubow illuminate the way multiracialism and nonracialism contributed to the ANC's factionalism.[6] Rob Skinner and Simon Stevens have even considered the ANC's relationship with international anti-apartheid organizations.[7] But the national project of South

---

[4] Gail Gerhart, *Black Power in South Africa: The Evolution of an Ideology* (Berkeley: University of California Press, 1978); Tom Lodge, *Black Politics in South Africa since 1945* (London: Longman, 1983).

[5] Stephen Ellis, *External Mission: The ANC in Exile, 1960–1990* (London: Hurst and Company, 2014); Paul Landau, "Controlled by Communists? (Re)Assessing the ANC in its Exilic Decades," *South African Historical Journal* 67:2 (2015): 222–241; and Landau, "The ANC, MK, and the 'turn to violence'," *South African Historical Journal* 64:3 (2011): 538–563.

[6] Hilda Berstein, *The Rift: The Exile Experience of South Africans* (London: Jonathan Cape, 1994); Hugh Macmillan, *The Lusaka Years: The ANC in Exile in Zambia* (Johannesburg: Jacana, 2013); and Scott Couper, *Albert Luthuli: Bound by Faith* (Scottsville: University of KwaZulu-Natal Press, 2010); Arianna Lissoni, "Transformations in the ANC External Mission and Umkhonto we Sizwe, 1960–1969," *Journal of South African Studies* 35:2 (2009): 287–301; Saul Dubow, "Were There Political Alternatives in the Wake of the Sharpeville-Langa Violence in South Africa?" *Journal of African History* 56:1 (2015): 119–142.

[7] Rob Skinner, *The Foundations of Anti-Apartheid: Liberal Humanitarians and Transnational Activists in Britain and the United States, c.1919–64* (London: Palgrave, 2010). See also Simon Stevens, "Boycotts and Sanctions against South Africa: An International History, 1946–1970" (PhD diss., Columbia University, 2016).

Africa has framed all of this literature, and most of these authors have probed the liberation struggle in order to historicize the country's turmoil in the twenty-first century.[8]

Farah's journey provides a different sort of starting point. While past scholars have tended to attribute splits within the liberation struggle to South Africa's internal divisions, this chapter flips that approach inside-out, arguing that external events shaped the organization's self-understanding. At the heart of the chapter is an obvious yet underexplored paradox. Forced into exile in 1960, the ANC's underground paramilitary wing, uMkhonto weSizwe, was defeated in 1963. This defeat effectively ended the organization's footprint within South Africa until the 1990s. Although ANC leaders continued to present themselves as spokesmen for an authentic, anti-racist South African nation – and stayed informed about events at home – the ANC existed primarily as a diasporic entity after the mid-1960s and many of its established truths lost the power to motivate the masses in these years. How could an organization that suffered so many setbacks maintain its place at the forefront of the anti-apartheid movement?

This chapter's argument is straightforward: analogies matter. It studies the ANC's road to and from the 1966 Tricontinental Conference and draws upon research from the ANC's Liberation Archive to suggest that external comparisons – not internal divisions – determined how the ANC explained what it stood for and what it wanted after the Sharpeville Massacre. Critically, these analogies changed over time. During the early 1960s, the ANC equated itself to the Front de Libération Nationale (FLN), which historian Jeffrey James Byrne critiques in Chapter 6. Initially, ANC leaders believed they could leverage diplomatic victories to defy minority white rule in South Africa. When the Algerian analogy faltered in the mid-1960s, the Cuban revolution became an alternative model for South Africa's future. Fidel Castro's apparent strength contrasted with the fate of Algeria's Ben Bella (and Ghana's Kwame Nkrumah), suggesting that *real* freedom required guerrilla warfare, not UN General Assembly resolutions. However, the ANC's embrace of Che Guevara's ideas set off a regional crisis that upended the organization in 1967, leading to the chapter's final section on Vietnam. Divided

---

[8] For an essential elaboration of this point, see the 7-volume *Road to Democracy* series, published by the South African Democracy Education Trust and 6-volume *From Protest to Challenge*, edited by Thomas Karis and Gail Gerhart and published by the Hoover Institution Press and Indian University Press.

internally by the late 1960s, the ANC responded to the Vietnam War by probing the logic and purpose of Third World solidarity, which offers a useful window to explore the relationship between revolutionary talk and revolutionary action after the Tricontinental Conference.

These shifting analogies served the ANC well. They helped the organization establish alliances with foreigners who never experienced apartheid, and they assuaged ANC expatriates who feared that Europeans would always rule South Africa. But most importantly, for the purposes of this book, the ANC's efforts provide a microcosm to consider how the Tricontinental Revolution changed the Third World project. By studying the context around Farah's rancorous encounter with the ANC in 1969, we can explain the tension between solidarity and revolution. After all, solidarity is what Farah was looking for in Lusaka. Yet he failed to obtain it because he was not a revolutionary. This chapter scratches at this tension while exploring how ANC leaders tangled with one of this volume's organizing questions: Was Tricontinental solidarity an end in itself or was it a means to foment violent change in the decolonized world?

EXCEPTIONALISM

As late as 1960, ANC leaders refused to compare themselves to foreigners. Because apartheid differed from European imperialism, the argument went, the ANC's struggle for majority rule had to be explained in the context of South Africa's past. The ANC's exceptionalism rested on a particular interpretation of history. An earlier rebellion against colonialism, fought in the late nineteenth century, pitted Dutch and British settlers against each other, and the forced migration of South Asians to the region significantly complicated the machinations of colonialism there. South Africa fit no mold, the argument went, and apartheid, which took shape after Afrikaner nationalists won power in 1948, elaborated British racism by repudiating Anglo-American liberalism, putting the country at odds with the rest of the English-speaking world after World War II. While apartheid's critics took inspiration from Indian independence in 1947, the ANC's 1952 Defiance Campaign, which imported Gandhian methods of civil disobedience to South Africa, neither changed government policy nor united the country's various ethnic groups under a common banner. By the mid-1950s, it appeared that South Africa was sui generis.[9]

[9] For classic treatments, see Saul Dubow, *Apartheid, 1948–1994* (New York: Oxford University Press, 2014); Leonard Thompson, *The History of South Africa* (New Haven:

This mindset created a distinct framework for political dissent. In South Asia, Jawaharlal Nehru spoke of a coherent Indian personality, channeled through the Indian National Congress. In South Africa, by contrast, the Congress Alliance, established after the Defiance Campaign's defeat, argued that *heterogeneity* had to be the wellspring of anti-apartheid politics.[10] Within the Congress Alliance, the African National Congress spoke for indigenous Africans, while the South African Indian Congress, the South African Congress of Trade Unions, the Coloured People's Congress, and the Congress of Democrats represented other anti-apartheid groups. The birth of this alliance went hand in hand with a Freedom Charter in 1955 that framed South Africa as a place that "belonged to all who live in it, black and white," accentuating the premise that South Africa would not follow the same path as India after 1947.[11] Rather than creating a racially homogeneous anti-colonial nation-state, the ANC would forge a politically plural and ethnically diverse democracy. If the Freedom Charter had an audience outside the country, it was probably the United Nations, a heterogenous organization invented to combat fascism, which had authored similar statements about politics after 1945. The Freedom Charter equated apartheid with fascism while dramatizing the difference between South Africa's near future and South Asia's recent past.

This approach began to buckle in the late 1950s. While the Congress Alliance struggled to gain traction within South Africa, Ghana's Kwame Nkrumah used Nehru's vision to spearhead the first successful anti-colonial movement in Sub-Saharan Africa.[12] After winning independence from Britain in 1957, Nkrumah called an All-African People's Conference in 1958, proclaiming the need for a continent-wide "African Personality based on the philosophy of Pan-African Socialism." Convinced that such a move would end the Congress Alliance, the ANC responded defensively. To comprehend "our aims

---

Yale University Press, 2001); William Beinart, *Twentieth-Century South Africa* (New York: Oxford University Press, 2001).

[10] For the place of India within the ANC, see Jon Soske, *Internal Frontiers: African Nationalism and the Indian Diaspora in Twentieth-Century South Africa* (Athens: Ohio University Press, 2017).

[11] For a succinct overview, Saul Dubow, *African National Congress* (Stroud: Sutton, 2000), chapter 5.

[12] For analysis, see Richard Rathbone, *Nkrumah & the Chiefs: The Politics of Chieftaincy in Ghana, 1951–1960* (Athens: Ohio University Press, 2000).

and objectives," ANC representatives informed Nkrumah and his supporters, outsiders needed to recognize South Africa's "political, economic, and social development," especially the fact that it was "the
only country in Africa with a very large settled White population."
Because of "this history," the statement continued, "our philosophy
of struggle is 'a democratic South Africa' embracing all, regardless of
colour or race who pay undivided allegiance to South Africa and
mother Africa." Although the ANC "support[ed] the cause of
National Liberation," it pointedly refused to adopt Nkrumah's political vocabulary. The ANC faced a problem called "national oppression" – not foreign imperialism – and the remedy was not
decolonization but "universal adult suffrage" within a democracy
based on the Freedom Charter.[13] This argument not only undercut
Nkrumah's call for an all-encompassing African nationalism – modeled
on Nehru's Indian nationalism – but also reified the premise that South
Africa was in but not of the African continent.

The ANC's exceptionalism crumbled spectacularly after the All-
African People's Conference. Just a few months later, Robert Sobukwe,
a former ANC Youth League leader who left the organization in the late
1950s, answered Nkrumah's clarion call by organizing a new group called
the Pan Africanist Congress (PAC).[14] The organization announced its
existence in 1959 and immediately attacked the ANC's multiracialism as
a "method of safeguarding white interests." The ANC conceptualized
South Africa's future on Europe's terms, Sobukwe argued, and failed to
recognize the continuities between settler colonialism in South Africa and
imperialism everywhere else. Part of the problem, in his mind, was the
ANC's relationship with the South African Communist Party (SACP),
whose members seemed to take inspiration from European
communists.[15] Because "South Africa [was] an integral part of the indi-
visible whole that is Afrika," Sobukwe wrote in 1959, it followed that
political power had to be "of the Africans, by the Africans, for the
Africans."[16] As the PAC cast the Freedom Charter aside, it attacked the

[13] Notes of the Delegates to the All-African People's Conference, December 1958, MF-
13332, *African National Congress Collection, 1928–1962* (microform).
[14] Gerhart, *Black Power*, chapter 6.
[15] Formation of the Pan Africanist Congress, in Thomas Karis and Gail Gerhart, eds., *From
Protest to Challenge: Documents of African Politics in South Africa 1882–1964*, vol. 3
(Stanford: Hoover Institution Press, 1977), 498–530.
[16] Robert Sobukwe, Opening Address at the Inaugural Conference of the PAC, in Karis and
Gerhart, eds., *From Protest to Challenge*, vol. 3, 512–513.

presupposition that universal suffrage would end national oppression, proclaiming that a *truly* independent South Africa would have to belong to the "Africanist Socialist democratic order" that would soon stretch from Cape Town to Cairo. Decolonization was not only in South Africa's future; it would arrive before 1963, Sobukwe declared in 1960. That was Nkrumah's target date for African liberation and Pan-African unification.[17]

The ANC lost control of events in early 1960. When British Prime Minister Harold Macmillan visited South Africa in February, he too attacked South African exceptionalism, albeit to critique apartheid's architects for failing to acknowledge the "national consciousness" of non-Europeans.[18] Intended to sting Afrikaners who opposed the "winds of change," Macmillan's barb also challenged the ANC's beleaguered worldview by conflating anti-apartheid activism with the movement that had recently ended British rule in Ghana. The Sharpeville Massacre, which featured so prominently in Farah's commentary ten years later, unfolded weeks after Macmillan's speech and culminated in the murder of almost seventy black South Africans. By April, no one on any side of the color line still believed that South Africa was sui generis. South African Prime Minister Hendrik Verwoerd insisted that the crisis had "to be seen against the backdrop ... of similar occurrences in the whole of Africa," and Nelson Mandela, who was emerging as a dynamic leader in the ANC, admitted, "In just one day, [the PAC] moved to the front lines of the struggle."[19] Neither Verwoerd nor Mandela knew what would happen next, but they interpreted Sharpeville as tacit confirmation of Sobukwe's worldview.

LIBERATION

In the aftermath of Sharpeville, the ANC took steps to reinvent itself. Verwoerd's government declared a State of Emergency in May 1960, arresting ANC and PAC leaders and forcing both organizations underground. However, the ANC's Deputy-President Oliver Tambo had

---

[17] Robert Sobukwe, "Time for Action," July 11, 1959, Robert Sobukwe Collection, University of Fort Hare Library (UFH): www.liberation.org.za.
[18] Harold Macmillan, "Wind of Change," in Nicholas Mansergh, ed., *Documents and Speeches on Commonwealth Affairs, 1953–1962* (London, 1963), 347–351.
[19] Nelson Mandela, *Long Walk to Freedom: The Autobiography of Nelson Mandela* (New York: Back Bay Books, 1995), 238.

already gone abroad, where he would prove a pivotal conduit to the outside world that year. Initially, Tambo found common ground with the ANC's rivals, forming a United Front (UF) that included the PAC.[20] Undergirding this fragile alliance was the shared assumption that the United Nations would confront apartheid because sixteen African countries joined the General Assembly that year. For the first time since 1946, sanctions seemed to be a possibility. African diplomats appeared to hold sway over the UN General Assembly's agenda, and the All-African People's Conference had inspired an impressive boycott of South African consumer goods in Britain and the Caribbean.[21] "[A] solution could only come from the outside," Tambo quipped in May 1960. Theoretically, a General Assembly resolution, labeling apartheid a clear threat to peace and security, would force the UN Security Council to punish South Africa, since the 1950 Uniting for Peace resolution had ostensibly vested the General Assembly with the power to supersede an obstructionist Security Council veto. Military intervention was an unrealistic goal. Yet economic sanctions seemed feasible, and the UF saw the United Nations as a tool to destabilize the apartheid system.[22] ANC President Albert Luthuli explained the situation succinctly in 1960: "I feel that ... when South African markets are affected, the people ... might feel that they would be better off with another form of Government."[23]

Obvious problems came into focus immediately. On the one hand, Verwoerd's government outmaneuvered the United Front abroad.[24] On the other hand, the PAC and ANC struggled to overcome their underlying differences. Sobukwe, whom Verwoerd imprisoned in May, hoped sanctions would destroy white rule, so South Africa could follow in Ghana's footsteps. Luthuli, also imprisoned that year (and awarded a Nobel Peace Prize), still clung to the ANC's vision of pluralist democracy, believing that sanctions would split European sentiment in South Africa.[25] That mindset dwindled outside Oslo as

[20] *African Digest*, September 1960; Scott Thomas, *The Diplomacy of Liberation: The Foreign Relations of the African National Congress since 1960* (London: I.B. Taurus, 2000), 28–37.
[21] Skinner, *Anti-Apartheid*; Ryan Irwin, *Gordian Knot: Apartheid and the Unmaking of the Liberal World Order* (New York: Oxford University Press, 2012), 44–59.
[22] Quoted in Irwin, *Gordian Knot*, 47.   [23] Quoted in Couper, *Luthuli*, 121.
[24] Irwin, *Gordian Knot*, chapter 2.   [25] Couper, *Luthuli*, chapters 4–5.

the year progressed, and the SACP did not pull its punches when Luthuli's underlings asked for feedback in the autumn. Most foreigners, the group explained, saw the ANC's multiracial rhetoric as a front that "concealed a form of white leadership of the African national movement."[26] African countries in particular were suspicious of the ANC and frequently nudged Tambo to accept the PAC's supremacy in South Africa's anti-colonial struggle. So, the ANC could either repudiate the SACP altogether – and tacitly acknowledge the validity of the PAC's criticism – or find a new way to frame its relationship to Pan-Africanism. Change was necessary.

Algeria offered one way forward. That country, Mandela explained in 1961, was "the closest model to our own in that the rebels faced a large white settler community that ruled the indigenous majority."[27] With help from the SACP, Mandela won support to create a paramilitary group called uMkhonto weSizwe (MK) that year and then spent most of 1962 in North Africa – his visit coincided with Algerian decolonization – where he received training from the Front de Libération Nationale (FLN).[28] In Mandela's mind, the juxtaposition between Ghana and Algeria could not have been clearer. Whereas Nkrumah had won sovereignty by mobilizing Africans within Ghana, the FLN had organized at home and abroad, waging a guerrilla campaign on the ground while turning French colonialism into a cause célèbre at the United Nations. The combination was important. In Mandela's private diary, he explained:

Your tactics will not only be confined to military operations but they will also cover such things as the political consciousness of the masses of the people [and] the mobilisation of allies in the international field. Your aim should be to destroy the legality of the Government and to institute that of the people. There must be parallel authority in the administration of justice.[29]

As the ANC adopted the FLN's playbook, three things happened. First, the ANC took over the Congress Alliance. For the architects of the 1955 Freedom Charter, plurality went hand in hand with universal adult

---

[26] Cited in Allison Drew, ed., *South Africa's Radical Tradition*, vol. 2 (Cape Town, University of Cape Town Press, 1997), 359–362.
[27] Report Sub-Committee to the African National Congress (External Mission) for Period December 29, 1962–January 31, 1963, Lusaka Mission, box 52, folder 2, ANC Archives, UFH.
[28] Mandela, *Long Walk*, 263–308.
[29] Nelson Mandela, *Conversations with Myself* (London: Macmillan, 2010), 103.

suffrage. However, at the Congress's first post-Sharpeville consultative conference, held in in Botswana in 1962, ANC representatives argued that universal suffrage could no longer assure South Africa's liberation. The country had to have a government controlled by people of African descent. To communicate this message abroad, the ANC declared it had to speak on behalf of the South African Indian Congress, the South African Congress of Trade Unions, the Coloured People's Congress, and the Congress of Democrats.[30] Second, the United Front collapsed. As the ANC recast the "African image," decoupling it from Ghana in order to dramatize Algeria's importance, the PAC-ANC rift became unbridgeable. With the creation of the Organization of African Unity (OAU), the two organizations began to openly attack each other's legitimacy, seeking sole support from the OAU's newly formed Liberation Committee.[31] Third, Mandela moved to import Algerian-style war to South Africa. UMkhonto weSizwe took steps to begin a sabotage campaign at home while Tambo established a quasi-government abroad to raise funds and speak at the United Nations. Although the effort might last years, an internal ANC memorandum said that year, minority rule could "collapse far sooner than we can at the moment envisage."[32] After all, the FLN had a government in Algiers, there was a UN peacekeeping force in the Congo, and African diplomats had just passed a resolution in New York that defined apartheid as a "clear threat" to international peace and security. Anything seemed possible.

But anything was not possible. Mandela was arrested immediately upon reentering South Africa in August, and MK was uprooted completely by July 1963. The ensuing Rivonia Trial has been chronicled extensively.[33] It overlapped with equally devastating setbacks in New York and The Hague, where the Security Council rejected the ANC's plea for sanctions, imposing a nonmandatory embargo on military weapons instead, and the International Court of Justice vacillated over the legal status of South West Africa. South African expatriates had overestimated the implications of African decolonization, and as the mid-1960s

---

[30] Report on the Lobatsi Conference October 1962, Lusaka Mission, box 52, folder 2, UFH.
[31] This split is chronicled in Karis and Gerhart, eds., *From Protest to Challenge*, vol. 5, chapter 2.
[32] Operation Mayibuye, in Karis and Gerhart, eds., *From Protest to Challenge*, vol. 3, 760–768.
[33] For introduction, Kenneth Broun, *Saving Nelson Mandela: The Rivonia Trial and the Fate of South Africa* (New York: Oxford University Press, 2011).

approached, it became increasingly apparent that salvation would not come through the United Nations.[34] With pessimism encroaching, the ANC's External Mission bifurcated between London, where white, Coloured, and Indian exiles clustered after 1960, and Lusaka, which attracted the lion's share of black South African expatriates, especially after Zambia's independence in 1964.[35] Once again, the situation felt tenuous.

For a time, Tambo bounced between Europe and Africa, maintaining a home in Britain and a headquarters in Tanzania. But criticism mounted as months turned into years.[36] Voices within the ANC's London Office called for changes after the 1964 Rivonia Trial. The organization had erred by putting so much emphasis on "the [African] majority" at the 1962 Botswana conference, respondents lamented in an internal survey in 1965, and "certain persons who [were] very important in their political organisations at home" had been sidelined since that gathering. In Zambia and Tanzania, meanwhile, black South African émigrés began to question Tambo's fitness as a military leader. Although he kept the organization afloat – mostly with aid from the Soviet Union, East Germany, and Sweden – uMkhonto weSizwe languished.[37] The relationship between the ANC and SACP remained poorly defined, and by 1965 Zambian officials were complaining among themselves that ANC freedom fighters simply wandered Lusaka's streets with nothing to do.[38]

To make matters worse, Algeria's appeal waned in the mid-1960s. As Byrne has explained, liberation proved elusive in the so-called Mecca of Revolution. By equating freedom with membership in an international organization, the FLN trapped itself in the existing nation-state system, and the same strategy that toppled French colonialism created problems after Algeria's independence. Guerrilla warfare had been justified, the FLN told the international community, because the French had no interest in economic development and human rights but redistributing resources while safeguarding human rights proved difficult.[39] It turned out that

---

[34] Irwin, *Gordian Knot*, chapters 4–5.

[35] Ellis, *External Mission*, chapter 3; Shubin, *ANC*, chapter 4; Macmillan, *Lusaka*, chapters 1–3.

[36] Luli Callinicos, *Oliver Tambo: Beyond the Engeli Mountains* (Claremont: David Philip, 2004), chapters 8–10.

[37] Vladimir Shubin, *ANC: A View from Moscow*, 2nd ed. (Johannesburg: Jacana, 2008), chapter 4; Callinicos, *Tambo*, chapters 8–10.

[38] Macmillan, *Lusaka Years*, 30–36.

[39] Jeffrey James Byrne, *Mecca of Revolution: Algeria, Decolonization, and the Third World Order* (New York: Oxford University Press, 2016).

economic development required unpopular taxes and foreign loans, which nurtured domestic resentments, muddied the FLN's reforms, and culminated in a military coup in 1965. (Ironically, Nkrumah, whose words had inspired the PAC, suffered the same fate a year later.) Mandela always recognized the Faustian bargain at the heart of the FLN's strategy. Before his arrest, he had promised to "make [the ANC] more intelligible – and more palpable – to our allies," implying that international recognition would somehow create the conditions for apartheid's collapse.[40] He had no way of knowing that postcolonial Algeria would fall apart instead. By the time the Tricontinental Conference assembled in 1966, the ANC had lost its most prominent leader and its symbolic lodestar in North Africa.

VIOLENCE

The gathering in Havana provided a different way to think about liberation, and the timing could not have been more propitious. Tambo hit a new low that year. In London, the South African Coloured People's Congress (CPC) left the fold. "The CPC has over the past three years patiently reasoned with the ANC leadership," but "we have had to witness" a "campaign of slander and disruption," perpetuated from the ANC's African headquarters.[41] At the same time, the SACP began pressuring Tambo to stop masquerading as an Africanist and ally openly with the Soviet Union. And to add fuel to the fire, key African countries on the OAU's Liberation Committee started to question the ANC's legitimacy as an international organization.[42] Looking back on this period a few years later, an ANC official wrote that the group's enemies "would have been able to wipe us out" if "not for the stubborn fact" that the ANC had "an army housed in campuses [in Lusaka] which everybody could see."[43]

However, the situation in Zambia was not ideal. Although Zambia's President Kenneth Kaunda supported the ANC, his government was divided and his aides grumbled loudly about South African expatriates who paraded around Lusaka "wear[ing] fur hats," promising a revolution

[40] Report Sub-Committee to the African National Congress (External Mission) for Period December 29th, 1962–January 31st, 1963, Lusaka Mission, box 52, folder 2, UFH.
[41] Statement of dissolution of the South African Coloured People's Congress, March 1966, in Karis and Gerhart, eds., *From Protest to Challenge*, vol. 5, 371.
[42] Shubin, *ANC*, 47–59.
[43] South African Revolution and Our Tasks, no date, Lusaka Mission, box 52, folder 1, UFH.

they never intended to fight. "I do not see how [the ANC] could go on and fight in South Africa," a Zambian official told Kaunda in these years. "Freedom fighters ... want to retire from the struggle. Management and leadership is being questioned." Even as Kaunda continued to blast apartheid publicly and cultivate his status within the newly created Non-Aligned Movement, his government put travel restrictions on the ANC and other organizations from Southern Rhodesia and Portuguese Africa. He supported these groups, in part, to avoid Ben Bella's fate in Algeria and Nkrumah's fate in Ghana. Zambia had no illusions about the ANC. After studying its operations in Morogoro and Lusaka, Zambia's foreign ministry summarized the government's mindset colorfully,

[T]he so-called leaders ... have forgotten about the fight. In Lusaka they are talking about buying farms, houses, furniture and cars. ... We should find if we should continue to give them money for their BEERS.[44]

Cuba offered a way out of this morass. The island's charismatic leaders – Fidel Castro and Che Guevara – positioned their revolution as a universal model for leftist anti-imperialism and armed revolt. In 1965, Guevara undertook a sojourn to Africa in a failed attempt to export this model to the Congo and Angola, and Cuban leaders retained an interest, if somewhat pessimistic, in the situation in Southern Africa.[45] Three ANC members attended the Tricontinental Conference in January 1966. While their reflections do not survive in the ANC's archives, the visit seems to have prompted two changes. First, ANC leaders began talking about their setbacks differently. Increasingly, they blamed neocolonialism, a term popularized initially in the OAU's 1963 charter and then embraced by the organizers of the Tricontinental meeting.[46] Nationalists had "gain[ed] political power through the mass anti-colonial struggle," an ANC editorial argued in 1966, but "when the masses of the people force[d] their national governments to make socio-economic reforms in the redistribution of wealth, the imperialists then resort[ed] to military dictatorships through their agents." Hence Algeria's coup. The ANC had no doubt who was pulling the strings. "Experience has shown that this imperialist

---

[44] Macmillan, *Lusaka Years*, 33.

[45] Piero Gleijeses, *Conflicting Missions: Havana, Washington, and Africa, 1959–1976* (Chapel Hill: University of North Carolina Press, 2003), chapters 4–8.

[46] Kwame Nkrumah, *Neo-Colonialism: The Last Stage of Imperialism* (London: International, 1966). For analysis of tricontinental politics, Ann Garland Mahler, *From the Tricontinental to the Global South: Race, Radicalism, and Transnational Solidarity* (Durham: Duke University Press, 2018).

technique was perfected by U.S. imperialism in Latin America and has
nowadays extended to Africa and Asia." However, Cuba, "chosen by the
peoples of these three continents as the seat of the Tricontinental
Organisation," proved that the "anti-imperialist revolution" could defeat
neocolonialism. Although the struggle had faltered since 1960, Cuba
"has remained the bane of all reactionary forces, especially
U.S. imperialism."[47] Because Washington responded to African decolonization with an "unholy" alliance in Southern Africa, it followed that the
ANC would only prevail if it remade itself in Cuba's image.[48]

Second, the ANC updated its ideas about guerrilla warfare. Initially,
Mandela's vision for the armed struggle focused on sabotaging South
Africa's physical infrastructure since that approach seemed to have
worked for the FLN. Although Mandela referred to national consciousness, he rarely explained how these methods would mobilize South
Africa's masses; he presented violence as an instrument to undercut the
apartheid government's *legitimacy*, which would inspire international
support and divide Europeans living inside South Africa.[49] Implicitly,
Mandela always believed that change required support from some white
South Africans. As historian Hugh Macmillan has noted, Che Guevara's
writings turned MK's theory of guerrilla warfare on its head. Guevara was
a celebrity by the mid-1960s. His theory of revolution suggested that
cadres of fast-moving militants could focus popular discontent, which
would then blossom into a widely supported national insurrection. The
resulting conflict would not require foreign recognition because credibility
would come from peasants and laborers within the targeted country.
Violence, by extension, would be an end in itself rather than an instrument
to change perceptions about the South African government's legitimacy,
and it would purge the country of neocolonial agents so that real liberation would be possible.[50] With Tambo's blessing in mid-1966, the
ANC's Lusaka office created a committee to implement this plan and
then sent militants into modern day Botswana in June, September, and

[47] "Hands Off Cuba!" *Spotlight on South Africa* 4:22 (June 1966).
[48] "The Unholy Alliance," *Sechaba* 3:7 (July 1969); Discussion Guide Con't, no date, Lusaka
    Mission, box 52, folder 2, UFH.
[49] Report of Sub-Committee on our Perspectives, no date, Lusaka Mission, box 52, folder 2,
    UFH.
[50] For context, Jon Lee Anderson, *Che: A Revolutionary Life* (New York: Grove, 2010),
    section 2; Robert Holden and Eric Zolov, *Latin America and the United States:
    A Documentary History* (New York: Oxford University Press, 2000), chapter 90;
    Max Boot, *Invisible Armies: An Epic History of Guerrilla Warfare* (New York:
    Liveright, 2013), chapters 49 and 54.

November. The goal was to "organise a machinery" to sort out "how people should be passing into South Africa."[51]

The subsequent Wankie and Sipolio campaigns, in which the ANC applied Guevara's theories to South Africa, were divisive. "[T]he whole concept," ANC political commissar Chris Hani explained, "was to build bridges, a Ho Chi Minh trail to South Africa."[52] The Vietnam War was expanding in real-time in 1966, and Guevara's ideas seemed to explain why Saigon's government was starting to collapse. However, ANC forces got bogged down in modern day Zimbabwe, and they were routed by the Rhodesian military first in August and again in December 1967. Ultimately, most MK soldiers were killed; Hani barely escaped to Botswana, where he was imprisoned for a year. In his absence, the ANC halted these "lightning strikes" altogether, and when Hani returned to Zambia in 1968, he claimed to barely recognize the organization. "There was no longer any direction," he recalled, and "there was general confusion or an unwillingness to discuss the lessons of the revolution."[53]

Tambo arguably mishandled the fallout from Wankie and Sipolio. "There were no medals," Hani's ally Joe Matthews later remembered. "[N]o official ceremony."[54] But the ANC's real problem cut deeper. Within South Africa, Verwoerd had been assassinated in 1966 and the country's new president, John Vorster, opened a secret correspondence with Kaunda after Sipolio. Kaunda did not outline the Lusaka Manifesto until early 1969, which acknowledged Pretoria's right to exist and asked anti-apartheid forces to negotiate with Vorster, but he disavowed violence and put severe restrictions on the ANC during 1968. For Hani, Tambo's acquiescence to Kaunda was tantamount to neocolonial collaboration. "Professional politicians rather than professional revolutionaries" had taken control of the organization, he wrote in a widely circulated memorandum in early 1969. "Careerism," he continued, had forestalled the revolution by creating a stagnant environment where ANC leaders attended conferences instead of waging war.[55]

Ironically, Hani's memorandum prompted a conference. The meeting was held in Morogoro in April 1969, just before Farah's visit to Zambia, and it resolved three issues. First, the ANC opened its membership to

[51] Macmillan, *Lusaka Years*, 35.
[52] Chris Hani, "The Wanki Campaign," *Dawn*, Souvenir Issue, 25th Anniversary of MK (1986): 34–37.
[53] Macmillan, *Lusaka Years*, 71.   [54] Ibid.
[55] Hugh Macmillan, "The Hani Memorandum: Introduced and Annotated," *Transformation: Critical Perspectives on Southern Africa* 69 (2009), 106–129.

non-Africans. The decision directly addressed the frustrations of Indian, Coloured, and white expatriates in London and consolidated Tambo's authority there as he confronted Hani's backers in Lusaka. Second, the ANC shrank the size of its governing council from twenty people to nine.[56] With considerable finesse, Tambo sidelined individuals who, in Macmillan's words, were "not guerilla leaders in the Castro mode," which tacitly acknowledged the legitimacy of Hani's complaint while assuring Tambo controlled the fallout.[57] Third, although membership in this smaller entity was still limited to black South Africans, Tambo created a Revolutionary Council that ignored racial identity altogether. The council formalized the SACP's place within the ANC and existed, in theory, to foster consensus around the ANC's long-term strategy. The decision had support among MK's rank-and-file, which had long accepted non-Africans in its ranks, and it was heralded later by ANC members and the ANC's historians as a turning point in the anti-apartheid movement. "[A]fter Morogoro we never looked back," Hani told an interviewer.[58] However, Jack Simons, a professor at the University of Zambia with close ties to the ANC, offered a more somber assessment. "Sometimes," he wrote in a private letter in mid-1969, "I feel that we are involved in some great charade, a play staged for the benefit of the outside world."[59]

SOLIDARITY

In truth, Morogoro was neither a turning point nor a charade. The ANC did not try to infiltrate South Africa again until Zimbabwe's independence in 1980, so Hani's conclusion is obviously incorrect; yet Simons's cynicism misrepresents Morogoro's impact. Before parting ways, conference attendees outlined a new set of strategic and tactical imperatives. Written by the SACP's Joe Slovo and Rusty Berstein with assistance from Joe Matthews and Duma Nokwe, these guidelines conspicuously recycled Marxist language, and journalists like Ellis have argued that Morogoro put the ANC on a course charted by the SACP.[60] But the document is better situated in a Tricontinental frame since its principal goal was to shift the ANC's focus away from Cuba. In a 2010 interview, Matthews

---

[56] For analysis, see Shubin, *ANC*, chapter 6, and Macmillan, *Lusaka Years*, chapter 6.
[57] Macmillan, *Lusaka Years*, 81.   [58] Ibid., 79.   [59] Ibid., 80.
[60] Stephen Ellis and Tsepho Sechaba, *Comrades Against Apartheid: The ANC and the South African Communist Party in Exile* (Bloomington: Indiana University Press, 1992), 59.

said explicitly that he wanted to reduce Guevara's intellectual footprint after Morogoro, and with considerable subtlety, his strategy and tactics paper eviscerated the logic behind the Wankie and Sipolio campaigns, suggesting that an "armed challenge" – spearheaded by a well-trained revolutionary vanguard – would not "achieve dramatic or swift success."[61] The ANC had to refocus attention on the masses at home, since "economic emancipation" required support from South Africa's "large and well-developed working class." This argument implied that Tambo had erred by sending MK soldiers into Rhodesia while shutting the door on another Hani-style intervention. Critically, the paper did not offer a timetable for South Africa's revolution. Because the whole world was "transition[ing] to the Socialist system," the strategy paper reasoned, the ANC did not have to rush things:

[The Freedom Charter], together with our general understanding of our revolutionary theory, provides us with the strategic framework for the concrete elaboration and implementation of policy in a continuously changing situation. It must be combined with a more intensive programme of *research* ... so that the flow from theory to application – when the situation makes application possible – will be unhampered.[62]

In the short-term, these words endorsed inaction, and the ensuing research program, which yielded papers on an array of topics, defended caution with considerable earnestness. Looking back on the past decade, one unnamed author lamented that the "political situation [had been] ripe" in South Africa but the ANC's "guerilla activities" were "premature because of the backward state of [its] technical and material preparations." Violence for the sake of violence had not accomplished anything. The paper asked the all-important question – "What then should be our approach on the question of timing?" – and argued for a flexible understanding of "what we are planning for." Perhaps the apartheid government would be defeated in battle – like the French at Dien Bien Phu – or maybe there would be an "unexpected break in the White front making some sort of negotiations possible" – à la the Évian Accords – or maybe there would be a Congo-style UN intervention. The ANC need not engage in "useless speculation" because it did not have to precipitate events. It

---

[61] Macmillan, *Lusaka Years*, 78; Strategy and Tactics, April–May 1969, in Karis and Gerhart, eds., *From Protest to Challenge*, vol. 5, 387–393.
[62] Strategy and Tactics, April–May 1969, in Karis and Gerhart, eds., *From Protest to Challenge*, vol. 5, 392–393.

merely had to gird itself for "a combination of some or all of these tactics."[63]

This conclusion existed in the context of a wider conversation about Vietnam. Initially, the ANC interpreted the National Liberation Front's (NLF) success as proof of Guevara's brilliance, hence its own campaign to establish a "Ho Chi Minh" trail from Zambia to South Africa. However, Vietnam's lessons were changing in the early 1970s. The NLF had not defeated the American military (and a second Dien Bien Phu was not imminent), but the NLF had sapped America's will to fight; it seemed to ANC strategists as if perseverance and *public relations* went hand in hand. Internally, this conclusion teed up several realizations. First, the ANC needed to align its ambitions with its capabilities. Whereas political plans were "timeless," and not easily defeated, the ANC could be – and had been – routed on the battlefield, and "it would be unrealistic" going forward to call upon uMkhonto weSizwe to undertake a project "large enough and effective enough to transform the situation." Second, the ANC had to distinguish fighting from the *appearance* of combat readiness, since planning for "guerilla operations" was "one of the most vital factors in creating a situation in which guerrilla warfare [might] take root."[64] Third, the ANC needed to accept that it was fighting one front in a global war to "overthrow imperialism, the reactionary ruling classes, and all other reactionaries who support the present South African regime." Against this backdrop, ANC planners could reframe the NLF's success as a turning point in a *transnational* war against neocolonialism. It followed that the United States' defeat in Vietnam would weaken Washington's support for apartheid, which would create a new status quo for the ANC.[65] Even if the details were fuzzy, the logic felt credible because such talk was so ubiquitous in the early 1970s.

Tambo and his backers were essentially theorizing their way out of a third direct fight with Pretoria. Unlike Algeria and Cuba, Vietnam was in the throes of an ongoing freedom struggle. By conflating South Africa's situation with Vietnam's war, Tambo shored up his revolutionary bona fides without ceding ground to Hani's supporters or Kaunda's lackeys. Yes, fighting was necessary to mobilize the masses in the long-term – and the Revolutionary Council reiterated this point at every opportunity – but

---

[63] Some Notes on Perspectives, no date, Lusaka Mission, box 52, folder 1, UFH; Discussion Guide Con't, no date, Lusaka Mission, box 52, folder 2, UFH.

[64] Reflections on Some Problems Connected with the Unfolding of our Armed Struggle, no date, Lusaka mission, box 52, folder 1, UFH.

[65] "Our Immediate Enemies," *Sechaba* 3:7 (July 1969); Discussion Guide Con't, no date, Lusaka Mission, box 52, folder 2, UFH.

the ANC could begin by allying with the "peace and progressive forces throughout the world," shorthand for anyone who opposed American foreign policy in those years. The NLF's "victories over United States imperialism," Tambo explained in 1973, would "forever be a fountain of inspiration and an example to all anti-imperialist forces."[66] The statement implied almost as much as it said. If the NLF's "solidarity actions" could successfully "galvanize ... large numbers of American people and [make] American imperialism's domestic base very unsafe," it followed that the anti-apartheid movement might mobilize those same forces "around the issue of colonialism and racism in Southern Africa."[67] Although South Africa's white population was recalcitrant, the United States was seething with discontent, and the NLF's apparent success in winning supporters there suggested that apartheid might be attacked effectively from within North America.

Mobilizing the world's "peace and progressive forces" presented obvious challenges but the ANC was no stranger to the complexities of solidarity politics. Since the 1966 Tricontinental Conference, it had expanded its horizon line dramatically. "Our allies are not always united," a research paper observed in the early 1970s. The Soviets and Chinese were at each other's throats, and African, Asian, and Latin American leaders rarely "agreed among themselves" even if they denounced white minority rule in unison.[68] Building inroads in the base of America's imperium, among leftists who despised Washington's support for right-wing governments, without losing credibility among socialists and nationalists would not be easy. Especially since the "malady of over-expansion" loomed over everything. "The whole world seems to be anti-apartheid," the ANC's Secretariat on External Affairs explained in another undated paper from this period. "Yet this world-wide campaign was diffuse, undirected and ineffective." Hearkening back to the theme of appearances, he suggested that the ANC had to focus on "regain[ing] tactical control over this vast and diffuse campaign of solidarity."[69] Going forward, the essential question was *how*.

It took the ANC another decade to settle on an answer, and the collapse of Portugal's African empire in 1975, outside the scope of this chapter,

---

[66] Tambo to Nguyen Huu Tho, June 1, 1973, Lusaka Mission, box 15, folder 67, UFH.
[67] Report on the International Situation, 1973, Lusaka Mission, box 52, folder 1, UFH.
[68] Discussion Guide Con't, Lusaka Mission, no date, box 52, folder 2, UFH.
[69] Report of the Secretariat on External Affairs, 1970, Lusaka Mission, box 52, folder 1, UFH.

arguably set the ANC's course. However, the seeds of a coherent mindset could be seen before Portugal's Carnation Revolution. Tapping into anti-apartheid sentiment was "inextricably interlinked with public relations," an undated memorandum from the early 1970s explained. The ANC could not "hope to raise money unless the image of the organization as a dynamic force is projected in its programmes." But there were too many differences among those who opposed apartheid to justify a cookie-cutter message. Critically, the organization looked outward, not inward, to determine an approach. It was "necessary to resuscitate in an intensive way the links with all the organizations we would like to raise funds from." In short, the ANC had to "fragment [its] appeals to suit the fragmented character of the organizations" it encountered abroad. When working with trade unions, the "whole struggle" had to be explained as a "struggle of the workers [and] peasants" against "anti-worker fascist laws." When reaching out to "political parties" from Asia, Africa, Europe, or the Americas, it was wiser to make "appeals on the basis of a national struggle." It was "all a question of" finding the right "balance to achieve maximum results."[70]

CONCLUSION

The ANC might have adopted a different strategy during the early 1970s. It could have embraced nontraditional warfare and followed the Palestinian Liberation Organization's example, or it could have launched a third invasion of South Africa, especially in the aftermath of Portuguese decolonization.[71] Instead, the ANC embraced the blanket claim that "imperialism [was] on the retreat" and began to tinker with its public relations toward the world's "peace and progressive forces."[72] This approach did not solve Tambo's problems overnight. Zambian officials continued to make life difficult, and while Hani rejoined the fold after Morogoro, other ANC members continued to lament that a "small clique" of non-Africans had "consolidated itself" and "reorganised representation of external missions to suit its aims."[73] Tambo sent some of

---

[70] Fund Raising Projects, no date, Lusaka Mission, box 52, folder 1, UFH.

[71] For reflections, see Paul Chamberlin, "The Struggle Against Oppression Everywhere: The Global Politics of Palestinian Liberation," *Middle Eastern Studies* 47:1 (2011): 25–41; Lien-Hang Nguyen, "Revolutionary Circuits: Toward Internationalizing America in the World," *Diplomatic History* 39:3 (2015): 411–422.

[72] The Report of the Secretariat Covering the Last Two Years, 1972, box 52, folder 1, UFH.

[73] Gerhart, *Black Power*, 401–413.

his critics to the Soviet Union, where they kept out of trouble and complained about the weather, and he unfurled extensive reeducation programs at the ANC's African camps in an effort to win the hearts and minds of his youngest followers.[74] When criticism surged again in 1975, the ANC expelled eight prominent leaders, but the stakes felt different this time. In a private letter that year, Simons wrote to a friend that he had "no clue ... what [Tambo's opponents] would undertake if they were in charge." They had no *analogy* for South Africa's future. The faction "just wanted to be leaders," Tambo recalled. "[T]hat is all. It was a power struggle."[75] One that Tambo won.

Was solidarity an end in itself or a means toward revolution? The question is useful because historical subjects offered different answers and changed their views over time. Like other diasporic organizations from the Third World, the ANC balanced solidarity and revolution in several ways as it implemented various plans and responded to events outside its control. Initially, the ANC believed that transracial unity would bring democratic reform to South Africa. When that argument crumbled in 1960, the ANC embraced the African image, or at least its Algerian variant. When that approach failed after 1963, the organization turned to Fidel Castro for inspiration. Many freedom fighters around the world venerated the NLF after 1968, but the ANC's overall trajectory shows that perceptions of the Third World project evolved after decolonization and interacted with specific debates about liberation, violence, and solidarity. In 1960, the ANC looked to a cluster of African states at the United Nations when acclimating to the vagaries of life-in-exile. A decade later, the organization's strategists had a sophisticated vocabulary to theorize and engage the so-called peace and progressive forces of the world.

The ANC is a useful prism through which to think about Tricontinentalism. Like other liberation movements, it adapted socialist ideas from Algeria, Cuba, and Vietnam. However, the ANC did not copy these models slavishly; it charted its own path, responding to setbacks that set it apart and learning lessons as events changed. This chapter has limited itself to the road to and from the 1966 Havana conference, and, admittedly, the shifts charted here were not as final as this narrative suggests. Voices within the ANC jockeyed with some of these issues for

---

[74] Lectures, Lusaka Mission, box 52, folder 2, UFH. For context, Shubin, *ANC*, chapter 7 and Macmillan, *Lusaka Years*, chapter 7.
[75] Macmillan, *Lusaka Years*, 93, 95.

another fifteen years. However, if analogies matter, and if they shaped the ANC's diasporic behavior, one conclusion seems obvious. *Political expediency*, more than age, temperament, or doctrine, informed the ANC's understanding of and interest in Tricontinentalism.

This conclusion should not come as a surprise. Since before the 1920s activists had appealed to Geneva and then New York, using universal claims in institutions recognized as global to establish their credibility on the world stage. The ANC's engagement with the Tricontinental Revolution extended this tradition, even as Farah's frustrations remind us that no one person or argument ever enjoyed a monopoly on solidarity politics. The sinews of the transnational world moved through and beyond international institutions, and it remains incumbent upon historians to recognize the diversity and opportunism that underlay this peculiar, important strand of twentieth century internationalism.

6

The Romance of Revolutionary Transatlanticism

Cuban-Algerian Relations and the Diverging Trends within Third World Internationalism

Jeffrey James Byrne

> But what harm is there in diversity, when there is unity in desire?
> - Sukarno's speech, Bandung Asian-African Conference, 1955[1]

By the early 1960s, a vociferous and coordinated critique of Western hegemony dominated political discourse across the Southern Hemisphere. So, it was hardly surprising when the prime minister of newly independent Algeria, Ahmed Ben Bella, addressing the United Nations General Assembly on October 9, 1962, firmly situated his country in this globe-spanning "Third Worldist" movement challenging the political and economic status quo. "In the structure of the contemporary world," he said, "Algeria is allied with an ensemble of spiritual families who, for the first time at [the 1955 Bandung Asian-African Conference], recognized the shared destiny that unites them." He vowed that Algeria would help in pursuing their shared goal of tearing up the "gentleman's agreements" (an expression commonly used in Algerian diplomatic communications at the time) by which the victors of World War II, chief among them the United States, created the structures that formalized and perpetuated their supremacy.

Referencing Algeria's own long and bloody war for independence from France between 1954 and 1962, he positioned his country in the more militant wing of that "spiritual family." Insisting that the Algerian revolution had "surpassed its national context in order to serve, henceforth, as

[1] "President Sukarno of Indonesia: Speech at the Opening of the Bandung Conference, April 18, 1955": www.fordham.edu/halsall/mod/1955sukarno-bandong.html.

FIGURE 6.1 A central tenet of Tricontinentalism was the interlinked revolutions of the three continents, which appeared in the iconography as unity between peoples of various non-white races. Even as states like Algeria moved away from direct invocations of militarism, the idea of multiracial struggle remained central to various political and economic challenges to the international system. OSPAAAL, Alfredo Rostgaard, 1968. Offset, 54x33 cm. Image courtesy Lincoln Cushing / Docs Populi.

a point of reference to all peoples still under colonial domination," Ben Bella dedicated his government to the eradication of colonialism "in classic or disguised form," pointing to nationalist struggles in places like Palestine and Angola as examples. He cautioned his audience against mistaking the high-minded and pacific doctrines of non-alignment and Afro-Asianism for policies of passivity; on the contrary, Ben Bella vowed, Algeria would be a responsible and engaged country "[f]or every concrete decision concerning major international problems, peace and global security."[2] As tangible proof of his active and "engaged" intent, Ben Bella traveled from New York to meet with John F. Kennedy at the White House before traversing the most dangerous Rubicon in international affairs – the 100 miles or so separating the United States from Cuba – in order to greet Fidel Castro as a revolutionary brother. Of course, nobody in the General Assembly Hall that day, least of all Ben Bella himself, realized that his first foray abroad would directly implicate his country in the incipient Cuban Missile Crisis.

Reporting on the speech and Ben Bella's interactions with the diplomatic community in New York, Western officials expressed general skepticism about Third Worldist rhetoric in general, as well as war-ravaged Algeria's ability to live up to its leaders' ambitious international agenda. A British observer condescendingly attributed Algerian ardor to the "first flush of enthusiasm" after independence. He suggested that with "the spotlight of Afro-Asian attention ... still very much on them ... [the Algerians] no doubt feel it necessary ... to live up to their reputation as fighters for freedom and to be that much more extreme in order to impress their Afro-Asian colleagues."[3] Kennedy's key advisor on the developing world, Robert Komer, expressed a similar tone a few days later when he briefed the president for the Algerian premier's visit. Warning that Ben Bella "still clings to a lot of naive ideas and thinks in terms of a melange of revolutionary clichés from Marx, Mao, Nasser and Che Guevara," Komer nonetheless judged that "basically ... he's much more pragmatic than doctrinaire." Komer believed that a pressing need for American economic assistance and food aid would soon temper Ben Bella's bellicosity.[4] United

---

[2] Ahmed Ben Bella, "Le Discours a l'assemblee generale des nation-unies," October 9, 1962, *Discours du Président Ben Bella du 28 Septembre 1962 au 12 décembre 1962* (Algiers: Ministère de l'information, 1963), 31–36.
[3] Campbell to Scrivener, November 8, 1962, UK National Archives (UKNA), Foreign Office Records (FO) 371/165654.
[4] Memorandum from Robert W. Komer of the National Security Council Staff to President Kennedy, October 13, 1962, *Foreign Relations of the United States (FRUS)*, 11, 102–104.

States officials felt that the Algerian government ought to dedicate itself to domestic concerns, not throw itself into ambitious plans to change the nature of international affairs.

But that is not what happened. Not only did the Algerians continue to push, fairly successfully, for an appreciable and disproportionate measure of influence in international affairs, but they were also unbowed by the diplomatic fallout from the Missile Crisis. Their warm relationship with Cuba quickly became an important – and controversial – facet of both countries' relations with the wider world. Algiers and Havana were advocates for one another in key diplomatic contexts; they also cooperated closely in transnational revolutionary training and subversion. Their ruling cliques had many traits in common: commitment to socialism, enthusiasm for supporting armed liberation and revolutionary movements in any part of the globe, and the desire to use the many organizing themes of Third World solidarity – Afro-Asianism, Pan-Africanism, non-alignment, and others – to surmount their own sense of local confinement and ideological isolation. Algiers sought to host the Second Afro-Asian Summit, or what they referred to as "Bandung II," in 1965, just as Havana hosted the Tricontinental Conference the following year. In fact, one of the main orchestrators of the 1966 Tricontinental Conference, Moroccan leftist Mehdi Ben Barka, was an intimate ally of the Algerian revolutionaries. (Ben Barka, infamously, was assassinated in still-murky circumstances in Paris before he could preside over the Havana Conference, as intended.) When Morocco briefly attempted to alter its border with Algeria by force of arms in November 1963, Fidel Castro immediately dispatched a Cuban tank unit to buttress Algeria's own armed forces. All told, throughout the early and mid-1960s, Cuban-Algerian Transatlanticism was one of the most substantive manifestations of Third Worldism's much-ballyhooed expansion from Asia and Africa into Latin America.

Yet the Algerian-Cuban relationship also reflected many of the complexities and contentions within the Third World solidarity movement. In their public diplomacy, postcolonial and Third World governments tended to formulaically invoke multiple expressions of solidarity – Afro-Asianism, non-alignment, Pan-Africanism, Pan-Arabism, and so on – which Western observers often interpreted as evidence of excessive ambition and insufficient substance. But such rhetoric reflected a desire to avoid publicly airing the many divergences of interest and priorities within the Third World; holding together a loose coalition of scores of countries necessitated some waffling diplomacy that did not always do justice to the seriousness of the participants' intent. None were more conscious than the Algerians of the need to make Third Worldism an effective foreign policy doctrine, which by necessity entailed real disagreements as well as real accomplishments. Often portrayed as an impetuous and unrealistic dreamer, Ben Bella himself was quite aware of the need to translate sweeping expressions of transnational solidarity into concrete supranational frameworks and bilateral gestures. Prior to his trip to the Americas in October 1962, which was rightly expected to be controversial even without knowledge of Soviet nuclear missiles in Cuba, he told Algeria's national assembly that "[f]or it to be effective and positive, neutralism must not be limited simply to statements of principle. The non-aligned countries must establish and develop a real solidarity between them, as much in the political domain as in the economic domain."[5] Privately, Algiers's diplomats deliberated over the actual meaning and relative urgency of each of the many expressions of solidarity that they publicly committed themselves to, including Arab, African, Afro-Asian, and Maghrebi (North African) solidarity projects, among others.

The Cuban-Algerian alliance in the early 1960s was a form of revolutionary solidarity that was a direct precursor to the Tricontinental Conference. Cuba and Algeria's willingness to cooperate closely in exporting armed revolution around the world was one of the most prominent and celebrated forms of Third World internationalism. However, it provoked criticism and controversy even within the postcolonial world. Cuban and Algerian support for armed revolutionary movements, especially those operating in African and Latin American countries that were objectively independent sovereign territories (rather than colonies), made many Third World elites nervous. India was the most prominent and powerful critic of support for guerrillas and terrorists, but other Latin America, African, and Asian governments agreed. Respect for national sovereignty and noninterference in one another's internal affairs was arguably the core principle of all Third Worldist diplomacy, prominent in all declarations by the Non-Aligned Movement and other such entities. Many saw how slippery a slope it was when the most radical countries, like Algeria and Cuba, argued that the compromised "neocolonial" status

---

[5] Ben Bella, "Declaration ministrielle a l'assemblee nationale constituante," September 28, 1962, *Discours du Président Ben Bella*, 16.

of some independent Third World countries – such as Congo under Moishe Tshombe in the early 1960s – legitimated fostering revolutionary activity in those territories without violating the principle of noninterference.

Additionally, the focus of Third Worldist diplomacy shifted markedly in the late 1960s and early 1970s toward global economic questions, rather than anti-colonial struggle. In that respect, the Tricontinental Conference's continued emphasis on revolution and political liberation was reflective of a concern that was gradually becoming a more marginal facet of international affairs in the Southern Hemisphere. The shift in focus toward economic affairs also brought Latin America firmly into the Third World coalition. With significant Latin American (but not Cuban) participation in the United Nations Conference on Trade and Development (UNCTAD), established in 1964, tensions between Cuba and some of its regional neighbors became a more prominent dynamic in Third World politics in the late 1960s and 1970s. While Cuba had been a participant in the founding of the Non-Aligned Movement (NAM) in Belgrade in September 1961, even the Algerians discreetly, if sympathetically, recognized that Cuba was emphatically Soviet aligned in Cold War terms. Consequently, the participation of Cuba in wider Third World meetings and associations generally required some diplomatic finesse, lest it be used to discredit non-alignment altogether. Last, Cuba's membership in the communist world was an even greater concern when the communist countries' internecine schisms and ideological battles, above all the Sino-Soviet split, threatened to pollute and spoil all attempts at Third World mobilization. The large majority of developing countries with no investment in such doctrinal disputes came to greatly resent communist bickering in the 1960s.

Algerian-Cuban friendship and the Tricontinental Conference of 1966 must be understood in this context. In many respects, the Tricontinental Conference marked the conclusion of the romantic era of decolonization, which Cuban-Algerian solidarity from 1959 to 1965 had exemplified. While they remained important partners in various Third World initiatives, in the late 1960s, there were increased divergences between Algiers and Havana that reflected divergences within postcolonial international affairs more broadly speaking. Algeria was a fine example of a country that was invested in the system, even if it sought to dramatically reform it. Like many postcolonial countries, Algeria sought to balance its support for the ongoing process of eliminating imperialist structures with the need to support an international system that was, ultimately, the guarantor of national legitimacy. By the 1970s, the global battle against imperialism was pursued chiefly by negotiators armed with briefcases and professional degrees, arguing over the global terms of trade and seeking to cast regimes like that in Pretoria as pariahs violating received morality. Cuba, in contrast, besieged by the United States and subsisting on Soviet benevolence, remained more stubbornly revolutionary and defiant of international norms. In the 1970s, Cuba's support for the anticolonial struggle abroad even progressed to the deployment of Cuban troops in significant numbers to places like Angola, Syria, and the Horn of Africa. In many respects, these initiatives were tremendous successes, but the perceived necessity of those direct interventions also undermined the narrative of historical inevitability that had powered anti-colonial struggle in previous decades. The very mixed record of the nationalist movements that featured prominently in the years of the Cuban-oriented Tricontinental – including cases like Angola and Mozambique, that suffered decades of civil war, or Western Sahara and Palestine that appear, as of the time of writing, simply to have failed – is poor in comparison to the 1940s–60s. A comprehensive autopsy of the Third World has yet to be performed, but an examination of Cuban-Algerian relations in the run-up to the Tricontinental Conference of 1966 sheds some light on how the era of anti-colonial romance ended, and how various divergences within the Third World project contributed to future disappointments.

THE EXAMPLE OF CUBAN-ALGERIAN TRANSATLANTICISM

After independence, one of Algeria's most insightful and successful strategies was to take advantage of its position at the intersection of multiple regions and geopolitical entities. The country bridged the Arab world and sub-Saharan Africa; considered part of metropolitan France for much of the colonial era, it also connected the two shores of the Mediterranean. Thus Yasir Arafat, cofounder of the Palestinian nationalist group Fateh, described Algiers in 1962 as the "window through which we appear to the West," while a senior official in Paris advocated productive postcolonial relations on the basis that Algeria could be France's "narrow doorway" into the Third World.[6] In

---

[6] Paul Chamberlin, *The Global Offensive: The United States, the Palestine Liberation Organization, and the Making of the post-Cold War Order* (New York: Oxford

addition to these historical connections, an activist vision of Cold War neutrality also encouraged Algeria and many other Third World countries to connect with both sides of the age's great ideological divide. Proclaiming themselves determined socialists (for the most part), Algeria's new leaders also decided that their country's future prosperity necessitated deepening and diversifying (in the sense of diluting France's overbearing role as a source of trade and development assistance) their economic ties to the West. It was entirely consistent, therefore, that Algerian diplomats called for convergence within the Third World space: for the Afro-Asian and non-aligned groups to merge, for Arabs to support Southern African liberation movements, for all Africans to support Palestinians, and indeed, for Latin America to be included fully in the Third World project. With this in mind, Algeria became probably Cuba's most important connection to Africa in the first half of the 1960s.

Even before the conclusion of the war in Algeria, the Algerian and Cuban revolutionaries had formed an enthusiastic bond in a remarkably short time, and with remarkably little direct interaction or exchange between them. From the very first encounter, in Cairo in early 1959, between a representative of the new Castro regime and those of the Algerian Front, the latter spoke of an instant sense of warmth, fraternity, and mutual recognition between true revolutionaries. A year later, the FLN's first visitor to Cuba wrote rapturously of the experience for the movement's main newspaper, *El Moudjahid*. "Under the sky of Cuba, pearl of the Antilles," he enthused, "in this Caribbean Sea lapping the equatorial shores of the South American continent, we have felt the ardent and fraternal hearts of millions of citizens, freed from the yoke of odious dictatorship, beating in unison with the Algerian Revolution."[7] If the demands of propaganda urged a poetic turn, the effusive substance of his piece was in fact wholly consistent, for the most part, with the Algerian revolutionaries' private, internal deliberations. Many cadres in the FLN's political apparatus saw Cuba's revolutionary project as an example for independent Algeria to follow in the social and economic spheres (albeit without

University Press, 2012), 52; Jean de Broglie, "Quarante mois de rapports franco-algériens," *Revue de Défense Nationale*, December 1965, 1833–1857.

[7] Chanderli's submission for El Moudjahid, March 25, 1960, Algerian National Archives, Birkhadem (ANA), Ministère des affaires extérieures du Gouvernement proviso ire de la République algérienne (GPRA-MAE), dossier 117.1.4.

going so far as to embrace outright communism), while also admiring the commitment to exporting revolution across the Latin American continent.[8] Could not Algeria be the "Cuba for Africa"? they asked, emphatically answering in the positive. Indeed, their widespread enthusiasm for Fidel Castro's Cuba is all the more notable for the fact that, in reality, Havana took only modest steps to demonstrate its solidarity with the Algerian cause, for fear of stoking the hostility of France as well as the United States. While the FLN leadership celebrated Castro's government for the largely symbolic gesture of taking in some Algerian refugees, they complained incessantly about the supposed inadequacy of the far more significant (and costly) support that they received from Arab governments such as Egypt, Morocco, and Tunisia.

Officers in the FLN's military bases in Tunisia soon started to imitate the Cuban revolutionaries' distinctive look by regularly wearing combat fatigues accessorized with pistols and even cigars. As would occur in student dorm rooms across the West, Cuban revolutionary posters and other paraphernalia proliferated in some of these bases. It is easy to mock these stylings, as some members of the FLN did, and to see a certain shallowness to such demonstrations of anti-imperialist solidarity and Third World internationalism.[9] But the early years of the Algerian-Cuban relationship show how the limits of such interactions – in truth, the two sides barely knew a thing about each other's countries or histories – did not curtail the intensity or significance of the sentiment. The relationship, however superficial, offered a sense of solidarity and reinforced the distinct revolutionary goals of two countries forging precarious paths in hostile environments. After all, in decolonizing Africa and the Middle East, dress and affection could be fraught and contested signifiers of cultural and political loyalties, or values.[10] Notably, FLN military bigwig Houari Boumédiène and his lieutenant, Abdelaziz Bouteflika, were two of the Front's most prominent Cubanophiles in the last years of the war. After independence, the former became the minister of defence and the latter the foreign minister, and they subsequently

---

[8] See Jeffrey James Byrne, *Mecca of Revolution: Algeria, Decolonization, and the Third World Order* (New York: Oxford University Press, 2016), chapter 2.

[9] Mohammed Harbi, *Le FLN: Mirage et réalité* (Paris: Editions Jeune Afrique, 1980), 290; Mohammed Harbi and Gilbert Meynier, eds., *Le FLN, documents et histoire* (Paris: Fayard, 2004), 171.

[10] For example, see the essays in Jean Allman, ed., *Fashioning Africa: Power and the Politics of Dress* (Bloomington: Indiana University Press, 2004).

orchestrated the successful coup that saw Boumédiène supplant Ben Bella in 1965.

Perhaps it was partly with a mind to appeasing such constituencies that Ben Bella took the dramatic decision to visit New York, Washington DC, and Havana in sequence in mid-October 1962, thereby unintentionally enmeshing independent Algeria's triumphant debut in world affairs with the hazardous acrimony of the Cuban Missile Crisis. It was at least equally important, however, to demonstrate the sincerity of Algeria's bold pronouncements on international affairs. While Ben Bella did not know that he would be meeting President John Kennedy at the White House on the same day that CIA analysts were poring over surveillance photographs of Soviet nuclear missiles deployed at his next port of call, he had certainly intended to flout one of the Cold War's most heated lines of fracture. The conversations between the Algerians and Americans during this trip directly addressed the fundamental issues of the Cold War in the Global South. On the one hand, the White House hoped that the Algerians would see Cuba as a warning of the perils of "Communist capture of indigenous national revolutions."[11] But Ben Bella's first foreign minister, Mohamed Khemisti (who was succeeded after his death several months later by Bouteflika), encapsulated his side's outlook by defending Cuba's right to pursue its "economic and social liberation" and criticized the United States for attacking the regime "chosen by the friendly people of Cuba."[12] Cuba's choice of communism, in the Algerian view, was first and foremost an expression of national sovereignty (the questionable reality of it being a free "choice" notwithstanding). This disagreement encapsulated the perpendicular divergence of perspectives between much of the Third World and the Kennedy administration: for all of Kennedy's genuine concern for the plight of the developing world, his sympathies could not exist outside of the Cold War paradigm. Moreover, the Cubans were greatly appreciative of their Algerian guests' willingness to endure Washington's ire by defying American efforts to isolate the island. Although the Kennedy administration accepted the Algerians' innocence with regards to the nuclear threat in Cuba, Ben Bella's trip to Havana unquestionably came at a cost.

Cooperation between Algiers and Havana flourished in the wake of the Algerian delegation's October 1962 visit. Fidel Castro appointed Jorge

---

[11] Memorandum from Komer to Kennedy, October 13, 1962, FRUS, 11, 102–104.
[12] "Algerian, at UN, Decries any effort to Overturn Castro," *New York Times*, October 13, 1962, 1.

Serguera to the new embassy in Algiers the following February, and Serguera arrived declaring that his role was not that of a traditional ambassador, but rather a revolutionary ally and "extra combatant in the service of Algeria."[13] At Havana's request, Ben Bella and Boumédiène agreed to take in a small group of Argentinian guerrillas-in-training who had overstayed their welcome in Prague, adding to a list that already included key leaders in African revolutionary movements from South Africa, Mozambique, and elsewhere in the continent. Shortly after, Algeria also received a delegation of the Venezuelan National Liberation Front and agreed to ship armaments to them across the Atlantic.[14] Operating under shell companies, an Algerian cargo vessel, the *Ibn Khaldun*, provided a circuitous yet effective supply line to Venezuela, thereby bypassing the United States' close surveillance of Cuba's efforts to export revolution.[15] In May, a grateful Castro sent a team of more than fifty doctors and nurses to help alleviate Algeria's severe health crisis and shortage of medical personnel. Visiting Moscow that spring, the Cuban leader urged Nikita Khrushchev to extend support to Algeria and to see the North African country as a properly revolutionary one that could well follow the Cuban example. Algiers took further action to alleviate Cuba's isolation by agreeing, in June, to serve as a refueling stop for Soviet aircraft bound for the Caribbean, which necessitated the enlargement of several runways with Moscow's assistance.[16]

Thus, the Cuban-Algerian relationship was quickly becoming very close in both substantive and atmospheric terms. When Guevara spent three weeks in Algeria in July, he received a rapturous reception in public and political circles alike. Essentially given license to wander at his leisure, the Argentinian enthused that "each time I see something new in Algeria, I am reminded of Cuba: there's the same esprit, the same enthusiasm, the same inexperience too."[17] It was a reflection of the unapologetic nature of the Cuban-Algerian friendship that US Senate Majority leader Mike Mansfield, who was also visiting Algeria at that time, unwittingly found

---

[13] Serguera interviewed in *El Moudjahid*, February 23, 1963; Jorge Serguera, *La Clave Africana: Memorias de un comandante cubano, emba- jador en la Argelia postcolonial* (Jaen: Liberman, 2008), 119–120.

[14] Jon Lee Anderson, *Che Guevara: A Revolutionary Life* (London: Bantam, 1997), 546–549.

[15] Serguera, *Clave Africana*, 184–187.

[16] "Note: Accord soviéto-algérien," June 5, 1963, Archives du Ministère des affaires étrangères, Paris, Secrétariat aux affaires algériennes (SEAA), carton 133; see also telegram from the Algiers embassy, June 5, 1963, SEAA, carton 130.

[17] Telegram from Argod, July 24, 1963, SEAA, chrono 20.

himself attending a state function on July 5th, the anniversary of Algerian independence, that featured Guevara and Egypt's Marshal Abdel Hakim Amer as joint guests of honor. The politically powerful senator was displeased to see his hosts fete the poster child of a revolution that, scarcely half a year prior, had threatened to obliterate his own country.[18] Unsurprisingly, Algerian requests for economic aid and commercial deals were meeting sizable and growing opposition in Washington.

By provoking Washington's ire, the Algerian government showed that it was willing to pay a significant price for its friendship with Cuba. On more than one occasion, State Department analysts confessed to being baffled by the Algerians' motivations, for they could see little benefit for Algeria in meddling in the controversies of another continent, half a world away.[19] Nevertheless, the Algerians' motivations do seem to have stemmed from the principles of revolutionary and anti-imperialist solidarity that American officials found hard to accept at face value; their internal records do not contradict their public statements in this regard. There was a clear ambivalence in the Algerian government's attitude to the United States: on the one hand, Algiers saw Washington as the most feasible alternative and competitor to France as a source of trade and development assistance; yet at the same time, Algerian officials consistently described American economic and strategic interests in the Third World as the most powerful and dangerous manifestation of "neo-imperialism." To the extent that cooperation with Cuba was pragmatic, the leaders of both governments believed that they could defend themselves best from American hostility by encouraging revolution elsewhere in Africa and in Latin America, which distracted Washington and created new allies for them. In any case, Algeria's friendship opened new vistas for Castro and his comrades. If Serguera was perhaps exaggerating the significance of the initial Cuban-Algerian subversive collaboration in Latin America by describing it as a breakthrough for the Afro-Asian world and a pioneering example of anti-imperialist solidarity, this unquestionably bold decision by Ben Bella's government would lead to more cooperative

[18] Memcon Kennedy and Guellal, July 24, 1963, John F. Kennedy Presidential Library (JFKL), Algeria country file, box 4b, Algeria general 6/63–9/63.

[19] Briefing Memorandum for Kennedy, "Presentation of Credentials by Algerian Ambassador Guellal," July 20, 1963, JFKL, Algeria country file, box 111, Algeria security 1961–1963; and Research Memorandum by the State Department Director of Intelligence and Research, "Ben Bella, Castro, and the Algerian Revolution," November 15, 1963, JFKL, Algeria country file, box 5, Algeria General 11/63.

ventures of a similar nature in the near future.[20] Likewise, as historian Piero Gleijeses has noted, besides strengthening the two countries' alliance, the medical mission in Algeria proved to be important to the history of Cuba's international relations because it was the first actual implementation of Havana's rhetorical commitment to humanitarian internationalism – the beginning of a long and proud tradition of providing assistance to other developing countries.[21]

Probably the most significant area of cooperation between Algeria and Cuba concerned supporting revolutionary and liberation movements in one another's continents. Algeria had a similar relationship with Yugoslavia, a country that in some respects shared Cuba's dilemma of being relatively isolated in its own region. In this period, the Algerians brought their Caribbean and Balkan allies into the self-identified revolutionary wing of postcolonial African politics, which included the likes of Egypt, Ghana, Mali, and Tanzania.[22] Countries such as these were more unrestrained than some of their African peers in supporting armed subversive movements. Cuba and Yugoslavia could more readily provide armaments, expertise, and transport than many of the African states, most of which were critically short on the requisite material and logistical resources. Algerian diplomats facilitated introductions and served as translators (linguistically and culturally) for the Cubans. For example, Alphonse Massemba-Débat, president of the Republic of Congo (Brazzaville), told Jorge Serguera that the presence of an Algerian diplomat at his side vouched for Cuba's revolutionary credentials.[23] Even if the sentiment was perhaps something of a diplomatic pleasantry, the fact is that geopolitically consequential relationships, crossing great distances, frequently resulted from brief and infrequent encounters such as these. Cuba was almost immediately assisting in the training of guerrilla fighters from numerous African territories, and probably also Palestine. In January 1965, the CIA reported the presence of Cuban officers at a camp in the mountainous Algerian region of Kabylia. The Algerians

---

[20] Serguera, *Clave Africana*, 184–187.

[21] Piero Gleijeses, *Conflicting Missions: Havana, Washington, and Africa, 1959–1976* (Chapel Hill: University of North Carolina Press, 2002), 53–56.

[22] See, for example, Reem Abou-El-Fadl, "Building Egypt's Afro-Asian Hub: Infrastructures of Solidarity and the 1957 Cairo Conference," *Journal of World History* 30:1 (2019): 157–192.

[23] Ajdali, "Rapport d'entretien entre le president Massemba-Débat et l'ambassadeur de Cuba à Accra," ANA, Archives du Ministères des affaires étrangères (MAE), 33/2000, box 323.

also assisted Che Guevara's ill-fated mission to take a column of Cuban soldiers into Congo that year, although they did not think it advisable to participate directly in the struggles of other nations.[24] The Cuban role in Africa's revolutions intensified in the early 1970s, culminating in the dispatch of thousands of soldiers to Angola in 1975, but the basis for that massive intervention was laid in the mid-1960s. Several small movements favored by the revolutionary network that the Algerians and Cubans participated in, such as the Angolan MPLA, Palestine's Fateh, or the Zimbabwean African National Union (ZANU), later played central roles in their country's politics.

But if these early years of Cuban-Algeria cooperation were testament to the potential and viability of Tricontinental solidarity, they also demystify the phenomenon. Indeed, the longer-term historical legacy of Cuban-Algerian cooperation is all the more remarkable for being based, in this initial stage, on scant apparatus or reciprocal knowledge. Guevara's rash venture into Congo was the result of a simplistic, ideological reading of Africa from afar. Rapid decolonization after 1960 and the emergence of armed revolutions in South Africa and Angola convinced the inveterate Argentinian militant that the continent was in the throes of unstoppable revolutionary change that was itself part of a greater global story. In the same vein, Algerian analyses of Latin America in the early-mid 1960s often amounted to little more than rephrasing Cuban agitprop. The Algerian foreign ministry's department for Asia and Latin America optimistically informed Bouteflika that "the revolutionary wind has blown strongly enough from Havana to have shaken up the situation in those countries where the United States' grip is still very strong, and it threatens to substantially change things even more."[25] At that time, the "department" for Asia and Latin America was meagerly staffed by people with little familiarity with either region. The section head, who had never visited Latin America, was delighted to be reappointed to the embassy in Bamako, Mali, in early 1965.[26] In comparison, a right-wing coup in Brazil

---

[24] CIA Intelligence Information Cable, "Presence of Cuban technical advisers at secret training camp for Algerian militia," January 26, 1965, Digital Declassified Documents Reference System (DDRS). Jorge G. Castañeda, *Compañero: The Life and Death of Che Guevara* (New York: Knopf, 1997), 290.

[25] See "Imperialisme US en Amérique Latine," a broad overview report by the MAE's Division Asie-Amérique Latine, from around mid-1964, probably for Bouteflika's attention, ANA, MAE, 32/2000, box 24.

[26] "Algerian Policy toward Latin America," telegram from Porter to Rusk, May 8, 1964, National Archives and Records Administration, MA (NARA), Record Group (RG) 59, Box 1882, General Records of the Department of State, Central FP files 1964–66.

in April 1964 put on hold Algerian plans to open a second embassy on the continent, after Havana, for narrow ideological reasons based on the Cuban perspective.

Still, despite the skepticism of many Western observers, leaders of both countries valued their relationship, in part for its ability to legitimize a diplomacy of revolutionary internationalism. Boumédiène's overthrow of Ben Bella in 1965 temporarily put a damper on the alliance, as Castro and his colleagues initially assumed the coup had a counterrevolutionary character akin to that seen in Brazil. Kwame Nkrumah's overthrow in Ghana the following February confirmed a pattern of early postcolonial regime changes. The Cuban government's decision to put on the Tricontinental Conference therefore occurred in the context of – and partly in response to – the loss of several valued allies as well as systemic, worsening schisms within the global anti-imperialist milieu. A key goal of the conference was to reinforce and formalize the kinds of alliances Cuba and Algeria had been forming in the early 1960s in light of these worrying trends.

SCHISMS IN THE GLOBAL ANTI-IMPERIALIST FRONT

The 1966 Tricontinental Conference in Havana took place in the context of intense divisions within what could be thought of as the worldwide "anti-imperialist front" – that is, those Third World countries and communist countries that claimed that anti-imperialism was a core tenet of their international relations. From the founding of the Non-Aligned Movement (NAM) in Belgrade in September 1961 to the late 1960s, heated debate reigned over the nature, purpose, and organization of the Third World project. A moderate/radical divide emerged among the Afro-Asian countries, chiefly over how militant a position to take toward violent crises of decolonization such as the war in Algeria and the complex conflict that consumed Congo in late 1960. The Belgrade Conference did not constitute a simple and harmonious sequel to Bandung: it was largely an initiative of countries that took a more militant stance toward those two crises than the likes of India and the Colombo countries, and the Non-Aligned Movement in these years actually had a more provocative and subversive tenor than the neutralism celebrated at Bandung.[27] At the same

[27] On the Colombo countries, see Cindy Ewing, "The Colombo Powers: Crafting Diplomacy in the Third World and Launching Afro-Asia at Bandung," *Cold War History* 19:1 (January 2, 2019): 1–19.

time, certainly the greatest impediment to the Third World's unity was the intensifying ideological and geopolitical rivalry between the USSR and the PRC. The Algerians and others saw competition between great powers as a boon for smaller countries, and the FLN had indeed already exploited Sino-Soviet tensions in the latter stages of their independence struggle. But after Belgrade, the Sino-Soviet split became a tedious obstacle even for those accustomed to profiting from such rivalries. China tried to squeeze its European rivals – the Soviets and Yugoslavs – out of the Third World coalition by emphasizing a more racially exclusive Afro-Asianism at the expense of a Non-Aligned Movement that the Chinese saw as a tool of the Yugoslavians and the Indians, the latter the primary antagonist in a fierce border dispute. As Nehru complained to Nasser regarding the extension of that territorial dispute into Third World affairs, "China's main purpose seems to be disrupt the policy of non-alignment which has gained widespread support, not only among the Afro-Asian countries, but also from the Great Powers. I think our own conflict with China should be seen against this background."[28]

Therefore, when Cuba attended the Belgrade Conference in 1961, it entered a Third World coalition already beset by complicated, overlapping tensions. China pitted Afro-Asianism against the NAM; India defended the NAM against China but also feared that the NAM was dominated by those too eager to support guerrillas and insurgencies in places like Congo. At the same time, China also had the sympathy of many leading NAM participants because of its own aggressive stance on supporting violent revolutionary struggles, which compared favorably in their minds to the Soviet Union's accommodating pursuit of "peaceful coexistence" with the West. As a further complication, some of the most militant Arab members of the NAM, notably Egypt and Algeria, worried that China's racial definition of the Third World might distance them from the rest of Africa. Therefore, Cuba, Algeria, Egypt, and Yugoslavia shared a willingness to directly assist violent anti-imperialist struggles, mostly in Africa, and shared a desire to emphasize a more expansive, diverse, and inclusive sense of Third World solidarity. While visiting Belgrade in March 1964, Ben Bella told Tito that Algeria's preference was to unite all "progressive forces" regardless of geographical,

---

[28] Mohamed Heikal, *The Cairo Documents: The Inside Story of Nasser and His Relationship with World Leaders, Rebels, and Statesmen* (Garden City, NY: Doubleday, 1973), 295–296.

ideological, or racial distinctions, and the Yugoslav premier agreed wholeheartedly.[29]

It was the emergence of this more assertive, revolutionary faction within the left wing of the Third World coalition that informed the articulation of Tricontinentalism. The proposal for a "Tricontinental Conference" issued from a January 1961 meeting of the Afro-Asian People's Solidarity Organization (AAPSO), headquartered in Cairo. The organization had started out three years prior as a Soviet initiative to harness the evident energy of the Bandung movement. But by proposing in 1963 to host this Tricontinental event, the Cuban government was hoping to formally extend the Afro-Asian bloc into Latin America, to blur the lines between the NAM and the AAPSO, to diminish its own isolation in Latin America as much as strengthen its connections further afield, and to reinforce its credentials as an autonomous Third World actor rather than a Soviet satellite. Indeed, regarding the final consideration, the Soviets initially preferred that Brazil host the Tricontinental – before the right-wing coup there in 1964.[30]

The Cuban desire to host the Tricontinental Conference reflected smaller and medium-sized countries' efforts to institutionalize Third Worldism in the face of the bigger powers' disruptive feuds. Yugoslavia and Egypt had mostly driven the founding of the NAM, despite Indian and, especially, Chinese and Soviet wariness of the project. While the Bandung Conference had been the product of a short-lived understanding between the two giants of Asia – India and China – Yugoslavian publicity material happily described the Belgrade summit as "a conference of small and medium-sized countries."[31] In that spirit, the likes of Algeria (still a liberation movement in 1961), Cuba, and Ghana enthusiastically came on board. Likewise, Nasser's government hosted a succession of Third World-related meetings after Belgrade – AAPSO meetings, non-aligned meetings, and the second summit of the Organization of African Unity in 1964. At the same time the Cubans were bidding to host the Tricontinental, the Algerians proposed, successfully, to hold the second

---

[29] "Zabeleske o Jugoslovensko-Alzirskim Razgovorima i Sastanku Pretsednika Tita i Ben Bela" (Minutes from the Yugoslav-Algerian talks and the meeting between President Tito and Ben Bella), March 11, 1964, Archives of Josip Broz Tito, Belgrade (AJBT), 837, Cabinet of the President of the Republic (KPR), 1–3-a/2–8.

[30] Jeremy Friedman, *Shadow Cold War: The Sino-Soviet Competition for the Third World* (Chapel Hill: University of North Carolina Press, 2015), 97–98.

[31] Quoted in G. H. Jansen, *Afro-Asia and Non-Alignment* (London: Faber & Faber, 1966), 306.

Afro-Asian heads of state summit, or "Bandung II," in 1965. Smaller countries saw the institutionalization of solidarity as a means to magnify their influence, especially if they achieved even greater prominence (and a real, though limited degree of influence over the agenda) by hosting major meetings and permanent secretariats. On the other hand, by dint of their sheer size, India, China, and the Soviet Union had little need of institutions that they could not closely control, with perhaps their ideal example being the interwar-era Communist International, or Comintern, through which Moscow had dominated communist parties worldwide. As a result, one constant dynamic of Third Worldist diplomacy in the 1960s was the tension between smaller organizing powers and the feuding major powers that wanted to weaponize organizing themes and institutions against one another.

The Sino-Soviet split, and related intra-communist schisms, damaged the vitality of AAPSO badly, even fatally. The animosity between Moscow and Beijing spilled out into the open in dramatic fashion at AAPSO meetings in Moshi, Tanganyika, in February 1963 and Algiers in March 1964.[32] Chinese and Soviet delegates belligerently strove to assert their ideological supremacy over one another while also competing, somewhat paradoxically, for the loyalty and support of the attending Third World governments, who were for the most part disinterested in and perplexed by the jargon-laden vitriol the communist delegates subjected them to. As one African attendee of the Algiers meeting memorably groused,

[M]ost of us haven't read a line of "The Capital." So what interest have we in your doctrinaire quarrels? I have had enough of this situation where whenever I eat my sandwich, I am accosted by someone who wants to know my opinion on the Soviet stand, and when I drink my coffee, by someone who asks me about the Chinese arguments. I want to be able to eat in peace![33]

If the Chinese scored points by criticizing the Soviet espousal of peaceful coexistence – which the Algerians, Yugoslavs, and Cubans, among others, suspected meant Moscow's conceding that Latin America was in the United States' "sphere of influence" and parts of Africa in Britain and France's – they also suffered from the increasingly off-putting, indecorous

---

[32] Omar Ali Amer, "China and the Afro-Asian Peoples' Solidarity Organization, 1958–1967" (PhD diss., University of Geneva, 1972), 120–121.

[33] Quoted in David Kimche, *The Afro-Asian Movement: Ideology and Foreign Policy of the Third World* (Jerusalem: Israel Universities Press, 1973), 185–186.

intensity of their attacks.[34] Other members of the anti-imperialist world now regularly complained of the "doctrinaire states," seeing them as losing their credibility as revolutionary vanguards through their preoccupation with insular arguments, even if the Soviet Union and China remained necessary allies for many developing countries. Indeed, general enthusiasm for AAPSO waned: after a discordant meeting in Ghana in 1965, the next one did not take place until 1972. Seeing opportunity in crisis, the Cuban government founded the Organization of Solidarity with the Peoples of Africa, Asia, and Latin America (OSPAAAL) at the 1966 Tricontinental meeting as a substitute for the foundering AAPSO.[35] However, the association with AAPSO helped limit the new organization's appeal, for the most part, to those nations that openly identified with communism, especially in its Maoist, peasant-oriented form. This lean to the left would become a defining element of revolutionary Tricontinentalism, eventually driving a wedge in the broad solidarity envisioned by Algerian ambitions for the Third World project.

Additionally, the Chinese government's willingness to use racial tensions against its Soviet and Yugoslavian rivals strained ambitions for an expanded Third World unity. The Chinese argument, expressed bluntly by officials and in propaganda material that primarily targeted sub-Saharan Africa, was that white Europeans like the Russians and Yugoslavs were simply not part of Asia and Africa. Moreover, questions of basic racial-geographic eligibility aside, Beijing argued that by dint of their mentality and experiences, white countries simply could not relate to or understand the problems of the non-Western world. "[W]hen we talk to you," Mao Zedong told Africans, "there is no feeling that I bully you or you bully me, nobody has a superiority complex, we are both of a colored race."[36] Showing their fear of China's racial arguments, a Soviet official fretted that Africans "now relate to all whites with suspicion," while Tito railed against the notion that "all blacks are good and all whites bad."[37]

---

[34] See, for example, Yugoslav comments to Algerian representatives on the proceedings of the Non-Aligned meeting in Cairo, October 1964, in Malek to Bouteflika, undated, "La Deuxième Conférence des Chefs d'état ou de gouvernement des Pay Non-alignés (Cairo, October 5–10, 1964)," ANA, MAE, 33/2000, dossier 23.

[35] Friedman, *Shadow Cold War*, 148–149 and 197–198.

[36] Sergey Radchenko, *Two Suns in the Heavens: The Sino-Soviet Struggle for Supremacy, 1962–1967* (Washington, DC: Woodrow Wilson Center Press, 2009), 82.

[37] Soviet official quoted in Friedman, *Shadow Cold War*, 55; Tito quoted in "Zabeleske o Jugoslovensko-Alzirskim Razgovorima i Sastanku Pretsednika Tita i Ben Bela," March 11, 1964, AJBT, 837, KPR 1–3-a/2–8.

This racial line of attack within the communist world's schism was especially worrying for some of the most enthusiastic participants in the Third World scene, above all the militant wing that included Algeria, Egypt, Yugoslavia, and Cuba. Each of those four countries was a prime mover in the Non-Aligned Movement as well as the transnational network of support for liberation movements and armed revolutionary groups. The latter activity was especially focused on Central and Southern Africa in this period, given the continued existence of Portuguese colonialism and other forms of white minority rule in South Africa and Rhodesia. The racial question also bore directly on the ongoing crisis in Congo-Léopoldville, which was one of the most pressing concerns for the NAM. Moishe Tshombe, the Western-backed leader of Congo who was loathed by the militant countries, strikingly protested against Algerian and Egyptian support for the rebels in his country by staging a reenactment of Arab slave raids in the main football stadium in Léopoldville (Kinshasa).[38] So, as Che Guevara prepared to lead a Cuban column into Congo in 1965, Nasser warned that he might appear like "another Tarzan ... a white man coming among black men, leading them and protecting them."[39] It was a revealing indication of how leading the international revolutionary vanguard could resemble a new sort of imperialist civilizing mission.[40]

China's rather brutal willingness to sow division on such profound lines also informed the Algerian and Cuban approaches to the two upcoming Third World meetings that were so important to them both: Bandung II in Algiers in 1965 and the Tricontinental in Havana in January 1966. The leaders of both countries sought to subsume the racialism that threatened to emerge from either cultural or geographic delineations of an Afro-Asian alliance within a secular, revolutionary solidarity that stretched across the Atlantic. They, as well as like-minded allies, advocated inclusive programmatic and political criteria for admission to the worldwide anti-imperial coalition. Ben Bella conceded to Tito that "we [Algerians] are white like you, maybe a little more brown," and agreed with the

---

[38] "Tshombe in Paris: Says Nasser Acts to Weaken Congo," *New York Times*, October 10, 1964; "Tshombe's Villlage Epic," *New York Times*, October 20, 1964.

[39] Muhammad Husayn Haykal, *Nasser – the Cairo Documents* (London: New English Library, 1972), 349; Castañeda, *Compañero*, 276–283.

[40] Guevara's mission did indeed become a disaster plagued by basic cultural misunderstandings, as recounted in his own lengthy report on the failed operation, Ernesto Che Guevara and Aleida Guevara, *Congo Diary: The Story of Che Guevara's "Lost" Year in Africa* (New York: Ocean Press, 2011).

Yugoslav's contention that "the wrongheaded idea of divisions according to race merits the [Non-Aligned states'] strongest censure."[41] Ben Bella's government favored including the Soviet Union in Bandung II and also desired expanding the NAM and the Afro-Asian group to include Latin America and beyond. Ben Bella told Tito that he desired "an enlargement of the circle of nonaligned states ... [I]n addition to Asian countries, Latin American and European countries ... [should] participate in the conference too. We also think that ideas about continents and skin color need to be overcome because progressive forces exist all around the world."[42] At the heart of this emerging ideology was an attempt to renegotiate historic inequalities between Global North and South, as well as countries great and small, by mobilizing a broad political coalition across all continents.

In the end, schisms within the Third World might well have ruined Bandung II, even if Boumédiène and Bouteflika had not chosen to overthrow Ben Bella on the eve of the conference in June 1965. China fought tooth and nail to prevent the Soviets from attending, while many African countries were inclined to stay away because the war of rhetoric between the communist countries gave rise to increasingly polarizing discourse. Boumédiène and his associates had removed Ben Bella from power before Bandung II took place because they feared, if the conference were successful, his augmented power and prestige would render him untouchable. The timing of the coup reflects how important postcolonial diplomacy was in bestowing political legitimacy: if hosting the conference might have made Ben Bella untouchable, those who deposed him likewise hoped that their hosting the conference instead might confirm and secure their assumption of power. Accordingly, the new government in Algiers attempted to hold the postponed conference a few months later, in November 1965, in order to enjoy the legitimization of the Third World. But China's disputes with the Soviet Union and with India, as well as the seeming loss of its Indonesian ally due to anti-communist massacres there, induced Beijing to successfully obstruct multilateral efforts to keep Bandung II alive.[43] In the skeptical view of the Indian delegation, China belatedly discovered "that Asian and African countries

---

[41] "Zabeleske o Jugoslovensko-Alzirskim Razgovorima i Sastanku Pretsednika Tita i Ben Bela," March 11, 1964, AJBT, 837, KPR 1-3-a/2-8.
[42] Ibid.
[43] See Jeffrey James Byrne, "Beyond Continents, Colours, and the Cold War: Yugoslavia, Algeria, and the Struggle for Non-Alignment," *The International History Review* 37:5 (2015): 912–932; Lorenz M. Lüthi, "The Non-Aligned Movement and the Cold War, 1961–1973," *Journal of Cold War Studies* 18:4 (2016): 98–147.

had a mind and will of their own ... As the Conference could not be bent to its will, China set about scuttling it."[44] As a meaningful organizing theme in Third World affairs, Afro-Asianism effectively died in Algiers in June 1965.

The same vicious factionalism greatly limited Cuba's success in ensuring that the expanded theme of Tricontinentalism might provide a genuine successor to Bandung. In many respects, the January 1966 Tricontinental Conference was a less ambitious and more narrow-minded event than the canceled Algiers conference had been intended to be. Castro's firm embrace of communism and the conference's origins in AAPSO, an organization created in order that Moscow might capture the energy of Afro-Asianism, meant the Tricontinental became a distinctly ideological event. Though it assembled representatives from all continents including both Europe and North America, the 612 delegates came mostly from communist parties or avowedly leftist organizations, including political parties, unions, liberation movements, and the like. An emphasis on militant, armed revolutions became a central component of the emerging philosophy guiding the conference. This characteristic alienated old guard Third Worldists even as it provided a platform for socialists such as Amílcar Cabral, the revolutionary nationalist from Portuguese Guinea who came to Havana in search of military and diplomatic support.[45] Communist infighting naturally influenced the proceedings greatly; the Soviets and Chinese fought over the invitation list beforehand, each trying to stack the crowd in its favor. At Chinese insistence, Yugoslavia was excluded, though the Egyptians subsequently facilitated the attendance of a Yugoslavian delegation with "observer" status, which was a particularly inconsequential achievement at a nongovernmental conference.[46]

All told, the Tricontinental's efforts to expand the geography of anticolonial revolution met severe challenges. Chinese objections greatly limited the actual participation of sympathetic Latin American movements, since these tended to be pro-Soviet rather than pro-Chinese. For the same reason, China opposed Cuba's proposal to institutionalize the Tricontinental by creating a new secretariat in Havana in the form of

---

[44] Report of the Indian delegation to Algiers, October 28–November 2 , 1965, as circulated to all missions by IJ Bahadur Singh on December 31, 1965, National Archives of India (NAI), Foreign Ministry records (FM), series 300, NY(PM)/162/3/64.

[45] Manuel Barcia, "'Locking horns with the Northern Empire': anti-American imperialism at the Tricontinental Conference of 1966 in Havana," *Journal of Transatlantic Studies* 7:3 (2009): 208–217.

[46] J.-J. Brieux, "La Tricontinentale," *Politique étrangère* 31:1 (1966): 19–43.

OSPAAAL. In this China failed but, in time, the influence of the new OSPAAAL would prove to be curtailed by more prosaic regional rivalries. Egypt was loath to see AAPSO, headquartered in Cairo, supplanted altogether. Many African attendees were also wary of Afro-Asianism acquiring too heavy a Latin American focus. The conference's emphatic emphasis on denouncing Yanqui imperialism in the strongest terms, with only cursory reference to European colonialism, encouraged their fears. The observing Indian chargé d'affaires concluded that,

If the Conference succeeded in creating a permanent secretariat in Havana, it created a house divided in itself, whose effectiveness and the wisdom itself of the choice of ... site was contested from the very start by the builders themselves. It will now be lived in by triumphant Latin Americans, disgruntled Africans, the warring partisans of the Soviet and Chinese camps, apart from the gullible many who are likely to be stampeded into submission in the Sino-Soviet war of nerves![47]

His analysis was itself an example of schism within the Third World, with Indian diplomacy eager to see Chinese ambitions foiled and the influence of militant revolutionary factions curtailed. In that respect, his report is doubly proof of the roiling rivalries within the anti-colonial solidarity movement, a mere decade after Bandung.

CONCLUSION

In the 1960s, the similarity of views and closeness of cooperation between Algeria and Cuba led many to equate the two revolutionary countries. Indeed, it was common for senior Algerian cadres themselves to describe their country as the "Cuba of the Maghreb" or even the "Cuba of Africa." The Soviet Union's increased economic and military assistance to Algeria reflected the hope, at least in Khrushchev's time, that it would follow the Caribbean country's political progression toward a full commitment to "scientific socialism." Such close association of the two countries concerned some sympathizers, such as the Yugoslavian ambassador in Algiers who fretted that "[t]he importance that the USSR wants to give to the Algeria-Cuba analogy has dubious value ... [because] the West and the reactionaries [will] use and amplify [it] in order to isolate Algeria."[48] His fears were well founded. However, rather than economic and ideological concerns, it was Algeria and Cuba's collaborative support for armed

---

[47] Soni to Sinh, February 10, 1966, NAI, FM, series 247, WII/162/14/65.
[48] Report from Dizdarević, June 22, 1964, Diplomatic Archives of the Ministry of Foreign Affairs of Serbia (DASMIP), Political Archives, 1964, folder 11, document 427425.

revolutionary movements that most displeased Washington. After all, there was no consensus in the Third World on openly supporting and abetting violent movements. The American official in charge of Algerian affairs admitted to a British colleague that "[t]he further up the State Department hierarchy you go, the more you hear the view that [Ben Bella] is 'no better than Castro'."[49] Kennedy had not wanted to concede Algeria to the Eastern bloc altogether, but by 1965, Algerian-Cuban cooperation in fomenting revolution in Latin America and Congo led many American national security officials to categorize Algeria as a hostile entity.

Nevertheless, the Cuban and Algerian positions in Third World affairs started to diverge somewhat in the second half of the 1960s. In part, this divergence was diplomatic fallout from the coup against Ben Bella, to which Castro initially reacted furiously. Assuming, as many did, that the military-orchestrated coup was a rightist counterrevolutionary development, Castro publicly warned that "events in Algeria affect us all, [Boumédiène and the coup's other instigators] have harmed the revolutionary movement in Africa and in all the world."[50] But the more fundamental cause of the growing distance between Algeria and Cuba was the fact that the former was more invested in the established structures and norms of the international order, while Cuba continued to act in more provocative, insurrectionary ways. Algeria continued to aid revolutionary movements opposed to colonial and minority regimes much of the world viewed as illegitimate, especially in Southern Africa and Palestine, but in the late 1960s, Algiers increasingly focused more on diplomatic approaches to addressing systemic economic inequalities. The presence of some Black Panthers in Algiers at the end of the decade attracted a lot of attention in the United States, but in practice the Algerian authorities were becoming more selective in their support for revolutionaries: they were increasingly skeptical of the Panthers' seriousness and secretly irritated that Algiers had become a destination of choice for hijackers.[51] As one of Algeria's senior diplomats explained to his colleagues in 1965, "Today, [the new nations'] essential

---

[49] Telegram from Owen to London, August 3, 1964, UKNA, FO 371/178770.

[50] Telegram from Algiers to Washington, "Algeria and the Sub-Saharan Radicals," March 10, 1966, NARA, RG 59, box 1882, General Records of State Department, Central Foreign Policy Files, 1964–66; "Etat des relations algéro-guinéenes," undated but seemingly from early 1966, ANA, MAE, 33/2000, box 332.

[51] For romantic American notions of Algiers as a haven of revolutionaries in this era, see Elaine Mokhtefi, *Algiers, Third World Capital: Freedom Fighters, Revolutionaries, Black Panthers* (Brooklyn: Verso, 2018).

goal is [to] gain access to the international responsibilities at the heart of the United Nations, and to make sure that their interests and economic imperatives are no longer subject to the whim of a few great powers."[52] There was no open schism between the two allies, who continued to collaborate on numerous issues, but Algeria began to place greater emphasis on broader-based Third Worldist cooperation, especially in the economic realm, and showed greater respect for the principle of noninterference in other developing countries' internal political affairs.

The January 1966 Tricontinental Conference, therefore, ran somewhat against the prevailing current of the Third World's general progression to more peaceful, more inclusive, and more economically oriented modes of collaborative mobilization. The UNCTAD and G-77 groups featured strong Latin American representation from the outset, not least in their intellectual and organizational apparatus, so the majority of the continent's governments voted for the initial exclusion of Cuba from these new entities, just as they also voted to expel it from the OAS around this time. Consequently, Cuba riposted by using the Tricontinental as an opportunity to promote a narrower and ideologically purer form of solidarity. Many of the Latin American delegates at the Havana Conference, being representatives of communist parties and other opposition groups, kept their identities secret. Unlike the core Afro-Asian, Non-Aligned, UNCTAD, or G-77 events, the Tricontinental was a nongovernmental, nonofficial gathering. Key Third World countries like India and Algeria were represented by ambiguously titled, nongovernmental entities such as the Algerian Committee for Afro-Asian Solidarity. The latter included at least one senior diplomat but kept an uncharacteristically low profile.[53] Western officials were not far off in portraying the Tricontinental as a communist gathering, for the event did have an overwhelmingly communist and like-minded fellow-traveling constituency. Prior to his abduction and assassination, Ben Barka himself had said that the conference "would blend the two great currents of world revolution: that which was born in 1917 with the Russian Revolution, and that which represents the anti-imperialist and national liberation movements of today."[54] Full-forced revolutionary resistance against Yanqui imperialism was the

[52] "Revision de la Charte des Nations Unies," undated think piece probably prepared for a May 1965 meeting of the senior Algerian diplomatic corps, ANA, MAE, 32/2000, box 24.

[53] Soni to Sinh, February 10, 1966, NAI, FM, series 247, WII/162/14/65.

[54] Quoted in Manuel Barcia, "'Locking horns with the Northern Empire': anti-American imperialism at the Tricontinental Conference of 1966 in Havana," *Journal of Transatlantic Studies* 7:3 (2009): 208–217.

central theme of the Tricontinental's discourse, with Guevara's memorably blood-curdling appeal to create "many Vietnams" representative of the tenor of proceedings.[55]

In contrast, the first G-77 ministerial meeting, held in Algiers in October 1967, gave Boumédiène's government the opportunity to position itself as a prime mover in the more consensual, legalistic, and institutional campaign to reform global economic structures that was quickly growing to encompass practically all the governments of the developing world. Though the G-77 group of developing countries had been formed at the first UNCTAD in 1964, it developed a permanent institutional structure at the first ministerial meeting, and Algeria's profile clearly benefited from the G-77's founding statement of principles being known officially as the "Charter of Algiers." This set out a program of action (including commodity cartels, price controls, and trade liberalization) that became the basis for the agenda of the New International Economic Order in the 1970s.[56] With its significant deposits of natural gas and oil, Algeria possessed commodities of significant value that were already the subject of intense political and intellectual scrutiny, and the North African country was thereby much better integrated into the mainstream of economic life in the Global South than its Cuban ally was.[57] The architect of Algeria's development project and hydrocarbon nationalization plans, Minister of Industry and Energy Belaïd Abdesselam, presented Algeria's critique of the global economic system at the 1967 meeting, and thereby exerted great influence over the content of the Charter of Algiers.[58] Perhaps no country boasted greater influence over the Global South's economic diplomacy over the next decade. Additionally, hydrocarbons bestowed Algeria with significant revenues to plow into its modernization drive, giving the country the appearance of genuine postcolonial socialist prosperity in the 1970s. It was on this basis that

---

[55] Vijay Prashad, *The Darker Nations: A People's History of the Third World, Reprint edition* (New York: New Press, 2008), 107–108.

[56] See the text of the Charter of Algiers in Mourad Ahmia, ed., *The Collected Documents of the Group of 77*, vol. 2 (New York: Oxford University Press, 2008), 9–32. Umut Özsu, "'In the Interests of Mankind as a Whole': Mohammed Bedjaoui's New International Economic Order," *Humanity: An International Journal of Human Rights, Humanitarianism, and Development* 6:1 (March 16, 2015): 129–143.

[57] For an excellent examination of Third Worldist economic intellectual exchange, see Christopher R. W. Dietrich, *Oil Revolution: Anticolonial Elites, Sovereign Rights, and the Economic Culture of Decolonization* (New York: Cambridge University Press, 2017).

[58] Robert A. Mortimer, "Algerian Foreign Policy: From Revolution to National Interest," *The Journal of North African Studies* 20:3 (2015): 466–482.

the peripatetic Polish appraiser of post-coloniality, Ryszard Kapuściński, described it as "the pivotal Third World State … a model, bright and entrancing."[59]

Together, the 1966 Tricontinental Conference in Havana and the 1967 G-77 meeting in Algiers set the course for international affairs in the Third World over the remainder of the Cold War. On the one hand, the Algiers Charter facilitated the construction of what became known in due time as the Global South: an assemblage of practically all developing countries, defined by inegalitarian global economic structures and the disparity in material prosperity between North and South. Conventional wisdom holds that the NIEO and UNCTAD projects ultimately failed, being blown apart by debt, structural adjustment, and neoliberal capitalist globalization in the 1980s and 1990s.[60] Yet the G-77's agenda still exerts influence, helping to stymie the most recent round of World Trade negotiations and informing the design of the Paris climate change treaty. In comparison, the Tricontinental's communist-led call for global insurgency was becoming more of a radical niche within the Third World movement, even in the late 1960s. Certain lingering anti-colonial struggles continued to command the sympathy of most of the Southern Hemisphere – South Africa, Palestine, and so on – but national political elites were also increasingly concerned that the controversy that inevitably accompanied armed struggle would jeopardize the greater cause of reforming global economic structures. Perhaps no event better encapsulates this divergence within the Third World than the terrorist attack on the OPEC headquarters in Vienna in December 1975: a small group of international terrorists, led by the notorious Venezuelan Ilich Ramírez Sánchez ("Carlos the Jackal"), took representatives of OPEC hostage in order to call attention to the Palestinian cause. The event demonstrated revolutionary anti-colonialists' frustration with the new postcolonial establishment.[61]

The Tricontinental agenda did leave a deep and lasting legacy, though perhaps one felt mostly in specific localities. Because of the Tricontinental's influence and the reduced participation of other postcolonial countries in violent causes, many of the major national liberation

[59] Ryszard Kapuściński, *The Soccer War* (New York: Vintage, 1992), 110.
[60] J. F. J. Toye, *Dilemmas of Development: Reflections on the Counter-Revolution in Development Economics* (Oxford: Blackwell, 1993).
[61] Giuliano Garavini, *The Rise and Fall of OPEC in the Twentieth Century* (New York: Oxford University Press, 2019), 254–266.

struggles of the 1970s and 1980s, such as those in Portugal's African colonies and Palestine, took on a more communist character than their predecessors elsewhere in Africa and Asia.[62] But the Tricontinental's undisguised purpose of confronting the United States also helped ensure that events in places such as Angola, Mozambique, and Palestine took a tragic and bloody turn, entailing decades of civil war and unresolved political impasses. For a time, Guevara's uncompromising vision of many Vietnams came to pass. But by the 1990s, the end of the socialist road was also accompanied by a decisive turn away from violent anti-colonialism. In Northern Ireland, Palestine, and South Africa, among other places, nationalist revolutionaries renounced both armed resistance and socialism. In that sense, Tricontinentalism and the Third World's vision of global economic transformation both shared the same fate.[63]

[62] The most thorough examination of Cuban involvement in Southern Africa is Piero Gleijeses, *Visions of Freedom: Havana, Washington, Pretoria, and the Struggle for Southern Africa, 1976–1991* (Chapel Hill: The University of North Carolina Press, 2016).
[63] For an interesting recent analysis of the Palestinian case, after the secular left-wing nationalist era, see Tareq Baconi, *Hamas Contained: The Rise and Pacification of Palestinian Resistance* (Stanford, CA: Stanford University Press, 2018).

PART III

SUPERPOWER RESPONSES
TO TRICONTINENTALISM

7

Reddest Place North of Havana

The Tricontinental and the Struggle to Lead the "Third World"

Jeremy Friedman

The significance of what would come to be known as the "Third World" was not obvious at first for communists. In the initial years after the Bolshevik revolution, the international attentions of men such as Lenin, Trotsky, and Zinoviev were squarely focused on revolution in Europe, particularly Germany, as both the logical site of socialist revolution and the political and economic prerequisite for the viability of their own project. It was only after their failure to bring revolution to the heart of Europe that they began to turn their attentions elsewhere, especially to Asia, with the hope of undermining the capitalist-imperialist system in its soft, colonial underbelly.[1] At first then, the significance of the developing world was secondary: it was a means of weakening the capitalist system in its North Atlantic heartland in order to inspire revolutionary upheavals there. The later Cold War as we know it, which became hot almost exclusively in Asia, Africa, and Latin America, therefore requires some explanation. Why were so many resources devoted to establishing and maintaining friendly and/or Marxist-Leninist regimes in these places? Why did acquiring the support of the developing world become so important to the Soviets, Chinese, and others?

The problem was that, in the aftermath of World War II, the capitalist countries failed to return to depression and, as they built new social

---

[1] See, for example, Karl Radek, "Address to the Baku Congress of the Peoples of the East," September 2, 1920: www.marxists.org/history/international/comintern/baku/cho2.htm; "Theses on the Eastern Question," Fourth Congress of the Communist International, December 5, 1922: www.marxists.org/history/international/comintern/4th-congress/east ern-question.htm.

welfare systems, the opportunities for revolutionary upheaval seemed to diminish. Instead, revolutionary energies exploded across the colonial and postcolonial world. The Soviets therefore had to find a way to lead a different revolution than the one they had anticipated. However, there were many political leaders and movements in Asia, Africa, and Latin America that espoused their own revolutionary ideologies, some claiming the terminology of socialism, a few of whom – figures like Nehru, Nasser, Sukarno, and Nkrumah – cast a wide shadow on the global stage. Others even sought to claim the mantle of communism, including Tito in Yugoslavia, some of the leaders of the Democratic Republic of Vietnam at times, and Fidel Castro of Cuba. The most dangerous threat to the Soviet claim to leadership of the world revolutionary process was the People's Republic of China (PRC). Each of these actors had its own agenda and rivalries, and the struggle for the political leadership of the developing world became a tangle of alliance politics, ideological compromises, and revolutionary agendas.

At first, the Soviets saw the new PRC as an asset in their attempt to play this role of leader of the "world revolution." Moscow envisioned a division of labor in which Beijing would act as a sort of subcontractor responsible for revolution in Asia, while it continued to focus on the West. Though the Chinese Communist Party (CCP) was excluded from the 1947 founding conference of the new Communist Information Bureau, or Cominform, which was limited exclusively to European parties, Mao broached the idea of China leading an "Asian Cominform" even before the proclamation of the PRC, which received a positive response from the Soviets.[2] Though the Asian Cominform idea never formally came to fruition, in practice China's leadership of the Asian revolution was forged in war – in Korea against the US-led UN forces and in Indochina against the French. The militant role fulfilled by the Chinese allowed for not only a geographic division of labor but a thematic one as well, as Soviet diplomacy pushed its "peace offensive" in postwar Europe, symbolized by the founding of the World Peace Council in Paris in 1949. Even during this arrangement, however, Chinese leaders saw it as more than just a convenient division of labor. As CCP theorist Lu Dingyi wrote in 1951, while the Russian October Revolution was a "classic example of revolution in the imperialist countries," the Chinese Revolution would be the model for the "colonial and

[2] Shen Zhihua and Xia Yafeng, "Leadership Transfer in the Asian Revolution: Mao Zedong and the Asian Cominform," *Cold War History* 14:2 (2014): 195–213.

semi-colonial countries."[3] Given that the sphere of "colonial and semi-colonial countries" was much larger than that of "imperialist countries," it would seem that eventually the importance of the example of the Chinese Revolution would eclipse that of the Soviet Union itself.

This arrangement between Moscow and Beijing would, however, be torn asunder by the different uses to which each hoped to put the developing world. The Soviets were chiefly concerned with demonstrating the superiority of socialism. Moscow never adopted a view that divided the world into three parts, or three "worlds," as many in the West and China did. Rather it saw the capitalist/imperialist system as being opposed by a unity of three forces: the working-class movement in the capitalist countries, the "national liberation movement" in the developing world, and the "socialist camp," which it led. Within a global framework of "Peaceful Coexistence," namely the avoidance of war between capitalist and communist countries, the victory of global socialism would be achieved through economic competition, and the Soviets therefore invested heavily in promoting socialism as a model of postcolonial development.

The Chinese leadership was far more skeptical of the possibility of building socialism in underdeveloped countries, comparing the situation in Africa in the early 1960s to that in China in the first decades of the twentieth century.[4] Instead, its primary goal was to create a broad, militant anti-imperialist front out of Asia, Africa, and Latin America (Figure 7.1). With American forces engaged in Korea, Taiwan, and Vietnam, the PRC felt itself to be under more direct military threat from the United States than the Soviets did, and without the same sort of nuclear deterrent to protect it. For Beijing then, creating such an anti-imperialist front was less about the ultimate victory of the socialist model than it was about survival, which meant the defeat of the imperialist system that threatened it.

The problem for Beijing was that it was not just the Soviets who wanted to avoid war in the developing world. Surrounded by American forces and excluded from the international power structure – particularly the United Nations – the PRC vision of the political role of the developing world was necessarily more militant and Manichean than that of many others. In

---

[3] Quoted in Qiang Zhai, *China and the Vietnam Wars: 1950–1975* (Chapel Hill: University of North Carolina Press, 2000), 21–22.
[4] Quoted in Charles Neuhauser, *Third World Politics: China and the Afro-Asian People's Solidarity Organization* (Cambridge, MA: Harvard University Press, 1968), 30.

FIGURE 7.1 "Resolutely support the anti-imperialist struggle of the Asian, African and Latin American people," declares this poster. China produced imagery in line with the Tricontinental iconography created by OSPAAAL and associated movements, but it hewed more closely to the socialist realism adapted from the Soviet Union. Shanghai People's Fine Art Publishing House, Zhou Ruizhuang, 1967. Offset, 77x106 cm. Image courtesy Lincoln Cushing / Docs Populi.

particular, Nehru and Tito sought to create their own blocs built around the concepts of "neutrality," "positive" or otherwise, and non-alignment. For the PRC, their efforts threatened to defuse the militancy of the developing world and leave Beijing isolated in its fight against US-led imperialism. Initially, especially given the legacy of the Cominform's battle against Titoist revisionism, Chinese leaders saw the Soviets as an ally against "neutralism," but as the Khrushchev-led Kremlin promoted "Peaceful Coexistence" ever more strongly, they began to see Moscow as part of the problem, not the solution.

The result was an open battle between Moscow and Beijing for dominance in the Afro-Asian, and eventually Latin American, spheres, where the stakes were prestige, legitimacy, and perhaps geopolitical viability. This battle took place particularly within the Afro-Asian People's Solidarity Organization (AAPSO), which the Chinese sought to use as their own bailiwick against the Soviet-dominated World Peace Council (WPC) and the Tito, Nehru, and Nasser-led Non-Aligned Movement (NAM). The competition culminated in the struggle over the Second Afro-Asian Conference, the sequel to Bandung to be held in Algiers in June 1965, which Beijing ultimately lost, though the conference itself was never held. The Tricontinental Conference of 1966 thus came at a time when Chinese fortunes were on the wane, but Soviet leadership of the Afro-Asian movement had been severely shaken. Both sides tried to determine the course of the conference in alignment with like-minded states. At the same time, the Cuban hosts sought to use the conference to rescue the project of Afro-Asian-Latin American solidarity from great power dominance and the Sino-Soviet rivalry that wrecked the AAPSO. The conference came near the peak of the Cuban attempt to make itself independent of Moscow and Beijing, a strategy which proved short-lived and of limited effectiveness. The impact of the conference and the resulting organization – the Organization of Solidarity with the Peoples of Africa, Asia, and Latin America (OSPAAAL) – proved smaller than the Cubans had hoped, in part because neither ultimately served the interests of Moscow or Beijing, who maintained their positions as the single most important patrons of Third World revolutionaries. In the end, the Tricontinental and its vision of global anti-imperial revolution turned out to be yet another casualty of the rivalries between multiple states to make the project of "Third World solidarity" serve their own needs.

SINO-SOVIET COMPETITION AND THE AFRO-ASIAN MOVEMENT

Before proceeding with the evolution of the AAPSO and the Afro-Asian movement, it is worth explaining how organizations like the AAPSO or WPC operated in practice. Both were officially "nongovernmental" organizations, which meant that their members were committees set up in various states, rather than the state governments themselves. In practice, the positions of not only the Soviet Afro-Asian Solidarity Committee or the Chinese Peace Committee, but also the committees of other countries such as India or Indonesia, were worked out with the relevant government and/or party institutions in those states, often requiring discussions at the highest level. While the conferences held by these organizations were their highest profile events, in reality most of the important work occurred behind the scenes and between conferences. This work often included the distribution of funds or other kinds of aid to various organizations, releasing statements on world events, and planning for future conferences, all of which entailed political jockeying among member committees. These committees would be represented by top officials in the organization's secretariat, such as the AAPSO's in Cairo, and as such the makeup of the Executive Committee for each organization was of paramount importance and was the subject of much maneuvering. In advance of a conference, the Executive Committee would organize a Preparatory Committee, whose duties normally involved setting the agenda, deciding whom to invite, and writing drafts of the resolutions that the conference was to adopt. In practice, the conferences themselves were usually highly choreographed, and the fiercest political battles had already taken place before the conference started, behind closed doors among the members of the Preparatory Committee. This structure gave the Soviets and Chinese outsized influence. Both were nearly assured to be on the executive committees of any such organizations, and they had the resources and leverage to muster allies to support their draft agendas and resolutions. Consequently, such conferences were often the product of an earlier struggle between Soviet and Chinese lines, and the results enabled a type of score keeping in terms of influence between the two.

The degeneration of the AAPSO conferences in particular into fora for Sino-Soviet battles only happened, however, once the stakes and divisions had become clear. As the Afro-Asian movement began to take shape in the mid-1950s, Moscow and Beijing approached it in a similar manner. They saw it as an opportunity both to separate the newly independent states from their former colonial masters and to create positive relations with countries whose leaders were being pressured by the West to avoid ties with the communist world. At this early stage, namely that of the Bandung Conference of 1955 and the New Delhi conference of Asian Nations held just a few weeks before, neither the USSR nor the PRC was ambitious enough to seek to turn the countries of Asia and Africa into full-fledged allies of the "socialist camp." Accordingly, Bandung was the scene of a masterful performance by Chinese Foreign Minister Zhou Enlai, whose conciliatory speech helped the PRC return to the world of Asian diplomacy, precisely what Nehru had intended by pushing for the PRC's invitation.[5] Though the New Delhi conference, as an officially nongovernmental event, would have a lower profile, it would ultimately have the greater institutional impact, since it would call for the creation of "Solidarity Committees" in each of the participating countries, which

---

[5] See Neuhauser, *Third World Politics*, 5–6.

would eventually come to form the Afro-Asian People's Solidarity Organization.

The first AAPSO conference, held in Cairo in December 1957, was dominated by the Egyptians, riding high off Nasser's nationalization of the Suez Canal and the subsequent events of 1956, and its militancy took both the Soviets and Chinese by surprise. The Soviets had gone seeking to focus on the "peace" struggle and economic aid, and Beijing had instructed its delegates to adhere closely to the Soviet line.[6] The militant tone of the conference, which reflected the rising wave of Arab nationalism, surprised and concerned the Soviets who worried that it would undermine their efforts to present the Afro-Asian countries as natural allies of the peace movement in Europe.[7] For the Chinese, meanwhile, the conference opened their eyes to the potential for a more militant orientation of the Afro-Asian movement than that of Bandung, one which dovetailed well with the radical turn in Chinese foreign and domestic policy that accompanied the launch of the Great Leap Forward in 1958. While the final conference resolution was significantly watered down from the opening statement, Liu Ningyi, the head of the Chinese delegation at the conference, took this to be a reflection of the fears the bourgeois-dominated governments of the newly independent states had regarding the militant feelings of their peoples.[8] In the Chinese view, opportunities for a more radical orientation of the Afro-Asian movement existed, and the obstacle was the conservatism of the new governments. In short, what the Soviets saw as a latent danger in the conference, the Chinese saw as an opportunity.

By the time of the second AAPSO conference in Conakry, Guinea, in April 1960, Sino-Soviet relations had deteriorated significantly, and the radical mood of the delegates had increased with the progress of African decolonization and the Algerian war for independence.[9] In spite of this, the Soviet delegation was determined to win adherence to its policy of

[6] Chinese MFA to all embassies, foreign trade representatives, consulates, December 18, 1957, Chinese Foreign Ministry Archive (CFMA) doc. 108–00004–07, 16–23.

[7] Report of State Committee on Cultural Ties (GKKS) to General Department of the Central Committee, March 22, 1958, Russian State Archive of Contemporary History (RGANI) f.5 0.30 d.272, 43–45.

[8] Report of Liu Ningyi to Central Committee, CCP from First AAPSO Conference, January 5, 1958, CFMA doc. 108–00004–07, 7.

[9] For more on Sino-Soviet relations in this period, see Lorenz Lüthi, *The Sino-Soviet Split* (Princeton: Princeton University Press, 2008), 114–156. See also Shen Zhihua and Xia Yafeng, *Mao and the Sino-Soviet Partnership, 1945–1959* (New York: Lexington Books, 2015), 307–343.

"Peaceful Coexistence," especially by promoting the idea that disarmament would liberate resources that could be employed for the economic development of the newly independent states. Meanwhile, the Chinese were worried about what they saw as the Indo-Egyptian hijacking of the conference in the name of "neutrality." In the words of the Chinese representative at the AAPSO secretariat in Cairo, Zhu Ziqi, the Indians and Egyptians were "conspir[ing] to boost the policy of so-called opposition to blocs and nonalignment ... in order to weaken and shift anti-imperialism ... in order to change the general character of the solidarity movement, replace it with reactionary content and have it led by the right wing of the bourgeoisie."[10] In the event, the rising tide of militant anti-imperialism among the African delegates carried the day, and the Chinese delegation left elated. The Indians and Egyptians, key players in the emerging non-aligned movement that would hold its first conference the following year, appraised the atmosphere of the conference and dropped their talk of "neutrality" following their opening statements.[11] At the same time, the Chinese understood that behind the efforts of the Indians and Egyptians stood the Soviet delegation, which tried to tack on a two-page addition to the General Secretary's speech with a list of pet Soviet issues, including peaceful coexistence and disarmament.[12] The dynamics at the AAPSO increasingly seemed to pit the USSR, allied with India and Egypt, in a sort of "peace" camp against the PRC, with many allied African delegations led by the Algerians, in the "militant struggle" camp.

Over the course of 1961 and 1962, the Sino-Soviet struggle began to dominate meetings of the AAPSO and WPC, including an Executive Committee meeting in Gaza in December 1961 and a meeting of the WPC in Stockholm two months later. It was at the Gaza meeting that the first serious steps were taken to organize a tricontinental conference, an idea that had been floated by the Cubans as early as January 1960.[13] The proposal quickly became a political battleground. The Soviets sought to hold the conference under the auspices of the WPC, where they and their European allies could control the agenda, while many African delegations argued that the WPC was "not an anticolonial, anti-imperialist

---

[10] Zhu Ziqi to Chinese Peace Committee, March 23, 1960, CFMA doc. 108–00106–01, 4.

[11] Liu Dingui and Liao Chengzhi to Zhou Enlai, Chen Yi, Liaison Department, Chinese Peace Committee, report from Second AAPSO Conference, April 10, 1960, CFMA 108–00106–01, 43.

[12] Zhu Ziqi to Peace Committee, March 24, 1960, ibid., 20.

[13] Letter of Embassy Cairo to MFA, January 20, 1960, CFMA doc. 111–00301–03, 6.

organization."[14] The Chinese made the same argument at the subsequent Stockholm WPC conference, though the Soviet position won the day there with the backing of the Europeans and Latin Americans. Far from a conclusive victory, however, this served merely to clarify positions and delineate turf, and the question of under whose auspices the Tricontinental would be held was far from decided.

The calling of a tricontinental meeting would take center stage at the next AAPSO conference, held in Moshi, Tanganyika, in February 1963. By this time the Sino-Soviet rivalry so overwhelmed the organization that Tanganyikan President Julius Nyerere felt it necessary to open the conference with an admonition to the Soviets and Chinese to keep their disputes to themselves.[15] The Soviets and Chinese both spent a lot of time feeling out and cajoling other delegations in advance of the conference in order to line up support, and the Chinese arrived feeling that they had Africa "in their pocket."[16] In a preconference meeting the Chinese taunted their Soviet colleagues, asking them "Why did you come? There is nothing for you to do here."[17] Anticipating the struggle over the Tricontinental at the conference, the Cuban ambassador to Mali Jose Carillo, who would be representing Cuba at the conference, met with Chinese officials to gauge their support for holding the conference in Cuba, and got a positive response.[18] Two weeks later, the Cuban ambassador in Cairo met with Yang Shuo, the new Chinese representative to the AAPSO Secretariat, reiterating Castro's eagerness to hold the Tricontinental in Havana as early as January 1964 in order to promote armed struggle in Latin America, particularly in Peru and Guatemala.[19] The Moshi conference came at a crucial juncture in the socialist camp when Soviet-Cuban relations were at their post-Missile Crisis nadir and the Chinese were trying to capitalize, as will be discussed in greater detail later. The Soviets therefore were afraid of a conference hosted by Cuba and tried to pressure the Cuban delegate not to propose Havana as the host city.

[14] Report of Anatoly Safronov to Presidium meeting of Soviet Committee of Solidarity of Asia and Africa (SKSSA), January 8, 1962, State Archive of the Russian Federation (GARF) f.9540 0.1 d.109, 54–55.

[15] Darryl Thomas, "The Impact of the Sino-Soviet Conflict on the Afro-Asian People's Solidarity Organization," *Journal of Asian and African Affairs* 3 (April 1992): 177.

[16] Report of SKSSAA chair Tursun-Zade on Moshi conference, February 18, 1963, GARF f.9540 0.1 d.129, 28.

[17] Ibid.

[18] Chinese Peace Committee to Embassy Mali, December 25, 1962, CFMA doc. 111-00375–04, 3–4.

[19] Yang Shuo (Cairo) to Peace Committee, January 11, 1963, ibid., 10.

Instead, they wanted the conference held under the auspices of the WPC in Brazil. The leftist government of João Goulart opposed armed struggle as the path to power, making Brazil a more acceptable location for the Soviets and the other Latin American observer delegations.[20] The Soviet effort failed, and a resolution was adopted to hold the conference in Havana. As the Chinese report described it, "The Soviet Union and its partners were completely on the defensive and isolated, in the end they slipped away in the middle of the night, heads bowed and discouraged."[21] However, the Chinese knew that the battle was far from over and told the Cubans that it would take a lot of work to get the resolution enacted.[22]

This work would be complicated by the fact that conferences and organizations attempting to speak for the developing world were now proliferating along with the increase in aspirants to leadership. While the Cubans, with help from the Chinese, were trying to organize a tricontinental meeting, Beijing's attentions increasingly focused on a second Bandung conference, while others were determined to hold a second non-aligned conference. The politics of these three conferences – who would be invited, where they would be held, what the agendas would be, and which would come first – became entangled with all sorts of rivalries. China and India were now bitter enemies following their wars over Himalayan borderlands. India and Pakistan were fighting over Kashmir. Egypt and Indonesia were rivals for the leadership of the Islamic world. Increasingly, India and Egypt worked with the USSR to oppose China, Indonesia, and Pakistan. The former promoted the WPC and Non-Aligned Movement (NAM) along with peace and disarmament (except on the issue of Israel), while the latter group focused above all on a second Bandung conference that would give rise to an Afro-Asian attempt to overturn the existing global power structure.

A preparatory conference for the second Bandung, held in Jakarta in April 1964, achieved mixed results. It did not invite the Soviet Union, a decision that was the PRC's chief objective. However, as the Soviet embassy in New Delhi reported, the Indians managed to get the conference pushed off to 1965 so that it would be held after the second NAM conference. They also got it moved to Africa rather than holding it in

[20] Zhonglianbu (Liaison Department) to PRC Embassy Cuba, February 23, 1963, ibid., 15–16.

[21] Report of Central Committee on Third AAPSO Conference to PRC representatives abroad, written by Liu Ningyi, February 17, 1963, CFMA doc. 108–00415–01, 6–7.

[22] Zhonglianbu (Liaison Department) to PRC Embassy Cuba, February 23, 1963, CFMA doc. 111–00375–04, 16.

Indonesia.[23] A year later, the Soviets managed to get invited to the Islamic Conference of Asia and Africa held in Bandung, despite Chinese protests that the USSR was "neither an Asian nor an African country."[24] The conference turned into a three-way struggle for leadership of the Islamic world between Indonesia (backed by the PRC and Pakistan), Egypt (backed by the Arab countries), and sub-Saharan Africa, which was fearful of Egyptian domination. The Soviets sought to maintain a low profile and make contacts in the name of a larger objective: getting invited to the second Bandung conference.

In early 1965, the issue of a second Bandung, specifically whether the Soviets should be invited, came to symbolize the battle between Moscow and Beijing for domination of the Afro-Asian movement. The USSR and the PRC pressured, cajoled, and bribed countries in order to get them to either support or oppose inviting the Soviets. In one instance, Zhou Enlai told Nasser to reject much needed grain from the USSR because one must "maintain principled struggle until the end."[25] Despite Chinese pressure, momentum was building in favor of inviting the Soviets, and by the beginning of June, Foreign Minister Gromyko reported to Politburo member Mikhail Suslov that of roughly 50 possible participants, 24 to 26 were thus far prepared to support Soviet participation.[26] A final decision on whether or not to invite the Soviets was not expected until a preparatory meeting of foreign ministers on the eve of the conference. The conference was to be held in Algiers at the end of the month, but it was postponed because of the coup that overthrew Algerian President Ahmed Ben Bella on June 19, 1965. Jockeying continued in the aftermath of the coup, as the PRC embraced the new government, led by Colonel Houari Boumédiène, in the hopes of convening a conference in the fall. Once it became clear that the USSR would be invited, the PRC backed out and the conference was never held, a major defeat for Beijing in its effort to establish itself as the leader of the Afro-Asian movement.

Nevertheless, the documents available in the Russian archives about this phantom conference are instructive with regard to the Soviet approach to such conferences and the Afro-Asian world at the time. A Central Committee resolution from June 1965 directed forty-three

---

[23] Report of Soviet ambassador to India I. Benediktov to General Department Central Committee, April 21, 1964, RGANI f.5 0.30 d.452, 109–113.

[24] Report of KGB to Central Committee, April 15, 1965, RGANI f.5 0.30 d.480, 44–47.

[25] PRC ambassador in UAR to MFA, June 22, 1965, CFMA doc. 109–03645–01, 17.

[26] Report of Gromyko to Suslov on Second Bandung, June 5, 1965, RGANI f.5 0.30 d.480, 126.

Soviet ambassadors to meet with their host governments on the question of the Second Afro-Asian Conference and laid out the Soviet agenda.[27] Disarmament and "peaceful coexistence" were now demoted to third and fourth place behind the "activization" of American aggression in Asia, Africa, and Latin America, specifically in the Dominican Republic, Congo, Cuba, and Indochina, and the battle against colonialism and neocolonialism.[28] In a directive to the Soviet delegation in case of participation in the conference sent from Gromyko to Suslov, the emphasis was placed on highlighting the Soviet role in Vietnam and putting the Soviets at the center of efforts to form an international anti-imperialist front in favor of North Vietnam and the National Liberation Front of South Vietnam (NLF), including China.[29] They were to vehemently deny any charge coming from the Chinese that the Soviets were pushing negotiations in Vietnam. In addition, the Soviet delegation was to play up Soviet anti-colonialism, especially in southern Africa. At the same time, the Soviets were to avoid any confrontation or condemnation of the PRC, for example if India tried to introduce a resolution condemning the Chinese nuclear test, despite Soviet promotion of the Nuclear Test-Ban Treaty. According to the directive, "polemics and fights with the Chinese delegations at the conference would not be in our interests, and so it would be desirable to avoid them." Rather, if they could not get China to agree on a "union of anti-imperialist forces, it is necessary that the participants in the conference see that not we, but rather the Chinese are the instigators of polemics and division, and that we strive for constructive solutions to the tasks facing the conference."[30] By 1965 then, the Soviet approach to establishing Moscow's leadership of the Afro-Asian movement was to embrace anti-colonial struggle, portray the Soviet Union as the patron of fighting oppression, and act above the fray of Sino-Soviet polemics.

Though the Second Afro-Asian Conference never took place, much of this approach would be evident at the Tricontinental only a few months later. For the Chinese, the Tricontinental would come as their one last, desperate chance. The second Bandung had been a failure, and with the events of October 1965 removing Beijing's most crucial ally in Indonesia, the Tricontinental offered one more opportunity to establish the PRC as the true leader of the anti-imperialist struggle of Asia, Africa, and Latin

---

[27] Materials for Foreign Policy Commission of CC CPSU to Suslov, June 18, 1965, ibid., 79–92.

[28] Ibid., 84.   [29] Gromyko to Suslov, June 17, 1965, ibid., 100.   [30] Ibid., 116–117.

America, although this time it would take place under the auspices of the Cubans, who were keen to take up the mantle of leadership themselves.

THE CUBAN ROLE

The decision to hold the Tricontinental Conference in Havana, made at the third AAPSO conference in Moshi a few months after the Cuban Missile Crisis, came at precisely the moment when Soviet-Cuban relations were at their most tense and Sino-Cuban relations were at their closest. At the time, this made the decision to hold the conference in Cuba a seeming victory for Beijing, one that Moscow rued. However, this constellation of relations would turn out to be very short-lived, and by the time the conference was held, Cuba was attempting to chart its own course as the leader of an anti-imperialist front in Asia, Africa, and Latin America. Cuban relations with both Beijing and Moscow were tense and, given the way that the Sino-Soviet dispute had torpedoed both the AAPSO and the second Bandung conference, Cuba was not alone in thinking that the success of Asia, Africa, and Latin America as a political force depended upon its independence from the USSR and PRC.

Soviet-Cuban relations got off to a more promising start than Havana's relations with Beijing, despite the fact that Fidel Castro's Cuban revolution had taken the path of armed struggle advocated by the PRC. This was in part because Castro's group had taken power without the cooperation of the communists in Havana, so his ideological allegiances seemed uncertain, and the early evidence was concerning from China's perspective. In January 1960, a Cuban delegation visited Yugoslavia – a country Beijing perceived as the fount of revisionism – and the two countries found a lot of common ground. They agreed on "active peaceful coexistence," the role of small states working together on the world stage, the need for economic cooperation, and the importance of the United Nations, from which the PRC was excluded.[31] Cuba and Yugoslavia talked about holding a conference for Asia, Africa, and Latin America to address economic cooperation, which the Chinese worried was just a gateway for Tito to bring the Cubans on board with a project to launch a "third force," specifically a political alternative to the capitalist and communist blocs. The PRC embassy in Cairo, where the Cuban delegation went before Belgrade, worried that the conference proposal was an attempt by the

---

[31] Report from Chinese ambassador in Yugoslavia to MFA, January 21, 1960, CFMA doc. 111–00301–03, 3–4.

Cuban "bourgeois nationalists" (资产阶级民族主义者) to unite with other bourgeois nationalists throughout Asia, Africa, and Latin America – in particular Nehru and Nasser – to create a "neutralist bloc" (中立主义集团).[32] Even Che Guevara was described by the Chinese as having only "advanced bourgeois democratic revolutionary thought" with some Marxist-Leninist influence.[33]

Moscow was much more sanguine in its evaluations of the Cuban revolution, and its aid relationship with Havana developed rapidly in 1960 and 1961. Politburo member Anastas Mikoyan visited Cuba in early 1960, and his positive report produced Soviet economic and military support. While Che Guevara's visit to Beijing in late 1960 convinced the Chinese that perhaps the Cubans were more revolutionary than previously thought, they began to worry that the extent of Soviet aid to Cuba would keep Cuba from publicly supporting Beijing on the issue of peaceful coexistence versus anti-imperialism. As Guevara told the Chinese, from his perspective "Soviet support for Cuba is a true indication of the Soviet policy of peaceful coexistence," meaning Moscow had not abandoned the struggle.[34] The chairman of the Soviet Solidarity Committee reported, following a trip to Latin America at the end of 1961, that

> In the course of this year, which has been difficult for the Cubans, they have become convinced that from the Chinese they can get only revolutionary slogans and loud yelling, but real aid from the Chinese is not visible and they couldn't see it, because the Chinese don't have the means and the possibilities to offer any kind of significant real aid. But our real aid there is very visible, it hits everyone in the face.[35]

Soon enough this aid would come to include the stationing of nuclear missiles in Cuba, but Khrushchev's removal of the missiles in the face of the American "quarantine" without consulting Havana deeply angered the Cuban leaders. The Cuban leadership saw this as both a betrayal and evidence of cowardice on Moscow's part, and Guevara claimed that had the missiles been under Cuban rather than Soviet control, they would have been fired.[36] Mikoyan returned to Havana in November 1962, but this

---

[32] Chen Jiakang, PRC Ambassador Cairo to MFA, January 20, 1960, ibid., 6–7.

[33] PRC MFA background on Che Guevara, November 13, 1960, CFMA doc. 204–00680–01, 5. See also Chinese Foreign Ministry documents on Cuba published and translated in *Cold War International History Project Bulletin* 17–18 (Fall 2012), 21–116.

[34] PRC representative in Cuba to Zhonglianbu and MFA, July 24, 1960, CFMA doc. 111–00301–04, 2.

[35] SKSSAA Presidium Meeting, February 22, 1962, GARF f.9540 o.1 d.110, 29.

[36] John Lee Anderson, "Castro's Defining Crisis," *The New Yorker*, October 16, 2012: www.newyorker.com/news/news-desk/castros-defining-crisis.

time to a cold reception: Guevara would not even greet him at the airport. When Mikoyan returned to Moscow to report on his trip, his colleagues called the Cubans "unreliable allies."[37] While it suddenly became much more difficult to distribute Soviet propaganda in Cuba, the Chinese capitalized by claiming that the Soviets had shown their true face, and that only the PRC was really willing to fight imperialism around the world.[38] In March 1963, the PRC began publishing a Spanish language edition of *Peking Review* known as *Pekin Informa*.[39] Cuba and China, as the two most militant advocates of armed struggle against imperialism, went to Moshi in February 1963 determined to make sure that it was their line that prevailed over the "peaceful," "neutralist" one of the Soviets and Indians. In addition to pushing for the Tricontinental in Havana, the Cubans told the Chinese that there would be a secret meeting on the side to discuss guerrilla warfare conducted by the Movimento Popular de Libertação de Angola (People's Movement for the Liberation of Angola, or MPLA) and invited the Chinese ambassador to make contact with them.[40] As noted above, the Soviets, together with Latin American communists who advocated a peaceful path to socialism in their countries and feared Cuban meddling, failed in their efforts to have the Tricontinental held in Brazil instead.

However, the Sino-Cuban honeymoon was short-lived. While the Cuban government may have been more ideologically compatible with the Chinese, it was dependent on economic and military aid from the Soviet Union, which China could simply not match. Castro visited the USSR in June 1963, and his conversations there with Khrushchev did much to repair the damage done the previous October, as well as to put some distance between Castro and Beijing.[41] Following Khrushchev's removal in October 1964, the Soviets tried to organize a new meeting of the international communist movement in order to resolve the Sino-Soviet dispute, or at least isolate the Chinese. In preparation for this effort, they helped organize a meeting of twenty-two Latin American communist

---

[37] Protocol of Presidium session October 14, 1962, in A. A. Fursenko, ed., *Arkhivy Kremlia: Prezidium TsK KPSS, 1954–1964* (Moscow: ROSSPEN, 2004), 663.

[38] Report of APN chairman B. Burkov to CC on situation of Soviet propaganda in Cuba, April 17, 1963, RGANI f.5 o.55 d.58, 73.

[39] Ernst Halperin, "Peking and the Latin American Communists," *The China Quarterly* 29 (January–March 1967): 134.

[40] PRC Embassy Havana to MFA, December 27, 1962, CFMA doc. 111–00375–04, 7.

[41] For Khrushchev's report on his conversations with Castro and Presidium discussion, see *Arkhivy Kremlia: Prezidium TsK KPSS, 1954–1964*, 720–731.

parties in November 1964, which the Cubans attended, that condemned "factionalism" and called for the end of Sino-Soviet polemics.[42] This meeting clearly showed Beijing that there was no hope Cuba would take its side in the Sino-Soviet dispute. It did not mean, though, that Havana was now on board with Moscow's agenda. The Soviets continued to support the "peaceful path" approach adopted by the Latin American communist parties that allowed it to maintain relations with sitting governments, while Cuba sought to promote armed struggle in Latin America and Africa. Moscow suggested that Cuba moderate its policies in order to establish relations with its neighbors for economic purposes, but the Cubans attacked the Soviets for insufficient militarism, especially in their support of the communist cause in Vietnam.[43] In the mid-1960s then, Cuba became a sort of wild card in the world of international communism.

On the eve of the Tricontinental Conference, Castro launched a public attack on the PRC. The previous November, Cuban Ministry of Foreign Trade officials visiting Beijing were told that the Chinese would be able to send Cuba only 135,000 tons of rice in 1966, as opposed to the 285,000 tons the Cubans had requested and the 250,000 tons they had been sent in 1965.[44] This shortfall was ostensibly because of the increased needs of North Vietnam, but it was clear that it was punishment for Castro's turn toward Moscow, and it might be reversed if he changed course. Instead, Castro decided to publicly announce the PRC's decision on January 2, 1966, the day before the opening of the Tricontinental. It was as good a way as any to demonstrate Cuba's independence on the eve of its biggest moment on the international stage.

THE WORLD COMES TO HAVANA

When the conference opened in Havana on January 3, 1966, the Soviets, Chinese, and Cubans had three very different versions of what they wanted out of it. The Soviets were essentially playing defense. As long as the conference did not turn out to be a rousing condemnation of

---

[42] See Report of European and American Department of MFA on foreign policy of new Soviet leadership in Latin America, February 11, 1965, CFMA doc. 111-00403-01, 1–8. See also William E. Ratliff, "Communist China and Latin America, 1949–1972," *Asian Survey* 12:10 (October 1972): 854.

[43] See, for example, Brezhnev's speech at CPSU Plenum, December 12, 1966, RGANI f.2 o.3 d.45, 69.

[44] Halperin, "Peking and the Latin American Communists," 150.

Moscow's policies, they would consider it a success, and the fewer institutional legacies left by the conference, the better. For the Chinese, the meeting represented a chance to achieve that which they had hoped but failed to achieve in Algiers, namely an explicit condemnation of the Soviet policy of "peaceful coexistence" in the name of armed anti-imperialist struggle, ideally with the PRC and Mao acknowledged as leaders of that struggle. For the Cubans, it was an opportunity to escape from the stale Sino-Soviet polemics, break their regional isolation, and rouse the forces of real anti-imperialist struggle around the world, which Cuba was fighting with men and arms, as opposed to the rhetoric that the PRC was supposedly fighting with. In the end, it would be the Soviets who would come closest to getting what they wanted.

Soviet behavior during the conference reflected this cautious, defensive approach. They wanted to seem welcoming of the conference and its agenda, while at the same time softening its sharper edges and not giving it too high of a public profile. Leonid Brezhnev and Aleksei Kosygin greeted the conference with a short statement on the front page of *Pravda* that spoke of imperialist aggression in Vietnam, South Africa, Rhodesia, the Dominican Republic, and Cuba, declaring that "The Soviet people ... faithful to their internationalist duty offer and in the future will offer all types of support to the people fighting for freedom and national independence."[45] They then went on to talk about the contribution the conference could make to the cause of economic development, ending by describing the struggle of the conference participants as one "against imperialism and colonialism, for freedom, national independence and social progress, for peace between peoples." A longer editorial in *Pravda* expanded upon these themes, not only talking of an economic focus of the conference but claiming that many of the delegations represented "newly developing countries which have launched on the non-capitalist, socialist path and are realizing deep social-economic transformations."[46] It tied the cause of economic development to that of peace:

The arms race, international tensions, the interference of imperialist powers in the internal affairs of peoples, military intervention, violations of state sovereignty, the use of tensions between peoples which remain as a consequence of imperialism – all these interfere with the unity of antiimperialist forces, divert the energy

---

[45] L. Brezhnev and A. Kosygin, "*Pervoi Konferentsii Solidarnosti Narodov Azii, Afrikim i Latinskoi Ameriki,*" *Pravda*, January 3, 1966, 1.
[46] "*Forum Trekh Kontinentov,*" *Pravda*, January 3, 1966, 3.

and means of young states from the most pressing and fundamental problems of their national development.[47]

Repeating the call to push for peaceful coexistence and nuclear disarmament, the editorial spoke of independence struggles both armed and peaceful, and added a note of caution: "It would be naïve to think that the coincidence of interests and goals of the struggle automatically create unity."[48]

The Chinese were livid at this Soviet attempt to tilt the conference agenda toward peace and economic development. A *Renmin Ribao* editorial summing up the conference gloated, "On the day the conference opened, the Soviet paper *Pravda* ... attempted to divert the attention of the conference with such stuff as 'universal peace,' 'total and complete disarmament,' and 'peaceful coexistence,' but the delegates saw through this."[49] The Soviet delegate at the conference, First Secretary of the Uzbek Communist Party Sharaf Rashidov, struck a more militant tone in his speech. Despite acknowledging the necessity of peaceful coexistence between sovereign states, he declared "it is clear that there is not, nor can there be, any peaceful coexistence between the oppressed peoples and their oppressors – the colonialists and the imperialists, between the imperialist aggressors and their victims."[50] He spoke these words two months before Brezhnev officially enshrined them at the 23rd CPSU Congress as the new Soviet approach to reconciling "peaceful coexistence" and anti-imperialist struggle.

As the conference went on, Soviet coverage of it diminished. The *Pravda* editorial was followed by short summary pieces that appeared daily during the first week of the conference and then nearly disappeared during the second week. The closing of the conference and the final resolutions adopted were given rather short shrift in the Soviet press, limited to short pieces in *Pravda* and *Izvestia*, and a three-page article in the CPSU theoretical journal *Kommunist*. The *Kommunist* piece returned to many of the themes of the original *Pravda* editorial but added a critical note about the events of the conference. It recognized that the complexity and heterogeneity of the anti-imperial movement created challenges but noted that such difficulties were exacerbated by the actions of "certain delegations" that championed a more radical agenda: "Their hysterical

[47] Ibid.   [48] Ibid.
[49] "Soviet Line Defeated at Havana Conference," Peking NCNA International Service in English, January 18, 1966.
[50] "Rashidov Speech," Moscow TASS International Service in English, January 6, 1966.

slogans, though devoid of real content, and obstructionist positions on a number of questions summoned the danger of a schism."[51] This was the closest the Soviets would come to acknowledging the difficult tone of the conference, where their calls for peace were not well-received by many. The important thing for them was that it was over, and the Chinese had not won the day.

Chinese coverage of the conference was a mirror image of Soviet reporting. While *Renmin Ribao* began slowly, with short articles limited mainly to naming speakers, the end of the conference was greeted with long celebratory pieces in *Renmin Ribao* and *Peking Review*, as well as a lengthy spread in *Shijie Zhishi*, the PRC's main foreign affairs journal at this time. In typically unsubtle terms, *Peking Review* triumphantly concluded,

> The Khrushchev revisionists' attempts to manipulate the conference and peddle their spurious "united action" to promote their capitulationist and divisive line were thoroughly exposed and firmly rejected. They failed, too, in their attempt to control the tricontinental and anti-imperialist solidarity organization in order to bring the national democratic movement in the three continents into the orbit of US-USSR cooperation for world domination.[52]

In particular, the *Peking Review* pointed to the defeat of the Soviet attempt to get "peaceful coexistence" included in the text of the political resolution and the adoption of a significantly more militant tone on Vietnam than that struck by the Soviets.

Vietnam was the issue on which the Chinese thought the Soviets most vulnerable and therefore the one they sought to exploit to the hilt to rally anti-imperialist sentiment against Moscow. The Chinese delegate Wu Xueqian repeatedly assailed the Soviets for supposedly seeking to negotiate an end to the war with the United States, while a parade of Asian delegations, not necessarily reflecting the positions of their governments, supported the PRC position: North Korea, Japan, Indonesia, Cambodia, Pakistan, Thailand, and "Malaya" (Beijing, in sympathy with Sukarno's policy, did not recognize Malaysia).[53] For the Chinese, it was not just a question of how much to support Hanoi and the NLF. It was about the

[51] Yu. Bochkarev, "*Gavanskaia Konferentsiia – Splochenie Antiimperialisticheskikh Sil*," *Kommunist* 3 (February 1966): 107.

[52] "Report from Havana: The First Afro-Asian-Latin American People's Solidarity Conference," *Peking Review*, No. 4, January 21, 1966, 19.

[53] "NCNA Reviews Delegates' Speeches, Raps USSR," Peking NCNA International Service in English, January 8, 1966.

opportunity that Vietnam presented to fundamentally undermine US power around the globe. As *Shijie Zhishi* wrote,

The victorious struggle of the Vietnamese people will also have a positive impact on the American domestic class struggle and development of its revolutionary movement. American imperialism's aggressive war has educated the American people, has made them more conscious ... Over the last year, the American people have surged on an unprecedented scale in a firm and unceasing movement against the aggressive war. This movement is closely uniting with the American black people's struggle for liberation, becoming a mighty torrent, creating a new front ... This shows that the American people are already awake as never before, are going down the path of struggle against their own country's imperialism, the prelude [序幕] to the American people's revolution has already begun.[54]

Therefore, in the eyes of Beijing, any Soviet attempt to negotiate an end to the war – even on Hanoi's terms – could mean only that the Soviets did not share the true objective of the struggle, namely the final destruction of American imperialism.[55]

Though Beijing sought to portray the conference as a victory since the Soviets did not gain official acceptance for their doctrine of "peaceful coexistence," it also failed to get any explicit denunciations of revisionism or acknowledgment of its revolutionary leadership. In the unequal conflict between the USSR and the PRC, a draw of this sort ultimately benefited the former more than the latter, since the Soviets had other sources of influence – the WPC, for one – while the PRC had lost yet another chance to build its own international base of support.

With the conference now behind them, the Soviets sought to distance themselves from it and bury the results. The Soviet delegation at the conference felt obliged to sign the final resolution calling for armed struggle against existing governments, but the Soviet government did not feel bound by that signature. Concerned about the Soviet signature on the conference resolution, the Chilean ambassador in Moscow asked Vice Foreign Minister Yakov Malik if it meant that "the USSR will support morally and materially the struggle in Peru, Venezuela, Colombia, Guatemala, and other countries of Latin America in accord with the results of the mentioned conference." Malik assured him that the USSR remained committed to "peaceful coexistence" and noninterference

---

[54] Hui Liqun, "风雷激动三大洲 [Wind and thunder excite three continents]," *Shijie Zhishi* [*Global Knowledge*], No. 2–3, 1966, 12.

[55] For more on the PRC's attempts to prevent negotiations on Vietnam during this period, see Qiang Zhai, *China and the Vietnam Wars*, 168–175.

and conveniently explained that the Tricontinental was attended by non-governmental representatives and did not reflect the positions of the Soviet state.[56] The head of the Soviet Foreign Ministry's Latin American division gave the ambassador an official Soviet statement to that effect, though he asked that the ambassador keep the statement private so as not to embarrass Moscow.[57]

To forestall the possibility of a new Tricontinental organization in Havana becoming a longer-term thorn in their side, the Soviets had managed to achieve one important goal at the conference: they got the next Tricontinental scheduled for Cairo in 1968. Cairo was already the headquarters of the AAPSO, and it had served as the location of the most recent NAM conference in 1964, so it was a place in which the Soviets felt comfortable operating. It was also one where a new Tricontinental organization would likely be subsumed by the existing "Third World" establishment. The secretariat set up in Havana after the conference was only meant to be temporary, and the question of a permanent secretariat for the new Organization for Solidarity with the Peoples of Africa, Asia, and Latin America (OSPAAAL) was to be decided in Cairo.

In the aftermath of the conference, the Cubans saw the potential move to Cairo as a threat, both because it meant their losing control of the organization and the possibility of OSPAAAL being effectively dissolved into the AAPSO. Osmany Cienfuegos, the new secretary of OSPAAAL, wanted to create an executive committee that would exclude both the Soviets and Chinese, arguing that such an organization would work better without them and would then be able to remain faithful to its mission of supporting armed struggle.[58] The Cubans therefore fought successfully to keep all Tricontinental organs in Havana, assuring that a second conference would never take place. After the Six Day War, Nasser and Cairo no longer had the prestige they had enjoyed in 1966 in any case. As a result, the second conference collapsed before serious negotiations had even begun.

For the next two years, the Soviets, along with AAPSO and the WPC, would conduct a propaganda battle with the Cuban-led OSPAAAL, remembering "not to exclude the possibility that our Cuban comrades

[56] Archivo del Ministerio de Relaciones Exteriores de Chile (AMREC), 1966 Embajda de Chile en Rusia: Oficios confidenciales no. 1, conf. no. 18, February 3, 1966.
[57] AMREC 1966 Embajada de Chile en Rusia: Oficios confidenciales no.1 conf. no. 21, February 12, 1966.
[58] SKSSAA Presidium session, March 15, 1967, GARF f.9540 o.1 d.225, 45–46.

might make some sort of contact with the decisions taken in Beijing."[59]
After 1968, the Cuban rapprochement with Moscow would make the
point largely moot, and OSPAAAL's relevance diminished accordingly.

CONCLUSION

The Tricontinental Conference in Havana took place at what might have
been the moment of peak fracture in the project of building an anti-
imperialist political vehicle to unite Asia, Africa, and Latin America. Sino-
Soviet cooperation in seeking to turn the AAPSO into such a vehicle had
collapsed amid polemical struggles that nearly tore the organization apart,
and that same rivalry prevented a follow-up conference to the original
Bandung Conference of 1955 from taking place. Other rivalries for various kinds of "Third World" leadership – Arab, African, Asian, Islamic,
etc. – and more standard political battles, such as that between India and
Pakistan, magnified the effect of the Sino-Soviet dispute by forming shifting alliances in the hopes of shaping agendas and appropriating resources.
Frustration with this state of affairs led some to seek a new beginning
beyond the control of Moscow and Beijing, but the Cuban effort to do
precisely that faltered on the grounds of its own precarious isolation and
militant sectarianism.

   Cuba would have a second opportunity to pretend to leadership of the
"Third World" when it held the presidency of the Non-Aligned
Movement following the 6th NAM summit in Havana in 1979. This
meeting came at the peak of Soviet-Cuban cooperation in the wake of
joint military efforts in Angola and Ethiopia, and for many it was the
moment when the Non-Aligned Movement ceased to be truly non-aligned
and became the ally of the socialist camp that the Soviets thought it should
have been all along. Ironically, given Soviet and Chinese claims about the
importance of their revolutionary leadership, it was the creation of Tito,
Nasser, and Nehru that would have the greatest longevity and come the
closest to instantiating the notion of a powerful anti-imperialist "Third
World" organization.

   The experience of the Tricontinental and the organization that it
spawned (OSPAAAL) demonstrated how difficult it was for a "Third
World"-ist movement to gain traction in a world of superpowers.
Convening the conference itself was hard enough, given the wariness of
the Soviets with regard to Cuba's militant "adventurism" and the PRC's

[59] Ibid., 42.

desire to turn the Afro-Asian solidarity movement into a vehicle for its own geopolitical ambitions. Nevertheless, the conference was convened, and Castro and his government put on a good show, passing more than 100 resolutions and frightening much of the Western press in the process. But the aftermath proved that these fears were unfounded. The Soviets, having done just enough to maintain their revolutionary credibility, quickly disavowed the conference and doomed the organization by pushing for the next conference to be held in Cairo. The Chinese, who had strongly resisted the establishment of a permanent tricontinental organization, poured their efforts into the organization of the next conference of the AAPSO, to be held in Beijing in 1967. Support for Hanoi and the NLF, so prominent rhetorically at the conference, still came primarily from Moscow and Beijing. The Cuban regime did not lose its desire to fight for its version of revolution around the world, but it would come to find that it could be much more successful doing so under Moscow's umbrella. It turned out that translating the power of "Third World" solidarity from rhetoric into action required the resources of a superpower, and those resources always came with strings attached.

8

"A Propaganda Boon for Us"

The Havana Tricontinental Conference and the United States Response

Eric Gettig

For US policymakers, the Havana Tricontinental Conference of January 1966 took place at a time of both confidence and vulnerability in US relations with the Third World. In the second half of 1965, the Lyndon B. Johnson administration believed that the prevailing winds in the Third World were blowing in its favor. The collapse of the "Second Bandung" African-Asian Conference at Algiers between June and October, the military coups against Algerian leader Ahmed Ben Bella and Indonesian leader Sukarno, and the collapse of the Chinese push for leadership of the Afro-Asian movement were all seen in Washington as a validation of US foreign policy and as heavy blows to several key antagonists. These perceived victories notwithstanding, however, US policymakers remained aware of the general unpopularity in much of the Third World of Washington's perceived support for European and white settler colonialism in Asia and Africa, of the US role in global capitalism, and of the recent US interventions (overt and covert) in Cuba, the Congo, the Dominican Republic, and above all, Vietnam.[1]

Unlike the Algiers conference, which was to have been a meeting of national governments across the political spectrum and including many Commonwealth and other governments broadly sympathetic to US and Western interests, the explicitly socialist and anti-imperialist Tricontinental

The author gratefully acknowledges the financial support of the Lyndon B. Johnson Foundation for providing a grant for research at the LBJ Presidential Library in the summer of 2010.
[1] On the Johnson administration's views of the Third World at this time see Robert B. Rakove, *Kennedy, Johnson, and the Nonaligned World* (Cambridge: Cambridge University Press, 2013), 236–240.

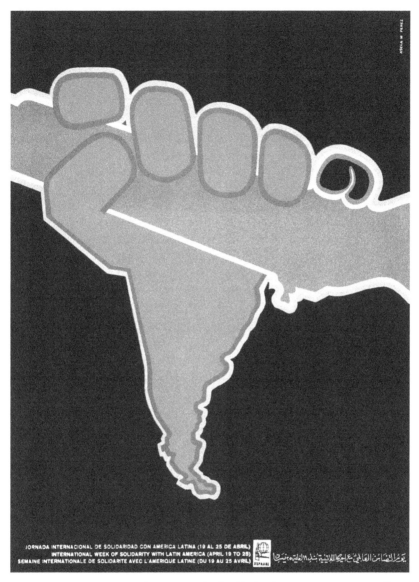

FIGURE 8.1 Tricontinental iconography highlighted imperial violence, offered satiric takes on Western icons like Uncle Sam, celebrated Global South cultures, and championed militancy. Their powerful simplicity mixed clear calls to action with historic references and inferred inequalities that continue to animate anti-imperial politics. OSPAAAL, Asela Perez 1970. Screen print, 53x33 cm. Image courtesy Lincoln Cushing / Docs Populi.

Conference would include no voices friendly to Washington and offered no
channel through which the United States might influence the conference
preparations or outcome. The Tricontinental's institutional predecessor,
the Afro-Asian People's Solidarity Organization (AAPSO), was technically
a nongovernmental organization; delegates participated on behalf of
national Solidarity Committees, umbrella organizations of mostly socialist
and communist groups and/or liberation movements. Some of these groups
worked with the blessings of their national governments, but others stood
in opposition to regimes with ties to the United States. Launched at Cairo in
1957 and sponsored by the Soviet, Chinese, and Egyptian governments,
AAPSO had articulated an increasingly militant and revolutionary message
at a series of conferences over the ensuing decade.[2]

The Tricontinental Conference aimed to extend AAPSO into the
United States' backyard through the inclusion of Latin American communist parties and guerrilla movements. The conference was to be the
largest gathering of self-identified revolutionaries in world history and
portended nothing but hostility to US interests. Furthermore, the conference's host, Washington's nemesis Fidel Castro, was the very embodiment
of left-wing revolutionary defiance of the United States, having already
survived almost a decade of efforts first to prevent him from taking power
during his guerrilla war of 1956–58 and then to undermine, isolate, and
overthrow his revolutionary government only ninety miles from US
shores.[3]

[2] David Kimche, *The Afro-Asian Movement: Ideology and Foreign Policy of the Third
World* (Jerusalem: Israel Universities Press, 1973), 126–213, based on press sources and
interviews with many participants, is the most well-documented and comprehensive his-
torical account of AAPSO's life from 1957 through 1967, and of AAPSO's extension into
Latin America at the Tricontinental Conference. See also G. H. Jansen, *Afro-Asian and
Non-Alignment* (London: Faber & Faber, 1966), 250–268; Charles Neuhauser, *Third
World Politics: China and the Afro-Asian People's Solidarity Organization, 1957–67*
(Cambridge: Harvard University East Asian Research Center, 1968); Robert Mortimer,
The Third World Coalition in International Politics, 2nd ed. (Boulder: Westview Press,
1984); and Vijay Prashad, *The Darker Nations: A People's History of the Third World*
(New York: The New Press, 2007), 51–61.
[3] The literature on US efforts to undermine Castro is voluminous. The Eisenhower adminis-
tration's efforts in 1957–58 to prevent Castro's "26th of July Movement" from coming to
power are best documented in Tomas G. Paterson, *Contesting Castro: The United States
and the Triumph of the Cuban Revolution* (New York: Oxford University Press, 1994).
The most comprehensive and useful studies of the decade after 1958 are Lars Schoultz,
That Infernal Little Cuban Republic: The United States and the Cuban Revolution (Chapel
Hill: University of North Carolina Press, 2009), and Morris H. Morley, *Imperial State and*

By defining the nature of the Tricontinental Conference agenda and invitees as they did, the organizers left few if any avenues for the United States to influence the preparations for or course of the conference through allied or sympathetic delegates. Washington's lack of leverage stands in contrast to successive US governments' efforts to shape the course of other Third World internationalist conferences from Bandung in 1955 through the non-aligned conferences at Belgrade in 1961 and Cairo in 1964 and the abortive "Bandung II" at Algiers in 1965. As several historians have shown, US diplomats played active roles behind the scenes before and often during each of these conferences. In general, these efforts followed a pattern. In advance of each conference, US officials viewed the prospective gathering as a threat with the potential to bring together anti-white, anti-Western, anti-imperialist, and anti-capitalist currents hostile to the United States and its allies. Washington feared that its most ardent antagonists in the Third World – above all the People's Republic of China but also at times Castro's Cuba, Ben Bella of Algeria, Ghana's Kwame Nkrumah, and Indonesia's Sukarno – would use the conference to try to unite the Third World behind a radical agenda inimical to US interests and turn it into a forum for propaganda and denunciation of the United States and its allies.

After considering, but discarding, the feasibility and desirability of trying to prevent the conferences from ever taking place by discouraging participation by governments sympathetic to US views, officials adopted (to varying degrees) a strategy of engagement with each conference to try to moderate its tone and outcome by ensuring that pro-Washington and pro-Western delegations attended and made their voices heard. US diplomats worked with and through sympathetic governments to shape the roster of invitees, the agenda and rules of procedure, and the tone of the eventual resolutions and declarations in order to minimize criticism of the United States and its allies, albeit with varying degrees of vigor and success. In the aftermath of each conference, US officials expressed relief that, from their point of view, things could have been worse. Washington was particularly sanguine in late 1965 given the fallout from the aborted Bandung II at Algiers; Johnson administration officials believed that their subtle but vigorous, behind-the-scenes diplomatic efforts to thwart the Sino-Indonesian push to radicalize Third World internationalism had

Revolution: The United States and Cuba, 1952–1986 (New York: Cambridge University Press, 1987).

been effective. "Moderate" and pro-US voices in the Third World had prevailed over the militant Afro-Asian left wing led by Beijing and Jakarta.[4]

The actions of the Johnson administration in response to the Tricontinental Conference would be largely consistent with the pattern set at these previous conferences. The Tricontinental presented the US government with both a revolutionary threat and a counterrevolutionary opportunity, and Washington responded with another vigorous but largely behind-the-scenes diplomatic effort to meet the challenge and exploit the opportunities it presented. The core of this strategy was to exploit the political and ideological divisions among the movements represented at Havana, largely indirectly and by proxy, in order to undermine the Tricontinental solidarity movement and isolate and harass Washington's enemies. While US officials considered their counteroffensive to be largely successful in short-term diplomatic and material terms, the push for Tricontinental revolutionary solidarity nevertheless highlighted the long-term challenges that Washington faced in seeking to suppress liberation movements across the Third World.

---

[4] On the Eisenhower administration's views of, and behind-the-scenes influence in, the 1955 Bandung Conference see Jason Parker, "Cold War II: The Eisenhower Administration, the Bandung Conference, and the Reperiodization of the Postwar Era," *Diplomatic History* 30:5 (November 2006): 867–892; Cary Fraser, "An American Dilemma: Race and Realpolitik in the American Response to the Bandung Conference, 1955," in Brenda Gayle Plummer, ed., *Window on Freedom: Race, Civil Rights, and Foreign Affairs, 1945–1988* (Chapel Hill: University of North Carolina Press, 2003), 115–140; and Matthew Jones, "A 'Segregated' Asia?: Race, the Bandung Conference, and Pan-Asianist Fears in American Thought and Policy, 1954–5," *Diplomatic History* 29:5 (November 2005): 841–868. On the Kennedy and Johnson administrations' responses to the non-aligned conferences at Belgrade in 1961 and Cairo in 1964, and to the non-aligned "Third World" more broadly, see Robert B. Rakove, "Two Roads to Belgrade: The United States, Great Britain, and the First Nonaligned Conference," *Cold War History* 14:3 (2014): 337–357, and Rakove, *Kennedy, Johnson, and the Nonaligned World*, esp. 62–93, 128–129, and 220–225. On US officials' views of and attempts to shape the non-aligned and Afro-Asian movements and the Cairo and Algiers conferences see Eric Gettig, "'Trouble Ahead in Afro-Asia': The United States, the Second Bandung Conference, and the Struggle for the Third World, 1964–65," *Diplomatic History* 39:1 (January 2015): 126–156. On how moderate Latin American governments had blocked an initiative by Castro's government in 1959–60 to host a global "Conference of Underdeveloped Countries" in Havana, see Eric Gettig, "Cuba, the United States, and the Uses of the Third World Project, 1959–67," in Thomas C. Field, Stella Krepp, and Vanni Pettinà, eds., *Latin America and the Global Cold War* (Chapel Hill: University of North Carolina Press, 2020), 241–273.

ANTICIPATING CONFLICT

Infighting along ideological, methodological, and regional lines had plagued AAPSO, and Third World revolutionary internationalism more broadly, ever since the late 1950s. At the heart of this struggle was the Sino-Soviet contest for leadership of the global revolution. The gradualist strategy of "peaceful coexistence," economic competition with the capitalist West, and the gradual achievement of socialism practiced by Moscow and the orthodox communist parties of Europe and Latin America conflicted with the more confrontational line of revolutionary armed struggle and militant anti-imperialism advocated by China, Maoist-inspired movements in Asia and Africa, and Fidel Castro and Che Guevara in Latin America.[5]

The potential for discord increased with the projection of AAPSO and ideological competition into Latin America. The Latin American Left in the 1960s was being simultaneously reinvigorated and fragmented by the victory of the Cuban Revolution and the export of Castro and Guevara's program of guerrilla warfare and revolutionary confrontation to the continent. The region's established orthodox communist parties continued to adhere to Moscow's gradualism but were challenged by new or splinter factions favoring direct guerrilla confrontation as advocated by Havana and Beijing. In a few cases, these more confrontational groups received material and ideological support from Havana. The deepening divisions prompted the Soviets and Cubans to convene a secret summit of Latin American communist parties in Havana in November 1964. Castro pledged to cease his rhetorical attacks against the orthodox parties, while Havana and Moscow pledged to increase their own support for the liberation struggle. The Tricontinental Conference would mark the culmination of these internal tensions and the efforts to overcome them within the Latin American and world communist movements, as the Cuban government continued its efforts to build and radicalize a coalition that united Second and Third World governments and nonstate movements behind a militant revolutionary

---

[5] The best study of the Sino-Soviet contest and its ramifications in the Third World is Jeremy Friedman, *Shadow Cold War: The Sino-Soviet Competition for the Third World* (Chapel Hill: University of North Carolina Press, 2015). See also Lorenz M. Lüthi, *The Sino-Soviet Split: Cold War in the Communist World* (Princeton, NJ: Princeton University Press, 2008); Sergey Radchenko, *Two Suns in the Heavens: The Sino-Soviet Struggle for Supremacy, 1962–1967* (Washington: Woodrow Wilson Center, 2010); and Odd Arne Westad, *The Global Cold War: Third World Interventions and the Making of Our Times* (Cambridge University Press, 2007), 158–180.

program.[6] It also came amid the period of most severe diplomatic and economic isolation for Cuba in the hemisphere, following its recent suspension from the Organization of American States (OAS), the imposition of an OAS-wide economic embargo, and the rupture of diplomatic relations between Havana and all the governments of the hemisphere save Canada and Mexico. It came, too, at a time when the Cuban government – economically dependent on the Soviet Union but ideologically more compatible with the Chinese and eager to see like-minded movements come to power in the hemisphere – found its balancing act between the two communist giants increasingly difficult.[7]

In response to the public revelation of the November 1964 Havana communist summit, US policymakers anticipated an increase in insurgent activity in the hemisphere, as Moscow sought to blunt Chinese and Cuban criticism and reassert its leadership of world revolution by more tangibly backing Latin American guerrillas.[8] The CIA predicted that Castro "personally attaches great importance" to the Tricontinental Conference and intended to use it to assert leadership among Third World liberation movements and ameliorate Cuba's diplomatic and economic isolation.[9] The Agency also predicted that "fireworks resulting from the Sino-Soviet dispute may well seriously disrupt the conference," but that it would nonetheless offer "a ringing indictment" of US policies.[10]

---

[6] For an account of these efforts, see Gettig, "Cuba, the United States, and the Uses of the Third World Project, 1959–67."

[7] Thomas C. Wright, *Latin America in the Era of the Cuban Revolution*, rev. ed. (Westport, CT: Prager, 2001); Hal Brands, *Latin America's Cold War* (Cambridge, MA: Harvard University Press, 2010), 1–128; Daniela Spenser, "The Caribbean Crisis: Catalyst for Soviet Projection in Latin America," in Gilbert M. Joseph and Daniela Spenser, eds., *In From the Cold: Latin America's New Encounter with the Cold War* (Durham: Duke University Press, 2008), 77–111.

[8] US Department of State (hereafter DOS) documents from the National Archives and Records Administration II, College Park, Maryland, are from the Subject-Numeric File, Record Group 59, and will be cited by: author, recipient, document type and number or title (if available), date, box number, NARA. DOS (Secretary of State Dean Rusk), Airgram CA-9072 to all Africa [AF], Far East [FE], and [Near East] NEA posts, March 4, 1965, Box 1828, NARA. See also W. Averell Harriman [Ambassador-at-Large, DOS], "Notes of my comments on my trip to ARA staff," May 10, 1965; Folder 11, Box 567, W. Averell Harriman Papers [WAHP], Library of Congress [LOC].

[9] CIA, Office of Current Intelligence, Weekly Summary #0317/65, November 26, 1965; Central Intelligence Agency Records Search Tool (CREST) database, NARA [hereafter CREST/NARA]. In addition to the US embargo, the first steps of which were imposed in 1960, as of 1964 Cuba had endured the breaking of diplomatic relations and an economic embargo from all members of the Organization of American States save Mexico.

[10] CIA, Office of Current Intelligence, Weekly Summary #[redacted], December 23, 1965; CREST/NARA.

Washington had monitored the effort in spring 1965 – spearheaded by Castro's government in cooperation with its closest Third World ally, Ben Bella's Algeria – to overcome the Sino-Soviet and other rivalries within AAPSO in order to proceed with the process of convening a tricontinental solidarity conference in Havana.[11] After the Johnson administration intervened in the Dominican Republic, Secretary of State Dean Rusk acknowledged in a cable to embassies in Latin America in early May that the "situation obviously provides exceptional springboard for conference propaganda on colonialism and imperialism, and most timely for AAPSO objective of extending its activities and influence in Latin America."[12] Rusk instructed diplomats in Asia, Africa, and the Middle East, meanwhile, "to expose this meeting for what it really is and whom it actually represents," that is, the most extreme and dangerous elements of their countries' political milieu. While "informal discussions" with local officials and other opinion leaders could be useful in this effort, Rusk instructed that this task should be carried out "preferably where possible through unattributable items in local media," in order to reach a broader public.[13]

The perceived gains from the Bandung II debacle at Algiers and the other critical Afro-Asian developments in the second half of 1965 do not seem to have fundamentally altered the US views of or approach to the impending Tricontinental. In December 1965, Undersecretary of State George Ball cabled all US embassies to instruct them to communicate with their host governments in order to expose the conference "for what it really is and whom it actually represents," while at the same time to "avoid building up or stimulating [public] interest in the Conference." Explaining these instructions, the cable predicted that, "The conference will be an anti-West, particularly anti-U.S., propaganda forum" that would denounce Washington for its support of reactionary governments in Rhodesia and the Congo, its embargo against Cuba, its escalating war in Vietnam and recent occupation of the Dominican Republic, and its "racial problems" at home. While Castro was expected to project his own

[11] DOS (Rusk), CA-1797 to all posts, March 25, 1965; US Embassy [hereafter USE] Algiers, embassy telegram [hereafter embtel] 856, March 27, 1965; USE Cairo, embtel 3417, March 30, 1965; USE Accra, embtel 966, April 28, 1965; USE Accra Airgram 431, April 29, 1965, all box 1551, NARA.
[12] Rusk, Circular 2130 to all American Republics Affairs [ARA] posts, May 4, 1965, box 1551, NARA.
[13] DOS (Rusk) airgram CA-2162 to all African and Asian posts, May 7, 1965, box 1551, NARA.

leadership of the Third World and the Latin American Left, the Soviets would seek to do the same, outflanking the Chinese in the process. Beijing, meanwhile, was expected to try to block the proposed merger of AAPSO into a single Tricontinental organization, since the addition of the pro-Moscow Latin American communist parties would dilute Chinese influence in the Afro-Asian bloc.[14] Therefore, before the conference began, Washington, while acknowledging its own vulnerabilities, had spotted potential weaknesses in the incipient Tricontinental movement and begun to foment opposition.

"NOISE" AND "PRACTICAL RESULTS"

In its critique of the geopolitical situation, the conference played out much as US observers predicted.[15] While celebrating that formal colonialism had retreated from most of Asia, the Middle East, and Africa, the conference called for the overthrow of the remaining Portuguese, British, and French colonies and of the white settler regimes in South Africa, Rhodesia, and Israel. The conference also denounced the turn to neocolonial economic exploitation and political control of Third World peoples through "reactionary" client governments and militaries in countries such as Nigeria, Saudi Arabia, Brazil, Guatemala, the Congo, and Thailand.[16]

While denouncing European colonialists, white settlers, and local collaborators, the Tricontinental aimed its main critique at the United States. Surprising the US National Security Council staff with his militancy, Cuban President Osvaldo Dorticós told the assembled delegates in his welcoming speech that, "U.S. imperialism, the center of world reaction

---

[14] DOS (Undersecretary George Ball), Airgram A-6200 to all posts, December 14, 1965, box 1551, NARA.

[15] The United States had no diplomatic presence in Cuba in this period, and there is no indication in the available sources that it had any intelligence presence inside the conference itself; Washington received inside information via the Canadian embassy in Havana and contacts in the Yugoslav and Egyptian governments, as well as from press accounts, and intelligence assets in Cuba and elsewhere. USE Belgrade, embtel 990, January 6, 1966; USE Cairo embtel 1701, January 7, 1966; USE Moscow embtel 2276, January 21, 1966, all in box 1554, NARA.

[16] "General Resolution of the Political Commission on Colonialism and Neo-Colonialism," *First Solidarity Conference of the Peoples of Africa, Asia, and Latin America* (Havana: General Secretariat of OSPAAAL, 1966), 80–87, with individual country resolutions to 124. This volume is one of two official published records of the conference's resolutions and declarations. The other is *Resolutions of the First Conference for Afro-Asian-Latin American People's Solidarity, 3rd–14th January, 1966, Havana, Cuba* (Cairo: Permanent Secretariat of AAPSO, 1966).

and the foremost enemy of peace and progress, unscrupulously carries out within the framework of a perfectly defined world strategy, any number of openly criminal actions." Washington, he said, funded and trained counterinsurgency forces; sustained Portuguese, South African, and Israeli colonialism; continued its efforts to overthrow the Cuban Revolution; and intervened militarily in Vietnam and the Dominican Republic.[17] Accordingly, the Conference's General Declaration proclaimed: "To destroy the domination of Yankee imperialism is an imperative issue for the complete and definitive victory of the anti-imperialist struggle in the three continents, and all efforts of the peoples should converge toward this aim."[18]

Caught up in the revolutionary spirit and pressured by militant hardliners, the Tricontinental delegates declared that globally coordinated armed struggle was the primary means to defeat Yankee imperialism. The militants prevailed in a hotly contested "Resolution on Peaceful Coexistence," which restricted this concept of relations between socialist and capitalist states, denied that coexistence was possible between imperialists and their victims or between the working and capitalist classes, and upheld the right of oppressed peoples to fight against their oppressors and to receive aid from others in their struggle.[19] The vote represented a victory for advocates of militant revolution such as the Cuban hosts and the Maoists, who rejected the gradualist Soviet vision of international revolution and favored instead a newly assertive brand that combined traditional Marxist readings of class warfare with a specifically Third World anti-imperialism. Pushing this more assertive reading of international revolution, Castro closed the conference with a two-hour speech in which he argued, "sooner or later all, or nearly all, of the peoples will have to fight, arms in hand, for their liberation."[20] The CIA called it Castro's "most explicit call for armed revolution" since his 1964 modus

---

[17] Speech of Osvaldo Dorticós to opening session, *First Solidarity Conference*, 31–35, quoted at 33; William G. Bowdler [National Security Council staff] to McGeorge Bundy [Special Assistant to the President for National Security Affairs], "Speeches by Fidel Castro and Dorticos," January 4, 1966, online in the Declassified Documents Reference System database [hereafter DDRS].

[18] "General Declaration," *First Solidarity Conference*, 153–159, quote 153.

[19] "Resolution on Peaceful Coexistence," *First Solidarity Conference*, 76.

[20] Fidel Castro, closing address, *First Solidarity Conference*, 165–177, quote 170; "Para los Revolucionarios Cubanos, el Campo de Batalla Contra el Imperialismo Abarca Todo el Mundo," *Granma* (Havana), January 16, 1966, 1, with speech on 3–5; "Castro Winds up Session," *New York Times*, January 16, 1966, 7; Jules Dubois, "Assisted Reds in Domingo, Castro Says," *Chicago Tribune*, January 17, 1966, A4.

vivendi with the pro-Soviet parties and warned of "renewed Cuban interest in insurgent activities throughout the hemisphere."[21]

The State Department noted the increasing theoretical divergence between the more measured revolutionary approach of the Soviet Union and the more aggressive rhetoric of Third World anti-imperialists led by Cuba and China. But in the words of a cable from Undersecretary Ball, the department saw this rhetorical battle mostly as "noise." Washington's focus moving forward was on the potential "practical results" of the Havana conference that could tangibly threaten US interests.[22] These included the creation of a Committee of Assistance and Aid to the National Liberation Movements – tasked with providing "moral, political, and material aid" to world revolutionaries – and a Tricontinental Committee for the Support of the Vietnamese People.[23] The twenty-seven Latin American delegations moved to support revolution in the hemisphere by creating a Latin American Solidarity Organization (*Organización Latinoamericana de Solidaridad*, OLAS), headquartered in Havana, to hold its inaugural meeting in 1967.[24] The new OSPAAAL secretariat, to be constituted in Havana, was to coordinate all these revolutionary efforts on a global scale and prepare for a Second Tricontinental Conference in Cairo in 1968.[25]

From Washington's point of view, however, the most important practical outcome of the conference was its demonstration of the deepening fissures in the socialist world. Ball perceived the "Sino-Soviet dispute visible in all proceedings" and noted that the "speeches by Soviet and Chinese delegates, as well as respective allies, [were] loaded with barbs and recriminations as two big powers struggled for domination." Many African and Arab delegations, meanwhile, were upset at the perceived neglect of their interests, according to the Department's intelligence reports.[26]

[21] CIA, Office of Current Intelligence, Weekly Summary #0273/66, January 21, 1966, CREST/NARA.
[22] DOS (Ball) telegram 1345 to all ARA posts, January 18, 1966, box 1554, NARA.
[23] Quotes in Resolution of the Organization Commission, *First Solidarity Conference*, 55–56; Resolutions of the Sub-Commission on Vietnam, *First Solidarity Conference*, 127–133; Reuters, "Help for Viet Cong is Urged at Havana," *New York Times*, January 14, 1966, 8.
[24] "Creado Organismo Latinoamericano de Solidaridad; Sede la Habana," *Granma*, January 18, 1966, 1.
[25] DOS (Ball) telegram 1345 to all ARA posts, January 18, 1966, box 1554, NARA.
[26] Ibid.; Thomas L. Hughes [Director of Intelligence and Research, DOS], Intelligence Note #792, "The Tri-Continent Conference at Havana: A Preliminary Assessment," January 19, 1966, DDRS.

A GLOBAL COUNTEROFFENSIVE

In response to the Tricontinental Conference, the US State Department launched a sophisticated and ultimately successful diplomatic effort to exacerbate those same divisions in order to discredit, divide, and undermine the Tricontinental project around the world. For the State Department, the Tricontinental Conference was as much a counterrevolutionary opportunity as a revolutionary threat. As recounted in the department's internal history of the period, and confirmed in the archival record, this counterrevolutionary effort had three main objectives. First, the Department endeavored to arouse anger in Latin America and the rest of the "Free World" in order to use the Tricontinental as a pretext for deepening Cuba's diplomatic and economic isolation, on the basis that Havana aspired to become a revolutionary base that could threaten noncommunist governments everywhere. Second and more successful was the effort to peel the Egyptian regime off from the Tricontinental coalition and abort the Second Tricontinental Conference scheduled for Cairo in 1968. Third, the principal and most elaborate effort was to use the OAS and United Nations (UN) as international fora to denounce the Tricontinental and exert diplomatic pressure on the Soviets. "The US basic tactic" in all of these efforts, the internal history states, "was to remain in the background and say little publicly, while quietly stimulating Latin American and other criticism and action against communist sponsors and participants. ... [I]t was particularly important to make certain that Latin American protests appeared as totally spontaneous, rather than as arranged or prompted by us."[27] Adopting these goals and tactics, ironically, the US government essentially conformed to the Tricontinental's depiction of US foreign policy as neocolonial and counterrevolutionary.

On January 21, 1966, as delegates made their way home from Havana (often clandestinely via third countries), Secretary Rusk cabled US embassies in Latin America, instructing them to suggest that their host governments put pressure on West European and Japanese governments to conform to the OAS embargo and curtail their trade with Cuba. The Tricontinental, they were to argue, highlighted the "basic inconsistency" between "free world" countries' trade and development programs in

[27] *The Department of State During the Administration of President Lyndon B. Johnson, November 1963–January 1969. Volume I – Administrative History: Western Hemisphere Security*, 34–36; DDRS.

Latin America and their simultaneous trade with Cuba, which was indirectly funding the "disruption" of those same Latin American countries. United States diplomats were to suggest that Latin Americans pressure the Free World's holdouts to purchase sugar from other sources and to deny Cuba access to credit and agricultural, transport, and communications equipment.[28] Rusk followed up individually with embassies in Guatemala City and Lima.[29] The absence of subsequent documentation suggests that this initiative did not amount to much, but the intent is indicative of the US effort to use the Tricontinental to further isolate and impoverish Castro's Cuba.

More sustained and successful was State's effort to drive a wedge between the Egyptian government and the rest of the solidarity movement. The AAPSO had been founded and headquartered in Cairo, and AAPSO Secretary-General Yusuf al-Siba'i had ties to the Egyptian regime of Gamal Abdul Nasser. Nasser's government, however, had grown increasingly disillusioned with AAPSO as Marxist sectarianism and Sino-Soviet infighting came to dominate the organization.[30] Egyptian discomfort deepened when the solidarity project's extension to Latin America threatened governments with which Nasser maintained friendly relations. The US ambassador in Cairo, seeing Egypt "reconsidering" its support for the movement, met with several Latin American diplomats in Cairo and "suggested timely representations might encourage this promising development."[31] Agreeing with the Colombian Foreign Minister's determination that "Nasser should be made to eat crow in some way" for his role in supporting Cuba and regional leftist movements, Undersecretary Ball instructed all Latin American posts to facilitate confrontation between their host governments and the Egyptians, while taking care to "avoid impression US taking initiative."[32] Ball believed that "stern LA reaction would serve as salutary lesson to such chronic meddlers as Nasser and Nkrumah that they

---

[28] DOS (Rusk) Airgram CA-1367 to USE Caracas, Lima, Bogotá, Guatemala City, London, Paris, Ottawa, Madrid, Tokyo, January 21, 1966, box 1554, NARA.

[29] USE Guatemala City, embtel 493, January 28, 1966; DOS (Rusk) telegram 706 to USE Lima, January 26, 1966, both box 1554, NARA.

[30] Kimche, *Afro-Asian Movement*, 162–193. In 1958, Egypt and Syria had formed a political union called the United Arab Republic (UAR); after Syria withdrew from the union in 1961, the term continued to apply to Egypt until 1971, after Nasser's death. This essay will use "Egypt," Egyptian, and "UAR" interchangeably.

[31] USE Cairo embtel 1972, February 4, 1966, box 1553, NARA.

[32] USE Bogota embtel 1098, February 18, 1966, box 1550, NARA; DOS (Ball) airgram CA-155 to all ARA posts, February 17, 1966, box 1550, NARA.

cannot with impunity support commie inspired intervention in LA or elsewhere as advocated in Tricon."[33] United States diplomats provided the supporting documentation behind several Latin American governments' formal protests.[34] Time would tell if the US-orchestrated pressure on Nasser would yield more significant results.

While working behind the scenes to isolate Cuba and Egypt, State maneuvered in similar ways against the Soviet Union, working through the Latin American delegations in the OAS and the UN. These moves, initiated while the Tricontinental delegates were still in Havana, sought to catch the Soviets in even greater contradictions than the Egyptians; not only had well-connected ruling party affiliates attended the conference, but in Moscow's case they had also publicly pledged – in contrast to their secret agreements at the 1964 Havana communist conference – to support the armed ouster of Latin American governments with which the Soviets maintained official diplomatic relations. Sharaf Rashidov, head of the Soviet delegation, was First Secretary of the Communist Party of Uzbekistan and an alternate member of the Presidium of the Central Committee in Moscow.[35] At the Tricontinental, Rashidov pledged "our fraternal solidarity with the armed struggle of the Venezuelan, Peruvian, Colombian, and Guatemalan patriots against the lackeys of imperialism."[36] It was a contradiction that the US government would productively exploit over the course of 1966.

The United States did not initiate the idea of action through international organizations; rather, the initiative can be traced to the Peruvian government, which requested and received US support for action

[33] DOS (Ball) airgram CA-155 to all ARA posts, February 17, 1966, box 1550, NARA.
[34] USE Cairo embtel 2129, February 21, 1966; DOS telegram 4743 to USE Cairo, February 23, 1966; US mission to the UN [hereafter USUN] embtel 3760, February 24, 1966; USE Bogota embtel 1126, February 24, 1966; USE Quito embtel 606, February 23, 1966; USE Montevideo, embtel 750, February 24, 1966; DOS (Rusk) telegram 352 to USE Montevideo, February 26, 1966; USE Lima embtel 1210, February 26, 1966, all Box 1550, NARA; USE Caracas, Airgram A-903 to USE Cairo, May 13, 1966, box 1554, NARA.
[35] DOS (Rusk) telegram 1576 to all ARA posts, February 18, 1966, box 1550, NARA.
[36] "Discurso Pronunciado por Sharaf P. Rashidov, Jefe de la Delegación Soviética, en la Sesión Plenaria del 6 de enero de 1966," in Organization of American States. Council. *Report of the Special Committee to Study Resolution II.1 and VIII of the Eighth Meetings of Consultation of Ministers of Foreign Affairs on the First Afro-Asian-Latin American Peoples' Solidarity Conference and Its Projections ("Tricontinental Conference of Havana"): New Instrument of Communist Intervention and Aggression* (Washington, DC: Pan American Union, 1966), vol. II: 75–85, quote 81 [hereafter OAS Council, *Report of the Special Committee*].

at the OAS and UN in an exchange of letters begun on January 15.[37] But State seized the opportunity provided by the Peruvian initiative and worked to broaden and intensify Latin American governments' condemnation of the conference and of the Soviet role in particular. The US embassy in Lima and US representatives at the OAS and UN encouraged the Peruvians to launch formal protests and to bring in other regional governments as co-sponsors.[38] After (as Ball wrote) "cooperating with Peruvian del[egate] to OAS in developing his presentation," US diplomats looked on approvingly as Peruvian Ambassador to the OAS Juan Bautista de Lavalle decried the conference and called for a special meeting of the OAS Council for January 24.[39] At that meeting, Lavalle took the lead in denouncing the Tricontinental as a whole and Soviet support for subversion in the hemisphere in particular. He submitted a resolution, drafted by the State Department, to have an OAS committee investigate the conference and refer the results to the UN.[40]

Radio Havana belittled the OAS as "the Yankee ministry of colonies," claimed that the "hysterical response from the North American imperialists and their obliging Latin American lackeys" was "to be expected," and vowed that the Tricontinental's resolutions would be carried out.[41] While knowing better than anyone the degree of truth behind Havana's invective, National Security Advisor McGeorge Bundy approved of the direction the Tricontinental's aftermath was taking. Bundy wrote to President Johnson of the "most welcome development" of the Latin Americans' action at the OAS and informed his boss, "We are encouraging them in these moves and capitalizing on the propaganda advantage which the Havana meeting affords ... We are working to get editorials and articles published in our

[37] Guillermo Gerberding [Chargé, Peruvian embassy, Washington] letter to Rusk, January 15, 1966; Robert M. Sayre [Deputy Assistant Secretary of State for Inter-American Affairs] to Celso Pastor [Peruvian Ambassador to US], January 21, 1966; USE Lima embtel 1015, January 17, 1966, all box 1554, NARA.

[38] DOS (Ball) telegram 1747 to USUN, USE Lima, Caracas, Bogota, Guatemala City, January 19, 1966; USUN embtel 3170, January 19, 1966; USE Rio de Janeiro embtel 1657, January 20, 1966; USE Lima embtel 1031, January 20, 1966; and USE Lima embtel 1041, January 21, 1966, all in Box 1554, NARA.

[39] Quoted DOS (Ball) telegram 1747 to USUN, USE Lima, Caracas, Bogotá, Guatemala City, January 19, 1966, box 1554, NARA; DOS (Rusk) telegram 692 to USE Lima, January 22, 1966, Box 1554, NARA.

[40] DOS (Rusk) airgram CA-1403 to all ARA posts, January 25, 1966; USE Bogotá embtel 947, January 24, 1966; and USE Buenos Aires embtel 1008, January 25, 1966, all Box 1554, NARA.

[41] AP, "Revolutionist Moves to Go on, Cuba Vows," *Los Angeles Times*, January 24, 1966, 11.

press, as well as the Spanish editions of *Life* and *Reader's Digest*. Through State and US I[nformation] A[gency], materials on the meeting will be reaching friendly editors, columnists, and writers" throughout the region.[42] In at least one case – that of Uruguay – a USIA-produced documentary on the conference aired on prime-time television.[43] From the highest levels in Washington down to Latin American newsstands and living rooms, the counterrevolution in the international public sphere was in full force within weeks of the Tricontinental Conference.

After subtle but firm arm-twisting by US diplomats in a number of Latin American capitals, meetings between Peruvian and US diplomats to finalize language, and a phone call and last-minute note from Rusk to stiffen Peruvian resolve, Lavalle submitted a resolution on the Tricontinental Conference that was approved by the OAS Council on February 2.[44] "This policy of intervention and aggression in the hemisphere on the part of the communist states," it declared, "constitutes a violation of the principles of non-intervention ... and of the self-determination of peoples" as upheld in UN General Assembly Resolution 2131 of December 21, 1965, and in the OAS Charter. The policy, furthermore, "endangers the peace and security of the hemisphere." The resolution condemned in particular the open participation of officially sponsored delegations from countries that voted in favor of Resolution 2131.[45] Ironically, the Soviets sponsored that resolution as a means of embarrassing the United States over its Dominican and Vietnamese interventions.[46] The OAS resolution was the first time the organization specifically and collectively denounced the Soviet Union and the first time it filed a resolution with the UN.[47] Diplomatically, the Soviets were caught in an awkward and rather unpleasant situation.

[42] McGeorge Bundy memo to the President, "Some Latin American Developments," January 27, 1966; Folder 4, Box 6, Bundy Memos, National Security File [hereafter NSF], Lyndon B. Johnson Library, Austin, Texas [hereafter LBJL].

[43] USE Montevideo embtel 769, February 25, 1966, box 1550, NARA.

[44] DOS (Rusk) airgram CA-1417 to USE Lima, Bogotá, Caracas, January 27, 1966; USE Caracas embtel 750, January 28, 1966; and USE Montevideo embtel 668, January 26, 1966, all in Box 1554, NARA; USE Lima, embtel 1079, January 30, 1966, Box 1554, NARA; DOS (Rusk) telegram 720 to USE Lima, February 2, 1966, Box 1553, NARA.

[45] DOS (Rusk) airgram CA-1465 to all ARA posts, February 2, 1966, Box 1553, NARA [includes text of resolution]. John W. Finney, "OAS Condemns Havana Meeting," *New York Times*, February 3, 1966, 4.

[46] Louis B. Fleming, "UN Sees Renewal of Latin American Unity," *New York Times*, February 21, 1966, 16.

[47] Dan Kurzman, "17 Latin States Back Bid to Censure Soviets," *Washington Post*, January 25, 1966, A19; AP, "OAS Charge Sent to U.N.," *Baltimore Sun*, February 3, 1966, A5.

While it stopped short of requesting action in the UN Security Council (where Moscow wielded a veto), the submission of the OAS letter of protest to UN Secretary General U Thant on February 7 escalated the international war of words over the Tricontinental.[48] On February 10, Castro sent an open letter to U Thant rebutting the OAS charges. Highlighting the "cynicism" of governments such as Costa Rica, Honduras, and Brazil that condemned "outside intervention" by Cubans and Soviets but actively participated in the US-led OAS intervention in the Dominican Republic, Castro labeled the American governments condemning the Tricontinental "the most servile instruments of Yankee imperialism in Latin America," who enabled the "exploitation of their own countries" by the United States.[49] Castro's (unsurprising) defiance suggested his continuing adherence to the OSPAAAL project.

Cracks were appearing, however, between the Soviet and Cuban positions. In the pages of *Izvestia*, Moscow had earlier labeled the OAS proceedings a "dirty farce" and claimed that the State Department was behind the action of its "satellites."[50] It continued in February to publicly defend Rashidov's actions and attribute the OAS furor to Yankee machinations.[51] Privately, however, Moscow appeared to be retreating. Rusk claimed that "Soviet diplomats in Latin America and UN now busily backpeddling [sic], when officially confronted by LA Governments, in attempt disassociate Soviet Government from militant resolutions and speeches of Tri-Continent Conference, particularly Rashidov's statements." He urged US embassies to take "appropriate steps . . . to expose Soviet doubletalk" and to encourage their host governments that maintained relations with the Soviets to formally confront the local Soviet ambassador.[52] The Brazilian and Uruguayan governments, at least, appear to have done so, and the Chilean ambassador to Moscow was notably recalled the next week "for consultations."[53]

---

[48] USUN airgram A-1364, February 11, 1966, Box 1553, NARA (includes full text of letter); USUN embtel 3820, February 28, 1966, Box 1550, NARA; USUN embtel 3809, February 28, 1966, Box 1550, NARA. In the US the events were reported in "Most Latin Members of U.N. Protest on Havana Parley," *New York Times*, February 8, 1966, 11, and Louis B. Fleming, "Red Solidarity Unit Hit by Latin U.N. Members," *Los Angeles Times*, February 8, 1966, 2.

[49] USUN embtel A-1395, February 15, 1966, Box 1550, NARA (letter enclosed).

[50] USE Moscow embtel 2353, January 28, 1966, Box 1554, NARA.

[51] USE Moscow airgram A-1317, February 18, 1966, Box 1550, NARA.

[52] DOS (Rusk) telegram 1576 to all ARA posts, February 18, 1966, Box 1550, NARA.

[53] USE Rio de Janeiro embtel 1896, February 25, 1966, Box 1550, NARA; USE Montevideo embtel 687, February 2, 1966, Box 1553, NARA; USE Moscow embtel 2614, February 25, 1966, Box 1550, NARA.

By the spring of 1966, the Soviets and Cubans, two of the most important players in the putative Tricontinental movement, appeared to US observers to be working at cross-purposes in Latin America. The Cuban media were conducting what struck the US press as a particularly strident propaganda barrage against hemispheric rivals.[54] By contrast, in March the State Department interpreted a pattern of Soviet trade initiatives in the region to be "one means of placating and 'buying off' Latin American protests and resentment over [the] Tri-Continental Conference."[55] After a rhetorical flirtation with armed struggle in response to Cuban- and Chinese-inspired pressure between 1964 and the close of the Tricontinental, the Soviets appeared to be reverting to their advocacy of the *vía pacífica* in the face of diplomatic pressure from Western Hemisphere governments. Latin American pressure over the conference, encouraged and facilitated by the United States, helped to distance Moscow from the Tricontinental program, limit its Soviet support, and exacerbate tensions between Havana and Moscow.[56]

As the OAS and UN actions and the divergence of Soviet and Cuban positions played out, Washington came to see the Tricontinental as a diplomatic success for the United States. The National Security Council informed the president that the conference continued to be a "propaganda boon for us in the Hemisphere," citing the OAS resolution and letter to U Thant, along with Moscow's perceived reversal.[57] Citing Castro's "insulting" letter to U Thant and the ensuing withdrawal in protest of a Chilean congressional delegation from a visit to Cuba, the NSC declared on February 18, "We are getting excellent propaganda

---

[54] Isaac M. Flores, "Latin Lands New Target of Cuba Hate," *Chicago Tribune*, April 10, 1966, A1.

[55] DOS Airgram CA-1728 to all ARA posts, March 10, 1966, Box 1553, NARA.

[56] James G. Blight and Philip Brenner point to the Tricontinental as the start of a rapid downward spiral of conflict over Third World revolution between Castro and the Kremlin, which ended in 1968 when Castro acquiesced to Moscow's coercive constriction of its oil subsidy to the island. James G. Blight and Philip Brenner, *Sad and Luminous Days: Cuba's Struggle with the Superpowers after the Missile Crisis* (Lanham, MD: Rownman & Littlefield, 2002). Using Soviet archival documents, Jeremy Friedman also illustrates Moscow's discomfort at the militancy of the Tricontinental and Cuban adventurism, and its efforts to quietly reassure Latin American governments and orthodox communists of its continued commitment to the peaceful achievement of socialism in Latin America and the rest of the Third World. Friedman, *Shadow Cold War*, 148–150, 155–164. See also Spenser, "Caribbean Crisis," 100–106.

[57] Bromley K. Smith [Executive Secretary, National Security Council], memorandum for the President, "Significant Latin American Developments," February 9, 1966; Folder 7, Box 6, Bundy Memos, NSF, LBJL. This document is also in the DDRS.

mileage from the Tri-Continental Congress, much of it generated by the Cubans and Soviets themselves."[58]

Washington did not declare victory, however. The OAS committee investigating the Tricontinental issued its preliminary report in April 1966, warning that OSPAAAL "constitutes a positive threat to the free peoples of the world, and, on the hemispheric level, represents the most dangerous and serious threat that international communism has yet made against the inter-American system." To defend against Cuban, Soviet, and other communist subversion, the report recommended that the American governments better "coordinate their security and intelligence activities" while undertaking "an intensive, coordinated, constant, and organized propaganda campaign in favor of democracy."[59] Publicly at least, hemispheric governments continued to express concern about the Tricontinental movement's revolutionary threat in order to keep the pressure on Havana.

That summer, the US Congress entered the picture as a new institutional player also emphasizing OSPAAAL's threat. In May the House of Representatives Republican Task Force on Latin America, chaired by Bradford Morse of Massachusetts and Donald Rumsfeld of Illinois, criticized the Johnson administration for not responding vigorously enough to "the magnitude of the danger of subversion to existing governments" that OSPAAAL posed.[60] In June, the Internal Security Subcommittee of the Senate released a study of the conference, anticipating "the immediate and massive intensification of terrorism and guerrilla activity throughout the Americas, as well as in Asia and Africa." It too questioned the administration's response:

It is humiliating enough to have the international communist conspiracy seize control of a country only 60 miles from American shores, and maintain itself in power despite all the pressures we have thus far brought to bear. It becomes a thousand times as humiliating when that country is transformed into a headquarters for international revolutionary subversion while the OAS and the mighty United States of America look on, helpless and apparently incapable of any decisive action.

---

[58] Bowdler to Bundy, "Tri-Continental Congress," February 18, 1966, DDRS.

[59] Organization of American States. Special Consultative Committee on Security. *The First "Tricontinental Conference," Another Threat to the Security of the Inter-American System*, April 2, 1966 (Washington: Pan American Union, 1966): 66–69; AP, "Red Threat Seen in Havana Talks," *Baltimore Sun*, April 29, 1966, A2.

[60] UPI, "Red Subversion Threat Is Seen," *Hartford Courant*, May 10, 1966, A10.

The recommended policy response, however, was essentially the same as that of the OAS committee: greater vigilance and enhanced cooperation between American governments on intelligence and counterinsurgency.[61]

In addition to pressuring the executive branch for a harder line in the hemisphere, Congress held one other card to play against the Tricontinental movement: foreign aid. As early as February, the House inquired to the State Department about the precise makeup of the conference delegations, whether any of those governments officially or semi-officially represented were receiving US aid, and, if so, whether an aid cutoff could be used as leverage against the movement.[62] Ball had urged US embassies in Africa to advise their hosts of possible congressional reprisals against African governments that had encouraged or even allowed their nationals to attend the Tricontinental, with a view toward promoting a crackdown on those delegates and their organizations.[63] In the summer of 1966, around the time of the Senate study and the House Republican outcry, Congress amended the Foreign Assistance Act in order to deny aid to "any country ... which hereafter is officially represented at any international conference when that representation includes the planning of activities involving insurrection or subversion." Rusk later urged all diplomatic posts to "drop a word to the wise" to foreign governments about the new rules of the aid game in advance of future solidarity events.[64] Just as the State Department had sought to use the Tricontinental Conference as a pretext to widen the "Free World" embargo on Cuba, Congress sought to use economic denial as a means to smother the nascent Tricontinental movement in other Third World countries.[65]

Washington's attempted use of economic leverage over its troublesome aid recipients demonstrates the essential conformity of its policies to the neocolonial caricature depicted at the Tricontinental. So, too, did State's

---

[61] US Congress. Senate. *The Tricontinental Conference of African, Asian, and Latin American Peoples: A Staff Study* (Washington, DC: Government Printing Office, 1966), quotes at 32.

[62] F. Bradford Morse letter to Rusk, February 4, 1966; Douglas MacArthur II [DOS, Assistant Secretary for Congressional Relations] letter to Morse, February 10, 1966; Armistead Selden, Jr. [Chairman, House Foreign Affairs Committee] letter #2870 to Rusk, February 4, 1966, all in Box 1553, NARA.

[63] DOS (Ball) airgram A-8298 to all Africa posts, February 16, 1966, Box 1550, NARA.

[64] DOS (Rusk) airgram CA-4661 to all posts, December 22, 1966, Box 1553, NARA (with excerpt of law).

[65] The efforts to exploit the Tricontinental controversy fit into the larger pattern of efforts to expand and globalize the economic denial program that Lars Schoultz identifies as one of the Johnson administration's chief priorities in its Cuba policy. Schoultz, *Infernal Little Cuban Republic*, 226–236.

behind-the-scenes maneuvering at the OAS and UN. The sum of these various initiatives by the summer of 1966 amounted to a two-track policy. Publicly, Latin American governments, the OAS, the Johnson administration, and Congress vehemently denounced the conference and trumpeted international communism's threat to hemispheric security. Behind the scenes, the national security and diplomatic apparatus was sensitive to the solidarity movement's internal divisions and viewed the conference as an opportunity to exploit. The CIA, for its part, was skeptical about a potential upsurge in Cuban aid to insurgencies in the wake of Castro's rhetorical escalation, reporting that "to date our information does not show that this interest is being translated into new levels of concrete Cuban assistance. Similarly," the CIA added, "it is uncertain if the Latin American and tri-continental organizations established at the recent Havana conference will be able to promote 'revolution by committee' any more effectively than Havana has unilaterally in the past." Castro seemed inclined to exploit the propaganda value of calling for revolution and to proclaim Cuban solidarity with the revolutionaries, but he appeared loath to incur actual risks by providing significant tangible support to the guerrillas. "Castro's more prudent subversion policy," the agency concluded, "means that now, more than ever, the burden of carrying out revolutions rests with the local revolutionaries themselves."[66] Therefore, it makes sense to view Washington's publicly expressed fear and outrage as utilitarian: the greater the alleged threat from Cuban and Soviet-sponsored insurgency, the more justified was the counterattack.

"COUNTERPRODUCTIVE"

By the end of 1966, this counterrevolutionary program appeared to be succeeding. The US press and State Department continued to warily observe Cuban efforts to foment guerrilla movements in Latin America, for example, through alleged gunrunning in Guatemala and landing guerrillas in Venezuela; but effective counterinsurgency and internecine divisions among the rebels, these observers claimed, meant that these efforts amounted to little.[67] Both the *New York Times* and the State Department

[66] CIA, Intelligence Memorandum #[redacted], "Castro and Communism: The Cuban Revolution in Perspective," May 9, 1966; Doc 71, Folder 2, Box 19, NSF, CF, LA, Cuba, LBJL.
[67] Jules Dubois, "Central American Anti-Red Moves Worry Castro," *Hartford Courant*, February 20, 1966, A39; Robert Berrellez, "Red Mountain Bands Beaten in Venezuela," *Chicago Tribune*, November 13, 1966, A1; "Guerrillas Wage Mountain War in Latin

noted OSPAAAL's announcement in November of its intent to establish schools in Cuba and North Korea "to train political cadres for revolutionary activity on the three continents."[68] However, Rusk's assessment was that, while keeping an eye on OSPAAAL's intentions, the "Department does not foresee OSPAAAL achieving immediate widespread increase [in] violence on any continent ... Moreover OSPAAAL decision provides more fuel for continuing attack on Tri-Continental activities." True to form, Rusk suggested "avoidance [of] direct American attribution" as embassies worked to drum up publicity and criticism in the local press.[69] Another round of OAS condemnation and Cuban rebuttal played out at the UN in November and December along much the same lines as before, with the OAS condemning communist subversion, urging security cooperation, and calling upon more states to join the blockade of Cuba, while the Cuban Foreign Minister denounced Yankee and OAS hypocrisy in reply.[70]

By the end of 1966, the Tricontinental revolutionary organization had failed to cohere as a tangible entity beyond the posters and journals being put out by the OSPAAAL publishing house in Havana and the unilateral initiatives of the Cuban government. Moscow continued to back away from its flirtation with armed struggle in Latin America and continued to expand its investment and diplomatic initiatives under the watchword of peaceful coexistence.[71] The US ambassador in Cairo observed that the Egyptian government was "embarrassed" by its pledge to host the Second Tricontinental Conference in 1968 and was resisting Cuban pressure to begin preparations while attempting "to either evade or postpone" it entirely. The Latin American embassies in Cairo, led by the Brazilians and Chileans, laid plans to jointly threaten the rupture of diplomatic relations with Nasser if the conference went ahead. Backed by the

America to No Avail," *Hartford Courant*, September 27, 1966, 8; Bowdler to National Security Advisor Walt Rostow, October 28, 1966, doc 0355, Box 1, NSF, LBJL.

[68] DOS (Rusk) airgram CA-4210 to USE Montevideo, December 2, 1966, Box 1553, NARA; "Cuba Reports Plans to Train Guerrillas," *New York Times*, November 20, 1966, 20.

[69] DOS (Rusk) airgram CA-91483 to all ARA posts and USUN, November 25, 1966, Box 1553, NARA.

[70] OAS Council, *Report of the Special Committee*, 95–99; DOS (Rusk) Airgram CA-4672 to all posts, December 22, 1966, Box 1553, NARA; Raúl Roa (Cuban Foreign Minister), *Cuba Answers OAS Document on Tricontinental Conference* [pamphlet] (Havana: Ministry of Foreign Relations, 1966).

[71] Spenser, "Caribbean Crisis," 100–106; Louis Fleming, "Soviet Extends Latin Relations Through UN," *Los Angeles Times*, January 19, 1967, 22.

Soviets, Cairo eventually withdrew its personnel from the OSPAAAL secretariat and ceased participating in OSPAAAL activities, although Nasser continued to support certain African and Arab liberation movements unilaterally. Meanwhile the Sino-Soviet and Sino-Indian rifts, the collapse into incoherence of Chinese foreign policy during the Cultural Revolution, and the likelihood of boycotts left the bi-continental AAPSO conference scheduled for Beijing in 1968 virtually dead as well.[72] Neither conference would ever take place. Internecine rivalries and the backtracking of key patrons, exacerbated by Latin American diplomatic pressure that was both spontaneous and facilitated by the United States, led to the stillbirth of an organized OSPAAAL movement in Africa and Asia and left Castro as its sole effective patron in the Americas.

Havana appeared to maintain its enthusiasm for promoting armed revolution in Latin America and the broader Third World. After Che Guevara's guerrilla column withdrew in failure from the (former Belgian) Congo at the end of 1965, the Cubans returned their principal focus once more to Latin America, as Castro prepared to host the first conference of the Latin American Solidarity Organization in 1967.[73] But with logistical support from Havana difficult to maintain and Bolivia's Communist Party and its Soviet patrons actively hostile, Guevara's next mission, in Bolivia, ended in failure and martyrdom.[74] The juxtaposition of Guevara being named chairman in absentia and "First Citizen of Latin America" at the OLAS conference of Latin American communists and guerrillas in Havana in July 1967, on the one hand, and his lonely death in the Bolivian outback at the hands of CIA-supported Bolivian rangers in October, on the other, encapsulates the fate of the Tricontinental organization as a patron of armed struggle.

The US government was largely unfazed by the OLAS conference and its aftermath. The CIA observed that "quarreling among the Latin American communists was at an all-time high" between the pro-Castro and pro-Moscow currents among the assembled revolutionaries and

---

[72] USE Cairo embtel 3368, December 15, 1966; USE Cairo embtel 3404, December 17, 1966; and USE Cairo airgram A-555, December 23, 1966, (quotation), all Box 1553, NARA. On the Cultural Revolution and China's Third World relations see Friedman, *Shadow Cold War*, 150–155.

[73] The leading historian of Castro's foreign policy argues that 1966–67 was the high point of Havana's efforts to foment revolution in Latin America. Piero Gleijeses, *Conflicting Missions: Havana, Washington, and Africa, 1959–76* (Chapel Hill: University of North Carolina Press, 2002), 215–224.

[74] Jon Lee Anderson, *Che Guevara: A Revolutionary Life* (New York: Grove Press, 1997), 670–739.

between them and those orthodox communists who stayed away entirely. Calling the bluff of several pro-Soviet delegates who threatened a walkout, Castro allowed a vote on a secret, unpublished resolution chastising "certain socialist countries" for their programs of trade credits and technical aid to Latin American governments, including dictatorships and oligarchies that repressed guerrilla movements and communist parties; the measure passed, fifteen votes to three, with nine abstentions. With this denunciation, the rift between Cuba and the Soviets over the guerrilla struggle in the Americas became definitive. The CIA accordingly believed that any plans laid for new guerrilla activities would be slow, sporadic, and undermined by infighting: "In short, the OLAS conference is not likely soon to lead to significant communist advances in the hemisphere."[75] Che Guevara's death in Bolivia in October seems to have reinforced US officials' confidence that insurgency in the hemisphere could be defeated and that support for it would fizzle out.[76]

Another OAS meeting in response to the OLAS conference condemned anew Cuban "acts of aggression" in Venezuela and Bolivia; expressed serious concern to those governments offering support for OSPAAAL; called upon them to withdraw their support for the organization and its subversive activities; urged OAS members jointly and individually to confront governments supporting subversion in the hemisphere; and renewed the appeal to free world governments to restrict their trade with Cuba. National Security Advisor Walt Rostow wrote to President Johnson, "These resolutions will not topple Castro, but they provide OAS-sanctioned levers for pressuring our European friends and Soviet bloc countries to put the heat on him."[77]

By 1968, therefore, the solidarity conferences and their message of Cuban-sponsored hemispheric revolution contributed to the further estrangement of Cuba from the hemisphere and the straining of Cuba's relations with those European and Soviet-bloc countries with which it maintained relations. With Cuban-Soviet relations at low ebb and the

---

[75] Central Intelligence Agency-Directorate of Intelligence, Special Report, "The Latin American Solidarity Organization Conference," September 22, 1967; DDRS.

[76] DOS (Rusk) telegram 57145 to all ARA posts, October 20, 1967; DOS Intelligence Note INR-837, "Castro Builds up a Hero," October 19, 1967; DOS Intelligence Note, INR-834, "Guevara's Death Invokes Tributes, Denunciations, Warnings in Latin America," October 18, 1967, all in Box 2019, NARA.

[77] Rostow, Memorandum for the President, "OAS Meeting of Foreign Ministers" (with enclosed resolutions), September 25, 1967; Doc 63, Folder OAS, Box 36, NSF, Subject Files, LBJL.

OAS governments increasingly diligent in coordinating and implementing counterrevolutionary programs, Castro was by 1968 in an exceedingly weak position to attempt significant tangible support to revolutionaries in the Americas.[78] For nearly a decade, Cuban encouragement and tangible support for guerrilla movements in Latin America would be considerably more circumspect and modest, and it would prioritize restoring economic and diplomatic relations with its neighbors.[79] Cuba's major military interventions in Africa in the 1970s and 1980s, while motivated in part by a sense of revolutionary internationalism, were undertaken as unilateral initiatives of national foreign policy, despite Soviet reluctance, to support recently established revolutionary governments rather than guerrilla insurgents.[80]

Assessing Cuba's foreign policy prospects in mid-1968, US intelligence analysts concluded that the entire OSPAAAL and OLAS project had proven "counterproductive" for Castro.[81] The State Department's internal history of the period asserts, "Because of the US activities, Latin American-OAS-UN opposition to both conferences was better organized, more completely documented, much stronger, and considerably more effective than it would have been otherwise."[82] Washington's counterrevolutionary activities certainly deserve some modest share of the credit or blame for the solidarity movement's struggles to coordinate support multilaterally and to achieve armed revolution in the Americas, Africa, or Asia. But Washington's primary role was to exacerbate and benefit from the internal contradictions already well established among the movement's various state and nonstate constituencies. By seeking to sow division and disillusionment among the diverse revolutionary forces of the world, US officials lived up to the nefarious image of them painted at the Havana conferences, with greater effectiveness than the assembled revolutionaries had hoped.

Maintaining a sense of perspective, however, is important when assessing the early history of the Tricontinental and Washington's response.

---

[78] Brands, *Latin America's Cold War*, 51–95.
[79] Tanya Harmer, "Two, Three, Many Revolutions? Cuba and the Prospects for Revolutionary Change in Latin America, 1967–1975," *Journal of Latin American Studies* 45:1 (February 2013): 61–89.
[80] See Piero Gleijeses, *Conflicting Missions and Visions of Freedom: Havana, Washington, Pretoria, and the Struggle for Southern Africa, 1976–1991* (Chapel Hill: University of North Carolina Press, 2013).
[81] Special National Intelligence Estimate #85–68, "Cuba: Castro's Problems and Prospects Over the Next Year or Two," June 27, 1968; DDRS.
[82] DOS, *Administrative History*, 36; DDRS.

US officials' principal concerns with the Tricontinental, OSPAAAL, OLAS, and the revolutionary project they represented were about what Marxists might call the objective conditions and the correlation of forces with respect to the prospects of revolution. Government officials in the United States were primarily concerned with questions of the movement's capacity to provide material support (funds, weapons, manpower, training) for guerrilla fighters; they were also focused on diplomatic questions at the UN and OAS of how to use the conferences as a cudgel with which to beat Havana and Moscow in order to further isolate Cuba economically and diplomatically from the "Free World" and, if possible, to isolate Havana from Moscow, Cairo, and other revolutionary governments. Through these lenses, the counterattack against the Tricontinental in 1966–68 does appear successful.

A distinction must be drawn, however, between OSPAAAL and OLAS's role as headquarters, clearinghouse, training ground, and support network for regional and global revolution, on the one hand, and the Tricontinental's role in articulating and inspiring a discourse of Third World solidarity and revolutionary internationalism, on the other. As several scholars, including some in this volume, have shown, the Tricontinental embodied and gave voice to a transnational discourse of revolution that continued to inspire revolutionaries around the world over the ensuing decades. With the exception of Southern Africa, where Cuba's contribution appears to have been of critical, even decisive, importance, the US government and its counterrevolutionary allies were fairly effective in undermining and containing OSPAAAL, OLAS, and the Cuban government as material supporters of revolution; but over the following two decades, from Palestine to Central America, Southern Africa to the Southern Cone of South America, Vietnam to US cities and college campuses, containing the idea and example of international and transnational revolutionary solidarity would prove to be a far more difficult task.

PART IV

FRUSTRATED VISIONS

9

Brother and a Comrade

Amílcar Cabral as Global Revolutionary

R. Joseph Parrott

In October 1972, Amílcar Cabral was in New York again. The bespectacled revolutionary was the leader of the Partido Africano da Independência da Guiné e Cabo Verde (African Party for the Independence of Guiné and Cabo Verde, or PAIGC). Since 1963 he had overseen an armed struggle for independence in the Portuguese colony of Guiné (Guinea-Bissau).[1] Cabral spent much of his time abroad, traveling the world in search of monetary and material support to oppose the better equipped military of the Portuguese empire. Most of this assistance came from Africa and Eastern Europe, where Cabral adopted the iconic Czech *zmijovka* hat that often covered his receding hairline. Nonetheless, Cabral continued to court Western populations. The countries of the North Atlantic Treaty Organization (NATO) supplied their Portuguese ally with weapons the dictatorship used to wage its colonial wars. But Cabral believed many US citizens sympathized with his party's push for self-determination and more could be won over.

Taking time from his latest trip to the United Nations, Cabral found himself in a small room packed with African American activists. Over the previous years, the PAIGC had become a model of self-determination for Black Americans and anti-imperial organizing for Western radicals (Figure 9.1), his writings part of a global canon of Third World leftists. For many in the room that day, Cabral stood out within this network of revolutionaries like Che Guevara and Mao Zedong because of his race. His identity as a "brother" created a Pan-African linkage, which made his words especially powerful for African-descended peoples. Yet as Cabral

---

[1] I refer to Guinea-Bissau simply as Guiné and Guinea-Conakry as Guinea for clarity.

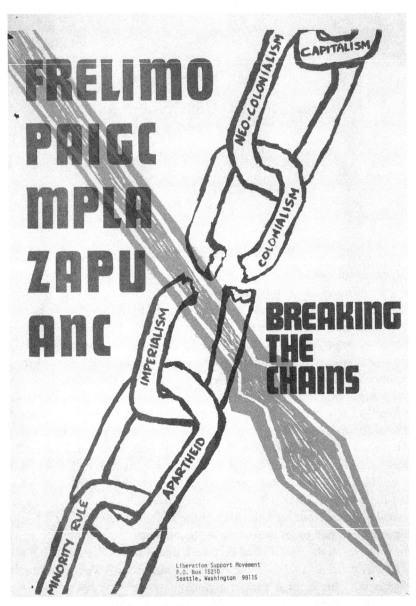

FIGURE 9.1 Westerners adapted and contributed to Tricontinental iconography while organizing solidarity movements. This American poster used the trope of broken chains to highlight the individual elements of imperialism and racism that Tricontinentalism challenged. It also reflects the cooperative diplomacy adopted by leftist liberation movements, especially in Africa, that encouraged Western activists to treat national revolutions as interconnected. Liberation Support Movement, Artist Unknown, 1972. Offset, 36x25 cm. Image courtesy Lincoln Cushing / Docs Populi.

answered questions from his audience, he offered a political challenge. "Naturally if you ask me between brother and comrades what I prefer," he explained, "if we are brothers it is not our fault or our responsibility. But if we are comrades, it is a political engagement. Naturally we like our brothers, but in our conception it is better to be a brother *and* a comrade."[2]

This concise statement captured Cabral's vision of solidarity but also some of its tensions. His nuanced, practical vision of anti-imperialism made him an icon in the 1970s and recently led to a resurgence of interest in his philosophy.[3] Yet how best to understand that philosophy remains open to debate. Many have seen Cabral as a Marxist who rarely quoted Marx and softened the edges of abstract dogmatism with a focus on concrete African realities.[4] Others have placed him in the Pan-African pantheon alongside Frantz Fanon and Kwame Nkrumah, men who drew upon African strands of radical politics.[5] A few scholars – notably Patrick Chabal and Mustafah Dhada – view Cabral as a pragmatic nationalist whose ideas developed primarily from the struggle in Guiné even as he drew elements from external sources.[6] These debates continue because Cabral never wrote a singular theoretical work laying out a cohesive set of ideas. He expressed his philosophy piecemeal in speeches and party documents, in which he revisited and refined concepts in response to domestic and international events. The result is an overarching intellectual

---

[2] Amílcar Cabral, *Return to the Source: Selected Speeches of Amilcar Cabral*, African Information Service, eds. (New York: Monthly Review Press, 1973), 76.

[3] See Amílcar Cabral, *Resistance and Decolonization*, trans. Dan Wood (New York: Rowman and Littlefield, 2016); Manji Firoze and Bill Fletcher, Jr., eds., *Claim No Easy Victories: The Legacy of Amilcar Cabral* (Dakar: CODESRIA, 2013); Carlos Lopes, ed., *Africa's Contemporary Challenges: The Legacy of Amilcar Cabral* (New York: Routledge, 2010).

[4] See Peter Karibe Mendy, *Amílcar Cabral: Nationalist and Pan-Africanist Revolutionary* (Athens: Ohio University Press, 2019), 202; Jock McCulloch, *In the Twilight of Revolution: The Political Theory of Amilcar Cabral* (London, Boston: Routledge and Kegan Paul, 1983).

[5] See for instance Reiland Rabaka, *Concepts of Cabralism: Amilcar Cabral and Africana Critical Theory* (London: Lexington Books, 2015), 204; and essays in P. Khalil Saucier, ed., *A Luta Continua: (Re)Introducing Amilcar Cabral to a New Generation of Thinkers* (Trenton: Africa World Press, 2016).

[6] Chabal's Cabral is a humanist, socialist democrat, while Dhada's measured approach highlights a unique "Cabralness" that emphasizes his nationalist reading of colonialism and empire. Patrick Chabal, *Amílcar Cabral: Revolutionary Leadership and People's War* (London: Cambridge University Press, 1983), chapter 6; Mustafah Dhada, *Warriors at Work: How Guinea Was Really Set Free* (Boulder: University of Colorado Press, 1993), 127.

trajectory complicated by a series of competing emphases and audiences, which has led to diverse interpretations.

This chapter contends that Cabral's ideas were centered on the practical needs of the Guinean struggle, but they aligned with a militant brand of anti-imperialism that emerged in the 1960s. Cabral was part of a generation of Third World leftists who believed coordinated, parallel national revolutions would erase inequalities between Global North and South, advancing the long fight against empire to a more aggressive phase. A dedicated nationalist, he viewed socialism as a toolkit for evaluating the international system and organizing an independent country. Change would come not via class struggle but rather through adoption of a common culture that provided the foundations for cross-class political action against foreign domination. This Third World revolution moved beyond European communism in hopes of finally erasing the manufactured economic inequalities and racism that marginalized the Global South.

As the PAIGC became enmeshed in the diverse solidarity networks that sustained its war for independence, Cabral refined his synthetic ideology to better explain his party's position at the intersection of Third World anti-imperial traditions, international socialism, and Pan-Africanism. Indeed, Cabral argued a month before the armed revolt began that the PAIGC "had lost its strictly national character and has moved onto an international level."[7] From its earliest stages, the PAIGC sought support from an array of international alliances, building connections as decolonization and shifting politics opened new avenues for solidarity. These networks not only funded the liberation struggle but also helped legitimize the party against competitors during its many years in exile. Tensions existed – racial solidarity versus ideological cohesion, philosophical purity versus practical compromise – yet Cabral managed them by focusing on the common imperial enemy, which he understood in both its colonial and neocolonial guises. The persistence of these frictions occasionally hampered the movement, especially at the granular level of interpersonal interactions, but PAIGC philosophy legitimized the creation of an inclusive revolutionary coalition and proved effective at building solidarity in both North and South. As a result, Cabral became, according to historian Jock McCulloch, "the leading political theorist of the second phase of the independence era," or what this volume argues might be better described as Tricontinentalism.[8]

---

[7] Amílcar Cabral, *The Revolution in Guinea* (New York: Monthly Review Press, 1969), 51.
[8] McCulloch, *In the Twilight of Revolution*, 10.

THE IDEOLOGY OF NATIONALIST REVOLUTION

Central to PAIGC philosophy was the search for unity amidst the social divisions created by Europe's oldest empire. Colonialism provided Portugal with power and prestige beyond its impoverished status, and Antonio Salazar made empire the centerpiece of his fascist Estado Novo from the 1930s onward. Extractive industries in the major colonies of Angola and Mozambique led to an expansion of the colonial state, but settlement remained light into the twentieth century, especially in the hinterlands of Guiné and Cabo Verde. In mainland Guiné, the Portuguese presence did not stretch far beyond administrative centers like the port capital of Bissau. Lisbon managed the colony by manipulating and reinforcing ethnic and social divisions, which included using Cabo Verdeans to fill minor bureaucratic positions. The Cabo Verde islands featured a creole *mestiço* population produced by centuries of intermingling between Portuguese administrators, sailors, and descendants of enslaved Africans. Creolized Cabo Verdeans, along with a small minority of "assimilated" mainland Africans hailing mostly from urban areas, had access to education and civil employment after modest colonial reforms in the early twentieth century. These advantages made them ideal middlemen in the empire, especially in Guiné, where islanders became symbols of empire.[9]

Cabral and the PAIGC leadership emerged from this context. Most were Cabo Verdeans by birth or lineage with ties to Guiné. Cabral was born to Cabo Verdean parents on the mainland, where his father served as a teacher. He attended island schools and witnessed the periodic starvation that Portugal allowed to occur in its drought-prone colony. Upon gaining admittance to university in Lisbon, Cabral diverged from the path of colonial administrator and embraced a distinctly African identity. He joined a community of young nationalists associated with the Casa dos Estudantes do Império (House for Colonial Students) that included Angolans Mário Pinto de Andrade and Agostinho Neto, as well as Mozambican Marcelino Dos Santos. This cadre – effectively a revolutionary salon in the metropolitan capital – explored foreign ideas suppressed by the dictatorship including Marxism, African nationalism, and the Harlem Renaissance's search for Black identity.[10] They also began organizing against Portugal's fascist empire.

[9] Chabal, *Revolutionary Leadership*, 27.
[10] Ibid., 40–44; Dalila Cabrita Mateus, *A Luta Pela Independência: A Formação das Elites Fundadoras da FREIMO, MPLA, e PAIGC* (Portugal: Inquérito, 1999), 66–75; Mario de Andrade, *Amílcar Cabral* (Paris: Francois Maspero, 1980), 32.

At the center of this nascent ideology was a conscious identification as Africans. The well-educated students were partially assimilated into the nominally race-blind culture of the Lusophone empire but found little sense of belonging in Portugal. Cabral later implied they were Europeanized "petite bourgeois" alienated from peasants at home (there being little to no colonial working class) but marginalized within the empire. Lacking a firm identity, they found a solution in the "re-Africanisation of our minds."[11] This process was the origin of Cabral's famous dictum that revolutionaries must "return to the source," rejecting the allure of European superiority to align with the "native masses." Yet Cabral believed this conversion took on historic importance only if resistance to cultural domination laid the groundwork for political solidarity that challenged "foreign domination as a whole."[12]

The middling classes therefore had a choice. They could enjoy their small privileges or commit class suicide by adopting a revolutionary consciousness that identified fully with the culture *and* goals of the majority in their homelands.[13] While Cabral referenced Marxist ideas, he did not desire class conflict but the creation of national unity across classes. This unity provided the foundation for a revolution forged around a shared African personality. Cabral carried this nascent ideology with him when he left Lisbon to serve as a colonial agronomist, using a surveying project to analyze Guiné's diverse communities. In 1956, party histories claim, Cabral founded the PAIGC alongside a core of Cabo Verdeans in Bissau. Later that year he was reportedly present at the formation of the Movimento Popular de Libertação de Angola (Popular Movement for the Liberation of Angola, or MPLA) in Luanda. The PAIGC organized clandestinely in Bissau, with some success among the city's dockworkers.[14]

Importantly, this "return to the source" did not mean adopting one dominant cultural tradition or ethnic identity but rather creating a new national consciousness. For the educated Africans of the Lisbon salon, returning wholesale to village traditions meant rejecting the useful elements that came with empire: advanced technology, industry, modern social relationships, and the nation-state. This last point was especially important in Guiné, which featured nearly a dozen ethnic groups with distinct

---

[11] Cabral, *Revolution*, 86.   [12] Cabral, *Return*, 63.   [13] Cabral, *Revolution*, 72 and 110.
[14] There is debate over Cabral's presence and the parties' founding dates, which were likely years later. See Julião Soares Sousa, *Amílcar Cabral: Vida e Morte de um Revolucionário Africano* (Lisbon: Vega, 2011), 184–191; Mendy, *Nationalist and Pan-Africanist*, 90–102; Chabal, *Revolutionary Leadership*, 54–57.

traditions and languages. Cabral believed this was the result of Portuguese imperialism "halt[ing] our history," exaggerating and formalizing anti-quated social formations or forging new ones to undermine a united resistance.[15] Europe developed nations and bureaucracies to manage modern economic and societal relations while keeping Guineans "prisoners of the medieval mentality of their political formulations."[16]

The process through which educated revolutionaries joined with the peasant majority offered a solution. It linked the nascent, authentic power of a mass movement with the knowledge and critical self-awareness of educated individuals like Cabral. For the PAIGC, the struggle against empire also offered Cabo Verdeans the opportunity for a renewed African identity as part of the formation of a modern Pan-African nation. Chabal argues that the party adapted sociopolitical structures from the large Balante ethnic group that provided many early recruits and which Cabral claimed was egalitarian and anti-colonial. Yet the party did not promote Balante nationalism.[17] Convinced that ethnocentric localism was anathema to revolution and unity amidst the diversity of Guiné, Cabral sought to forge a new identity.[18] With his party acting as a gatekeeper, Cabral envisioned a movement that promoted "positive cultural values" derived from shared African traditions while discarding inherited practices that hindered solidarity such as sexism, sectarianism, and racism.[19] Cabral contended that a successful movement could not simply displace colonialism with old ideas; it needed to create a nation that represented all citizens.

Therefore, Cabral and the PAIGC built their party at the intersection of two political avenues: an aspirational form of African identity politics and a practical socialism that provided concrete material benefits. Both were vital to party ideology but sometimes caused tension within the movement.[20] Regarding the former, the PAIGC's desire to forge a common identity

[15] Amílcar Cabral, *Unity and Struggle: Speeches and Writings* (New York: Monthly Review Press, 1979), 32–33.

[16] PAIGC, Communicado analisando a origem da luta na Guiné, n.d. (c. 1963), Folder: 07073.132.001, Arquivo Amílcar Cabral, Fundação Mário Soares, Casa Comum: http://casacomum.org/cc/arquivos?set=e_2617. Hereafter, Cabral Archive.

[17] Chabal, *Revolutionary Leadership*, 69–70, 201.

[18] Aristides Pereira maintained ethnic differences were generally "much stronger" than the mainland-islander divide. Aristides Pereira, *O Meu Testemunho* (Lisbon: Noticias, 2003), 103.

[19] Cabral, *Return*, 48.

[20] The PAIGC concept of African identity has similarities to the way Mahler argues Tricontinentalism used color as a metonym linking Afro-Asian-Latinx identity to anti-imperial action. Anne Garland Mahler, *From the Tricontinental to the Global South: Race, Radicalism, and Transnational Solidarity* (Durham: Duke University Press, 2018), 65.

using positive aspects of an idealized African culture meant it consciously rejected unity based on anti-imperial racism. The party's official position was that it opposed Portugal, not its people.[21] Yet this nuance faded at the operational level when PAIGC operatives used emotional appeals to mobilize disaffected Africans. "The BLACK MAN lives in misery because the WHITE MAN exploits him," wrote PAIGC President Rafael Barbosa, who recruited in Bissau until his arrest in 1962. "[I]n Africa as a whole," added Barbosa, "we are driving the Whites out because they treat us poorly."[22] Cabral himself occasionally blurred the lines connecting whites to empire when addressing PAIGC cadres, but the party generally avoided such rhetoric.[23] Cabral repeatedly expressed his strong opposition to organizing around race, arguing "we can not answer racism with racism."[24] Yet tension remained, since such appeals were powerfully convincing to many Guineans whose experiences of empire were visibly tied to white Europeans.

Indeed, competing parties saw value in adopting racial appeals. By the late 1950s, an array of nationalists competed with the PAIGC to win followers. Prominent among them was François Mendy, a Senegalese soldier of Guinean descent that historian Mustafah Dhada describes as "rabidly racist."[25] In 1960, he founded the Senegal-based Movimento de Libertação da Guiné (MLG), which became a primary alternative to the PAIGC.[26] Despite living most of his life in French territory, Mendy argued the PAIGC's Cabo Verdean leadership were interlopers. He built his party using black racial appeals that attacked both imperial Portugal and creole islanders, arguing PAIGC leaders were using the Guinean people to free their island home and replace Portuguese domination with "Cabo Verdean neocolonialism."[27] In response to these attacks, the PAIGC denounced "intransigent enemies who, guided by an opportunistic and selfish spirit, try to confuse our people" by dividing Guineans and Cabo Verdeans in ways that served Portuguese goals.[28] Linking African identity

[21] Cabral, *Revolution*, 18.

[22] Zain Lopes, A Verdade, n.d. (c. 1960–61), Folder 07063.036.077, Cabral Archive.

[23] See Cabral, *Unity*, 35.   [24] Cabral, *Return*, 76.   [25] Dhada, *Warriors at Work*, 7.

[26] The MLG launched an unsuccessful armed revolt in 1961 but never received much African support outside Dakar. Peter Karibe Mendy and Richard A. Lobban Jr., *Historical Dictionary of the Republic of Guinea-Bissau*, 4th ed. (Lanham: Scarecrow Press, 2013), 270–271.

[27] FLING, "Appel Aux 'Guineens'," n.d. (after 1960), Folder 07059.024.018, Cabral Archive; see also Letter, Luís Cabral e Aristides Pereira to Cabral, November 17, 1960, Folder 04605.043.067, Cabral Archive.

[28] Alexandre Carvalho et al., Mensagem aos jovens guineenses e caboverdianos, n.d. (likely early 1960s), Folder 04602.007, Cabral Archive.

with anti-imperialism downplayed the racial and xenophobic rhetoric that had the potential to rebound on the Cabo Verdean-dominated PAIGC. For Cabral, "African" necessarily denoted an evolving political nationalism that contrasted with the exclusionary identarian politics proposed by the Dakar-based MLG.

This less racialized idea of African identity worked hand in glove with Cabral's reading of socialism, which sought rapid modernization while complementing the oft-cited idea of African communalism. As with much of Cabral's philosophy, the origins of his socialist thought dated to his time in Lisbon, where collaborators – notably Agostinho Neto – had ties to Portuguese communists. Cabral was attracted to the socialist worldview and Lenin's definition of empire as the highest form of monopoly capitalism. But rather than adopting the one-world socialism of Portuguese communists, who were equivocal about the national question and initially hoped Africans would act as extensions of the metropolitan party, Cabral aimed for the revival of African polities capable of self-determination.[29] As Cabral explained later, African revolutions needed to gain control of the "mode of production" – and by extension, political institutions – to create "new prospects for the cultural development of the society . . . by returning to that society all its capacity to create progress."[30] The Marxist worldview helped identify strategies for reestablishing control of their own history. The PAIGC defined itself from the beginning as a "workers' political organization" (*uma organizaçao politica da classes trabalhadores*) and focused on urban organizing, but Cabral avoided the communist label.[31] Rather, he used the theoretical tools socialism provided to unite disparate African peoples against imperial domination.

Cabral's socialist worldview led him to define self-determination broadly, reaching beyond political or flag independence to embrace national control of economics and culture. "Independence," he argued in 1961, was "just one indispensable step to attaining this objective [of national progress]."[32] Other European states were allowing political independence while retaining effective economic and diplomatic control of former colonies. Cabral assumed (correctly) that allies like the United States were encouraging Salazar to embrace this approach as a way of

[29] Chabal, *Revolutionary Leadership*, 41.   [30] Cabral, *Return*, 43.
[31] Estatutos do PAI, 1956, Folder 04999.001, Cabral Archive; Cabral, *Revolution*, 67.
[32] Cabral, "Rapport géréral sur la lute de libération nationale," July 1961, in Ronald H. Chilcote, ed., *Emerging Nationalism in Portuguese Africa: Documents* (Palo Alto: Hoover Institution Press, 1972), 309.

retaining influence and pro-Western stability in Africa.[33] Cabral feared "attempts by imperialists and colonialists to re-establish themselves, in new forms," specifically warning of business penetration.[34] This broad idea of imperialism encompassing both formal colonialism and socioeconomic neocolonialism became central to Cabral's ideology.

The conceptualization of empire had two effects. The first was to expand beyond Portugal to criticize Western countries that supported Lisbon, notably the economic powerhouses of the United States and Germany. This allowed the PAIGC to find allies opposed to common foes, ranging from Vietnamese communists to the British working class. Second, it highlighted the threat of "African traitors," whom Cabral described as the "self-styled heads of state" and unprincipled nationalists willing to accommodate foreign economic or political domination in exchange for personal power.[35] Effectively, the PAIGC dismissed opponents not just as rivals but also as agents of empire. In 1962, Cabral warned, "We must strengthen our vigilance against the attempts to install a new form of colonialism among us, against the opportunists, the ambitious, and all the enemies of the unity of freedom and progress of our peoples."[36] As a result, dueling accusations of neocolonialism became an inescapable part of nationalist politics.

The PAIGC promised a modern, united socialist state in direct opposition to the history of imperial division. In Guiné, where ethnicity and race were contested topics, a shared future and the struggle to achieve it provided the foundation for solidarity. In early 1962, the party laid out its program for achieving independence and building a Pan-African polity. Plans included a government based on "democratic centralism," the development of "modern industry and commerce" through state intervention, compulsory public education, religious freedom, and the "elimination of man's exploitation of man" responsible for poverty, ignorance, sexism, and a host of other social maladies.[37] After the armed revolt began in 1963, the creation of schools, hospitals, and "people's stores" became

---

[33] See Telegram, State to Lisbon, March 10, 1961, Box 1813, Central Decimal File, 1960-63, RG 59 Records of the State Department, National Archives and Record Administration (College Park, MD).

[34] PAIGC, Proclamation, November 1960, in Chilcote, ed., *Emerging Nationalism*, 361.

[35] Cabral, *Revolution*, 16.

[36] Cabral, Sobre a situação actual da luta de libertação na Guiné "Portuguesa" e Ilhas de Cabo Verde, January 20, 1962, Folder 04607.051.004, Cabral Archive.

[37] PAIGC, "Statuts et Programme," n.d. (c. early 1962), 23-26, Arquivo Andrade, Casa Comum: http://casacomum.org/cc/visualizador?pasta=10191.002.007#!11.

major components of party policy – and propaganda – in newly liberated territory. These services grew from one of Cabral's key insights: "the people are not fighting for ideas, for things in anyone's head. They are fighting to win material benefits, to live better and in peace ... to guarantee the future of their children."[38] Rather than building the nation solely on racial or ethnic identity, the PAIGC claimed legitimacy by promising material benefits.

As a result, visible and sustained action was a necessary component of selling this political movement. Early efforts focused on labor organizing in Bissau, mirroring the ways unions mobilized against empire in British and French territories. Yet Portugal would not abandon its empire. In 1959, a strike by workers at Bissau's Pidjiguiti Docks invited a deadly crackdown that forced the party into exile.[39] Denied the ability to pursue non-violent political action, Cabral gravitated toward models offered by militant Afro-Asian liberation movements.

This shift marked the final element establishing the direction of the PAIGC. Cabral was not opposed to armed conflict, but neither did he seek it. In statements preceding and following Pidjiguiti, Cabral stressed his willingness to negotiate with Portugal for independence.[40] Though these appeals came as the PAIGC prepared for war, there is reason to take Cabral at his word. As late as 1972, he stated he was "not a great defender of the armed fight" even though it was necessary in Guiné.[41] Cabral did not fetishize violence but embraced fighting as the necessary response to Portugal's stubborn use of force to sustain its empire. In justifying this idea, he looked abroad to the "lesson" offered by "the case of Algeria" – that "armed struggle is the necessary corollary to the impossibility of resolving this conflict through the ballot [*voix politique*]."[42] Additional models from China and Cuba encountered after Pidjiguiti bolstered the Algerian model.[43] Progress was necessary to build a movement, and with no other avenues, only armed conflict could achieve concrete victories. With it came an opportunity to unite the nation's disparate peoples through the crucible of war.[44]

---

[38] Cabral, *Revolution*, 86.
[39] Chabal, *Revolutionary Leadership*, 56–57; Sousa, *Vida e Morte*, 186.
[40] See Memorando enviado ao Governo Português pelo Partido Africano da Independência, n.d. (c. December 1960), Folder 04602.010, Cabral Archive.
[41] Cabral, *Return*, 79.
[42] Cabral, Declaração por ocasião da independência da Argélia, July 1, 1962, Folder: 04612.063.006, Cabral Archive.
[43] Cabral first encountered Maoism in 1960 or 1961. Cabral, *Return*, 87.
[44] Cabral, *Return*, 79.

After recruiting and training small cadres, the PAIGC invaded Guiné from neighboring Guinea in January 1963. The invasion revealed one final element of Cabral's ideology drawn from the Algerian example. The National Liberation Front's (FLN) successful diplomacy revealed that "the strengthening of real and active solidarity of oppressed peoples is an indispensable condition for the common struggle against imperialism and colonialism."[45] By linking material and political solidarity with local anti-colonialism, the exiled PAIGC found the power to challenge Portugal's empire and build its socialist, African nation. With domestic organizing impossible, Cabral understood that the international dimension became "the most important point of our struggle. Without resolute and frank support from the Afro-Asian nations, nothing can be done."[46]

A TRANSNATIONAL AFRICAN STRUGGLE

International support was vital for the PAIGC for two main reasons. It legitimized the PAIGC against competing parties and provided material aid for the guerrilla war and reconstruction of occupied territories. Cabral identified potential allies by drawing on the ideas that informed internal PAIGC solidarity: shared ideological goals and an identity based on common histories, values, and ambitions. He believed concentric circles of collaboration formed beginning with Lusophone liberation groups and then extending progressively to "solidarity on the African, Afro-Asian and international levels."[47] Cabral tapped into the currents of the global process of decolonization and developed increasingly broad networks of support as the party's ambitions expanded.

Because Guiné and Cabo Verde were hinterlands even within Portugal's empire, the PAIGC used ties to important colonies such as Angola to bolster its position. Cabral achieved this goal by institutionalizing the personal contacts and ideological affinities of the Lisbon salon.[48] In 1958, he spearheaded the formation of the Movimento AntiColonialista with MPLA leaders, which evolved into the Conferência das Organizações Nacionalistas das

---

[45] Cabral, Declaração por Argélia.
[46] Mensagem do MLGCV para Abel Djassi, July 30, 1960, Folder 07063.036.026, Cabral Archive.
[47] Cabral, Declaration Sobre a situação actual da luta de libertação na Guiné "Portuguesa," January 20, 1962, Folder 04607.051.004, Cabral Archive.
[48] PAIGC, Amílcar Cabral – O Homem e a sua Obra, July 1973, Folder 04602.130, Cabral Archive.

Colónias Portuguesas (Conference of Nationalist Organizations of the Portuguese Colonies, or CONCP) three years later. This latter group united all the major socialist-inclined nationalist parties in the Lusophone world, including the MPLA, activists from Portugal's Indian enclave of Goa, and the Frente de Libertação de Moçambique (Mozambique Liberation Front, or FRELIMO) after its formation in 1962. These organizations amplified the power of the individual parties by loosely linking the political and military challenges to Portugal. Among its first actions, the CONCP used the international attention focused on the Angolan rebellion to press its broader case against Portuguese imperialism. Later, the existence of three distinct military fronts – Angola from 1961, Guiné after 1963, and Mozambique after 1964 – prevented Portugal from concentrating its forces in any one country (Map 9.1).[49]

Yet the CONCP parties lacked military materiel, international prestige, and refuge from Portuguese crackdowns, meaning they needed allies among newly independent states. Cabral actively cultivated such support from the PAIGC's founding, attending the All-African People's Conference and other gatherings, but decolonization was vital. The PAIGC needed a safe haven from repressive Portuguese authorities. When Sékou Touré led neighboring Guinea to independence in 1958 (a year before Pidjiguiti forced the PAIGC into exile), Cabral reportedly exclaimed, "That's it! Now I have my country."[50] An ardent nationalist and champion of Pan-Africanism, Touré embraced a leftist vision of state development that gave him access to Eastern European largesse. Touré was wary of provoking Portugal, but he opposed colonialism and saw the PAIGC as the best prospect for achieving decolonization. He allowed the PAIGC to establish their headquarters in his country in May 1960.[51]

This transnational solidarity was vital for the party in the years before it was capable of waging revolution, enhancing PAIGC legitimacy as it competed with other nationalist groups. The party's emphasis on material progress and the promise of a new nation required action to legitimize its claims, whereas groups like Mendy's MLG could fall back on static identarian politics. Such problems were not uncommon. In Angola, the Congo-based, Bakongo-dominated Frente Nacional de Libertação de Angola (National Liberation Front of Angola, or FNLA) attacked the socialist MPLA as *mestiços* and over-educated

[49] See Cabral, *Unity*, 48. [50] Quoted in Chabal, *Revolutionary Leadership*, 57.
[51] Dhada, *Warriors at Work*, 12–14.

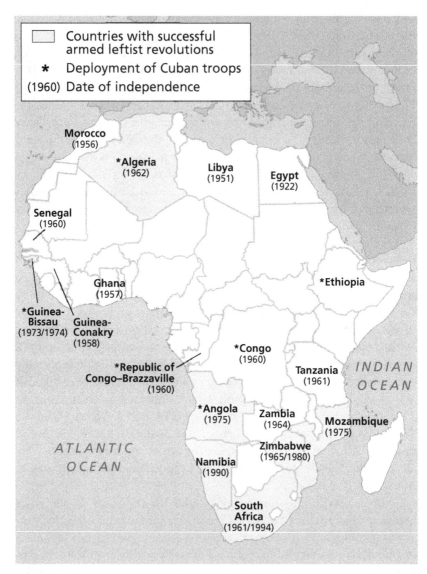

MAP 9.1 *Africa, leftist liberation, and Cuban intervention, 1960–1980*
Note: Cabo Verde (1975) – not pictured – sits roughly 600 kilometers West of
Cap-Vert, Senegal. South Africa became a sovereign state in 1934, declared itself a
republic independent from the British monarchy in 1961, and ended apartheid
with free elections in 1994. Rhodesia unilaterally declared independence as a
white republic in 1965; an international agreement recognized Zimbabwe in 1980.

cosmopolitans disconnected from the African masses.[52] These challenges likely informed the formation of the CONCP, since recognition by other socialists lent credibility and provided political momentum before a successful armed revolt could legitimize the individual parties. Later, such connections offered a sense of progress in the up-and-down war against Portugal so long as one CONCP member was making military gains.

The support of independent countries, however, was more concrete: they empowered individual movements through direct political and material aid. This reality was apparent in the period before the armed revolt began in 1963. After failing to establish a broad front, the PAIGC competed with Mendy's MLG to be the voice of Guinean nationalism. From different exile capitals – Mendy in Dakar and the PAIGC in Conakry – each sought to win the contest by assembling international support. The PAIGC focused first on Touré in what became known as the "Battle of Conakry."[53] Unable to fully resolve the mainland-islander divide, they sought assistance to limit the influence of local MLG proponents by asking the government to admit only party approved Guineans. They warned officials of a "small group of would-be Africans ... [who] fostered the politics of racism in the native races and exploited some resentment existing with other Africans, for example Cabo Verdeans."[54] Cabral's able diplomacy and successful navigation of domestic politics gradually won over Touré. He permitted the PAIGC to open training facilities, and Conakry became the conduit for shipments of goods and arms from North African states and Eastern Europe. Cabral achieved less success in Senegal due to Mendy's ties to President Leopold Senghor. Still, MLG efforts to have Senegal champion its position among African states reaped few rewards, so the PAIGC outpaced its rival as Cabral cultivated new alliances, notably with Kwame Nkrumah in Ghana.[55]

The expanding list of allies gave the PAIGC momentum, but it needed a successful military campaign to demonstrate progress. The outbreak of armed hostilities in Angola in 1961 put Portugal on the defensive, but Cabral concluded a second front was necessary to "divide the forces of our

---

[52] John Marcum, *Angolan Revolution: Exile Politics and Guerilla Warfare, 1962–1976* (Cambridge: MIT Press, 1978), 49, 169.

[53] Pereira, *O Meu Testemunho*, 122.

[54] Memo, Seidi Camará e Tcherno Mané to Djallo Sheyfoulay, n.d. (c. 1960–61), Folder 07063.036.097, Cabral Archive.

[55] See Dhada, *Warriors at Work*, 12–18 and appendix C.

common enemy."[56] The PAIGC concentrated on achieving long-term results rather than short-term political impact, patiently infiltrating small cadres across the border to observe conditions, cultivate relationships with village leaders, and prepare for a sustained war. In January 1963, the armed campaign began in the densely forested southern portion of the territory. The PAIGC expanded its influence in rural areas over the next decade. Lisbon maintained control of Bissau thanks to a military advantage largely supplied by NATO countries, both bilaterally and through illegal Portuguese transfers of material meant for Western defense.

The armed revolt opened what Julião Soares Sousa has argued was the second phase of Cabral's foreign policy.[57] The PAIGC used its newfound legitimacy to expand its web of support to become the leading party in Guiné and, after the collapse of the revolt in Angola, the Lusophone movement. Arms and money came from several African states, notably Algeria and Egypt.[58] After its founding in 1963, the Organization of African Unity (OAU) further enhanced the PAIGC's profile. Its Liberation Committee sought to organize continental support for decolonization by identifying and aiding nationalist parties capable of waging active liberation campaigns. In the Portuguese colonies, the OAU chose the PAIGC and fellow CONCP member FRELIMO. It initially favored the more active FNLA, which launched the 1961 revolt, but it split its support after 1965 between that party and the MPLA once the latter became the preferred partner of the wider Afro-Asian movement.[59] The messy Angola situation aside, the OAU decision affirmed the PAIGC's position as the preeminent nationalist party for Guiné. Even Senegal gradually warmed to the party, admitting in 1964 (according to PAIGC propaganda) that it was "the most serious" movement.[60]

Pan-African solidarity solidified the PAIGC's position and allowed it to launch the revolution. The party hoped that the OAU promise to coordinate aid would counter the assistance Portugal received from the West.

[56] Comunicado sobre os acontecimentos de Luanda, n.d. (c. 1961), Folder 07073.132.002, Cabral Archive.
[57] Sousa, *Vida e Morte*, 463.
[58] Registo de entrega de armamento e munições, August 12–24, 1964, Folder 07065.084.019, Cabral Archive.
[59] The MPLA lobbied communist and non-aligned allies to freeze the FNLA out of international meetings, including the 1966 Havana Conference, which influenced OAU decisions. Marcum, *Angolan Revolution*, 93–99, 171–173.
[60] PAIGC, Comunicado sobre a atitude das autoridades da República do Senegal em relação à luta de libertação e ao Partido, n.d., Folder 04612.064.063, Cabral Archive.

Yet the reality was that OAU recognition was primarily a diplomatic victory. The Liberation Committee had difficulty securing meaningful commitments from donors and was slow to distribute supplies, most of which came from states like Algeria that already championed liberation. The reality was that as the PAIGC transitioned from a revolt into a full-scale war of independence, it needed more extensive aid than its postcolonial allies could provide.

BRIDGING THIRD WORLD REVOLUTION AND COMMUNISM

Given the limitations of postcolonial Africa, the PAIGC relied heavily on communist states. The Eastern bloc provided the weaponry and services needed to confront the power of Euro-American imperialism, but the PAIGC was more ideologically aligned with Tricontinental anti-imperialists such as Vietnam and Cuba. Cabral viewed Marxism, in Patrick Chabal's pithy phrasing, as "a methodology rather than an ideology."[61] It explained the basic realities motivating empire, but the PAIGC's main goals – national independence, antiracism, democratization under party guidance, and economic progress to provide social welfare – only partially aligned with the hierarchical, proletariat-driven universalism of the Soviet Union. The PAIGC's most natural allies were Third World leftists, who had experienced colonialism and were in some cases transforming their societies through militant struggles for independence. Cabral found early lessons in Algeria and Patrice Lumumba's Congo and drew parallels further afield to Vietnam and Palestine as his party grew in stature. There was informal collaboration with North Vietnam and short-lived assistance from China, but most states had too few resources and too many local demands to send much aid.[62]

Alone among non-African Third World countries, Cuba provided substantial support. Cooperation began in earnest after the PAIGC impressed Che Guevara during his unsuccessful Congo campaign. The PAIGC received shipments of food, arms, and medicine from 1965 onward. Cuba offered training and sent advisors that numbered between 50 and

---

[61] Chabal, *Revolutionary Leadership*, 169.
[62] Dhada, *Warriors at Work*, 182–186. Relations with China suffered due to Beijing's attempts to pull the PAIGC into its ideological competition with the Soviet Union. See Julião Soares Sousa, "Amílcar Cabral, the PAIGC and the Relations with China at the Time of the Sino-Soviet Split and of Anti-Colonialism," *International History Review* 42:6 (2020): 1274–1296.

60 in any given year.[63] Cabral gladly accepted this assistance, but on terms that reveal his understanding of solidarity. First, he kept tight reins on the struggle and did not replicate Cuban models. There was danger in "blindly applying the experience of others." Referencing Che's statements about the value of mountains for guerrillas, Cabral explained, "[Guiné] has no mountains ... We had to convert our people themselves into the mountain."[64] Cabral looked abroad for ideas, but the PAIGC had to wage its own revolution and articulate its own philosophies in response to local conditions.[65] Second, it had to do so with its own people. Cabral welcomed Cuban expertise, but he turned down offers of large Cuban deployments: "A basic principle of our struggle is counting on our own forces, our own sacrifices, our own efforts."[66] Since the struggle itself would give shape to the aspirational nation, combatants had to be locals. Aid in the form of material and expertise addressed the "disparity of means" between empire and colonized, empowering Guineans and Cabo Verdeans to free their country.[67]

In addressing this disparity, one of the key accomplishments of the Third World network was raising the PAIGC's profile and giving it an international voice. Cuba invited the party to the 1966 Tricontinental Conference alongside a select group of leftist revolutionaries from Southern Africa that included fellow CONCP members, the African National Congress (ANC), and the Zimbabwe African People's Union (ZAPU). Cabral's rousing "Weapon of Theory" speech in Havana introduced the nascent West African revolution to the world and sketched a roadmap for Third World socialist revolution. Cabral argued peasant countries needed a vanguard party like the PAIGC, in which an educated elite (identifying with the masses) parsed the difference between a "fictitious political independence" and true self-determination.[68] The party led a revolution that transformed economic, political, and cultural relationships in order to displace an empire that maintained its power by operating at all three levels.[69] Though these goals were not military in nature, events in Algeria, Vietnam, and Lusophone Africa demonstrated that militancy was needed to combat determined imperialism. The

---

[63] Piero Gleijeses, *Conflicting Missions: Havana, Washington, and Africa, 1959–1976* (Chapel Hill: University of North Carolina Press, 2003), 186–196.

[64] Cabral, "Determined to Resist," *Tricontinental* 8 (September 1968), 117–118.

[65] Pereira, *O Meu Testemunho*, 125.   [66] Cabral, *Revolution*, 147.

[67] Cabral, *Unity*, 180.   [68] Cabral, *Revolution*, 105; Cabral, *Unity*, 84–85.

[69] Cabral, "Problemas fundamentais da luta," January 15, 1964, Folder 07070.112.004, Cabral Archive.

"criminal violence" that sustained colonialism and empire, Cabral argued, required "liberating violence" in response.[70] Given status alongside representatives of the USSR, China, Cuba, and North Vietnam, the nationalist leader from a small West African colony asserted his place at the forefront of the growing Tricontinental movement.[71]

Cabral's critique of the international system drew from the experiences of the Global South to contend the world's major problem was not class division but the inequality imperialism created between nations. He believed the postwar welfare state blunted the hard edges of capitalism in the North, where technological progress and an emphasis on consumption "enabled vast strata of the population to rise." But the imperial structures that enriched European nations did so at the expense of the colonized, directing investments narrowly and creating extractive relationships in colonies that "instigated, fomented, inflamed or resolved social contradictions and conflicts."[72] Western capitalism was problematic, but imperialism separated the rising living standards of the Global North from the stubborn poverty and war typical in the South.

This worldview aligned the PAIGC with radical Third World nationalists, but its concept of revolution also provided the foundations for relations with the wealthier Eastern bloc. Cabral saw the nascent Tricontinental movement as the successor to international communism, now centered on the needs of the long-marginalized Third World. Cabral praised the October Revolution as "the first major blow to imperialism," though the Soviet model no longer represented the vanguard. In 1961, Cabral cast the Tricontinental idea as the "final phase of the elimination of imperialism":

even more than class struggle in the capitalist countries and the antagonism between these countries and the socialist world, the liberation struggle of the colonial peoples is the essential characteristic, and we would say the prime motive force, of the advance of history in our times; and it is to this struggle, to this conflict on three continents that our national liberation struggle against Portuguese colonialism is linked.[73]

---

[70] Cabral, *Revolution*, 107.
[71] Cabral's collected works and radical publications, republished speeches and *Tricontinental* interviews. See Cabral, "The Power of Arms," *Black Panther* III:20 (September 6, 1969), 16.
[72] Estudos relativos à luta armada e ao seu desenvolvimento, January 1964, Folder 07070.112.004, Cabral Archive.
[73] Cabral, *Revolution*, 13–14.

The PAIGC needed the wealth and arms of the East, but the radicals of the Global South had to guide this generation's revolution. Cabral borrowed principles from Marxism – the distribution of international power, confidence in the masses, and egalitarian justice – and deployed them within the colonial context to create a cohesive ideology. "We changed the names," Cabral told a Soviet audience, "and adapted the discourse to the essential reality of the history of our day: the struggle for life against imperialism."[74] The Soviet Union set the stage for contemporary movements by shifting the balance of power in the world toward revolution.[75] Its primary role in the 1960s was to be banker and armorer of Third World struggles led by Vietnam, Cuba, and now the PAIGC.

Nonetheless, the Soviet Union was cautious when Cabral first requested assistance in 1961, likely wary to back armed revolt during a tense period with the United States. It did not, however, object to its allies working with liberation parties. The first linkage was with Czechoslovakia, whose shipments of arms in 1961 helped make the war possible. Philip Muehlenbeck and Natalia Telepneva argue this relationship emerged from ideological solidarity and a consensus among Eastern satellites that the PAIGC was a "serious movement" with prospects for rolling back colonialism.[76] The party built relationships with Romania, East Germany, and Yugoslavia, which supplied materiel, medical assistance, and other goods for liberated territories in Guiné.

Early interactions with socialist states paved the way for expanded ties to the Soviet Union as the PAIGC's status rose. The relationship began with professional training and scholarships requested by the PAIGC and MPLA, which Eastern states hoped would guide socialist economies after independence.[77] A year after launching the revolt, Cabral sought to expand these ties, requesting grants in medicine, food, and arms from

---

[74] Cabral, Une lumière feconde éclaire le chemin de la lute, 1970, 11, Folder 04602.118, Cabral Archive.

[75] Cabral, *Unity*, 256.

[76] Philip Muehlenbeck, *Czechoslovakia in Africa, 1945–1968* (New York: Palgrave Macmillan, 2016), 106; Natalia Telepneva, "Our Sacred Duty: The Soviet Union, the Liberation Movements in the Portuguese Colonies, and the Cold War, 1961–1975" (PhD diss., London School of Economics, 2014), 59.

[77] See letter, Cabral to Valentin Ivanov, September 26, 1960, Folder 07057.011.003, Cabral Archive; letter, Cabral to Secretary of the Central Council of Unions, May 11, 1961, Folder 04606.046.031, Cabral Archive; and various documents requesting safe passage for militants studying in USSR, Czechoslovakia, etc. in Cabral Archive, 04. PAI/PAIGC, Relações Internacionais, Guiné Conakry, Salvo-Condutos/Títulos de Viagem.

Nikita Khrushchev.[78] The Soviets became more responsive as the armed struggle proved durable.[79] Cabral benefited from Khrushchev's promotion of "different roads to socialism" as a way of combating Chinese influence in the Third World. Telepneva argues that the Soviets, having had uneasy relationships with both Nkrumah and Touré, also appreciated that Cabral distanced himself from "African socialism."[80] Cabral had strong relationships with both leaders and was no strict communist, but he did stand out among African radicals. His "scientific socialism" clearly drew from Marxism and, as historian Jock McCulloch notes, more actively embraced modernization, technology, and solidarity with Northern working classes than either Fanon or Nkrumah.[81]

These tendencies and Cabral's active pursuit of Eastern bloc aid proved attractive to Soviet officials.[82] Other chapters in this volume detail how the Soviet Union's competition with China pushed it in more anti-colonial directions in the 1960s, but Portugal's pariah status and the PAIGC's growing international reputation made the alliance palatable. Rather than fomenting a revolution, the USSR was aiding one. Mustafah Dhada notes that from 1964 onward, the Soviet Union provided military training and an estimated 30–40 percent of light and heavy arms, or what one party document called "articles of primary necessity" for the war.[83] As early as 1965, Cabral – after lamenting the "very inadequate" assistance from well-intentioned African governments – stated that "we rely mainly on the help of our friends, the socialist countries," specifically referencing the USSR.[84] These weapons, including anti-aircraft guns delivered in the early 1970s, allowed the PAIGC to counter the Portuguese military advantage and occupy the majority of the country by 1973.

As with the Lusophone and Tricontinental networks, the alliance helped legitimize both sides. This fact became apparent at the International Conference of Solidarity with the Peoples of Southern Africa and the Portuguese Colonies held in Khartoum in 1969. With the

[78] Letter, Cabral to Nikita Khrushchev, May 26, 1964, Folder 07057.011.007, Cabral Archive.
[79] Dhada, *Warriors at Work*, 13.   [80] Telepneva, "Our Sacred Duty," 85–86.
[81] McCulloch, *In the Twilight of Revolution*, 7.
[82] Dhada counts nine trips to the Soviet Union, more than Cabral took to any country outside West Africa. Dhada, *Warriors at Work*, appendix C, tables 3–5.
[83] Ibid., 186. See also Cabral, Breve Relatório sobre a Luta em 1971, January 1972, Folder 04602.069, Cabral Archive.
[84] Cabral, Relatório sobre a situação da luta de libertação nacional em 1965, November 8, 1965, Folder 07057.011.010, Cabral Archive. This attitude remained consistent into the 1970s, see Cabral, *Return*, 84, 89–90.

Soviet-supported Afro-Asian Peoples Solidarity Organization, the USSR sponsored the event to burnish its revolutionary credentials after its controversial intervention in Czechoslovakia the year prior. The conference highlighted its aid to African independence movements by mobilizing international support behind what it called the "sole official and legitimate authorities of the respective countries." These parties – the leftist nationalists of the CONCP, the ANC, and ZAPU – included all those invited to the Havana Conference three years earlier.[85] More overtly ideological than the OAU's preferred list, the conference established a clearly delineated set of "authentic movements" worthy of global support, with Cabral and his party heralded as the most successful examples.

Cabral joined individuals such as Che Guevara in providing an intellectual bridge between Global South anti-imperialism and Marxism, ably managing tensions as Tricontinentalism diverged from Soviet bloc communism. Cabral tacked left, but the PAIGC celebrated non-alignment and carefully guarded its sovereignty even as it sought foreign aid.[86] The Soviets and their Eastern allies accepted this ideological independence, since an international coalition of anti-imperial governments served their purposes almost as well as a cohesive communist international. The result was an alliance that, according to one East German official, represented "the cohesion of the three great revolutionary currents of our times ... world socialism, the movement for national liberation, and the people's struggle for peace, security, national independence, and social progress."[87]

WESTERN SOLIDARITY AND THE PROBLEM OF RACE

Cabral's integration of Third World nationalism with Marxism worked well internationally, but tensions remained at the granular level, particularly where theoretical concepts informed localized action. These tensions were particularly visible in Cabral's attempts to build a broad, multiracial solidarity network in the West. Both race and ideology were contentious matters in Guiné, but they faded at the international level. Militant Afro-Asian leaders shared a vaguely racialized anti-colonial identity while

---

[85] "Guidelines for Solidarity Movements," *Sechaba* 3:4 (April 1969), 3. See Telepneva, "Our Sacred Duty," 178–185.

[86] Pereira, *O Meu Testemunho*, 125.

[87] Cabral, Comunicado sobre a visita da delegação do PAIGC à RDA, October 31, 1972, Folder 07197.160.002, Cabral Archive.

Soviets elided it by focusing on class and empire; all shared ideological proclivities. Yet both issues were front and center in the Western experience of the 1960s, and Cabral clarified the relationships between identity, culture, ideology, and revolution as he pursued a flexible non-alignment that courted support in Europe and the United States.

That Cabral bothered appealing to Western activists at all reflected his concept of imperialism. He believed the global system of exploitation and dehumanization included marginalized European and North American populations alongside the colonies. Portugal itself was ripe for revolution since Salazar's fascist state preserved order and stability at the expense of living standards. Militarily and economically dependent on NATO allies, Lisbon was effectively "employed by world imperialism," argued Cabral.[88] Revolutions were necessary in both colonies and metropole, though these would be parallel movements because they operated in unique contexts and articulated distinct if overlapping goals.[89] This idea became the basis for the PAIGC's effort to mobilize "all the progressive forces" in support of the anti-colonial struggle.[90] Westerners could identify with the political programs of African revolutions, even if they could not become part of the armed revolt or African culture. The PAIGC welcomed government support as it did in the East, but Cold War fears of instability and Soviet involvement led most Western states to ally with Portugal. However, there were hints that civil society groups might be receptive as decolonization and the Vietnam War fueled social disruption.

After all, many Westerners were coming to believe they too suffered under empire. As part of the attempt to "rationaliz[e] imperialism" after World War II, Cabral contended, capitalists created a "false bourgeoisie to put a brake on the revolution" in the colonies and took similar action in metropoles through the creation of the postwar welfare state. The hope was that slight material progress would weaken demands for economic and social justice.[91] Cabral rejected this temptation during his time in Lisbon, and he saw Westerners grappling with similar calculations during the 1960s. Youth raised amidst the dissonance of material luxury, racial

[88] Cabral, "The Death Pangs of Imperialism," July 1961, in Chilcote, ed., *Emerging Nationalism*, 302.

[89] See Cabral, *Unity*, 76, 216.

[90] PAIGC Statement on Proclamation of Independence, Material Support Conference 1973, February 18, 1973, Folder 2, Committee for Freedom in Mozambique, Angola, and Guinea Papers, Bishopsgate Institute (London, United Kingdom). Hereafter CFMAG Papers.

[91] Cabral, *Revolution*, 73.

inequality, and the threat of nuclear destruction rejected the status quo. Many embraced instead a program for reform of social and economic relations associated with the New Left. Their models came not from classical labor philosophers but from Tricontinental revolutionaries such as Fanon who focused on the problems of the day: empire, social inequality, self-determination, and the spiritual malaise of the middle class.

The PAIGC actively cultivated support from this movement. Efforts began in neutral Sweden as early as 1965, where Cabral found a warm reception from Social Democrats under Olof Palme, who approved humanitarian support to PAIGC projects after he became prime minister in 1969. But the rise of New Left activism promised possibilities in the heart of NATO. In 1970, Cabral built on the Soviet-backed Khartoum meeting by spearheading the Rome Conference, a three-day gathering aimed at coordinating nonstate aid to the PAIGC and its leftist CONCP allies.[92] The goal was broad solidarity uniting "effective people of all the tendencies" from across the political spectrum.[93] Because Western support for an armed revolt against Portugal was unlikely, Cabral encouraged aid to rebuild occupied territory. He also asked allies to mobilize political pressure to isolate Portugal and legitimize the PAIGC enough to avoid post-independence interventions. The goal, Cabral told a group of Italian communists, was not armed European resistance but allies who could "find the best means and the best forms of fighting against our common enemy."[94] Dozens of organizations responded, ranging from German Marxists to British churches.

Support for the PAIGC was especially strong from two sources: radical youth and the Black diaspora. Regarding the former, activist students gravitated to the PAIGC's social reconstruction of liberated territories and practical ideas for self-determination that included local control of education and healthcare, economic reform, and gender equality. Cabral's advice "to tell no lies . . . claim no easy victories" became a popular dictum reminding activists to keep their actions constant and grounded in reality.[95] Cabral promoted these aspects of the struggle through extensive travel and publications. Collections of writings and speeches began appearing in 1969, a few years after he became a subject for magazines

---

[92] "Guidelines for Solidarity Movements," *Sechaba* 3:4 (April 1969), 3.

[93] "Missão de Onésimo Silveira à Suécia, Escandinávia e Bélgica," August 19, 1968, Folder 07198.169.151, Cabral Archive.

[94] Cabral, *Revolution*, 75.   [95] Ibid., 86.

such as *Tricontinental* and *The Black Panther*. The PAIGC also invited Westerners to visit Guiné to see the revolution in action. Films and books, such as Stephanie Urdang's *Fighting Two Colonialisms* about women in the struggle, highlighted the most progressive elements of Cabral's philosophy and connected them to Western debates over changing social relationships.[96] Judy Tzu-Chun Wu has described this phenomenon of idealization and application as "radical orientalism," but the PAIGC encouraged these glosses and lionized Cabral to promote solidarity.[97] While activists supported the MPLA and FRELIMO, Cabral emerged as the face of Lusophone revolution and, according to Swedish writer Per Wästberg, "an idol to many."[98]

Cabral's status peaked among the Black diaspora in Europe and North America. Especially in the United States, Cabral was a true *African* revolutionary with whom many identified. His experience of alienation and rediscovery of African identity spoke to the Black Power Movement, while his theorization of "class suicide" legitimized its many middle-class activists. Militants lauded the success of the PAIGC's armed campaign, and Cabral's warning that revolutions were "not exportable commodities" allowed more moderate Black nationalists to argue for assertive but peaceful political organizing.[99] The key for Cabral was using the analytical toolbox provided by Third World socialism to mount a cultural and political response to empire based on local "geographical, historical, economic, and social conditions."[100] In articulating this concept of flexible transnational revolution based on local conditions, Cabral necessarily waded into issues of race, which haunted Western politics during this period.

Cabral's view of race was complex, and he used the term sparingly. He understood identity primarily through the lens of culture. Culture reflected the interaction of genetic, historical, political, economic, and geographic factors, and Cabral believed that "the sociological factors are more determining than the biological."[101] As a result, identity was

[96] Stephanie Urdang, *Fighting Two Colonialisms: Women in Guinea-Bissau* (New York: Monthly Review Press, 1979).
[97] Judy Tzu-Chun Wu, *Radicals on the Road: Internationalism, Orientalism, and Feminism during the Vietnam Era* (Ithaca: Cornell University Press, 2013), 4–6.
[98] Interview with Per Wästberg, in Tor Sellström, ed., *Liberation in Southern Africa: Regional and Swedish Voices* (Uppsala: Nordiska Afrikainstitutet, 2002), 355. FRELIMO's Eduardo Mondlane was popular in the West, but his assassination in 1969 left Cabral the most visible leader during the height of solidarity activism.
[99] Cabral, *Revolution*, 92.   [100] Cabral, "Determined to Resist," 117–118.
[101] Cabral, *Return*, 65.

always in flux as social conditions and material realities changed, and the African continent included a multitude of identities that could be described as forming "several Africas."[102] Racial conceptualization essentialized these complex identities, and Cabral implied it was a byproduct of imperial strategies promoting disunity. Indeed, when the PAIGC leader used racial terms, it was generally while attacking practices of imperialism, apartheid, and segregation. His concept of an African people, which he referenced often, did not automatically designate blackness but rather a combination of geographically defined linkages, historical experiences, and common values or traditions that existed across cultures and provided opportunity for collaboration. Indeed, Cabral dismissed the common delineation between the light-skinned Islamic north and darker sub-Saharan Africa when it was made by one African American interlocuter.[103]

This distinction between fluid cultural conceptions of identity and more static racial categorization is vital for understanding Cabral's Pan-African appeal in the West. Cabral understood Pan-Africanism as a sociopolitical project more than a strictly racial one, which did not automatically exist but was built on the common experiences and aspirations of *anti-imperial* African peoples. In this way, it fit with his humanist concept of a gradual evolution of societies toward larger and more effective party, national, and ultimately transnational groupings.[104] It was practical and political in nature rather than exclusive and ancestral. This idea sometimes caused confusion in the diaspora, especially among Black Americans, because strictly enforced racial borders promoted a race-based theory of Pan-Africanism in which membership was intrinsic and action should occur immediately at the transnational level.[105] Cabral's concept of Pan-African revolution reflected two key components of Tricontinentalism – socio-historical commonalities and ideological solidarity, the brotherhood and comradeship referenced above. He recognized the powerful emotional appeal of the former but emphasized the necessity of political action embedded in the latter.

By conceptualizing Pan-Africanism as a sociopolitical project rather than merely an ethnic brotherhood, Cabral reaffirmed the necessity of cooperative, multiracial solidarity organized at both the international and

---

[102] Ibid., 51.   [103] Ibid., 84.
[104] Cabral noted "before being Africans, we are men, human beings, who belong to the whole world." Cabral, *Unity*, 80.
[105] See Cabral, *Return*, 90–91.

local levels. During one British tour, Cabral explained that "racism is always opportunism," and he urged Black audiences to embrace political action alongside white activists.[106] In response, many Black Power nationalists softened their stance on race in ways that mirrored PAIGC practice, retaining assertive calls for local self-determination and racially exclusive leaderships but cooperating with reformist whites. This process is most apparent in the experience of the African Liberation Support Committee (ALSC), which sponsored nationwide African Liberation Day celebrations in the United States beginning in 1972. Partially under Cabral's influence, the nationalist ALSC drifted left, adopting a platform in 1973 that emphasized socialism and opened avenues for multiracial coordination. This decision reflected nationwide political shifts, dramatized by the conversion of the Newark-based cultural theorist Amiri Baraka into a Third World Marxist willing to use democratic structures to take control of local government.[107] This transition from brothers into comrades in a multiracial revolution linking North and South expanded the scope of solidarity organizing in the early 1970s. Successful multiracial campaigns targeting Portugal's colonial economy included the Dutch Coffee Boycott and the Gulf Oil Boycott in the United States.[108]

Political organizing in the West produced inconsistent but valuable results for the PAIGC. A year after Sweden became the first Western state to provide medical and educational aid, the World Council of Churches launched its Program to Combat Racism with grants going to each of the CONCP parties. Groups such as the American Committee on Africa and the Dutch Angola Comité sent smaller shipments of clothes, medicine, vehicles, and other supplies for social projects in the liberated territories. Popular organizing also changed official policies. In 1970, the Dutch government began donating to African liberation groups, and the minority UK Labour Party passed a resolution favoring moral and material support.[109] The PAIGC slowly gained acceptance, highlighted by the 1972 visit to the liberated territories by a UN panel consisting of

---

[106] Polly Gaster, Skype interview with author, August 7, 2013.

[107] See R. Joseph Parrott, "'We Are an African People': The Development of Black American Solidarity with Portuguese Africa" (MA thesis, University of Texas at Austin, 2014), 57–69.

[108] R. Joseph Parrott, "Boycott Gulf: Angolan Oil and the Black Power Roots of American Anti-Apartheid Organizing," *Modern American History* 1:2 (July 2018): 195–220.

[109] See R. Joseph Parrott, "Struggle for Solidarity: The New Left, Portuguese African Decolonization, and the End of the Cold War Consensus" (PhD diss., University of Texas at Austin, 2016), chapter 3.

representatives from Ecuador, Sweden, and Tunisia. Its report noted the "marked progress achieved" in liberating territory and building up local services, recommending support for the PAIGC and "concerted action by the international community to exercise pressure on the Government of Portugal."[110] While this declaration did not end the Portuguese war, it affirmed the PAIGC's status as a government-in-waiting and provided the party with highly effective propaganda when it unilaterally declared independence in September 1973.

The growth of Western solidarity alongside earlier Third World and Eastern support reveals that the PAIGC crafted an effective strategy at the international level. Cabral defined a socialist theory of anti-imperialism that traversed both North-South and East-West political divides. Yet at the grass-roots level, this inclusive revolution continued to face challenges from ideological, racial, and ethnic divisions. These contradictions appeared clearly in the Western context, where divergent identarian and political motivations for anti-imperialism hampered organizing. The Tricontinental tendency toward localized political analysis and varied modes of revolution fueled sometimes rancorous debates, especially where no dominant party existed to guide discussions. In one European example, hardcore Marxists unwilling to compromise with capitalists criticized the coalition of humanitarians, liberal reformers, and pragmatic radicals, who favored peaceful campaigns on "easily understandable" issues like forced labor on coffee plantations.[111] The CONCP parties desired mass movements that could achieve tangible results, but – focused on their own armed struggles – their irregular interventions did not stop the internecine conflicts that weakened anti-imperial organizing in key countries like Germany.

So too did the embrace of Cabral's theories reveal the uneasy balance between exclusive Third World identities and universal leftist ideologies that defined the Tricontinental movement. Tension between diasporic visions of Cabral as an *African* revolutionary fighting white racism and his leftist philosophy reinforced the bitter divide between race-conscious nationalists and the growing socialist wing of Black Power. In the United States, this view manifested dramatically in the division of the ALSC in

---

[110] United Nations, Report of the Special Committee on the Situation with Regard to the Implementation of the Declaration on the Granting of Independence to Colonial Countries and Peoples, A/8723/Rev.1, vol. III, chapter X, Annex I (New York, 1975), 105–106.

[111] See the debate over the Dutch coffee campaign, in which German groups directly reference Cabral: Minutes from Morning Session, Lund Easter Conference, April 2, 1972, Folder 3, CFMAG Papers.

1974. One witness to the debate noted that Cabral represented the "major theoretical author ... popular with all tendencies in the black movement for their own reasons."[112] For leftists, Cabral was an accessible voice of anti-imperialism and self-determination, promoting practical methods to empower Black leaders within the heart of global capitalism. By contrast, racial nationalists deeply skeptical of multiracial alliances situated Cabral's writings on culture within a Pan-African pantheon of leaders stretching from Marcus Garvey through Nkrumah. They rejected broader ideas of Tricontinentalism, with the influential poet Haki Madhubuti dismissing PAIGC allies Castro and Guevara (along with Lenin) as "another sect of white people ... using their special system of control, both steeped in and based on white supremacy."[113] Continued unity between these trends proved impossible, and the bifurcation of the ALSC undermined one of the largest Black anti-imperial organizations in the West.

The development of the Western solidarity movement thus represented both the ambition and the limitations of PAIGC philosophy. In September 1973, the PAIGC unilaterally declared independence after a decade of war, seven months before the Carnation Revolution toppled the Lisbon regime. Nearly sixty countries recognized the declaration, but all were from the Global South or Communist East. Even those Western states providing aid did not officially recognize free Guiné until the new Portuguese government accepted decolonization in 1974. Still, Cabral had praised the Western assistance that filled stores in liberated territories and isolated Lisbon. These partial victories implied a de facto acceptance of PAIGC governance that smoothed the transition after Portugal's collapse and had great symbolic value. As Tanzanian Ambassador Salim Salim told Swedish Premier Olof Palme, in the "context of the North-South divide," aid to the PAIGC demonstrated that many Westerners supported "the struggle against colonialism and racialism."[114]

CODA

Cabral did not live to see independence, partly because of the identarian conflicts that his philosophy never fully overcame. In January 1973,

[112] Phil Hutchings, "Report on the ALSC National Conference," *The Black Scholar*, July–August 1974, 51.
[113] Maoism was no less problematic, being the "intermediate step to pull us into the *real-white thing*." Haki Madhubuti, *Enemies: The Clash of Races* (Chicago: Third World Press, 1978), 56, 75.
[114] Interview with Salim Ahmed Salim, in Sellström, ed., *Liberation in Southern Africa*, 245.

a former party officer assassinated him in Conakry. Though debate continues over circumstances surrounding the event, the officer was a Guiné mainlander who, among other issues, resented the party's majority Cabo Verdean leadership. Yet Cabral had fashioned a movement bigger than himself. Portugal recognized the PAIGC's claim to Guinean independence in 1974, only months after young military officers disillusioned by their time fighting in Guiné toppled the Lisbon regime. In July 1975, Cabo Verde received independence. The two shared the ruling PAIGC, a flag, and an anthem, with constitutions that established national unity as their end goal. Without the charismatic Cabral and the cohesion demanded by the military campaign, however, the PAIGC could not make the Pan-African project last. Difficulty transitioning the colonial system to the socialist state and poor economic conditions inspired criticism of the PAIGC in Guiné, and intraparty tensions focused on outsider "mestiços" dominating leadership. In November 1980, a military coup ousted Cabral's half-brother, Luís, and ended plans for union.[115] Amílcar Cabral and the PAIGC liberated both Guiné and Cabo Verde, but they remained separate nations.

These events do not negate Cabral's ideology, but they reveal the challenges faced by, and inherent in, Tricontinentalism. Third World radicalism did not fit the boundaries established by colonialism or the international system. Cabral and the PAIGC merged ideology and identity in the hopes of forging a unity between traditionally distinct but inter-related colonies in Guiné and Cabo Verde. They situated the revolution within overlapping ideological currents, adapting foreign ideas to define the movement and using international aid to enable the struggle against Portugal. More difficult was using these same relationships to overcome the economic and cultural legacies of imperialism without the powerful solidarity provided by war. Though ultimately unsuccessful and perhaps overly optimistic, this was not quixotic utopianism. It was an attempt to restore the sense of agency that imperialism denied colonial subjects while working within inherited social and diplomatic realities. This project was common to postcolonial nations, and it proved difficult because the fight for political self-determination was just one step in a larger project seeking the more diffuse goals of economic and cultural liberation.

Few of Cabral's ideas related to revolution were wholly unique, but his ability to unite different strands into a cohesive global vision made him

---

[115] Joshua Forrest, "Guinea-Bissau," in Patrick Chabal, ed., *A History of Postcolonial Lusophone Africa* (Bloomington: Indiana University Press, 2002), 250–251.

a leading figure in the Tricontinental movement. His socialist-inspired nationalism coincided or preceded similar programs pursued by others such as Nelson Mandela. Still, Cabral's emphasis on national unity and the power of culture as the foundation for political action spoke eloquently to the context and desires of the Third World. Few individuals more clearly conceptualized these relationships and explained them, especially in the Pan-African context. Part of this had to do with the fact that he led a revolutionary movement in the Tricontinental era, which provided the PAIGC access to alliances in and beyond Africa denied to those who came before and after. The popularity of his philosophy encouraged him to enact and refine specific intellectual ideas because global revolution seemed possible and doing so expanded potential networks of support. Cabral balanced competing tensions by harnessing hope for the future and legitimizing political organizing through the material benefits it promised ordinary people. Cabral's premature death preserved for many around the world the unrealized potential of this ambitious vision of global revolution, even as his assassination and the fate of the Guiné-Cabo Verde union highlight the barriers that obstructed Tricontinentalism.

"Two, Three, Many Vietnams"

Che Guevara's Tricontinental Revolutionary Vision

Michelle D. Paranzino

Our every action is a battle cry against imperialism, and a battle hymn for the people's unity against the great enemy of mankind: the United States of America.[1]

Ernesto "Che" Guevara, January 1966

Ernesto "Che" Guevara's message to the Havana meeting of the Organization of Solidarity with the Peoples of Africa, Asia, and Latin America (OSPAAAL) – also known as the Tricontinental Conference – was the clearest elucidation of his Tricontinental vision of revolutionary warfare. The speech lauded the Vietnamese people for their courageous struggle against US imperialism and called for the creation of many other Vietnams. Guevara's conviction that the international proletariat shared a common enemy led him to promote a strategy for guerrilla warfare on the continents of what is now widely referred to as the "Global South." Though the nomenclature took a while to catch up, this shift in the conceptual construct of the developing countries, from the "Third World" to the "Global South" tracked an evolving understanding of the ways in which the world was divided. Guevara, among others (Figure 10.1), came to believe that the most salient divisions were not between the capitalist and communist blocs, but between the Global North – the industrialized economic powers, including the Soviet Union and other highly developed economies of the Eastern bloc – and the Global South. The latter term was understood as including not only the peoples of Africa, Asia, and Latin America – in other

[1] Che Guevara, *Message to the Tricontinental* (Havana: Executive Secretariat of the Organization for Solidarity of the Peoples of Africa, Asia, and Latin America, 1967).

FIGURE 10.1 Che Guevara's death in 1967 affirmed his position as a global revolutionary icon. He became the most familiar face in a pantheon of Tricontinental martyrs that included Patrice Lumumba, Mehdi Ben Barka, and Amílcar Cabral. OSPAAAL posters memorialized these contemporaries while also drawing linkages to older revolutions with celebrations of Cuba's José Martí and the Nicaraguan Augusto Sandino. OSPAAAL, Olivio Martinez, 1971. Offset, 54x33 cm. Image courtesy Lincoln Cushing / Docs Populi.

words, the decolonizing world – but also the subject peoples within the industrialized countries, particularly African Americans in the United States.[2]

Guevara's views on this subject put him at odds with revolutionary Cuba's superpower ally, the Soviet Union. Cuban leaders, particularly Fidel Castro, found themselves caught between conflicting strategies: to cultivate the solidarity of the developing world, with Cuba playing a leading role, and to develop an alliance with the Soviet Union as the only great power capable of protecting the Cuban Revolution against US aggression. While Castro struggled to balance on this tightrope of competing imperatives, over time Guevara became more outspoken in his criticism of the Soviet Union. This tendency is ironic in light of his earlier self-identification as a communist and the role he played in radicalizing the Cuban Revolution beyond the more moderate visions of noncommunist and anti-communist members of the 26th of July Movement.

This chapter traces the development of Guevara's beliefs, ideas, and actions, particularly as they evolved within three unfolding and inter-related historical contexts: the shifting Cuban-Soviet alliance, the deterioration of relations with the United States as the Cuban Revolution confronted the realities and legacies of US imperialism, and the deepening yet ultimately quixotic quest for Third World solidarity. Guevara both embodied and foreshadowed a pattern that would play out elsewhere in the developing world – admiration and emulation of the Soviet Union, followed by disillusionment with the model on offer in Moscow and a shift toward emphasizing the commonalities and solidarities of the Third World. His internationalism, idealism, and optimism ultimately contributed to the failure of his Tricontinental revolutionary vision, as they led him to seriously underestimate the heightened appeal of nationalism among the peoples of the newly decolonizing states.

---

[2] On the evolving concept of the "Global South," see Anne Garland Mahler, *From the Tricontinental to the Global South: Race, Radicalism, and Transnational Solidarity* (Durham, NC: Duke University Press, 2018). On solidarity between the Cuban Revolution and radicals in the United States, see John A. Gronbeck-Tedesco, "The Left in Transition: The Cuban Revolution in US Third World Politics," *Journal of Latin American Studies* 40:4 (November 2008): 651–673; Teishan Latner, *Cuban Revolution in America: Havana and the Making of a United States Left, 1968–1992* (Chapel Hill: University of North Carolina Press, 2018); and Rafael Rojas, *Fighting over Fidel: The New York Intellectuals and the Cuban Revolution* (Princeton, NJ: Princeton University Press, 2016), 165–194.

BECOMING "EL CHE"

Born in 1928 in Argentina to a downwardly mobile family of aristocratic background, Ernesto Guevara de la Serna was raised in an atmosphere of intellectual and political debate. As a medical student at the University of Buenos Aires, he came into contact with militant communists and accompanied them to at least one communist youth meeting, where he witnessed the destructive sectarianism of Argentina's radical left. These experiences compounded his innate skepticism and distrust of established authority, while inculcating disdain for the factionalism of Latin America's communist parties. Though sympathetic to communism, he never became a formal member of the Argentine communist party or any other political party. Moreover, he criticized Latin America's reformist left-wing parties for their anti-communism and amenability to cooperating with the United States. Guevara's extensive travels around Latin America brought him face to face with the dreadful living conditions of poor peasants and urban workers in the countries he visited. He came to believe that the revolutionary struggle of *"Nuestra América"* was a shared one against US imperialism. Only by breaking Latin American dependence on the United States could the region truly decolonize and fulfill the promise of genuine freedom. Even at this early stage, Guevara's outlook was international. He would repeatedly be frustrated by what he viewed as the parochial nationalism of many Latin American regimes and political parties.

In assessing the prospects for revolution in Latin America, Guevara was most impressed by Guatemala under Colonel Jacobo Arbenz Guzmán. The second democratically elected president in Guatemalan history, Arbenz came to power in 1951 and began to enact reforms that alienated powerful US interests and threatened the prerogatives of key sectors of Guatemalan society. Arbenz drew resentment not only from US business interests and domestic stakeholders but also from regional strongmen. The struggle between dictators and democrats in Central America and the Caribbean had been underway since before the end of World War II, with tyrants like Trujillo in the Dominican Republic and Somoza in Nicaragua conspiring to topple democratic reformers like Arbenz and his predecessor, Juan José Arévalo.[3] Guevara became

---

[3] See Charles Ameringer, *The Democratic Left in Exile: The Antidictatorial Struggle in the Caribbean, 1945–1959* (Miami, FL: University of Miami Press, 1974); and Aaron Coy Moulton, "Building Their Own Cold War in Their Own Back Yard: The

steeped in the Guatemalan revolutionary milieu, embarking upon an intellectual journey into Marxism-Leninism with his soon-to-be wife Hilda Gadea, a Peruvian and member of the American Popular Revolutionary Alliance and the Alliance of Democratic Youth, the mass organization of the Guatemalan communist party, the Partido Guatemalteco del Trabajo (PGT).[4] Arbenz had recently legalized the party, and Guevara applauded Arbenz's willingness to cooperate with communist leaders.[5] For Guevara, it was Arbenz's willingness to work with the communists that distinguished him from other Latin American leaders who were leftist and reformist yet still anti-communist. Through the PGT, Guevara came into contact with exiled Cubans who were plotting a return to their home island to overthrow the increasingly tyrannical regime of Fulgencio Batista. Guevara was in Guatemala City when a ragtag band of exiles led by Colonel Castillo Armas and backed by the CIA, which coordinated a devastatingly effective psychological warfare campaign against Arbenz, launched a coup. The CIA's propaganda, especially radio broadcasts, convinced Arbenz that a much larger army, including US troops, was on its way. He capitulated without firing a shot and fled to Mexico City.[6] This was a profound moment for Guevara, one that would shape his later attitudes and experiences. He had been fully prepared to fight on behalf of the Arbenz government, expecting the regime to arm the peasants and workers. Guevara was crushed when he found out that Arbenz had failed even to put up a fight.[7]

Guevara's assessment of the events in Guatemala tracked closely with that of the Guatemalan communists and Soviet officials. Nikolai Leonov,

Transnational, International Conflicts in the Greater Caribbean Basin, 1944–1954," *Cold War History* 15:2 (2015): 135–154.

[4] Michael Lowy, *The Marxism of Che Guevara: Philosophy, Economics, and Revolutionary Warfare* (New York and London: Monthly Review Press, 1973), 11. See also Hilda Gadea, *Mi vida con el Che* (Lima: Arteidea Editores, 2005).

[5] Carta a Tita Infante, March 1954, in Ernesto Guevara Lynch, *Aquí va un soldado de América* (Buenos Aires: Sudamerica/Planeta, 1987), 44–45.

[6] For more on the Guatemalan coup, see Nick Cullather, *Secret History: The CIA's Classified Account of Its Operations in Guatemala, 1952–1954* (Stanford, CA: Stanford University Press, 2006); Piero Gleijeses, *Shattered Hope: The Guatemalan Revolution and the United States, 1944–1954* (Princeton, NJ: Princeton University Press, 1991); Richard H. Immerman, *The CIA in Guatemala: The Foreign Policy of Intervention* (Austin: University of Texas Press, 1982); and Michelle Denise Getchell (Paranzino), "Revisiting the 1954 Coup in Guatemala: The Soviet Union, the United Nations, and 'Hemispheric Solidarity'," *Journal of Cold War Studies* 17:2 (Spring 2015): 73–102.

[7] Guevara Lynch, *Aquí va un soldado de América*, 39, 44–45, 54–58.

a KGB officer whose later career would include multiple stints in various Latin American countries and who served as an information officer at the Soviet embassy in Mexico City in the early 1950s, observed that across Latin America, opposition to authoritarian regimes was increasing. He predicted that because of US support for regional dictators, this opposition could potentially spill over into a general protest against the "imperialistic policies" of the United States.[8] Arbenz himself had sent an urgent plea to Moscow for help in rebuffing US imperialist pretensions. In a communiqué that was circulated in the International Department of the Soviet Communist Party (CPSU) Central Committee, Arbenz claimed that his economic policies, particularly agrarian reform, had threatened "such powerful monopolies as United Fruit," which had then petitioned the Eisenhower administration to lend "moral and material" support to their invasion plans. The United States was waging a campaign of slander and lies, tarnishing Guatemala as a "threat to the security of the American continent" and a "bridgehead of international communism" in order to create a pretext for "open intervention" in Guatemala's internal affairs, with the ulterior motive of depriving the country of its sovereignty and independence.[9]

Though many Soviet officials and representatives of trade unions and other party organizations sympathized with Arbenz, the highest-ranking leadership in the CPSU still adhered to a more dogmatic view of revolution that characterized Guatemala under Arbenz as "bourgeois-democratic" because it was not led directly by the Guatemalan communist party. This rigid ideological orthodoxy undermined Soviet influence on Latin America's radical left and pointed to a critical divergence from the views of Guevara, who understood that Arbenz's attempts to cultivate a measure of independence by allowing the Guatemalan communist party to operate legally represented a clear break from US-imposed definitions of "hemispheric solidarity." Soviet propagandists, based on information supplied by the communist parties and trade unions, assumed that the US intervention was designed to protect the monopoly status of United

[8] Posol'stvo SSSR v Meksike 24 dekabrja 1953 g. Zavedujushhemu otdelom stran Ameriki MID SSSR spravku stazhera N.Leonova "Panamerikanskij kongress pechati," Fond 5, Opis' 28, Delo 48, List 135, Rossijskij Gosudarstvennyj Arhiv Novejshej Istorij, Moscow, Russian Federation [Russian State Archive of Contemporary History, hereafter, RGANI].

[9] Kommjunike Sekretariata prezidenta respubliki Gvatemala o namerenijah SShA k sverzheniju demokraticheskogo pravitel'stva respubliki, 29 janvarja 1954 g., F. 5, Op. 28, D. 253, L. 5, RGANI.

Fruit, and they discerned no difference between the interests of the Eisenhower administration and those of the company.[10] Guevara's analysis of the Guatemalan coup was similar to that of Soviet officials, even though he had greater faith in Arbenz's reforms. He believed that the US State Department and the United Fruit Company were virtually indistinguishable. The coup had proven that victory could only be gained through "blood and fire" and that the "total extermination" of the reactionaries was the only way to achieve justice in America.[11] This oversimplified view of US-Latin American relations would later contribute to Guevara's unraveling in Bolivia.

Guevara's experience in Guatemala shaped the development of his revolutionary strategy. Specifically, he learned three key lessons from the Guatemalan coup. First, given that factions of the armed forces had turned against Arbenz, it seemed obvious that for a revolution to consolidate its gains in the face of US imperialism and its local lackeys, the army needed to be purged and created anew. A revolutionary regime had no reason to expect the support of the existing armed forces. Second, the leaders of the revolution must arm the populace in order to defend the revolution. Guevara sincerely believed that if only Arbenz had provided weapons to his supporters in the labor unions and the peasantry, he could have vanquished Castillo Armas even without the help of the regularly constituted armed forces. Finally, the experience of Arbenz even more firmly convinced Guevara that US imperialism could only be defeated via armed violence.[12]

After fleeing Guatemala, Guevara traveled to Mexico City, where he linked up with Fidel Castro and the Cuban exiles. They received training from Alberto Bayo, a Cuban-born Spanish military officer who had conducted guerrilla operations with the Republican forces in the Spanish Civil War. Bayo, whom Guevara later described as the only real teacher he ever had, counted among his influences Augusto César Sandino, who led the insurgency against the US occupation of Nicaragua from 1927 to 1933.[13] Sandino's guerrilla strategy attacked

---

[10] O polozhenii v Gvatemale i dejatel'nosti Gvatemal'skoj partii truda / po materialam pechati / 25 ijunja 1954 g., F. 5, Op. 28, D. 194, L. 104, RGANI.

[11] "El Dilema de Guatemala," in Guevara Lynch, *Aquí va un soldado*, 69.

[12] Paul J. Dosal, *Comandante Che: Guerrilla Soldier, Commander, and Strategist, 1956–1967* (University Park: Pennsylvania State University Press, 2003), 42.

[13] General Alberto Bayo, *Mi Aporte a la Revolucion Cubana* (Havana: Imp. Ejercito Rebelde, 1960), 10 (Prologo del Comandante Dr. Ernesto Guevara); see also "Una Revolucion que Comienza," in Guevara Lynch, *Aquí va un soldado*, 160.

the morale of US combat forces as well as the American public's will to fight. From his mountain outposts, he spread the struggle into the cities, protracting the conflict and refusing to engage US troops head on.[14] Bayo also borrowed heavily from the consummate theorist of guerrilla warfare, Mao Zedong, though there were profound differences between the two. Mao's strategy was aimed at a foreign aggressor; Bayo's aimed instead at a domestic authoritarian regime. Mao's strategy combined conventional with irregular warfare, whereas Bayo advocated an entirely guerrilla campaign on the Sandino model. The two agreed on the crucial importance of cultivating the active support of the local peasantry. For Bayo, success in guerrilla warfare could be achieved only when "a people suffer, whether from foreign invasion, the imposition of a dictatorship, the existence of a government which is an enemy to the people, an oligarchic regime, etc." If such conditions were lacking, Bayo asserted, "the guerrilla war will always be defeated."[15] Holding the United States responsible for installing and supporting regimes that caused so much suffering in Latin America, Guevara left Mexico dedicated to applying Bayo's strategies to the "armed struggle against Yankee imperialism" in Cuba.[16]

THE VANGUARD OF THE LATIN AMERICAN REVOLUTION

Though the voyage and landing of the *Granma* was an utter disaster, the Castro brothers, Guevara, and several others survived and escaped into the Sierra Maestra mountains, where they waged guerrilla warfare against Batista's forces for almost three years. Relations between the leaders of the urban underground and the leaders of the rural insurgency were tense at best, especially as Castro moved to consolidate his control over revolutionary strategy and tactics. Perhaps in large part due to the dispute between the urban and rural revolutionaries, Guevara assigned insufficient importance to the urban struggle in his theoretical writings on

---

[14] Donald C. Hodges, *Intellectual Foundations of the Nicaraguan Revolution* (Austin: University of Texas Press, 1986), 134–135.

[15] Alberto Bayo, "One Hundred Fifty Questions to a Guerrilla," in Jay Mallin, ed., *Strategy for Conquest: Communist Documents on Guerrilla Warfare* (Coral Gables, FL: University of Miami Press, 1970), 319.

[16] Guevara Lynch, *Aquí va un soldado*, 136. For more on Che's time in Mexico, see Eric Zolov, "Between Bohemianism and a Revolutionary Rebirth: Che Guevara in Mexico," in Paulo Drinot, ed., *Che's Travels: The Making of a Revolutionary in 1950s Latin America* (Durham, NC: Duke University Press, 2010), 245–282.

guerrilla warfare. The *foco* theory attributed to Guevara was popularized by Regis Debray, who oversimplified much of Guevara's writings on revolutionary warfare.[17]

Almost immediately upon consolidating power in Cuba, the revolutionaries of Castro's 26th of July Movement began to look outward. Guevara, as one of the movement's most committed internationalists, played a key role in planning for the earliest expeditions to spread the revolution to Cuba's neighbors, especially those governed by brutal dictators like Somoza in Nicaragua and Trujillo in the Dominican Republic. These expeditions were motivated by ideological revolutionary romanticism as well as pragmatic security concerns. The Cubans sought not only to liberate their neighbors suffering under the tyranny of dictatorships but also to create a regional environment conducive to the consolidation of their own revolution.[18] Though all expeditions were either aborted or ended in spectacular failure, they demonstrated the regional outlook of the Cuban Revolution.

In June 1959, Guevara was dispatched on a tour of African and Asian states, many of which had been represented at the first Afro-Asian conference in Bandung in 1955. He also spent a week in Yugoslavia, his first visit to a socialist country. Although he found his trip fascinating, he was skeptical of the regime's commitment to communism and frustrated by its refusal to grant a Cuban request for an arms deal.[19] Though raising some doubts about the socialist world, his travels solidified an ambition to unite the struggles of the peoples of all three continents – Asia, Africa, and Latin America. Che sensed that he was living at a crucial juncture in world history, when "the liberated people are becoming conscious of the great deceit they have been subjected to, the so-called racial inferiority." Cuba's identification with the Third World and integration into what would become known as the Non-Aligned Movement was, for Che, "the result of the historic convergence of all oppressed peoples." The Cuban Revolution could be a catalyst for this convergence. Upon returning to Cuba from his travels around Africa and Asia, Che declared that "our

---

[17] Julia Sweig, *Inside the Cuban Revolution: Fidel Castro and the Urban Underground* (Cambridge, MA: Harvard University Press, 2002); Samuel Farber, *The Origins of the Cuban Revolution Reconsidered* (Chapel Hill: University of North Carolina Press, 2006).

[18] Jorge G. Castañeda, *Compañero: The Life and Death of Che Guevara* (New York: Vintage Books, 1998), 146–148; Jonathan C. Brown, *Cuba's Revolutionary World* (Cambridge, MA: Harvard University Press, 2017), 47–72.

[19] Castañeda, *Compañero*, 160–166.

continents will unite and destroy, once and for all, the anachronistic presence of colonialism."[20]

Guevara believed this global revolution would be summoned through armed violence and would result in a structural economic reordering in favor of small, postcolonial states, with Cuba serving as a model for both. In extrapolating the experience of the Cuban Revolution outward, Che acknowledged the existence of very few "exceptional" factors in the success of the revolution. The most important was that "North American imperialism was disoriented and unable to measure the true depth of the Cuban Revolution." Future insurrections would not be able to count on such disorientation because "imperialism ... learns from its mistakes."[21] Yet Guevara remained confident of the hemisphere's revolutionary prospects, because there existed, as Bayo had argued, common plights motivating the "colonial, semicolonial, or dependent" countries toward revolution. The "underdeveloped" world suffered from "distorted development" due to imperialist policies that encouraged raw material production and monocultural economies. Dependence on a single product, with a single market, was the result of "imperialist economic domination."[22] In Cuba, the most basic fact of the economy was that it "was developed as a sugar factory of the United States."[23] The revolution had been waged not merely to topple Batista but to reorder such unequal economic relations.

As head of the Department of Industrialization within the National Institute of Agrarian Reform (INRA) and then as president of the National Bank, Guevara further developed his ideas about economic planning. Although his thinking was deeply influenced by Marxism-Leninism, he ultimately came to reject the economic prescriptions of the Soviet Union and other socialist states in Eastern Europe. He believed that the Soviet system had failed to advance the consciousness of the workers that was

---

[20] "Latin America as Seen from the Afro-Asian Continent," in Rolando E. Bonachea and Nelson P. Valdes, eds., *Che: Selected Works of Ernesto Guevara* (Cambridge and London: MIT Press, 1969), 44–45.

[21] "Cuba: Exceptional Case or Vanguard in the Struggle against Colonialism?" [*Verde Olivo* (Havana), April 9, 1961], in Bonachea and Valdes, eds., *Che: Selected Works of Ernesto Guevara*, 59.

[22] Ibid., 62.

[23] "The Cuban Economy: Its Past and Its Present Importance" [*International Affairs* (London), October 1964], in Bonachea and Valdes, eds., *Che: Selected Works of Ernesto Guevara*, 137.

a prerequisite for the construction of genuine socialism.[24] Even before visiting the Soviet Union, he had read Soviet industrial manuals that referred to the law of value, which for Marx was at the center of the capitalist mode of production. The Soviet Union, in attempting to build communism from a pre-capitalist level of development, relied on the law of value, and hence the profit motive, to achieve efficiencies and thereby accelerate the development of productive forces. Guevara rejected this Soviet solution to the dilemma of industrialization, which he argued merely adopted the tools of capitalism but without the efficiency of the "free market."[25] He further argued that the law of value should never operate in trade between the countries of the socialist bloc.[26] Specifically, he objected to the use of material incentives for production, maintaining that they must be replaced by moral incentives in order to undermine the law of value and achieve a truly socialist consciousness.[27] This idea would form one of the main planks in his critique of Soviet economic policy toward the developing world.

In August 1961, a special meeting of the Inter-American Economic and Social Council of the Organization of American States in Punta del Este, Uruguay, provided an ideal venue for Che to expound upon his economic ideas. First of all, he argued that economic planning was not possible until political power was in "the hands of the working class." Second, the "imperialistic monopolies" must be "completely eliminated." Finally, the "basic activities of production" must be "controlled by the state." Only if those three preconditions held could real economic planning for development begin.[28] Che's policies stood in stark contrast to the terms of the Alliance for Progress as presented by Kennedy administration officials at Punta del Este. Whereas the Alliance for Progress apportioned financial aid in the hopes of spurring moderate political and economic reforms, Che envisioned a revolutionary restructuring of the historically unequal

[24] Helen Yaffe, "Che Guevara and the Great Debate, Past and Present," *Science & Society* 76:1 (January 2012): 11–40.

[25] Helen Yaffe, "Che Guevara's Enduring Legacy: Not the Foco but the Theory of Socialist Construction," *Latin American Perspectives* 36:2 (March 2009): 51.

[26] Helen Yaffe, *Che Guevara: The Economics of Revolution* (London: Palgrave Macmillan, 2009), 41.

[27] Ibid., 66.

[28] "On Growth and Imperialism," Speech at the Special Meeting of the Inter-American Economic and Social Council of the Organization of American States in Punta del Este, Uruguay, August 8, 1961, in John Gerassi, ed., *Venceremos! The Speeches and Writings of Ernesto Che Guevara* (New York: The Macmillan Company, 1968), 168.

economic relations across the Americas. He believed that it was necessary to protect Latin American businesses from foreign monopolies and that the United States must reduce tariffs on the industrial products of Latin American states. Furthermore, any foreign investment should be indirect and not subject to political conditions that discriminated against state enterprises. The interest rates on development loans should not exceed 3 percent, and the amortization period should be no less than ten years, with the possibility of extension in the case of balance of payments issues. Che also called for reforms to lighten the tax burden on the working class.[29] Additionally, he urged the US delegation to cease pressuring OAS member states not to trade with the socialist bloc.[30] As head of the Cuban delegation to the meeting, Guevara refused to sign onto the Alliance for Progress, arguing that it completely neglected the fundamental economic problems facing Latin America.[31]

At the United Nations Conference on Trade and Development (UNCTAD) in Geneva in 1964, Che continued to develop his economic platform. He declared that the "only solution" to the problems of humanity was to bring an end to the "exploitation of the dependent countries by the developed capitalist countries."[32] Noting that the "socialist camp" had "developed uninterruptedly" at rates of growth much higher than its capitalist counterpart, he lamented the "total stagnation" of the under-developed world.[33] In Guevara's view, this stagnation was a direct legacy of colonialism, and the decisive defeat of the imperialists was a necessary precondition for economic development.[34] Though the vast majority of his ire was reserved for the United States, by placing the socialist bloc within the developed world and counterposing the developed world with the decolonizing countries, Guevara gestured toward a different understanding of economic exploitation from the one offered by the Soviet Union. Guevara's views on this issue were more closely aligned with those of the Chinese communists in positioning anti-imperialism – as opposed to class conflict – at the center of the struggle for economic liberation.

---

[29] Ibid., 170.   [30] Ibid., 171.

[31] "On the Alliance for Progress," Speech delivered at the Punta del Este Conference of the OAS Inter-American Economic and Social Council, August 16, 1961, in Gerassi, ed., *Venceremos!*, 182–189.

[32] "Discurso en la Conferencia de Naciones Unidas sobre Comercio y Desarrollo," Ginebra, 25 marzo de 1964, in Ernesto Che Guevara, *Escritos y Discursos Vol. 9* (La Habana: Editorial de Ciencias Sociales, 1985), 256.

[33] Ibid., 260.   [34] Yaffe, *Economics of Revolution*, 55.

BETWEEN THE THIRD WORLD AND THE SOVIET UNION

From the outset, Cuban leaders positioned the revolution between the Third World and the Soviet Union. A combination of ideological convictions, geopolitical realities, and domestic political pressures conditioned early Cuban foreign policy. Castro sought to consolidate power in his hands domestically, using the Cuban communist party's ties to Moscow to court the Soviet Union while simultaneously seeking to export the revolution to Cuba's authoritarian neighbors in a bid to shore up regional security. In the looming confrontation with the United States, it was critical that Cuba's neighbors not become a convenient launching point for a US invasion. Yet these oft-conflicting imperatives required a careful balancing act. Castro could announce his intentions to establish an alliance with the Soviets only once the more moderate factions of the revolutionary movement had been sidelined or eliminated. At the same time, the Cubans had to send reassuring signals to Moscow regarding the strictly tactical nature of their temporary compromises with the national bourgeoisie.[35]

Castro repeatedly urged greater unity and emphasized the power of Cuba's revolutionary example for the rest of Latin America.[36] In a speech at the UN, Castro declared that the "case of Cuba" is the "case of all underdeveloped, colonialized countries."[37] At the same time, the Cubans were embarking upon what would ultimately become a highly contentious relationship with the Soviet Union. In March and April 1959, Cuban emissaries began making overtures; one emissary told the Soviet ambassador to Mexico that the Castro regime was striving to emulate the accomplishments of the Soviets and that the restoration of formal diplomatic relations between the two countries was "only a matter of time."[38] It was

---

[35] Brown, *Cuba's Revolutionary World*, 20–46.

[36] "Fidel Castro Speaks to Citizens of Santiago," speech by Fidel Castro, Santiago, January 3, 1959. Castro Speech Database: http://lanic.utexas.edu/project/castro/db/195 9/19590103.html; "Means for Ibero-American Unity Suggested," interview with Fidel Castro, Caracas, January 26, 1959. Castro Speech Database: http://lanic.utexas.edu/pro ject/castro/db/1959/19590126.html.

[37] "Let the Philosophy of Plunder Disappear and War Will Disappear: Denunciation in the U.N.," Address by Prime Minister Fidel Castro at the 15th Session of the General Assembly of the United Nations, September 26, 1960 (La Habana: Editorial en Marcha, 1962), 37.

[38] Soviet embassy in Mexico, March 25, 1959, Record of conversation with the wife of Cuban ambassador Salvador Massip, from the diary of Soviet ambassador V. I. Bazykin. Fond 110, Opis' 9, Papka 43, Delo 5, List 55, Arhiv Vneshnej Politiki Rossijskoj Federacii, Moscow, Russian Federation [Foreign Policy Archive of the Russian Federation,

not long, however, before Cuba's efforts to export the revolution created tensions between the Soviet Union and countries in Latin America. Mexican officials expressed their disapproval of Cuban expeditions in the Caribbean to the Soviet ambassador in Mexico City in August 1959. The Mexican government had detained and deported three separate groups of Cubans who had been captured in Mexican territorial waters.[39] The Soviets had no interest in destabilizing the Mexican government, but they approached the Cuban Revolution with cautious optimism. The visit of Anastas Mikoyan to Havana in February 1960 to open the Soviet cultural and technical exhibit presented an opportunity for Moscow to evaluate the "character and path" of the Cuban Revolution and the possibilities for further Soviet-Cuban cooperation.[40]

In October 1960, Che headed the first official Cuban delegation to the Soviet Union. His travels around the socialist bloc left his admiration for the Bolshevik revolution intact, but he also witnessed a clash between Soviet plans and Cuban revolutionary ambitions. According to Anatoly Dobrynin, Che requested Soviet assistance in constructing a steel mill and an automobile factory in Cuba in order to spur the industrialization of the economy. He was informed that what the Cuban economy really needed was hard currency and that the best way to obtain it was through continued sales of sugar.[41] Due in part to the continued operation of the law of value in intra-socialist bloc trade relations, as well as the Soviet prioritization of raw material imports over industrialization in its economic relations with Cuba, Che ultimately came to believe that the Soviet Union was complicit in the continued exploitation of decolonizing states.[42]

Yet the Cubans needed the support of a great power patron like the Soviet Union in their confrontation with US imperialism. The case of Arbenz's Guatemala seemingly proved that this confrontation would inevitably involve violence. Cuban leaders therefore sought to safeguard the security of the revolution by strengthening ties with the socialist bloc and the non-aligned world. Though Cuban ambitions most closely

hereafter, AVPRF]; Diary of 3rd Secretary V. I. Andreev: Report on Prime Minister of Cuba Fidel Castro's press conference at the Washington Press Club, April 20, 1959. F. 104, Op. 14, P. 5, D. 1, L. 19, AVPRF.

[39] Soviet embassy in Mexico, record of conversation with acting MFA Mexico Jose Gorostiza, August 18, 1959, from Bazykin's diary. F. 110, Op. 9, P. 43, D. 5, L. 107, AVPRF.

[40] Nikolai S. Leonov, *Likholet'e: Sekretnyie Missii* (Moscow: Russkii Dom, 2003), 52.

[41] Richard N. Goodwin, *Remembering America: A Voice from the Sixties* (New York: Harper and Row, 1988), 172.

[42] Castañeda, *Compañero*, 256–258, 267–268.

paralleled those of Third World radicals, only the Soviets and their Eastern European allies had the financial, industrial, and military resources that Cuba needed. This balancing act created tensions with Soviet leaders, who occasionally chastised the Cubans for their "revolutionary adventurism," while some members of the Non-Aligned Movement viewed the Cubans as aligned with the communist bloc.[43] After the Bay of Pigs debacle of April 1961, which confirmed for the Soviets the fundamental inability of the United States to coexist peacefully with the Cuban Revolution, Havana amplified its requests for Soviet military assistance.[44]

Fortunately for Castro, Cuban requests came at a time when Khrushchev was pursuing a more active approach to spreading Soviet influence in the decolonizing world. At the 22nd CPSU Congress in October 1961, Khrushchev lauded the "revolutionary struggle" of the peoples of Asia, Africa, and Latin America, expressing his conviction that "the 1960s will go down in history as the years of the complete disintegration of the colonial system." Yet "remnants" of the colonial system remained; Khrushchev singled out "the Guantanamo military base on Cuban soil," occupied by the imperialists "against the will of the Cuban people." The Soviet Union was "unswervingly fulfilling its internationalist duty."[45] Khrushchev backed up this rhetoric with the provision of military aid to Cuba, including medium-range ballistic missiles capable of reaching targets in the United States and in some Latin American capitals.

These missiles would open a divide between the Soviets and their revolutionary clients during the October Crisis, more familiar as the Cuban Missile Crisis in Washington and the Caribbean Crisis in

---

[43] Michelle D. Getchell (Paranzino), "Negotiating Non-Alignment: Cuba, the USSR, and the Non-Aligned Movement," in Thomas Field, Stella Krepp, and Vanni Pettinà, eds., *Latin America and the Global Cold War* (Chapel Hill: University of North Carolina Press, 2020). Anxieties about the pro-Soviet stance of the Cubans had been present among some members of the Non-Aligned Movement since its inception – see Michelle Getchell (Paranzino) and Rinna Kullaa, "Endeavors to Make Global Connections: Latin American Contacts and Strategies with Mediterranean Non-Alignment in the Early Cold War," *Verbindungen zwischen Südosteuropa und Lateinamerika* 4:2 (2015): 25–35.

[44] Telegram to Soviet Foreign Minister Gromyko from Osvaldo Dorticós and Fidel Castro, April 28, 1961. F. 104, Op. 16, P. 8, D. 9, L. 34, AVPRF; Telegram from Havana, October 11, 1961, to Minister of Foreign Affairs Gromyko. F. 104, Op. 16, P. 8, D. 9, L. 93, AVPRF.

[45] Nikita Khrushchev, Report of the Central Committee to the XXII CPSU Congress, October 17, 1961; in Alexander Dallin, ed., *Diversity in International Communism: A Documentary Record, 1961–1963* (New York: Columbia University Press, 1963), 10.

Moscow.[46] The idea of installing missiles in Cuba originated with Khrushchev, and some Soviet officials were skeptical that Castro would accept the deal, as it contradicted his identification of Cuba with the non-aligned world. The Cubans believed that the Soviet provision of nuclear weapons could protect the revolution from US aggression while enhancing the strategic position of the entire socialist bloc. Yet during the crisis itself, when Castro urged Khrushchev to consider launching the weapons in the event of a direct US invasion of Cuba, the Soviet premier balked. Khrushchev's failure even to consult the Cubans regarding negotiations with the Kennedy administration infuriated Havana and ushered in a chilly period of Soviet-Cuban relations.[47] Mao was quick to capitalize on Khrushchev's "great power chauvinism," accusing the Soviets of kow-towing to the imperialists and selling out the Cuban Revolution.[48] After blinking into the nuclear abyss, the Soviets actively sought to reduce tensions with the United States, and Chinese hostility escalated to the point of considering Soviet influence as akin to a second form of imperialism.[49]

Despite the greater ideological affinity of the Cubans with the Chinese, Havana was still dependent on Soviet aid, requiring Cuban leaders to continue their balancing act. The November 1964 conference of Latin American communist parties hosted in Havana illustrated one such com-promise with Moscow. Although Beijing-oriented regional communist parties were excluded from the gathering, the delegates proclaimed sup-port for the armed struggle in several Latin American countries – Colombia, Guatemala, Haiti, Honduras, Panama, Paraguay, and Venezuela – while continuing to pursue the peaceful path to power in the rest of the region.[50] Mao was reportedly furious about the conference; he railed against the "three demons" of "imperialism, the atomic bomb,

[46] James G. Blight and Phillip Brenner, *Sad and Luminous Days: Cuba's Struggle with the Superpowers after the Missile Crisis* (Lanham, MD: Rowman & Littlefield, 2002), 247.

[47] For more on the missile crisis, see Aleksandr Fursenko and Timothy Naftali, *"One Hell of a Gamble": Khrushchev, Castro, and Kennedy, 1958–1964* (New York: W.W. Norton & Co., 1997); Sergo Mikoyan, *The Soviet Cuban Missile Crisis: Castro, Mikoyan, Kennedy, Khrushchev, and the Missiles of November* (Stanford, CA: Stanford University Press, 2012); and Michelle Getchell (Paranzino), *The Cuban Missile Crisis and the Cold War: A Short History with Documents* (Indianapolis/Cambridge: Hackett, 2018).

[48] Enrico Maria Fardella, "Mao Zedong and the 1962 Cuban Missile Crisis," *Cold War History* 14:1 (2015): 73–88.

[49] Richard L. Jackson, *The Non-Aligned, the UN, and the Superpowers* (Westport, CT: Praeger, 1983), 191–200; see also Jeremy Friedman, Chapter 7 in this volume.

[50] "Havana Meeting of Latin American Communist Parties, and Other Evidence of Cuban Alignment with Soviet Bloc," Joint State-USIA Message, March 3, 1965, Cuba,

and revisionism," with the Soviet Union epitomizing the last of these.[51] The goal was clearly to discredit the predominantly white, industrially advanced Soviet Union in the eyes of the Third World, but Guevara seemed to reject the political implications of this "theory of the two imperialisms." The Soviet Union was reliably anti-imperialist and played an invaluable role in sustaining Cuba in a hostile region, he believed, even if Cuban and Soviet priorities did not fully align in terms of economics, the transition to socialism, and support for armed revolutionary movements.

Though Cuba did not abandon its Soviet patron, Guevara critiqued the communist superpower for what he saw as its divergence from the revolutionary path. While celebrating the anniversary of the Russian Revolution in Moscow in November 1964, he criticized the Soviet model of industrial success before a crowd of local students, suggesting that the "Soviet Man" was not so very different from, for instance, a Yankee. This assertion reflected his belief that the continued operation of the law of value would perpetuate a capitalist consciousness and thereby prevent the emergence of a fundamentally new socialist outlook. The students, recognizing this opinion as an attack from the left, accused him of "Trotskyism." Che rejected the epithet.[52] But upon his return to Cuba, he indulged in a lengthy attack on the notion of "goulash communism," arguing that the reason the socialist bloc was falling behind the West was not because it was following the tenets of Marxism-Leninism but because it had abandoned them. The Soviets had succumbed to the law of value and adopted all manner of capitalist methods.[53] Many in the Cuban leadership, however, did not share Guevara's views and sometimes criticized his extreme ideological purity.

The following month, Guevara departed for a three-month tour of several African countries and China, where he continued this line of attack. At the second economic seminar of Afro-Asian Solidarity, held in Algiers in February 1965, Che criticized the Soviets as "accomplices" of the West in the exploitation of the underdeveloped world, and he asserted that the socialist countries had a "moral duty to liquidate their tacit complicity with the exploiting countries of the West." He urged the

Subversion, Volume 1, Part 1, 12/63–7/65 [1 of 2], National Security Files, Country File, Cuba, Box 31, Lyndon Baines Johnson Library, Austin, Texas [hereafter, LBJL].

[51] "Visit to Peiping of Latin American Leaders Following the November Conference in Havana," CIA Intelligence Information Cable, March 24, 1965, Cuba, Subversion, Volume 1, Part 1, 12/63–7/65 [1 of 2], National Security Files, Country File, Cuba, Box 31, LBJL.

[52] Lowy, *The Marxism of Che Guevara*, 66–67.   [53] Castañeda, *Compañero*, 269–270.

socialist bloc to use its power to transform international economic relations.[54] At the heart of the matter was Che's belief that ongoing, global revolution was necessary if small states like Cuba were ever to attain true political and economic independence. Though less racialized, this theory of Third World revolution aligned with much of China's rhetoric and created tensions with the countries of the socialist bloc. Raul Castro, in an effort to patch things up, privately suggested to at least one Eastern European diplomat that Che's proposals were "too extreme."[55] Nevertheless, Guevara would soon avail himself of the opportunity to back up his rhetorical exhortations to tricontinental solidarity with meaningful action, as he turned his sights to the ongoing struggle in Africa for liberation from European colonialism.

THE CUBAN VISION OF GLOBAL REVOLUTION

Guevara believed that a global revolution was necessary to achieve a socialist transformation of the international system. Obtaining power via armed force was an essential prerequisite for eliminating the continuing vestiges of imperialism and transforming global economic relations. The spread of armed revolts would inevitably weaken the United States as it aided reactionary governments and became directly involved in counterinsurgency. Though the Cubans came to power with ambitions of fomenting revolution in the Americas, Africa seemed more fertile ground after a wave of decolonization swept the continent in the early 1960s. While Che's erstwhile adventures in the Congo proved frustrating, the 1966 Tricontinental Conference helped establish a shared Third World vision of socialist revolution that would provide the impetus for new insurgencies in Latin America.

The Cuban revolutionaries exhibited an early and intense interest in the African liberation movements, particularly in the struggle of the Algerian National Liberation Front (FLN) against French colonialism. As Piero Gleijeses has shown, "Algeria was Cuba's first love in Africa," and

---

[54] "Discurso en el Segundo Seminario Economico de Solidaridad Afroasiatica," February 24, 1965, in Guevara, *Escritos y Discursos*, Vol. 9, 343–344.

[55] Statement of Raul Castro Ruz Pertaining to Cuba's Minister of Industry, Ernesto "Che" Guevara, March 1, 1965, History and Public Policy Program Digital Archive, Records of the Polish United Workers Party Central Committee [KC PZPR], Sygnaatura 237/XXII/1399, Archiwum Akt Nowych [AAN; Archive of Modern Acts], Warsaw, Poland. Obtained by the National Security Archive and translated for CWIHP by Margaret K. Gnoinska: https://digitalarchive.wilsoncenter.org/document/116563.

exchanges of weapons and medical assistance began as early as December 1961.[56] These exchanges demonstrated just how quickly the Cuban regime acted upon its vision of global revolution. Connections between Cuba and Africa stretched beyond material interests. Intellectually, the Cuban leadership – particularly Che – was profoundly influenced by Frantz Fanon, the radical psychologist and FLN member of French West Indian descent, whose philosophical writings continue to inform postcolonial studies. One can note striking similarities in the views of the two revolutionary thinkers. They both viewed the world in Manichean terms and disdained the national bourgeoisie that served as handmaidens to Western imperialism. Neither saw the possibility or even desirability of rapprochement with the capitalist world. Perhaps most importantly, both men were humanists; they emphasized the commonalities linking oppressed peoples everywhere and sought to build solidarity by transcending the class, racial, ethnic, religious, and sectarian divides that have long plagued humankind.[57] They believed this could happen only if a people's national consciousness evolved to a higher level – that of "a common cause, of a national destiny, and of a collective history."[58] They shared an emphasis on the tricontinental nature of the revolutionary struggle, and both believed that in order to build a new society, the structures of the colonial system must be destroyed and a new consciousness created.

As for how the countries of the Third World should conduct themselves in an international system divided between capitalism and socialism, Fanon and Guevara agreed: "The Third World ought not to be content to define itself in the terms of values which have preceded it. On the contrary, the underdeveloped countries ought to do their utmost to find their own particular values and methods and a style which shall be peculiar to them."[59] Che held a deeper respect for communism than did Fanon, but he agreed that the Soviet model did not fit seamlessly with the conditions of Latin America and Africa. For him, it was impossible "to realize socialism with the aid of the worn-out weapons left by capitalism" because the "economic base has undermined the development of

---

[56] Piero Gleijeses, "Cuba's First Venture in Africa: Algeria, 1961–1965," *Journal of Latin American Studies* 28:1 (February 1996): 159–161. For more on the Cuban-Algerian relationship, see Jeffrey James Byrne, Chapter 6 in this volume.

[57] Clive W. Kronenberg, "Manifestations of Humanism in Revolutionary Cuba: Che and the Principle of Universality," *Latin American Perspectives* 36:2 (March 2009): 66–80.

[58] Frantz Fanon, *The Wretched of the Earth* (New York: Grove Press, 1963), 93.

[59] Ibid., 99.

consciousness." In order "to construct communism simultaneously with the material base of our society, we must create a new man." Che sought a merger of socialism and Third World internationalism, wherein the mobilization of the masses would be achieved by moral rather than material incentives.[60] Indeed, for Che, the "ultimate and most important revolutionary ambition" was "to see man liberated from his alienation," a theme common to Third World theorists.[61] Both Fanon and Che argued that their parties would be the vanguard. They rejected the necessity of waiting for the "objective conditions" of a revolution to ripen and argued that such conditions could be created by revolutionary movements. "Africa will not be free through the mechanical development of material forces," Fanon wrote in 1960, "but it is the hand of the African and his brain that will set into motion and implement the dialectics of the liberation of the continent."[62]

If Algeria offered the first concrete example of solidarity, then the Congo became the prime illustration of why such cooperation was needed, especially after the 1961 assassination of Patrice Lumumba. Many progressives and socialists around the world viewed Lumumba as a symbol of the anti-imperialist struggle, and many Cubans interpreted his assassination as evidence that the forces of imperialism would not relinquish power without a fight. Though Che blamed Lumumba's murder on the "imperialists," he acknowledged that the Congolese prime minister had made some mistakes. He put too much trust in the United Nations and international law and failed to understand that the imperialists could be defeated only via force of arms.[63] Guevara would go on to lead an advisory mission to the Congo in support of Congolese revolutionary Laurent Kabila. In order to blend in with the Africans, the mission was composed overwhelmingly of Afro-Cubans, including Che's second-in-command, Víctor Dreke.[64]

Guevara's dream of a Cuban-aided African revolution would not be realized until after his death. Although the Cubans were successful in

---

[60] Ernesto Che Guevara, "Socialism and Man in Cuba," in Bonachea and Valdes, eds., *Che: Selected Works of Ernesto Guevara*, 159.

[61] Ibid., 162. See also R. Joseph Parrott, Chapter 9 in this volume, on Amílcar Cabral.

[62] "Unity and Effective Solidarity are the Conditions for African Liberation" [*El Moudjahid*, No. 58, January 5, 1960] in Frantz Fanon, *Toward the African Revolution* (New York and London: Monthly Review Press, 1967), 173.

[63] Piero Gleijeses, *Conflicting Missions: Havana, Washington, and Africa, 1959–1976* (Chapel Hill: University of North Carolina Press, 2002), 77.

[64] Víctor Dreke, *De la Sierra del Escambray al Congo: En la Vorágine de la Revolución Cubana* (New York: Pathfinder, 2002), 123–124.

infiltrating 150 men into eastern Congo in early 1965, they found Kabila's forces undisciplined, surprisingly small in number, and divided along ethnic and political lines. There was little sense of shared struggle or will to coordinate forces. Though Che tried to instill the lessons of the Cuban guerrilla experience, he found students inattentive and overly attached to superstitions he perceived as limiting their interest in training.[65] With more Cuban instructors than recruits, Che left the Congo before the year was out.[66] The only bright spot in this "history of a failure" was that Che made contact with Agostinho Neto, leader of the People's Movement for the Liberation of Angola (MPLA).[67] Neto requested instructors, weapons, and equipment to train and arm MPLA cadres and showed interest in fighting alongside experienced Cuban guerrillas.[68] In agreeing to these requests, Guevara unknowingly laid the groundwork for the later Cuban military intervention in the Angolan Civil War, which pitted the MPLA against US-backed anti-communist forces after the country's independence in 1975. At the height of Cuban involvement in sub-Saharan Africa in the 1980s, nearly 40,000 Cuban combat troops actively protected the MPLA from both domestic foes and the neighboring South African military. The psychological and material costs of this war contributed to the ultimate collapse of apartheid.[69]

Guevara's failure in the Congo did not blunt the Cuban commitment to revolution. Though Che was the most vocal proponent of guerrilla tactics, much of the Cuban leadership shared his belief that only revolution on a global scale would transform the international system and that Cuba functioned as the vanguard for this global revolution. This was the motivation for the Castro regime to work together with Algeria's Ahmed Ben Bella (until his ousting in mid-1965) to organize the first Tricontinental Conference, convened in Havana in January 1966. The conference sought to define and organize a tricontinental revolution by integrating the "two great contemporary currents of the World Revolution" – the Soviet-led socialist revolution and the "parallel current of the revolution for national

[65] Edward George, *The Cuban Intervention in Angola, 1965–1991: From Che Guevara to Cuito Cuanavale* (London and New York: Routledge, 2005), 29–30.
[66] Gleijeses, *Conflicting Missions*, 111-115.
[67] Ernesto "Che" Guevara, *The African Dream: The Diaries of the Revolutionary War in the Congo* (New York: Grove Press, 1999), 1.
[68] George, *The Cuban Intervention in Angola*, 22–23.
[69] See Piero Gleijeses, *Visions of Freedom: Havana, Washington, Pretoria, and the Struggle for Southern Africa, 1976–1991* (Chapel Hill: University of North Carolina Press, 2013), and George, *The Cuban Intervention in Angola*.

liberation."[70] The goal, then, was to bridge the ideological differences that fueled the Sino-Soviet split, replacing it with revolutionary unity on the Cuban model. Accordingly, Castro openly criticized the Chinese leadership in his remarks, even as the general commitment to armed struggle adopted elements of the more aggressive Maoist approach to revolution that made the Soviets uneasy.[71] The peoples of Asia, Africa, and Latin America, the conference collectively concluded, "must answer imperialist violence with revolutionary violence."[72] This was the type of revolutionary syncretism, drawing on a wide base of support from the Second and Third Worlds, that informed the Cuban model of revolution, which Che was attempting to export.

Still abroad weighing his next move after the Congo debacle, Guevara's absence was notable, but the message he sent epitomized his vision of Tricontinental unity. Disunity hobbled Kabila's Congolese revolution, and it had undermined the prospects for global revolution. As the Soviet Union, China, and the nations of the Third World squabbled in the years preceding the Tricontinental Conference, the United States deployed troops in the Dominican Republic and South Vietnam. Would-be revolutionaries had to recognize that "Yankee imperialism" – the "fortress of colonialism and neocolonialism" as the Cubans described it – represented the "greatest enemy of world peace" and constituted "public enemy number one of all the peoples of the world."[73] Che argued that resistance to the United States was the locus of unity for the struggles of the world's downcast. Those on the frontlines of the struggle required the support of both the Third World and the socialist countries – what he and others referred to as the "progressive forces of the world." Specifically, he lamented the "sad reality" that Vietnam "is tragically alone," putting most of the blame for the plight of the Vietnamese people on the shoulders of US imperialism but also condemning those "who hesitated to make Vietnam an inviolable part of the socialist world." The Tricontinental strategy aimed at the complete destruction of imperialism and the creation

[70] "Introduction," *First Solidarity Conference of the Peoples of Africa, Asia, and Latin America* (Havana: General Secretariat of OSPAAAL, 1966).
[71] See Jeremy Friedman, Chapter 7 in this volume. See also his monograph, *Shadow Cold War: The Sino-Soviet Competition for the Third World* (Chapel Hill: University of North Carolina Press, 2015).
[72] "Antecedents and Objectives of the Movement of Solidarity of the Peoples of Africa, Asia, and Latin America," in *First Solidarity Conference of the Peoples of Africa, Asia, and Latin America*, 22.
[73] Ibid., 26.

of truly independent nations, but to achieve this goal, progressive govern-
ments had to encourage and support those actively fighting against the
United States and its capitalist allies; there had to be "two, three ... many
Vietnams."[74]

The conference established the Latin American Solidarity Organization
(OLAS), which was to be permanently headquartered in Havana. Castro
used the August 1967 OLAS conference to snub the Soviets, ensuring that
most delegations were headed by noncommunist revolutionary leaders
and issuing provocative statements that were clearly aimed at Moscow. In
his closing speech, Castro criticized those who suggested the possibility of
a peaceful transition to socialism and asserted that armed violence was the
irrevocable course of the revolution in Latin America.[75]

THE ILL-FATED BOLIVIAN ADVENTURE

Guevara chose Bolivia to launch the continental campaign because he
viewed it as ripe for revolution. In 1964, General René Barrientos had
staged a coup against President Víctor Paz Estenssoro of the leftist
Movimiento Nacionalista Revolucionario (MNR). Víctor Paz had come
to power in 1952 after an insurrection of armed tin miners, Indian
peasants, and labor unionists forced a reluctant military to honor his
democratic election two years prior. Guevara, who had visited the country
in 1953, believed that the MNR was insufficiently radical, even though
Víctor Paz had enacted meaningful agrarian reform, nationalized the tin
mining companies, and granted universal suffrage.[76] After the coup,
Barrientos pledged to continue these reforms but kept the peace through
increasingly repressive measures, alienating key rural constituencies from
the government in La Paz.

Rising political frustration combined with several other factors to
make revolution seem feasible. First, Guevara believed that the Bolivian
army and security forces were too small and weak to effectively confront
a guerrilla challenge. Second, he believed that the United States would be
slow to react to an insurgency there, despite evidence of intense US interest

---

[74] Guevara, *Message to the Tricontinental*.

[75] Fidel Castro Speech at LASO Closing Session, August 11, 1967. Castro Speech Database:
http://lanic.utexas.edu/project/castro/db/1967/19670811.html

[76] Thomas C. Field, *From Development to Dictatorship: Bolivia and the Alliance for
Progress in the Kennedy Era* (Ithaca and London: Cornell University Press, 2014), 5;
Carta a Tita Infante, Lima, setiembre 3, 1953, in Guevara Lynch, *Aquí va un soldado*, 21–
22.

in Bolivia in the framework of the Alliance for Progress.[77] Guevara seemed to hope that that the *foco* would inspire others throughout South America, so that if the United States did intervene, it would sink into a quagmire. Third, the geographical location of the country in the heart of South America was seen as a strategic center from which the revolution could spread. Fourth, Mario Monje, General Secretary of the Bolivian Communist Party, agreed to provide logistical support, contacts, and cadres to the effort.[78] Finally, the political circumstances of Bolivia's neighbors were not viewed as favorable. Though Che initially hoped to launch a *foco* in his homeland under the command of his friend and fellow Argentine Jorge Masetti, the column was destroyed by the harsh climate of northern Argentina, its inability to attract local support, and ruthless Argentine security forces. Neighboring Peru, meanwhile, boasted a popularly elected civilian government that was embarking upon a program of moderately progressive reforms and an army that had effectively suppressed several guerrilla insurgencies in the two years before Che set out for Bolivia.[79]

From the outset, though, Che found the conditions for revolution had been greatly exaggerated. At the Tricontinental Conference, Monje, as head of the Bolivian delegation, deceived the Cubans about the revolutionary potential of Bolivia and about the Bolivian Communist Party's own intentions to launch a guerrilla *foco*. Bolivia's communist left had split into two factions, with Monje's Bolivian Communist Party remaining loyal to Moscow and the New Bolivian Communist Party aligning with Beijing. Moreover, the majority of Bolivian Marxists identified with neither of these parties, but instead belonged to an array of other groups – most of them more powerful than the two communist parties – ranging from the Trotskyite Workers' Revolutionary Party to the governing MNR. The rigidly orthodox Monje added to Guevara's frustrations, insisting that any revolution must be party led. He refused to recognize the authority of a commander who was not a card-carrying communist and prevented the Bolivian communists who trained in Cuba from joining

[77] Gordon H. McCormick and Mark T. Berger, "Ernesto (Che) Guevara: The Last 'Heroic' Guerrilla," *Studies in Conflict & Terrorism* 42:4 (2019): 349; Field, *From Development to Dictatorship*.

[78] "'Red Beard,' Che's Compañero, Interview by Claudia Furiati," in Manuel "Barbarroja" Piñeiro, *Che Guevara and the Latin American Revolution* (Melbourne: Ocean Press, 2006), 50; "CNN Interview with Lucia Newman," ibid., 66–67.

[79] Richard Harris, *Death of a Revolutionary: Che Guevara's Last Mission* (New York: W. W. Norton & Co., 1970), 65–66.

Che's group. The communists promised aid and support that they never had any intention of delivering, and they may have even provided the Bolivian authorities with information regarding Che's whereabouts.[80]

Ultimately, the Bolivian disaster demonstrated that Che's model of guerrilla warfare, based on a selective reading of the Cuban experience, was not readily generalizable and that he neglected the unique aspects of the Cuban Revolution to his own peril.[81] In addition to discounting the key role urban revolutionaries played in the 26th of July Movement, Guevara's overweening dedication to militant confrontation led him to eschew the sort of tactical compromises that Castro had pursued in order to broaden cooperation among the various anti-Batista elements. Most importantly, Guevara overestimated Bolivian popular revolutionary sentiment and ultimately failed to gain local support. Even though Barrientos had seized power via a military coup, he was then popularly elected in 1966 (albeit facing little opposition). He traveled extensively through Bolivia, giving speeches to the Indians in Aymara and Quechua and promising further economic and social programs. Che viewed these and earlier reforms as insufficiently radical, but many Bolivian workers and peasants disagreed. Most remained invested in their society and felt they had already experienced their revolution for national liberation under Víctor Paz. Ultimately, perhaps the fundamental ingredient missing from Che's *foco* was that its cause was not viewed as just by the majority of Bolivians.

Furthermore, the response of the Barrientos regime to the presence of the guerrillas was highly effective. The Bolivian president requested the assistance of the CIA in the counterinsurgency campaign to eradicate Che's *foco* but was still able to portray the campaign in a nationalist light because most members of Guevara's group were Cuban and not Bolivian. He repeatedly drew attention to the foreign nature of the guerrilla movement and portrayed himself as a staunch defender of Bolivian law and order. In a deft move to appeal to Bolivia's radical left, Barrientos even appointed four Marxists to his cabinet during the period of Che's guerrilla activity in the country. Though he faced criticism from right-wing circles, he explained that he was not opposed to Marxists so long as they worked within the democratic process. With limited popular

---

[80] "CNN Interview with Lucia Newman," in Piñeiro, *Che Guevara and the Latin American Revolution*, 70–71, "Che and Bolivia, Interview with Italian journalists Ana María Lobouno and Francesco Loquercio," ibid., 98–99; Harris, *Death of a Revolutionary*, 159.
[81] McCormick and Berger, "The Last 'Heroic' Guerrilla," 354.

support, Guevara's early success in battles against the Bolivian security forces gave way to months of frustration. On October 9, 1967, he was captured and executed by a Bolivian Ranger unit that had received counterinsurgency training from US Army Special Forces.[82]

AFTERMATH AND LEGACIES

Though there was a tremendous outpouring of grief among Latin America's radical left, Che's capture and execution were virtually ignored in Moscow. A brief *Pravda* obituary praised his "deep devotion to the cause of the revolutionary liberation of the peoples and great personal courage and fearlessness," but the only public commemoration of Che's life was a rally held by a small group of Latin American students from Moscow's Patrice Lumumba People's Friendship University.[83] Soviet news media continued to disparage the brand of revolutionary "adventurism" that Che exemplified, and a month after his execution, Brezhnev gave a speech in which he declared that socialist revolutions should only be launched in countries where the necessary objective conditions for revolution had already been fulfilled. The message was a clear reference to Che's failure in Bolivia. Orthodox communist parties in Latin America followed suit, issuing denunciations of armed struggle and declaring their loyalty to the CPSU line.

The death of Che and the obliteration of the nascent Bolivian *foco* he had nurtured, combined with guerrilla defeats in Guatemala, Colombia, and Venezuela, contributed to an improvement in Cuba's relations with the USSR. Though Castro continued to aid revolutionary movements, he was more selective in determining which ones to support. He continued to advocate the armed struggle but softened his rhetoric about the inevitability of violence.[84] By refusing to condemn the 1968 Soviet invasion of Czechoslovakia, Castro signaled his support for Moscow's foreign policy. Though his speech about the episode contained several veiled criticisms of the Soviets, it marked a turning point after which Soviet-Cuban relations were closer and less contentious. In 1972, Cuba became a member of the

---

[82] Felix I. Rodriguez and John Weisman, *Shadow Warrior* (New York: Simon and Schuster, 1989), 9–18; Harris, *Death of a Revolutionary*, 126–130.

[83] "In Memory of Ernesto Che Guevara," *Pravda*, October 18, 1967, *The Current Digest of the Russian Press*, 1967, No. 42, Vol. 19.

[84] Soviet embassy in the Republic of Cuba, November 21, 1967. Cuban press coverage of the 50th anniversary of the Great October Socialist Revolution (press review). F. 104, Op. 22, P. 18, D. 9, L. 30, AVPRF.

Council for Mutual Economic Assistance (CMEA), the Soviet-led economic assistance organization comprising the socialist bloc countries.
Later in the year, a series of bilateral trade, economic, and financial
agreements reshaped the Cuban economy along Soviet lines, eventually
making the island's economic dependence on Moscow almost total.
Cuban officials now loyally defended Soviet policy positions in international organizations, especially the Non-Aligned Movement and the
United Nations, but so too did the USSR become a key backer of Cuban
support for Third World nationalism, actively aiding Castro's support for
communist governments in Angola and Ethiopia in the 1970s and 1980s.

Che's radicalism and his fierce devotion to spreading the revolution
would continue to inspire armed revolutionaries in Latin America, even
after the fall of the Berlin Wall and the complete collapse of Soviet-style
communism in Europe. Yet Che's ideals and actions had exacerbated
tensions in the Cuban-Soviet alliance and provoked the wrath of
Washington. The ideological and theoretical hair-splitting that distinguished the *Fidelistas* from the Maoists from the pro-Soviet factions
undermined the unity and cooperation necessary for effective action.
The United States, unwilling to tolerate the rise of any leftist regime,
happily took advantage of divisions by consolidating alliances with
a range of Latin American dictatorships. The Pentagon designed and
disseminated counterinsurgency tactics to stamp out the spreading influence of *Fidelista* and other Marxist-inspired guerrilla groups. The
Vietnams that Che sought to inspire in South America failed as US
counterinsurgency doctrine and training spread across the continent,
culminating in Operation Condor, a transnational network of right-
wing violence and oppression of the Marxist left.[85] In the United States,
though some radical groups answered Che's call (perhaps most infamously, the Weathermen), ultimately US society managed to cleave together
in the maintenance of the status quo.[86]

Nevertheless, the internationalism and solidarity that Che epitomized
continue to animate Cuban foreign policy into the twenty-first century.
Cuba provides humanitarian aid to dozens of countries in Africa, Asia, the

[85] For more, see John Dinges, *The Condor Years: How Pinochet and His Allies Brought Terrorism to Three Continents* (New York: The New Press, 2004); Peter Kornbluh, *The Pinochet File: A Declassified Dossier on Atrocity and Accountability* (New York: The New Press, 2013); and J. Patrice McSherry, *Predatory States: Operation Condor and Covert War in Latin America* (Lanham, MD: Rowman & Littlefield, 2005).
[86] See Jeremy Prestholdt, "Resurrecting Che: Radicalism, the Transnational Imagination, and the Politics of Heroes," *Journal of Global History* 7:3 (2012): 506–526.

Middle East, and Europe alongside emergency support, especially medical and health workers, to countries suffering from natural disasters. Thousands of students from all over the world received free medical education at the Latin American School of Medicine in Havana. Cuba even provided health care to children affected by the 1986 nuclear accident in Chernobyl.[87] Moreover, Che distinguished himself as an economic philosopher whose ideas shaped the Cuban economy and continue to inspire progressives worldwide. Many of the items on his agenda would appear in the 1970s in the guise of the New International Economic Order (NIEO), a political project aimed at enshrining the economic sovereignty of the postcolonial states. The major proponents of the program advocated a complete restructuring of global economic relations along lines similar to those Che sketched out at the 1961 Punta del Este conference.[88] The NIEO ultimately suffered the same fate as Che's Tricontinental revolutionary vision. Both fell victim not only to the dominance of the industrialized capitalist world, headed by the United States, but also to the continuing appeal of nationalism and the enduring primacy of national interests.

---

[87] Richard L. Harris, "Cuban Internationalism, Che Guevara, and the Survival of Cuba's Socialist Regime," *Latin American Perspectives* 36:3 (May 2009): 36–37.

[88] Nils Gilman, "The New International Economic Order: A Reintroduction," *Humanity* 6:1 (Spring 2015): 1–16; Johanna Bockman, "Socialist Globalization against Capitalist Neocolonialism: The Economic Ideas behind the New International Economic Order," *Humanity* 6:1 (Spring 2015): 109–128.

I I

From Playa Girón to Luanda

Mercenaries and Internationalist Fighters

Eric Covey

> Marx discovered and history has confirmed that the capitalist and the
> worker are the principal opposed personages of our time, and the mercenary
> and the internationalist fighter embody the same irreconcilable opposition.
>
> Raul Valdez Vivo[1]

In some ways, the year 1976 represented the peak of Tricontinental
solidarity. Cuban soldiers operating halfway around the world in the
former Portuguese colony of Angola helped consolidate power for the
leftist Movimento Popular de Libertação de Angola (People's
Movement for the Liberation of Angola, or MPLA) in the face of
concerted opposition. They repelled a coalition of local nationalist
parties, South African soldiers, and covert Western assistance that
sought to deny the MPLA its claim to authority in the months after
independence. By the time Fidel Castro visited Guinea in June 1976,
much of the world recognized the MPLA as the legitimate government
of Angola, and the trial of thirteen mercenaries in Luanda revealed the
extent of intervention. In Conakry, Castro hailed the victory as a blow
to global imperialism with a distinct regional importance (Figure 11.1).
"In Angola," he claimed, "the white mercenaries were destroyed along
with their myth and so was the myth of the invincibility of the South
African racists."[2]

---

[1] Raul Valdes Vivo, *Angola: An End to the Mercenaries' Myth*, trans. Anonymous (New
Delhi: People's Publishing House, 1976), 90–91. Quotations throughout are from the
English-language edition of this text.

[2] Ibid., 9.

FIGURE 11.1 "Angola is for the US imperialists an African Girón," asserts this poster. Both Cuba and Angola viewed the MPLA's victory over US-backed forces as a black eye for Washington, and many in the United States agreed. Southern Africa was the major arena for Cuban foreign policy for the next decade, and Southern African revolutionaries praised Cuban efforts opposing apartheid. Departamento de Orientación Revolucionaria, 1976. Image from private collection of Richard Knight; reproduced under fair use guidelines.

During the prior decade, mercenaries emerged as one of the most persistent challenges to socialist revolution in Africa. In the Congo, white soldiers of fortune hailing from South Africa, Rhodesia, and former metropoles subdued rebellions and led the armies of Western-aligned governments. A myth of invincibility grew up around these forces as they won major victories with small numbers. When Cuba first began to envision a global revolutionary solidarity, it consciously sought to combat this mercenary challenge, which Castro described in his speech closing the 1966 Havana Conference as "one of the most subtle and perfidious stratagems of Yankee imperialism."[3] Yet the reference was not merely to soldiers of fortune or mercenary companies like the one Mike Hoare assembled in the Congo. Rather, Castro targeted a range of figures working on behalf of Euro-American interests, including the forces of South Vietnam in 1966 and the failed exile invasion of Cuba at Playa Girón in 1961.

For Cuba, mercenarism represented the violent edge of neocolonialism: the coalition of Western advisors, local allies, covertly funded exiles, and soldiers-for-hire that limited the expansion of revolution through force. As the Cuban official Raul Valdez Vivo explained, "as long as there is imperialism, there will be mercenaries."[4] This expansive definition never became widely adopted, but it reflected an inescapable reality. The wealthy United States and its powerful allies had a spectrum of options to respond to revolution. They used different forces in order to balance strategic necessity, material cost, and the effects on US prestige. Soldiers-for-hire offered Western governments ways to augment local forces while maintaining "plausible deniability," but so did the use of covert forces and to some extent the arming of client states.[5]

The Cuban concept of mercenarism sought to capture the calculations behind these options and was central to the militant Tricontinental worldview. Opposite mercenaries were revolutionary internationalist fighters, embodied in the figure of Che Guevara. Both these opposing forces consisted of foreign militants fighting alongside rebels or for governments, but they had different motivations and relationships to allied movements or states. Cuban leaders believed there was a distinctly unequal power

[3] Fidel Castro, "At the Closing Session of the Tricontinental Conference," January 15, 1966, US Information Agency: http://lanic.utexas.edu/project/castro/db/1966/19660216.html.
[4] Vivo, *Angola*, 70.
[5] Klaas Voß, "Plausibly Deniable: Mercenaries in US Covert Interventions During the Cold War, 1964–1987," *Cold War History* 16:1 (2016): 40.

relationship between mercenaries and their employers. Wealthy Western governments – or sometimes companies – retained anti-revolutionary agents to protect their interests either by direct payments (traditional mercenaries) or indirect benefits provided to local clients or client states, which included assurances of power, weapons, or other forms of aid. These local clients were motivated by self-aggrandizement, individual gain, or class promotion. By contrast, revolutionary solidarity drove the internationalist fighter, who sought to support the global struggle against empire and capitalism. Internationalist fighters operated not independently but rather as representatives of formerly colonized states or liberation movements (considered postcolonial governments in waiting). As Cuba's internationalist fighters confronted mercenaries in Africa, the nation's leaders emphasized identarian politics to further reinforce the distinction between Global North and South. Thus, by the 1970s, the internationalist fighter became a politicized symbol of cross-racial solidarity in the struggle against the necessarily interlinked "white mercenary," imperialism, and neocolonialism.

Scholars have paid little attention to the ideologies that animate opposition to mercenaries and mercenarism. Yet thinking about the Castro government's conceptualization of these phenomena and Cuba's actions in Africa (see Map 9.1) reveal important elements about how a key branch of Tricontinentalism understood neocolonialism, internationalism, and the distinct power dynamics that damned the former while legitimating the latter. This chapter will consider this concept through four lenses: the Cuban response to the Playa Girón invasion, the extended challenge of mercenaries in the Congo, the Cuban intervention in Angola, and finally efforts to establish a body of law to control the use of mercenary force.[6] Taken together, these events reveal that, despite setbacks, Cuba's internationalist fighters scored significant victories against mercenaries, particularly in Angola. But Cuba's articulation of this spectrum of neocolonial violence, in which mercenarism was a key strategic part, struggled to gain support beyond Castro's immediate allies. As events in the Congo and Angola raised global concern about freelance soldiers, states responded by drafting international laws that ignored Cuba's expansive view and ultimately failed to resolve the challenge of mercenary

---

[6] I argue, following Cynthia Enloe, that mercenary force "is not just a legal phenomenon but also a historical and cultural one, with strong connections to nationalism and capital" and an ambiguous relationship to states. Eric Covey, *Americans at War in the Ottoman Empire: US Mercenary Force in the Ottoman Empire* (London: I.B. Tauris, 2019), 3, 5.

force. Nevertheless, this Cuban conceptualization of mercenarism provides a window into Tricontinentalism: its global vision, concrete solidarity, and ultimate inability to change the structure of the international
system.

MERCENARIES AND TRICONTINENTAL SOLIDARITY

The shifting role of mercenaries in the modern world has been well
documented by scholars.[7] The once common practice of hiring soldiers
from elsewhere became controversial amidst the nationalist revolutions
of the nineteenth century. Yet soldiers-for-hire did not wholly disappear, and mercenaries thrived as instruments of neocolonialism in
Latin America.[8] They served as security for US companies – effectively
extralegal armies – protecting and promoting national interests in
between regular invasions and occupations by marines. In effect, Latin
America anticipated the reality many postcolonial nations in Asia and
Africa confronted during the Cold War. The Cuban concept of mercenarism evolved from this context, linking Cold War interventions to
this longer history of foreign adventurism, filibustering, and economic
domination.

The US-supported invasion at Playa Girón, known in English as the Bay
of Pigs, led the Castro government to begin articulating its Tricontinental
definition of mercenarism. On April 17, 1961, about 1,500 CIA-trained,
anti-Castro exiles – the military wing of the Frente Revolucionario
Democrático (FRD), self-styled as Brigade 2506 – landed at Bahía de
Cochinos. When internal uprisings failed to materialize and President
John Kennedy declined to provide US naval and air support, the Castro
government overpowered the invasion force and captured about 1,200
members of Brigade 2506. Cuba subsequently tried and convicted the
exiles for treason. Though many returned to the United States in exchange
for prisoners and medicine in late 1962, a handful were executed.[9] The

---

[7] See, for example, Janice E. Thomson, *Mercenaries, Pirates, and Sovereigns: State-Building
and Extraterritorial Violence in Early Modern Europe* (Princeton, NJ: Princeton University
Press, 1994).

[8] See, for example, Lester D. Langley and Thomas David Schoonover, *The Banana Men:
American Mercenaries and Entrepreneurs in Central America, 1880–1930* (Lexington:
University Press of Kentucky, 1995).

[9] See James G. Blight and Peter Kornbluh, eds., *Politics of Illusion: The Bay of Pigs Invasion
Reexamined* (Boulder: Lynne Rienner Publishers, 1998); Juan Carlos Rodriguez, *The
Inevitable Battle: From the Bay of Pigs to Playa Giron* (Havana: Editorial Capitan San
Luis, 2009).

members of Brigade 2506 viewed themselves as representatives of a legitimate anti-Castro political movement – "freedom loving, Cuban patriots from all walks of life" – but Cuba labeled them mercenaries.[10] Though mercenaries remained undefined in international law, the Castro government used the term to delegitimize political opposition by linking it to outside meddling.

At the center of the issue was the question whether the members of Brigade 2506 acted on their own or on behalf of the United States. The Castro government believed the latter, laying out its logic in a collection of documents published in Havana as *Historia De Una Agresión: El Juicio a Los Mercenarios De Playa Girón*. The March 1962 indictment stated that the "mercenary brigade" was "trained, armed, directed, and paid by the imperialist Government of the United States of America."[11] In fact, the CIA spent a year and $4.4 million molding disparate exile groups into a cohesive opposition.[12] *Historia De Una Agresión* took pride in uncovering the agency's central role, detailing secret meetings from Havana to New York and a string of Caribbean training camps from Puerto Rico through Louisiana to Guatemala.[13] Collaboration with the imperial power immediately called into question the legitimacy and authenticity of the nationalism claimed by Brigade 2506, with the Cuban government arguing its members represented foreign interests. It noted that many members of the brigade planned to recover nationalized property. For Cubans, these counterrevolutionary goals meant that the invaders' motives were "purely economic, purely at the service of a foreign country."[14] For Castro, who warned of "mercenary armies" as early as 1960, these actions confirmed that opponents of the revolution had become paid agents of the United States determined to undermine Cuban sovereignty.[15]

Cuba argued that the mercenary was a vital component of the neocolonial variety of imperialism practiced by the United States.

---

[10] Haynes Johnson, *The Bay of Pigs: The Leaders' Story of Brigade 2506* (New York: Norton, 1964). "The Brigade," 2018, Bay of Pigs Veterans Association: www.bopva.org/the-history.

[11] *History of an Aggression: The Trial of the Playa Giron Mercenaries* (Havana: Ediciones Venceremos, 1964), 39. Quotations throughout are from the English-language edition published two years after its Spanish counterpart.

[12] Jack B. Pfeiffer, *Official History of the Bay of Pigs Operation*, Vol. I: Air Operations, March 1960–April 1961 (Central Intelligence Agency, 1979), V, 408–413.

[13] *History of an Aggression*, 76, 81, 131.   [14] Ibid., 201.

[15] Tad Szulc, "Castro Resumes Talk of Invasion," *New York Times*, March 27, 1960.

The use of mercenary force allowed the United States and allied capitalist states to intervene against revolution with limited responsibility or liability.[16] Long familiar to Latin America, this practice became common across the 1960s Third World as decolonization ended European political control without dissolving the strong economic ties of empire. The first flashpoint in this new reality was the former Belgian Congo. When the country gained independence in June 1960 under the leadership of the outspoken Prime Minister Patrice Lumumba, the powerful Anglo-Belgian mining company Union Minière du Haut-Katanga encouraged the secession of the mineral-rich southeastern province of Katanga under the businessman Moïse Tshombe. Tshombe accused Lumumba of communist sympathies and built a local gendarme under the leadership of Belgian officers, many of whom remained as mercenaries when colonial troops withdrew after independence. Worried Lumumba might lean toward the Soviet Union, Belgium and the United States quietly supported the assassination of the independent-minded nationalist by Katangan authorities in January 1961. Lumumba's death caused international outrage, and fellow African leaders criticized Tshombe for seceding with the aid of white mercenaries, implying a betrayal of carefully intertwined racial and anti-imperial solidarities that helped bind together postcolonial states. On February 21, 1961, less than two months before the invasion of Cuba, the UN Security Council sought to calm tensions by urging foreign forces, including "mercenaries," to withdraw from the Congo.[17]

Cubans understood the regime's victory at Playa Girón in this broader context. As the United States and its Western allies turned to mercenary force to police imperial boundaries where they had no direct control, the small Caribbean island fought back and won. Though isolated within its own hemisphere, where the Organization of American States (OAS) suspended the country because its "Marxist–Leninist government" was "incompatible with the principles and objectives of the inter-American system," Cuba found new allies.[18] First among these was the Soviet Union, which aided the island and adopted some of its ideological

---

[16] *History of an Aggression*, 288.
[17] Security Council, "Resolution of 21 February 1961," *S/4741* (United Nations: 1961).
[18] Eighth Meeting of Consultation of Ministers of Foreign Affairs, Punta Del Este, Uruguay, January 22–31 (Washington, DC: Pan American Union, 1962).

language in order to needle the United States. In a March 1962 Security Council meeting, the Soviet ambassador claimed that the United States was "preparing within its own armed forces units of mercenaries to engage in a new intervention against Cuba."[19] So too did Africans, Asians, and even North Americans see in small, embattled Cuba an example of resistance to Euro-American empire.[20] After Playa Girón, the Cuban regime posited that the nation had become "a symbol, an emblem of the anti-imperialist struggle."[21]

Isolated as it was, Cuba looked to this new international status to safeguard its revolution. The Soviet Union's decision to deploy nuclear missiles on the island was, according to Che Guevara, linked to the insecurity created by "the mercenary attack at Playa Girón."[22] Yet while the resolution of the Cuban Missile Crisis included a modicum of protection from US invasion, the revolutionary government envisioned a global movement of small states that could take the offensive against the United States in a way the Soviets were not willing to undertake. Detailed in other chapters within this volume, notably those by Hernandez and Hosek, Byrne, and Friedman, this struggle took Cuba into the orbit of the Afro-Asian People's Solidarity Organization (AAPSO) and eventually led to the Tricontinental meeting in Havana of 1966. Key postcolonial leaders viewed European attempts to preserve economic and political power in their former colonies as analogous to the Latin American context, so they looked to Cuba as a model for reinforcing independence. The Moroccan leftist Mehdi Ben Barka predicted it would require either "Castroism" (revolution) or progressive political alliance to assure Africa would not become a neocolonial outpost for the Western powers.[23] In many ways, Cuba anticipated the problems its African allies would face. As a result, many states gradually adopted Castro's conception of neocolonial force as Africa became the center of mercenarism.

[19] Sam Pope Brewer, "Soviet Tells U.N. U.S. Perils Cuba," *New York Times*, March 16, 1962.

[20] North Vietnam regularly referenced Cuba, as did the Lusophone liberation parties discussed below.

[21] *History of an Aggression*, 365–366.

[22] Che Guevara, "At the United Nations (December 11, 1964)," in David Deutschmann, ed., *Che Guevara Reader: Writings on Politics & Revolution* (North Melbourne: Ocean Press, 2003), 325–339, quoted 333.

[23] Mehdi Ben Barka, *Écrits Politiques, 1957–1965* (Paris: Syllepse, 1999), 190.

THE MERCENARY AND THE INTERNATIONALIST FIGHTER
IN THE CONGO

For Cuba, mercenary force was part of a larger problem: wealthy Western countries feared socialist revolutions in the Third World and could choose from a range of options to undermine them. In terms of military responses, mercenaries involved minimal commitment but transgressed international norms, which inspired Cuba's liberal use of the term to denigrate US actions. Their sudden appearance in the Congo spoke directly to the Western decision to intervene in the Third World to protect economic and strategic interests. Postcolonial nations, long subsumed within Euro-American empires and lacking the resources to protect state sovereignty, struggled to respond to mercenary force. "Only the protégés of Yankee millionaires, representatives of slavery and wealth, representatives of fortune and privilege," Castro said, "can obtain the support of a navy or an army."[24] Even Soviet support failed to address this power imbalance, especially after the Cuban Missile Crisis illustrated the limits of Moscow's commitment to confronting the United States. Cuban leaders therefore concluded that Third World states had to unite to confront this capitalist imperial challenge. They would organize within the Non-Aligned Movement and United Nations to draft new legal frameworks for the international system, but there was a need for active defense in the short-term. The result was what became known as the internationalist fighter.

Two main characteristics distinguished the internationalist fighter from the mercenary, as these terms were understood in radical Third World circles. First, the internationalist fighter was a socialist.[25] Mercenaries were motivated by greed and personal gain. Cubans believed anti-communism was generally either ideological window dressing for or intertwined with these base motives. Internationalist fighters, by contrast, were selfless. They fought to defend a global revolution waged by Third World socialists for national self-determination and the transformation of the international system. This "new revolutionary subject," as Anne Garland Mahler describes it, was a direct refutation of the degradations of empire, including colonialism and neocolonialism.[26] "If the Yankee imperialist[s] feel free to bomb anywhere they please and send their

---

[24] *History of an Aggression*, 20.
[25] Richard L. Harris, "Cuban Internationalism, Che Guevara, and the Survival of Cuba's Socialist Regime," *Latin American Perspectives* 36:3 (May 2009): 27–42.
[26] Anne Garland Mahler, *From the Tricontinental to the Global South: Race, Radicalism, and Transnational Solidarity* (Durham, NC: Duke University Press, 2018), 97.

mercenary troops to put down the revolutionary movement anywhere in the world," Castro explained at the Havana Conference, "then the revolutionary peoples feel they have the right, even with their physical presence, to help the peoples who are fighting the Yankee imperialists." He went on to pledge "our revolutionary militants, our fighters, are prepared to fight the imperialists in any part of the world."[27]

Second, as the quote above shows, the internationalist fighter operated in solidarity with the world's oppressed people, not as a tool of domination. Governments employed mercenaries when they lacked legitimacy and sufficient support from local peoples to field a national force. Therefore, mercenaries fought against the best interests of the people (as revolutionaries saw it) on behalf of the Western powers, who either controlled client governments or undermined the independence of revolutionary states. In either case, mercenaries became agents of foreign domination. By contrast, the internationalist fighter fought alongside nationalist movements and governments in a bid to protect their rights to political and economic self-determination. At least in the ideal, this was a relationship of equals. Solidarity sought to bolster the nascent power of postcolonial governments.

The Congo became the first test of the worldview pitting the internationalist fighter against the neocolonial mercenary. Following the formation of the Democratic Republic of the Congo in 1964, the former head of secessionist Katanga, Moïse Tshombe, became prime minister. Faced with a rebellion by leftist supporters of the assassinated Lumumba, Tshombe turned to the West, specifically the United States, for aid. Fearing a "Commie field day in the Congo" but hesitant to intervene directly, Washington acted covertly.[28] It cajoled Belgium and employed mercenaries, repackaged as "military technicians" and volunteers, to prop up the weak government and defeat the Simba rebellion.[29] Recruited heavily from South Africa and Rhodesia (modern Zimbabwe) despite US preference for more Belgians and other Europeans, the mercenaries served as officers for the poorly trained Congolese army. They also formed the "cutting edge" of the government's military response as part of the all-white 5th Commando

---

[27] Castro, "At the Closing Session of the Tricontinental Conference."

[28] Telegram, Congo Station to CIA, August 10, 1964, Nina D. Howland et al., eds., *Foreign Relations of the United States, 1964–1968, Volume XXIII, Congo, 1960–1968* (Washington: United States Government Printing Office, 2013), 301. Hereafter, *FRUS*.

[29] Piero Gleijeses, "'Flee! The White Giants Are Coming!' The United States, the Mercenaries, and the Congo, 1964–65," *Diplomatic History* 18:2 (1994): 216–217, quoted 222.

unit under Colonel "Mad" Mike Hoare, an Indian-born Irish veteran of the British army who settled in South Africa and worked for Tshombe during the Katanga secession.[30] Though meant to operate quietly, the mercenaries gained notoriety in 1965 working alongside Belgian paratroopers to retake Stanleyville (Kisangani), where rebels held hundreds of European nationals hostage. The United States was essential in these efforts, providing funds, planning operations, and supplying transport for mercenaries and Belgian troops.[31] The CIA also arranged for air support and maritime interdiction of rebel aid, hiring Cuban exiles as contractors in order to limit US personnel to mostly advisory and technical roles.[32]

Castro's government believed the Congo confirmed its critique of US policy, including the mercenary nature of Cuban exiles, and provided an opportunity for the internationalist fighter. African governments were concerned about events in sub-Saharan Africa's largest country, and aid from radical states like Algeria increased after white mercenaries became involved. The Tshombe government appeared weak. "Northeast Congo," one US official noted in early 1965, "is really being held by only 110 mercenaries, supported by a peanut airforce."[33] Washington officials worried a small band of "well-trained 'enemy' mercenaries could conceivably take it all back again."[34] That such a small band was able to secure the large territory owed more to the exaggerated reputation the mercenaries acquired fighting poorly trained rebels over the past months than their actual military might. Believing the African continent ripe for revolution, Castro sent Che Guevara to organize a more effective rebellion.

Guevara found mostly frustration. With Cubans in the Congo at the joint request of the rebels and neighboring Tanzania, notes historian Piero Gleijeses, Guevara was constrained by respect for his hosts and the Congolese fear that public knowledge of the revolutionary icon's presence might draw a forceful Western response. And Guevara found that Cuba had overestimated the potential of the rebellion. He complained of poorly organized troops, questionable leadership, and little fighting spirit. Finally, African countries proved willing to accept the Western-backed

---

[30] Telegram, State to Congo Embassy, August 10, 1964, *FRUS*, 298.

[31] Telegram Congo Station to CIA, 10, 1964, *FRUS*, 301.

[32] Piero Gleijeses, *Conflicting Missions: Havana, Washington, and Africa, 1959–1976* (Chapel Hill: University of North Carolina Press, 2002), 134–135.

[33] Memo, Robert Komer to President Johnson, January 8, 1965, *FRUS*, 552.

[34] Memo, Komer to Bundy, April 3, 1965, *FRUS*, 597. United States officials used quotes or qualified when talking about the potential of "mercenaries" aiding the rebels, hinting at the different motivations of the internationalist fighter.

government in the Congo. When President Joseph Kasa-Vubu dismissed the controversial Tshombe and pledged to send all the "white mercenaries" home, the Organization of African Unity (OAU) withdrew aid from the Simba rebels. Tanzania, which served as Cuba's forward operating base, made peace with Congo in order to focus its support for the anti-colonial revolution in southern neighbor Mozambique. It requested Cuba end its operations in the Congo, and Havana agreed.[35]

Guevara's Congo venture did not go as planned, but there are two points worth noting. First, it illustrated a distinct contrast between Cuba's militant internationalism and Western intervention. Cuba's internationalist fighters were there as allies in solidarity with the leftist rebellion opposing the Tshombe regime, which many Africans viewed with suspicion due to its political and economic ties to Europe. While Che's reputation and Havana's assistance provided Cuba with influence, it generally deferred to the desires of its African allies even when these desires clashed with Cuban priorities. This approach contrasted with US involvement, wherein Washington knew the "kind of leverage we have" over the Congolese government and was not above threatening to "cut aid or pull out some planes."[36] While the United States did not always get its way, it achieved most of its goals in the Congo, in part by cajoling a reluctant Belgium to deploy troops and using powerful diplomatic tools to keep critical African governments at bay.

Second, Cuba did find partners in Africa, particularly among Lusophone revolutionaries. The strongest relationship developed with Amílcar Cabral and his successful Partido Africano da Independência da Guiné e Cabo Verde (PAIGC). Castro provided the party with important military and technical aid over the next decade, which likely encouraged Cabral to adopt Castro's concept of mercenaries. By 1970, he identified "mercenaries of various nationalities" as responsible for training counter-revolutionary forces in the Republic of Guinea and criticized the "African mercenaries" who supported the Portuguese attack on the PAIGC's exile home in Conakry.[37] Yet Cabral, though grateful for Cuban support, rejected Castro's offers for larger numbers of troops even as Portugal turned to mercenaries. His emphasis on the role revolution played in the construction of the new nation precluded the involvement of foreign

[35] Gleijeses, *Conflicting Missions*, 117–118, 139–140, 155–156.
[36] Memo, Saunders to Bundy, October 16, 1965, *FRUS*, 631.
[37] Amílcar Cabral, *Unity and Struggle: Speeches and Writings*, trans. Michael Wolfers (New York: Monthly Review Press, 1979), 184, 198–199.

soldiers, as R. Joseph Parrott notes in Chapter 9. Castro accepted this logic, adapting the idea of the internationalist fighter to the needs of the ally in question. Thus, the many doctors and technicians sent to train PAIGC operatives would be the most important contribution Cuban internationalists would make to an African revolution before the 1970s.[38]

A 1974 military coup that ended Portuguese colonialism created a new opportunity for Cuba. Castro had ties to the PAIGC's ally, the MPLA, the most avowedly socialist but least successful of the major leftist parties fighting Portuguese rule.[39] Over the next year, the MPLA vied militarily for control of Angola with two opposing parties linked to the West. The Cuban government agreed to provide aid to the Forças Armadas Populares de Libertação de Angola (FAPLA), the party's armed wing, when competition turned increasingly toward military confrontation. As the November transfer of power neared, it became clear that the MPLA's enemies were slowly uniting into a coalition supported by the Congo, South African troops, US weapons, and hired soldiers. Militant Tricontinentalism and the internationalist fighter finally had the chance to confront a Western intervention.

ANGOLA AND THE DEFEAT OF THE "WHITE MERCENARY"

The sudden end of Portugal's empire presented a number of geopolitical challenges. Scholars often explain US involvement, which aided the Frente Nacional de Libertação de Angola (FNLA) and the União Nacional para a Independência Total de Angola (UNITA), as a response to the arrival of Cuban forces in the country. But as Piero Gleijeses's exhaustive research shows, the CIA and South Africans were active in Angola before Cuba deployed its internationalist brigades in November 1975. President Ford authorized a covert war against the MPLA on July 18, 1975, beginning with a CIA investment worth $24.7 million.[40] Wary of deploying troops following the Vietnam War, US strategy again looked to allies and proxies, including mercenaries recruited to fight in northern Angola. Once it became clear that the United States and South Africa were in the process of intervening in Angolan affairs, MPLA head Agostinho Neto requested

---

[38] Gleijeses, *Conflicting Missions*, chapter 9.
[39] On the longer history of "Cuban-Angolan transatlanticism," see Stephen Henighan, "The Cuban Fulcrum and the Search for a Transatlantic Revolutionary Culture in Angola, Mozambique and Chile, 1965–2008," *Journal of Transatlantic Studies* 7:3 (2009): 233–248.
[40] Gleijeses, *Conflict Missions*, 12.

Castro's assistance. Cuba responded with what historian Jonathan Brown describes as "religious fervor."[41]

Cuban aid proved invaluable in helping the MPLA establish control of Angola. The few dozen advisors present in August 1975 grew to 500 officers and instructors by October. They brought with them rifles, trucks, and pilots to fly the MPLA's small air force. Supported by this Cuban assistance, the MPLA won some early victories, but the South African intervention aiding UNITA in the south and FNLA forces backed by the CIA and Portuguese mercenaries in the north pressed toward Luanda. In response, Cuba sent two planeloads of troops to fight alongside the MPLA.[42] With Soviet aid, Cuban troops helped the MPLA hold the capital of Luanda until independence on November 11. They pushed back two more offensives over the following months as the number of Cuban troops swelled past 15,000. Increased military success, combined with a strong global reaction to South African intervention, turned the tide in favor of the MPLA, which gained widespread recognition as Angola's ruling party by February 1976.

Cuban solidarity played a vital role in reinforcing MPLA sovereignty in the face of foreign intervention. The presence of internationalist fighters was no secret; news reports and sympathetic Westerners remarked on their presence, the latter differentiating them from mercenaries by referring to "Cuban volunteers."[43] The key difference was their identification with the MPLA and its cause. Neto argued they were "comrades who have felt the problems of our revolution, of our struggle, the problems of our people."[44] American officials also noted the foreign fighters' impact. CIA Director William Colby remarked cynically that Cuban soldiers had become the "mercenaries of the Communist world." Yet even Washington officials recognized that the motivation, organization, and public avowal of the Cuban deployment set them apart. "These are not mercenaries," the CIA's Africa chief reminded Colby, "they are regular Cuban troops." All admitted they had a powerful impact on events in Angola.[45]

---

[41] Jonathan C. Brown, *Cuba's Revolutionary World* (Cambridge, MA: Harvard University Press, 2017), 195.

[42] Gleijeses, *Conflicting Missions*, chapters 13–14.

[43] See, for example, Ole Gjerstad, *The People in Power* (Richmond, BC: Liberation Support Movement, 1976), 35.

[44] Agostinho Neto, *Speeches* (Luanda: DEPPI, 1980), 32.

[45] Memo for the Record, November 21, 1975, in Myra F. Burton, ed., *Foreign Relations of the United States, 1969–1976, Volume XXVIII, Southern Africa* (Washington, DC: U.S. Government Printing Office, 2011), 346–352. Hereafter, *FRUS* Southern Africa.

By contrast, the American-backed intervention proved a disaster. The covert aid provided by the United States became a global spectacle after South Africa intervened. The alliance between Angolans and the apartheid state elicited immediate regional condemnation. The sudden appearance (and capture) of white mercenaries, whom one MPLA official noted were "frequently" encountered in battle, caused additional consternation.[46] A US Congress still smarting from the Vietnam War moved to constrain a policy that lacked legitimacy, passing the Clark Amendment that barred covert activities in Angola without prior legislative approval. South Africa soon withdrew its troops, though it continued to support UNITA's guerrilla war for over a decade. The MPLA held a trial in Luanda for thirteen captured mercenaries, including three Americans, that heightened Western embarrassment by publishing details of the failed intervention.

Cuba embraced events in Angola as not just a blow to US empire but also as a defeat of mercenary force, dramatized by the Luanda Trial. Cuba's global vision of mercenarism and the internationalist response found its clearest explanation in the publication *Angola: Fin Del Mito de Los Mercenarios* (1976), a sustained analysis of the Western intervention written by Raul Valdes Vivo, the head of the General Department of Foreign Relations of the Cuban Central Committee of the Communist Party.[47] Taking an expansive view, Vivo identified a spectrum of US agents: Israel, "traitorous Arab rulers," South Vietnam, and UNITA's Joseph Savimbi. But he argued that Angola represented a new stage in US policy after its inglorious defeat in Vietnam. Washington resorted to mercenaries, asserted Vivo, "so as to avoid the need for a full frontal attack by imperialism."[48]

While Vivo simplified the Angolan situation, he was accurate in many respects. White mercenaries were just one component meant to strengthen the resolve and ability of the FNLA and UNITA alongside assistance from the CIA, Zaire (formerly Congo), and South Africa. US policymakers were more reluctant to use soldiers-for-hire than they had been a decade prior, but the shadow of Vietnam pushed them in that direction. When one military official recommended increasing CIA operatives to help reinforce anti-MPLA forces, he was quieted with the rhetorical "General, did you

[46] George Houser, Report on the Havana Seminar (February 25–29, 1976), March 1976, Africa Activist Archive, Michigan State University: https://africanactivist.msu.edu/index.php.
[47] I have located Spanish, English, Portuguese, German, Russian, Hungarian, and Polish editions of Vivo's book.
[48] Vivo, *Angola*, 48.

ever hear of Laos?" Strategy immediately shifted to mercenaries. Much like earlier in the Congo, the United States sought to shape events with minimal involvement, including reaching out to former Portuguese colonials who "have a heart for Angola and want to help out."[49] Portugal proved reluctant to assist these efforts, and Brazil flatly refused, leaving the United States to depend on local proxies and South Africa. The United States funded some mercenaries alongside France, though both operated more subtly than they had in the Congo.[50]

As a result, the mercenary network that cohered in Angola was more diffuse and less professional than a decade prior. Klaas Voß argues that Angola was the beginning of a shift in American recruitment strategies, from the organized method that partially reproduced colonial relationships to a "laissez-faire approach" that depended on "recruitment agencies and mercenary networks."[51] One (in)famous node in this network was *Soldier of Fortune*. Founded in 1975 after former army officer Robert K. Brown visited Rhodesia, the magazine became a clearinghouse for information about mercenaries in Southern Africa, including recruitment notices.[52] Vivo interviewed the captured US mercenary Gary Acker, who found his way to Angola through his own ad in the magazine. A Vietnam veteran with anti-communist views, he gravitated to the mercenary life after failing to find a peacetime job. While such economic motivations were real, historian Gerald Horne contends that many veterans like Acker also saw Angola as an opportunity to flip the script from Vietnam. They welcomed the chance to fight against real communists after Cuban participation became public.[53] This anti-communist connection led Vivo to suspect CIA connections to *Soldier of Fortune* and the recruiting offices that appeared in Western nations.[54] While the United States certainly funded mercenaries in Angola, the government apparently did opt for the "laissez-faire" approach. Records show less of the recruitment, coordination, and transportation that typified the Bay of Pigs invasion or the Congo episode.[55]

---

[49] Memo for the Record, November 14, 1975, *FRUS Southern Africa*, 341.

[50] See documents 138 and 186 in *FRUS Southern Africa*.

[51] Voß, "Plausibly Deniable," 47, 49.

[52] Kyle Burke, *Revolutionaries for the Right: Anticommunist Internationalism and Paramilitary Warfare in the Cold War* (Chapel Hill: University of North Carolina Press, 2018), 108–109.

[53] Gerald Horne, *From the Barrel of a Gun: The United States and the War against Zimbabwe, 1965–1980* (Chapel Hill: University of North Carolina Press, 2001), 56–63.

[54] Vivo, *Angola*, 69. Gerald Horne also investigated the role of the magazine in Rhodesia. Horne, *From the Barrel of a Gun*, 233–236.

[55] Vivo, *Angola*, 87–88.

While reinforcing some Cuban arguments about mercenarism, the Angola conflict also promoted a subtle change in the Cuban approach to the topic. Castro's claim that Angola had witnessed the destructions of "the white mercenaries ... along with their myth" implied a new emphasis on race in Cuban ideas of Tricontinental solidarity.[56] This shift in Cuban rhetoric directly reflected an increased involvement in Africa. Events in the Congo during the previous decade created an aura of invulnerability around the white soldiers drawn heavily from minority-ruled Southern African states. It began with the Katanga secession but transformed into myth when the mercenaries, rarely numbering more than 1,000, defeated the Simba rebellion.[57] African concern with white mercenaries served two conflicting purposes. On the one hand, it linked small bands of unaffiliated soldiers with institutional power associated with the colonial system, subconsciously attaching the mercenary to a long history of martial success. Simultaneously, this rhetoric united a diverse set of majority-black African states behind an anti-imperial cause. It also enabled them to argue that mercenaries exacerbated racial strife, which Westerners feared would harm their standing on the continent.[58] The myth provided white mercenaries with exaggerated power in the 1960s, but their defeat in Angola provided a rallying cry for anti-imperial solidarity.

Cuba's rhetorical shift is important because the Castro government had previously resisted making race central to Tricontinentalism or its concept of mercenarism. Not only were light-skinned Cuban leaders, including Argentinian Che Guevara, sensitive about race, but this formulation excluded local collaborators like Tshombe and the FNLA. In the Congo, Guevara criticized the rebels for blaming their losses on white mercenaries rather than fellow Africans. Mercenaries from Belgium and Southern Africa trained and led the army, but much of the fighting was undertaken by formidable Congolese soldiers in the employ of a black-led government.[59] When the Cubans finally withdrew, Che worried less about the challenge posed by the handful of whites than the fact that the rebels would have to confront "mercenary" Africans acting as agents of imperialism and neocolonialism.[60]

---

[56] Fidel Castro, "At the Closing Session of the Tricontinental Conference."

[57] Memo, Rostow to President Johnson, July 6, 1967, *FRUS*, 743.

[58] The United States expressed concern that "racist feeling which is mounting rapidly against white mercenaries ... may grow to include all whites." Ibid.

[59] Ernesto Che Guevara, *Congo Diary: Episodes of the Revolutionary War in the Congo*, ed. Che Guevara Studies Center (North Melbourne: Ocean Press, 2012), 95, 75, 86, 223.

[60] Ibid., 179, 183, 206.

Still, Cuba knew race had the power to promote solidarity, especially at the interpersonal level. Victor Dreke, Guevara's Afro-Cuban second-in-command in the Congo tasked with recruiting Cuban volunteers, recalls being told "the compañeros were to be black – 'very black'."[61] As Dreke's comment implies, the increased emphasis on the racial elements of solidarity emerged as Cuban collaboration with Africans increased. Allies like Cabral sought to balance race and ideology in conceptualizing revolution, and his statement that Cubans were "a people that we consider African" likely encouraged the shift.[62] Moreover, African opposition to minority rule provided a ready source of solidarity partially defined along racial lines. It had been the public revelations about the South African intervention, after all, that undermined UNITA and the FNLA while forcing African states to overwhelmingly condemn the intervention.

Invoking this racialized specter aligned Cuba with African allies and further differentiated its soldiers from mercenaries. Vivo's *Fin Del Mito de Los Mercenarios* emphasized this new racial frame. He dismissed *Soldier of Fortune* as bigoted, one node in the network connecting Washington and its "mercenary thugs" to the hated minority states of the continent.[63] The magazine adopted a rhetoric of nominal racial equality, but its fawning coverage of Rhodesian and South African soldiers reinforced the mythic power of armed whites, which Vivo compared to depictions of Tarzan in "US racist literature."[64] Destroying this threat struck a blow against empire *and* white dominance. "The 30 year-long myth of the white mercenaries, arriving by the legion or emerging suddenly from nowhere as vast armies," Vivo declared, "was destroyed in a matter of three weeks, and neocolonialism lost one of its sharp fangs."[65] Castro declared Angola no less than the Playa Girón of Africa; there was now proof that "white mercenaries" were subject to defeat and that the mighty South African government was vulnerable.[66]

Wedding aspects of black self-determination to the socialist revolution served one final purpose. Race had long been a mark of status in Cuba, but officials downplayed domestic divisions by promoting a "Marxist exceptionalism" that claimed racism to be impossible in the socialist state.[67]

[61] Mary-Alice Waters, ed., *From the Escambray to the Congo: In the Whirlwind of the Cuban Revolution* (New York: Pathfinder, 2002), 125.

[62] Amílcar Cabral, "Determined to Resist," *Tricontinental* 8 (September 1968), 125.

[63] Vivo, *Angola*, 69–70.   [64] Ibid., 91.   [65] Ibid., 77.   [66] Ibid., 9.

[67] Mark Q. Sawyer, *Racial Politics in Post-Revolutionary Cuba* (New York: Cambridge University Press, 2006), 28–31. See also Christabelle Peters, *Cuban Identity and the Angolan Experience* (New York: Palgrave Macmillan, 2012).

This rhetoric did not erase inequalities. Nor did it fit comfortably with the mindset of African and Asian leaders, whose non-white identities became increasingly central to their national oppositions to empire. Aligning itself with African states against white invaders encouraged the Castro government to embrace an Afro-Cuban identity. Vivo captured the idea in striking prose:

In Angolan soil, the soil of many of their ancestors, remain the bodies of the internationalist fighters killed in combat, followers of Che Guevara, eternal heroes of two homelands, giving new life to the Latin-African roots of which Fidel spoke.[68]

As Mark Sawyer observes, "involvement in Angola opened the issue of race."[69] The embrace of this Afro-Cuban identity further tied the nation to the global anti-imperial movement while realizing – abroad if not always at home – the power of a multi-ethnic state.[70] Whereas mercenaries were outsiders intent on prolonging foreign domination, Cuba claimed a diasporic solidarity opposed to alien white empires and racism writ large. This formulation of mercenarism addressed foreign and domestic priorities of the Cuban state but ultimately limited its ability to shape wider global norms.

MERCENARY FORCE AND INTERNATIONAL LAW

If Angola in 1976 was a prime example of Tricontinental solidarity and the evolution of the Cuban concept of mercenarism, its aftermath demonstrated the limitations of the philosophy, namely its inability to win sufficient support to transform the international system. Cuba and the MPLA sought to use the Luanda Trial to legitimize its power and set legal precedent against foreign intervention and the use of mercenaries. With support from African governments, the MPLA's Ministry of Justice invited approximately fifty-one individuals from thirty-seven countries to make up the International Commission of Enquiry on Mercenaries. Headed by André Mouélé of the Congo-Brazzaville, the commission included among its members three Cubans including Vivo, two Soviets, and three Americans from the National Conference of Black Lawyers. The MPLA charged the commission with drafting a statement on the legal status of mercenaries and monitoring the trial, which most analysts deemed politicized but procedurally fair. More troubling, perhaps, these

---

[68] Vivo, *Angola*, 95–96.   [69] Sawyer, *Racial Politics*, 78.
[70] Mahler, *From the Tricontinental to the Global South*, chapter 4.

observers concluded that "being a mercenary" was not a legally recognizable crime. They agreed that the international community should intervene to solve this problem.[71]

International law had indeed been slow to tackle the problem of mercenaries. Though they fell out of favor during the 1800s when nationalism became the preferred tool for recruiting armies, mercenaries remained valuable contributors to small, distant wars and found new state imprimaturs under guises like the French Foreign Legion. Few legal documents mentioned mercenaries. The 1907 Hague and 1949 Geneva Conventions assumed such soldiers – without using the term precisely – to be lawful combatants and privy to the same humane treatment as other prisoners of war.[72]

After Playa Girón in 1961, Cuba intermittently sought to institutionalize the vague distaste for mercenaries into international law, ultimately hoping to declare foreign intervention by mercenaries illegal. Attorney General Jose Santiago Cuba Fernández cited elements of the 1928 Havana convention, the 1936 Inter-American Peace Conference, and the charters of the UN and OAS to claim the United States violated international law. These documents discouraged indirect intervention in the affairs of sovereign states. Fernández's choice of the emotionally powerful term *mercenaries* dramatized the extent to which the United States had funded and guided the exile invasion.[73] Cuba ultimately convicted the exiles of treason, but they structured the colorful hearings around mercenarism in an attempt to try the United States in "the Court of the Peoples of the world."[74]

Castro argued in 1962 that the lack of international law regulating mercenarism allowed the use of mercenaries to continue.[75] Thus, Cuban rhetoric and the multilingual publication of documents like *Historia De*

---

[71] Lennox S. Hinds and Hope R. Stevens, *The Trial of the Mercenaries, June 7–19, 1976: A Special Report* (New York: National Conference of Black Lawyers, 1976), 15–19, 96–97. Robert E Cesner Jr. and John W. Brant, "Law of the Mercenary: An International Dilemma," *Capital University Law Review* 6:3 (1977): 339–340, 345–351, 358. George H. Lockwood, "Report on the Trial of Mercenaries: Luanda, Angola June 1976," *Manitoba Law Journal* 7:3 (1977): 183–184, 190, 194, 197, 201. Mike J. Hoover, "The Laws of War and the Angolan Trial of Mercenaries: Death to the Dogs of War," *Case Western Reserve Journal of International Law* 9:2 (1977): 349. "Mercenaries in South Africa: Interview with Professor Lars Rudebeck, Uppsala University, Sweden, Member of the International Commission of Enquiry on Mercenaries, Angola, 1976," *Review of African Political Economy* 6 (1976), 71, 73.
[72] James M. Doty, "International Law and Private Military Firms," *GPSolo* 25:2 March (2008): 38–39.
[73] *History of an Aggression*, 301–302.   [74] Ibid., 312.   [75] Ibid., 14.

Una Agresión and Vivo's *Fin Del Mito de Los Mercenarios* sought not just to win propaganda victories but also to influence international law. In this respect, these publications and gatherings like the Havana Conference were part of the larger anti-imperial project that sought to forge solidarity in order to integrate concerns of the Global South into an international system built on European and North American priorities and precedents. As Vijay Prashad notes, the Tricontinental "rehearsed the major arguments – so that they could take them in a concerted way to the main stage, the United Nations."[76] Cuba wanted to put neocolonial intervention on the docket in New York. Yet by defining mercenaries as products of specific ideological and (later) racial contexts, Cuba delimited the legal value of the concept it sought to universalize.

Rather, it was African states that led the push to revise international law to discourage the use of mercenaries. Events in the Congo unnerved many of these young nations, especially after the munity of white mercenaries in 1966 threatened regional stability. The next year at Kinshasa, the OAU passed a resolution demanding the withdrawal of mercenaries from the Congo.[77] Events such as the Biafran secession from Nigeria, which led to a civil war in which mercenaries played a small role, reinforced the need for change as governments on both the left and right felt threatened. As a result, the OAU, meeting in Addis Ababa in 1971, drafted a convention against mercenaries that was finalized six years later.[78] It declared that mercenarism was a crime that could be "committed by the individual, group or association, representative of a State and the State itself who with the aim of opposing by armed violence a process of self-determination stability or the territorial integrity of another State" engage in a number of different actions.[79] The convention did not use the politicized language of intervention favored by Cuba, but the OAU went beyond merely defining the mercenary as an individual and articulated a definition of a crime for which states might be guilty. It further demanded that states prohibit within their territories "any activities by persons or organisations who

---

[76] Vijay Prashad, *The Darker Nations: A People's History of the Third World* (New York: New Press, 2007), xvi.

[77] The Fourth Ordinary Session of the Assembly of Heads of State and Government, "Resolution on Mercenaries," *AHG/Res. 49 (IV)* (Kinshasa: Organization of African Unity, 1967).

[78] The convention's authors attended the Luanda Trial. International Committee of the Red Cross, *Commentary on the Additional Protocols of 8 June 1977 to the Geneva Conventions of 12 August 1949* (Geneva: Martinus Nijhoff Publishers, 1987), 573fn7.

[79] OAU Convention for the Elimination of Mercenarism in Africa, *CM/817(XXIX) Annex II Rev. 1* (Libreville: Organization of African Unity, 1977).

use mercenaries against ... the people of Africa in their struggle for liberation."[80] This formulation directly responded to the implicitly racialized use of mercenaries by and from the white minority regimes that aimed to frustrate self-determination of postcolonial states. These OAU efforts were a catalyst for international action before the Luanda Trial.

The UN responded to OAU efforts by formulating the first truly intercontinental definition of a mercenary. Begun in 1974 and adopted in 1977, Article 47 of the Additional Protocols to the 1949 Geneva Convention stripped these figures of the legal protections extended to legal combatants and prisoners of war.[81] But it lacked much of the language of the OAU convention, specifically the attempt to hold states accountable for employing mercenaries. These more radical elements present in the OAU text fell victim to UN deliberations, where the need for majority approval empowered moderate states and allowed powerful Western countries to promote acceptably banal language. Blessing Akporode Clark, Nigeria's Permanent Representative to the UN, described Article 47 as a "compromise text" that owed much to the US delegation, "who had conducted the negotiations leading to the adoption of the new article."[82] International law finally ruled on mercenaries, but it did so in a way that failed to address the inequalities of power that led to their use. Cuba was deeply disappointed. As Minister of Foreign Affairs Juana Silvera explained, his country favored "an exact definition and prohibition that would clearly reflect the truth of mercenary activities, the aims of which are to hamper and thwart the struggle of peoples to free themselves. These aims," Silvera continued, "reflect political interests of the imperialist countries and their lackeys, which have ... ignored this truth, thus helping to build up the mercenary system."[83] Such an overtly political definition of mercenary activity was unlikely to gain traction, but the reality was the OAU conventions fared only marginally better because they targeted practices used by *both* the Western powers and their Third World allies.

---

[80] "OAU Convention for the Elimination of Mercenarism in Africa."

[81] Diplomatic Conference on the Reaffirmation and Development of International Humanitarian Law applicable in Armed Conflicts, *Protocol Additional to the Geneva Conventions of 12 August 1949, and Relating to the Protection of Victims of International Armed Conflicts (Protocol I)* (United Nations: 1977).

[82] *Official Records of the Diplomatic Conference on the Reaffirmation and Development of International Humanitarian Law Applicable in Armed Conflicts.* Volume 6. (Bern: Federal Political Department, 1978), 156–157.

[83] Ibid., 184–185. The representatives from Mozambique placed the new article squarely in the context of events in Angola. Ibid., 193–194.

Agitation against mercenary force became an ongoing theme at the UN as the practice grew increasingly common. Ten years after passage of the UN convention, the Red Cross lamented, "there has scarcely been any conflict involving military operations in which the presence of mercenaries has not played a part in one way or another."[84] As a result, efforts increased to address the recruitment, use, and financing of mercenaries. African states again took the lead. In December 1979, Nigeria pushed successfully for a new convention against the recruitment, use, financing, and training of mercenaries. Likely referencing the Western obsession with the violent international struggle of the Palestinian Liberation Organization, Clark explained that "efforts by the international community to reduce the problem of international terrorism cannot be said to be complete without focusing attention on the menace these soldiers of fortune bring to many nations in Africa."[85] A month later, at the start of its new session, the General Assembly formed a committee to draft the new convention, with nine of the thirty-five members coming from African nations. Cuba was not initially selected as a member of the committee by the Latin American group of nations. But just a few days after the committee was announced, Panama, under the control of the socialist-leaning Democratic Revolutionary Party, withdrew in favor of Cuba.[86]

Cuba seemed to have finally gained the international standing to promote its theory. The successful defense of the MPLA in Angola affirmed Cuba's claim to be a revolutionary state with global aspirations. Its troops remained in Angola while doctors and technicians streamed in to help build the infrastructure of the state. In late 1977, Cuban troops again deployed to the African continent, this time to protect the communist Derg in Ethiopia from a Somali invasion.[87] As Paul Thomas Chamberlin shows in Chapter 3, this was the apex of Tricontinental solidarity. Cuba parlayed its standing among leftist Third World governments to finally take the chairmanship of the Non-Aligned Movement beginning in 1979

---

[84] *Commentary on the Additional Protocols of 8 June 1977 to the Geneva Conventions of 12 August 1949.*

[85] "Request for the Inclusion of an Additional Item in the Agenda of the Thirty-Fourth Session: Drafting of an International Convention against the Activities of Mercenaries," A/34/247 (United Nations: 1979).

[86] "Drafting of an International Convention against the Recruitment, Use, Financing and Training of Mercenaries," A/35/793/Add.1 (United Nations, 1981).

[87] Gebru Tareke, "The Ethiopia-Somalia War of 1977 Revisited," *The International Journal of African Historical Studies* 33:3 (2000): 635–667.

with hopes of moving the loosely organized conference in more radical directions. With nominal leadership of the UN's largest voting bloc, Cuba seemed poised to shape the conversation on mercenarism. Yet Cuba was ultimately frustrated. This history illustrates the extent to which Cuba's expansive view of mercenarism – and Tricontinentalism itself – struggled to gain and maintain widespread support.

Cuba had lost its position as head of the NAM by the time the two working groups of the drafting committee consolidated their efforts in 1984. Cuba struggled to steer the loose conference, stymied on various occasions by conservative oil states in the Gulf region, moderates like Nigeria, and even by allies like Vietnam whose zeal for revolution took a backseat to its interest in managing regional and global politics. Cuba's UN vote against censuring the Soviet Union for its invasion of Afghanistan further eroded its standing. Yet the country remained committed to Tricontinentalism, and the Cuban delegation contributed a proposed draft convention to the committee that situated the problem of mercenary force squarely within this context. The preamble identified mercenaries as antagonists of liberation and decolonization, citing earlier efforts by the OAU and NAM to promote "progressive development of international law towards regarding mercenarism as international crime." Cuba's expansive definition of mercenarism provided an alternative to the individual-focused UN Additional Protocols of 1977, declaring that states, along with their representatives and agents, were culpable for the crime of mercenarism if they organized, financed, supplied, equipped, trained, promoted, or employed forces that oppose national liberation, independence, or self-determination movements.[88] This language drew on and expanded the 1977 OAU convention, but Cuba's draft garnered sparse support. As deliberations stretched on, the financial crisis of the 1980s led to the decline of G-77 power and forced many UN-member states to court donations from Washington and the international financial institutions it controlled. There was little appetite for a radical challenge to international norms, even when the subject was mercenaries.

The committee's final draft neglected most of the Cuban language. The focus was on mercenaries as individuals and the goal of maintaining "friendly relations" between states, rather than protecting liberation movements. The Convention against the Recruitment, Use, Financing and Training of Mercenaries adopted in 1989 did update the Additional Protocols of 1977

---

[88] "Cuba: Draft Convention against the Recruitment, Use, Financing and Training of Mercenaries," *A/AC.207/L.22* (United Nations, 1985), 1–2.

by adding a second definition of mercenaries that recognized them as a threat to the constitutional order and territorial integrity of a state. Still, the UN maintained a narrow vision of who constituted a mercenary: an outsider "neither a national or resident of the State" in which they were operating, who acted outside official state forces.[89] The Cuban definition of both exile invasions and foreign-backed proxy governments as examples of a broader, neocolonial concept of mercenarism had no support from international law. The convention discouraged states from recruiting, using, financing, or training mercenaries, but all the offences specified in the convention were acts committed by persons.

Ironically, even this watered-down convention failed to win much support. After nearly three decades, only thirty-six states had ratified it by 2021. The United States, France, and Britain – major purveyors of mercenary force from the Cold War to the present – are not among them. Neither is Angola, which signed the convention in 1990 but never ratified it. Three years later, the country became a launching point for a generation of soldiers-for-hire. Still involved with its prolonged civil war with UNITA, the MPLA government – without Cuban troops thanks to the end of the Cold War – employed the private, South Africa-based military company Executive Outcomes (EO) to help it defend major assets, including oil infrastructure operated by multinationals like Gulf Oil.[90] Cuba's Tricontinental vision of international fighters opposing capitalist mercenaries was lost. In the following decades, employment of these corporate security contractors became common as states like Angola chose to defend elite political and economic interests rather than continue down the path of Tricontinental revolution.

The private contractors employed by EO and similar companies, which some observers see as modern mercenaries, fit well with the competitive neoliberalism of the 1990s.[91] The delimited, much ignored anti-mercenary laws formulated after the Luanda Trial did little to slow the growth of these companies, and prosecutions of all but their worst excesses remain rare.[92]

---

[89] "International Convention against the Recruitment, Use, Financing and Training of Mercenaries," *A/RES/44/34* (United Nations, 1989).

[90] Kevin A. O'Brien, "Private Military Companies and African Security 1990–98," in Abdel-Fatau Musah and 'Kayode Fayemi, eds., *Mercenaries: An African Security Dilemma* (London: Pluto Press, 2000), 51–54.

[91] See, for example, P. W. Singer, *Corporate Warriors: The Rise of the Privatized Military Industry* (Ithaca: Cornell University Press, 2008).

[92] Hin-Yan Liu argues that private military companies are characterized by their impunity under the law; law has in fact evolved to ensure the survival of mercenary force. Hin-Yan

In the twenty-first century, the United States used dozens of private firms such as Blackwater to provide security, training, and operations support during its extended wars in Afghanistan and Iraq.[93] Though the underlying logic had changed from anti-communism to anti-terrorism, essential calculations about cost and culpability remained constant in producing these new coalitions between Western forces, local allies, and soldiers-for-hire. So too did this coalition both respond to and encourage networks of opposing transnational fighters, though the identarian fundamentalism of groupings like the Islamic State contrasted sharply with the Tricontinentalism of the Cold War era.

CONCLUSION

As a radical, revolutionary nation, Cuba conceptualized mercenarism – understood to be an explicit form of imperialism – to help organize and assist Third World peoples to challenge colonial and neocolonial domination. As a consequence of what Mahler calls "the totalizing perspective," anyone acting against Cuba or its Tricontinental partners was a mercenary.[94] Dreke summed up this global contest in 2017: it was as simple as capitalists versus socialists.[95] Emergent formulations of international law viewed mercenaries more simply, as individual legal violations rather than components of a larger system aimed at policing the edges of North-South power disparities. Cuba's broad formulation of mercenarism and inherently ideological motivations proved controversial even at the time. This contention prevented the adoption of these ideas even as a majority of African states sought to rein in this destructive and unpredictable practice. Tricontinental thought was too radical to achieve a consensus among Third World states, let alone to reshape the rules of international law. With no sufficient legal apparatus limiting the use of mercenaries or intervention in the Global South, Tricontinental advocates – and subsequent generations of anti-imperialists – responded to force with force.

Liu, *Law's Impunity: Responsibility and the Modern Private Military Company* (Oxford: Hart Publishing, 2015).

[93] See, for example, Jeremy Scahill, *Blackwater: The Rise of the World's Most Powerful Mercenary Army* (New York: MJF Books, 2008).

[94] Mahler, *From the Tricontinental to the Global South*, 103.

[95] Ron Augustin, "No Other Choice but to Unite: An Interview with Victor Dreke," October 7, 2017, *Monthly Review*: https://mronline.org/2017/10/07/no-other-choice-but-to-unite-an-interview-with-victor-dreke/.

This does not mean that Cuban soldiers became mercenaries for the left. Christine Hatzky, among others, argues that the Cuban government profited from its deployment of military and civil forces in Angola, making them mercenary in nature.[96] Hatzky is correct that Angola paid for decades of Cuban assistance, and internationalist deployments became a point of national pride for Castro's government, almost mythic in nature. However, these payments were considered parts of Tricontinental solidarity, in which marginalized states pooled their limited resources to fight a common revolution. Cuba lent military and civil assistance to Angola, but it required payments to subsidize these deployments. Two points argue against understanding this as a mercenary relationship. First, Hatzky herself admits that most Cubans were motivated by solidarity and commitment to the revolution, not by the possibility of individual gain.[97] Exchanges occurred between governments as part of international diplomacy. Second, understanding Cuban concepts of mercenarism reveals that the limited inequalities of power between the parties prevented the creation of such a dynamic. Cuba and Angola negotiated their relationship in ways that allowed each country to benefit.[98] Cuba could not bankroll its foreign mission, but neither could it dictate terms. This arrangement contrasts with both traditional mercenary relationships wherein money buys loyalty and the expansive definition that Cuba applied to the United States, whose wealth allowed it to provide generous aid but wielded this power to control clients such as Congo and South Vietnam.

This is not to say that Tricontinental solidarity was wholly superior to mercenary force. Internationalist fighters thrived in the postcolonial era because of their role within the militant ideological conflict of the Cold War. When the conflict ended, the internationalist fighter became untenable even as US empire remained. Cuba began reducing its Angolan deployment after the MPLA claimed victory over South African troops at Cuito Cuanavale, but it is no coincidence that the final withdrawal occurred between 1989 and 1991. Moreover, the departure of Cuban and

[96] Christine Hatzky, *Cubans in Angola: South-South Cooperation and Transfer of Knowledge, 1976–1991* (Madison: University of Wisconsin Press, 2015).

[97] According to Hatzky, interviewees were surprised or unresponsive to the idea that Cuba even accepted payments.

[98] Abdel-Fatau Musah and J. 'Kayode Fayemi conclude simply, "The official involvement of Cuban forces in Angola in the 1970s and 1980s by invitation of the Angolan government exclude such a force being described as a mercenary involvement," *Mercenaries: An African Security Dilemma*, 36.

other foreign troops did not resolve the factors that led to internal unrest and the use of mercenaries; indeed, decades of Cold War conflict exacerbated it. Especially in Africa, leaders such as Angola's José Eduardo Dos Santos grew dependent on foreign soldiers – be they politically inclined or paid – to prop up governments whose legitimacy was limited by political, regional, and historical divisions. Like mercenaries, internationalist fighters provided weak governments with an effective fighting force whose allegiance was only tangentially related to domestic competence and whose foreign makeup militated against the creation of competing domestic power blocs. It is this reality that helps explain Angola's shift toward corporate mercenaries after the Cold War ended. As a result, Che and his fellow internationalist fighters have become largely symbolic, while mercenaries soldier on.

AFTERWORD

Patterns and Puzzles

Mark Atwood Lawrence

The organizers of the 1966 Tricontinental Conference exuded certainty. They were certain of their purpose. "It is obvious that the militant solidarity of the peoples of the three continents is a necessity which cannot be postponed," asserted a statement of objectives written in advance of the meeting. The organizers were certain, too, of their methods. The peoples of Asia, Africa, and Latin America must join with the socialist bloc as well as "progressive" forces in Europe and the United States to oppose both colonialism and neocolonialism – categories they carefully teased apart – by whatever means were necessary, including "armed struggle," asserted the statement. And the organizers were certain that their endeavor marked something new in the annals of anti-colonial activism. "The celebration of this Conference in Havana is an event of world-wide importance," declared the statement, which promised that cooperation among the world's downtrodden and exploited peoples would deal no less than "a severe blow to the backbone of imperialism."[1]

In some respects, the conference, like the movement it announced, corresponded to the rhetoric, however overheated the latter may have been. As R. Joseph Parrott establishes in the Introduction to this volume, the new phase of activism announced at Havana possessed several characteristics that distinguished Tricontinentalism from other strands of the anti-imperial project dating back to the early twentieth century and made the new movement a distinct departure in the history of Third World

[1] "Antecedents and Objectives of the Movement of Solidarity of the Peoples of Africa, Asia and Latin America," in *First Solidarity Conference of the Peoples of Africa, Asia and Latin America* (Havana: General Secretariat of the OSPAAAL, 1966), 17, 22, 26.

organizing. Perhaps most conspicuously, leaders uniting under the Tricontinental banner embraced violence more explicitly than earlier architects of the Third World movement. Numerous chapters highlight the belief that Western rapaciousness could be defeated only through direct confrontation and the tendency to celebrate armed resistance, most notably North Vietnam's struggle against US intervention in Southeast Asia. The era of the heroic liberation fighter was at hand.

Related to this enthusiasm for direct action was a notably expansive view of the challenges that must be overcome on the road to global justice. Whereas earlier generations of Third World leaders had concentrated on the evils of formal "flag" colonialism, the Havana conference fixed attention on the pernicious ways in which the United States and Europe continued to wield economic and cultural supremacy even after colonial territories had won their independence. Cuban primacy in the Tricontinental movement, highlighted in several of the preceding chapters, made this adjustment practically inevitable since most of Latin American had, after all, gained its independence decades before; Cuba's prominence made sense only if US behavior in the Western Hemisphere could be linked to the territorial domination that still prevailed in many parts of the Eastern. But the emphasis on neocolonialism also appealed to revolutionary leaders in Asia and Africa by explaining problems that lingered after imperial ties were severed and providing a rationale for global cooperation. Furthermore, the concept of neocolonialism helped assure ideological homogeneity by disqualifying nations that had gained their independence but hewed closely to the West, a condition that ipso facto reflected stunted progress on the road to postcolonial consciousness.

The architects of Tricontinentalism also conformed to the rhetoric of the Havana conference by downplaying non-alignment, a major theme of earlier strands of Third World organizing, and casting their lot firmly with the communist bloc. Pragmatic considerations contributed to this shift. Cooperation with communist nations, particularly the Soviet Union and China but also smaller powers such as East Germany and Czechoslovakia, enabled small nations to close the yawning gap between their material capabilities and those of Western nations hostile to revolution. But, as several chapters show, the embrace of Marxism also flowed from ideological convictions that now, rather than geography or historical experience with colonialism, provided the key criteria of membership. Above all, proponents of Tricontinentalism saw capitalist exploitation as the principal cause of the Third World's woes, including the economic backwardness, racial inequality, cultural marginalization, and political fragmentation that had long inhibited effective resistance against the West. To be sure, various chapters reveal the profound ways in which the Sino-Soviet split disrupted and limited, if not actually destroyed, the Tricontinental project. But consensus prevailed among the proponents of Tricontinentalism on the basic notion that the Third World revolution would be built on the foundations laid by communist revolutionaries in earlier times.

This emphasis on ideology was intertwined with another hallmark of Tricontinentalism championed at the Havana conference and well-illustrated in this book. The movement went further than any earlier variant of Third Worldism in embracing nonstate movements and parties alongside governments of independent states. As Map 0.2 makes clear, nonstate groups ranging from South Vietnam's National Liberation Front to Amílcar Cabral's African Party for the Independence of Guiné and Cabo Verde to Puerto Rican nationalists had seats at the table in Havana. This diversity reflected the fact that common purposes and tactical preferences, rather than geography or historical experience of colonialism, provided the glue that held the movement together. It reflected, too, the movement's fascination with aiding fledgling revolutionary groups – often romanticized as beleaguered Davids facing off against Western Goliaths – along the path to power in fully sovereign nations. By 1966, enough Third World nations had gained their independence and accumulated sufficient power to exert political influence, if not material support, beyond their borders and to form networks of mutual assistance. But the wide variety of participating entities also resulted from the subtle ways in which race figured into Tricontinentalism. As Parrott argues in the Introduction (and as numerous chapters bear out), adherents of Tricontinentalism sought to generate solidarity on the basis of a shared non-white identity and the hostility they ascribed to the Anglo-American world. Yet this non-white identity was, in Parrott's words, "a fluid, often symbolic element within Tricontinentalism." It was, that is, a loose and expansive concept that encompassed a vast array of the world's populations and served more as a proxy for the larger political agenda than as any sort of fixed category.

If the essays in this volume underscore the principles and practices that lent coherence to Tricontinentalism, they also, however, point out any number of ambiguities that hover around the phenomenon. Of course, it is no surprise that such vagaries can be discerned. A worldwide movement organized around a complex array of ideals and tactics was bound to give rise to inconsistencies and contradictions that enable latter-day historians to draw differing conclusions. Indeed, one of the principal strengths of Tricontinentalism, like any plausible movement with global ambitions, was surely its adaptability to sharply different geographical, historical, and political circumstances. Digging into these areas of ambiguity thus promises to reveal some of the reasons why Tricontinentalism resonated so powerfully across diverse spaces. What might appear to be weaknesses often were strengths. But exposing these uncertainties, along with the differences of interpretation that have arisen from them, also promises both to highlight the nascent debates swirling around the history of the Third World movement in the 1960s and 1970s and to lay out at least the broad contours of the research agenda that awaits future scholars concerned with the matters addressed in this collection. The essays point in particular to three broad questions that drive interpretive uncertainty: What were the origins of Tricontinentalism? How should we understand the trajectory of the movement that gave rise to, and followed from, the Havana conference? And how should we evaluate Tricontinentalism's overall successes and failures?

With respect to the origins of the Tricontinental Conference, the organizers' statement of objectives could hardly have been more definitive: the meeting represented a heroic effort by enlightened political forces to deliver decisive blows at a moment when the imperialist system was "in crisis," succumbing to its own "internal contradictions."[2] A few of the essays in this volume highlight the confidence with which Tricontinentalism reflected this sense of historic opportunity and coherence of purpose. Perhaps most strikingly, Michelle D. Paranzino's chapter reveals Che Guevara's confidence that Latin America, if not a wider swath of the world, was poised to defeat "Yankee imperialism" through the right political tactics and proper application of force. Parrott describes Amílcar Cabral as a more nuanced thinker but also leaves little doubt that the PAIGC leader viewed the Tricontinental movement as a vehicle for achieving his own objectives as well as anti-colonialism on a global scale. Rafael Hernández and Jennifer Ruth Hosek similarly see coherence and foresight at the heart of Tricontinentalism, even suggesting that it gave rise to a "grand strategy" to advance Third World interests. For the most part, though, the essays in this collection show that the Tricontinental Conference emerged from a sense of setback, even crisis, within the communist and developing worlds, not within the capitalist West. In Jeremy Friedman's words, early 1966 even represented the moment of

[2] Ibid., 18.

"peak fracture" in post-1945 efforts to build an effective Third World movement.

In making this point, the essays are on target in ways that none of them explicitly acknowledges. Although the West may plausibly have entered a moment of "crisis" by 1968 due to the Vietnam War and burgeoning social unrest, only hints of this deterioration were visible in the period leading up to the Havana conference. On the contrary, 1965 stood out as perhaps the zenith of US power in the post-1945 era. Western economies, above all that of the United States, soared to unprecedented heights, while liberals scored major successes in passing transformative domestic reforms that enhanced American prestige abroad. In the military realm, moreover, the United States possessed staggering nuclear capabilities, a planet-encircling archipelago of bases, and massive air and naval forces that enabled Washington to project power virtually anywhere. All in all, according to a later study, US military power in 1965 was more than nine times greater than that of the Soviet Union. For its part, Moscow possessed little capacity to use force beyond Soviet border areas and acquired a credible nuclear arsenal capable of surviving a US first strike only in 1966.[3]

More closely connected to the purposes of this book, various developments in the Third World during 1964 and 1965 suggested that Asia, Africa, the Middle East, and Latin America, far from uniting to promote global revolution, were in fact tipping toward the West. As several chapters suggest, coups in Brazil (April 1964), Algeria (June 1965), and Indonesia (October 1965) destroyed or diminished governments that had recently held leadership roles in Third World forums and vigorously challenged Western hegemony. The 1966 coup that overthrew Kwame Nkrumah in Ghana only confirmed what Jeffrey James Byrne calls, with notable understatement, the "worrying trend" against Third World radicalism. Facing a particularly gloomy situation in Latin America, several authors agree, Castro's government – already reeling from a sense of abandonment by Moscow during the Cuban Missile Crisis – felt increasingly isolated within the Western Hemisphere. As Eric Gettig puts it, Cuba faced its "most severe diplomatic and economic isolation" since the revolution of 1959 as a consequence of its suspension from the Organization of American States and the imposition of an OAS-wide economic embargo. To the considerable extent that the Cuban

---

[3] Gareth Porter, *Perils of Dominance: Imbalance of Power and the Road to War in Vietnam* (Berkeley: University of California Press, 2005), 4–5, 7.

government led the drive for the Tricontinental Conference, then, it did so out of weakness and a sense that legitimization of its revolutionary pretensions would have to be found in the Eastern Hemisphere, particularly through cooperation with African liberation movements on battlefields thousands of miles from the island.

To the extent that African nations responded to Cuban initiative and lined up behind the Tricontinental project, they also appear to have acted largely from a position of weakness, if not outright desperation. In his analysis of the African National Congress, for example, Ryan Irwin notes that Cuban activism offered a way out of the "morass" of setbacks afflicting the ANC in the years before the Tricontinental Conference. At Havana, Irwin argues, ANC officials latched onto Cuban theories about "neocolonialism" as a way to explain their problems and embraced the Tricontinental's acceptance of violence as a way to revitalize their fortunes. Byrne's analysis of Algeria suggests, too, that Tricontinentalism sprang more from weakness than confidence about the future. Although the Algerian-Cuban relationship formed the axis around which the whole movement coalesced, contends Byrne, leaders of the two countries barely knew anything about each other. Their ritualistic invocations of solidarity, he writes, were useful mostly as a way of stirring a glimmer of hope at a time when both faced dire challenges. Of the chapters examining Tricontinentalism in specific national settings, only Pierre Asselin's analysis of Vietnam fails to note the ways in which transnational solidarity appealed as a way to offset profound weaknesses. Asselin's essay is, however, an exception that proves the rule since North Vietnam had a steady source of supply and political support from the communist superpowers. Third World solidarity was, in this anomalous case, more a bonus than a necessity.

Authors who focus on the roles of the communist powers offer a similarly critical assessment of the origins of Tricontinentalism, emphasizing the ways in which the Sino-Soviet rivalry drove the radicalization of the Third World movement in the mid-1960s. To be sure, Friedman acknowledges the central role of the Cuban government, which sought to overcome its isolation through leadership of a worldwide revolutionary effort. But he argues that both the Chinese and Soviet regimes drove the Tricontinental agenda by contributing in important ways to the confrontational approach announced at Havana. For the Chinese government, radicalism promised to bolster Beijing's claim to leadership of the Third World movement following the collapse of the Bandung II conference scheduled for June 1965. In the best case for Chinese leaders, writes

Friedman, the conference would denounce Soviet revisionism and embrace Mao as the undisputed leader of militant anti-colonialism on a global scale.

The Soviet goal, meanwhile, was to downplay the overall significance of the conference and to assure that it did not veer in excessively militant directions that would play into Chinese hands. For the latter reason, Moscow initially hoped that the conference would take place in Brazil, where the left-leaning government aligned with Soviet preferences until its overthrow in an April 1964 military coup. But Friedman also highlights Soviet efforts to blunt Chinese advantages with Third World radicals by accentuating their own dedication to revolution. There could never be peace between colonial aggressors and their victims, declared the chief Soviet representative, a comment that prefigured Leonid Brezhnev's declaration two months later officially reconciling peaceful coexistence in superpower relations with Soviet support for revolution in the Third World.

None of these explanations for the impetus behind the Tricontinental Conference – genuine ideological commitment, desperation to overcome weakness and isolation, and competing efforts to impose leadership – are mutually exclusive. Indeed, all three appear to hold significant explanatory power. The challenge posed by this volume is to strike the right balance and to appreciate the complex interplay of factors in analysis of local settings, where narrow motives and opportunism are often easy to see, and in the history of the Tricontinental movement as a whole. Privileging ideological dedication to social justice and economic development, after all, tends to cast these histories in a relatively sympathetic light. Stressing the ways in which self-interest drove individual actors – whether Fidel Castro, the African National Congress, East Germany, or the Soviet Union – to embrace a common agenda might lead to a more mixed overall assessment. Meanwhile, attaching central importance to the roles of the communist giants in shaping the agenda at Havana might contribute to a gloomy story of exploitation by the two dictatorships whose brutality in the second half of the twentieth century immeasurably dwarfed that of the United States.

With respect to the second area of uncertainty – What was the trajectory of the Tricontinental movement? – the essays offer more starkly contradictory answers. All of them, it is true, reinforce the notion that Tricontinentalism was just one strand in a complex web of ideas and movements that comprised Third World activism in the decades following World War II. The collection makes clear that teasing apart those strands is no small challenge. Yet each chapter, with varying degrees of explicitness, offers at least a broad sense of the chronology that Tricontinentalism followed. Anne Garland Mahler's essay stands apart in extending that chronology far backward in time, arguing that the Tricontinental had its roots in the interwar League Against Imperialism and especially its branch for the Western Hemisphere, the All-American Anti-Imperialist League. In taking this approach, Mahler deftly shows that notions of solidarity between the Western Hemisphere and the colonial territories of the Eastern hardly originated in the 1960s. The rest of the essays do not directly dispute this possibility but leave the distinct impression that the core ideas of Tricontinentalism coalesced in the aftermath of the Cuban and Algerian revolutions. It was in those years that Cuban isolation, Algeria's powerful example, the quickening pace of decolonization, perceptions that the moderate brand of Third World organizing pioneered at Bandung had produced meager returns, and the dynamics of the Sino-Soviet split all combined to generate calls for precisely the blend of objectives proclaimed in January 1966 at Havana.

The sharpest disagreements center on the question of what ensued thereafter. Several essays suggest that Tricontinentalism, enshrined in the OSPAAAL, followed a rise-and-fall pattern, with the Havana conference opening an era that prevailed for a time before giving way to something different. But how should we date this rise and fall, and what is the "something different" that replaced Tricontinentalism? Paul Thomas Chamberlin answers both these questions in elegant fashion. The era of "cosmopolitan revolution" announced at Havana persisted from the mid-1960s to the second half of the 1970s, when a new era of "ethno-sectarian" revolution gradually eclipsed it. If African revolutionaries, Vietnamese guerrillas, and Palestinian Liberation Organization fighters – secular forces fighting for national independence – were the face of the earlier period, writes Chamberlin, religiously motivated groups ranging from Hezbollah to the Afghan Mujahideen to Ayatollah Khomeini's student radicals embodied the latter. According to this scheme, which Parrott largely embraces in the Introduction as the basic framework for the collection, Tricontinentalism drew on earlier strands of radicalism associated with the Chinese-led Afro-Asian People's Solidarity Organization (AAPSO) but represented a discernible phase of militancy between the Bandung era dominated by Afro-Asian non-alignment and a new period characterized by identarian radicalism and religious fundamentalism.

Several essays suggest that the start of what might be called the Tricontinental era was hardly clear-cut. Chamberlin notes that the anti-colonial movement in the Third World had always been a relatively "slapdash" affair, and in any case, key elements of the program proclaimed at Havana were already circulating among Third World nations well before the conference of January 1966. Only Byrne goes so far, however, as to challenge the idea that the Tricontinental Conference somehow heralded the start of a new era in the development of the Third World movement. In his view, in fact, the conference marked the "conclusion of the romantic era of decolonization" that Cuban-Algerian cooperation epitomized from the late 1950s until 1965. By 1966, Byrne suggests, Algeria, once Fidel Castro's main partner in Africa, was shedding its more radical tendencies as it bought into an "international system" rooted in conceptions of sovereignty and territorial integrity that meshed poorly with the Tricontinental's dedication to overthrow and upheaval. By the end of the 1960s, Byrne continues, Algeria – presumably representative of other influential Third World nations – had diverged from Cuba and refocused on achieving its revolutionary goals through political and economic avenues. "The global battle against imperialism," Byrne memorably asserts, "was pursued chiefly by negotiators armed with briefcases and professional degrees, arguing over the global terms of trade and seeking to cast regimes like that in Pretoria as pariahs violating received morality."

Authors who allow that the Havana conference gave rise to a clearly discernible Tricontinental movement differ markedly in their contentions about timing. Some argue that the Tricontinental moment lost its luster relatively quickly. Friedman contends, for instance, that the collapse of Egyptian influence as a consequence of the Six Day War, combined with Cuban-Soviet rapprochement around the same time, undermined the notion of a truly independent Tricontinental alliance and made revolutionary states and movements more reliant on Soviet power. Gettig posits that Che Guevara's death in October 1967 symbolized the collapse of the movement only twenty months after it had been launched at Havana. Other authors, however, join Chamberlin in suggesting a much longer life for Tricontinentalism. Indeed, Eric Covey argues that the "apex" of Tricontinentalism came as late as 1976 or even 1977, years when Cuban troops first helped the communist MPLA gain power in Angola and then defended the communist Derg in Ethiopia from Somali invasion. Thereafter, adds Covey, the Cuban government exploited its prestige among Third World governments to win the chairmanship of the Non-Aligned Movement starting in 1979, a position the Castro regime sought to use – unsuccessfully, as it turned out – to move the loosely organized Third World bloc in more radical directions.

Who's right? Much depends, of course, on how one conceives the defining characteristics of Tricontinentalism. If Tricontinentalism, at its core, entailed partnerships among key nations that had long wielded power in Third World forums, it might be reasonable to suggest that the initiative suffered an early demise. Algeria, Egypt, and Ghana, to name just three of the governments that participated in the Havana conference, abandoned much of their revolutionary ardor for an array of reasons in the years around the Tricontinental Conference. The Indo-Pakistani War of 1965 and the Six Day War of 1967 contributed to this drift by highlighting fractiousness within the Third World that could not always be plausibly blamed on the West. If one views Tricontinentalism more as an expression of Cuban foreign policy, designed to offset the Castro regime's weaknesses through the cultivation of allies and opportunities for intervention elsewhere in the world, it might be reasonable to see a much longer heyday and even a peak, as Covey suggests, as late as 1976 or 1977. And if, like Parrott, Irwin, and Mahler, one sees Tricontinentalism more as an ideal that offered inspiration and sustenance to radical organizations, no matter how small or weak, it might arguably have endured still longer. Another possibility is that Tricontinentalism – a deliberately loose endeavor, as several essays observe – was more than one of these things. Or it might have changed over time, giving rise to one heyday around the time of the Havana meeting and another later heyday linked more directly to successful African revolutions or perhaps the North Vietnamese capture of Saigon in 1975.

Part of the challenge of settling on one of these possibilities lies in the difficulty of assigning Tricontinentalism an appropriate weight compared to other Third World ideals that circulated alongside it in the 1960s and 1970s. The establishment of the United Nations Conference on Trade and Development (UNCTAD) in 1964 no doubt focused attention on matters of economics and trade, but Byrne's suggestion that men with briefcases thereafter displaced the men brandishing machine guns may not hold up outside the case of Algeria and perhaps a few other established Third World nations whose once-radical governments increasingly found security in an orderly international system. The story of Tricontinentalism's rise and fall might also depend on the role assigned to more conservative Third World nations in the Organization of Petroleum Exporting Countries (OPEC) or the far looser network of relationships among Iran, South

Africa, Brazil, Argentina, Thailand, Malaysia, Indonesia, Anwar Sadat's Egypt, and other counterrevolutionary governments. More research is necessary to expose the ways in which these linkages, which are even less thoroughly examined than the history of Tricontinentalism, eclipsed radical forms of organizing by the early 1970s and amounted to an equally formidable, if not dominant, strand of transnational activism in the Third World.[4] Better understood is the rise of what Chamberlin calls ethno-religious or ethno-sectarian forms of Third World activism in the late 1970s, though the displacement of the Tricontinental movement's secular militancy is more asserted than demonstrated in this collection. What accounts for this trend, and what forms did it take outside the Middle East and Southwest Asia, where it is easiest to see in cases like Lebanon, Iran, and Afghanistan? How did political forces committed to the older secular radicalism react to the emerging phenomenon? Historians have their work cut out for them in delving into such questions and fleshing out Chamberlin's tantalizing periodization.

   Closely related to the question of the Tricontinental movement's trajectory is disagreement about its overall success. How, in short, did the movement fare in realizing the grand vision enshrined in the statement of its purposes and principles crafted ahead of the Havana meeting? Historians who see a relatively quick demise naturally tend toward skeptical views, while those who see a longer life offer more positive assessments. But the correlation is not exact, and, in any case, success can be measured by standards other than longevity. Byrne offers perhaps the most critical assessment, highlighting not only the movement's short duration (if it had any duration at all) but also reasons why, in his view, the movement produced paltry results. Above all, Byrne contends that the pro-communist orientation of Tricontinentalism drove a "wedge" in the broad solidarity envisioned by at least Algerian leaders. Whereas Map 0.2 suggests a remarkably broad array of participation in the Havana conference, Byrne notes that the 612 delegates came mostly from communist parties or leftist groups, including political parties, unions, and liberation movements. All in all, writes Byrne, the meeting was a "distinctly

---

[4] Pathbreaking works exploring the rise of this counterrevolutionary network include Kyle Burke, *Revolutionaries of the Right: Anticommunist Internationalism and Paramilitary Warfare in the Cold War* (Chapel Hill: University of North Carolina Press, 2018); Carl Forsberg, "A Diplomatic Counterrevolution: The Transformation of the U.S.-Middle East Alliance System in the 1970s" (PhD diss., University of Texas at Austin, 2019); and Wen-Qing Ngoei, *Arc of Containment: Britain, the United States, and Anticommunism in Southeast Asia* (Ithaca, NY: Cornell University Press, 2019).

ideological event" that Western delegates were correct to dismiss as a communist gathering. The event alienated "old guard Third Worldists" and proved a "more narrow-minded and less ambitious event" than the "Bandung II" meeting would likely have been if it had gone forward as planned in 1965.

Friedman similarly blames "militant sectarianism" for Tricontinentalism's short duration and limited appeal. But he goes in a different analytical direction by stressing the difficulties of maintaining a distinctly Third World voice in a world dominated by major powers determined to assert their influence. Friedman shows that China's eagerness to exploit racial differences to question Soviet participation in Third World forums (and to marginalize Yugoslavia) damaged prospects for solidarity around the time of the Tricontinental Conference. But Friedman also delves into the Tricontinental itself, contending that the conference, though conceived as a forum for crafting a truly Third World vision, devolved into an exercise in Sino-Soviet jockeying. More specifically, Friedman interprets the conference as a clash among three different visions of what should be achieved there – the Cuban desire for affirmation of the militant program that the Castro government espoused, the Chinese desire for a condemnation of Soviet "revisionism," and the Soviet desire to affirm its own leadership in the Third World and avoid any significant Chinese victories. Perhaps Friedman's harshest condemnation of the conference is his judgment that the proceedings resulted in a "draw" that amounted to a victory for Moscow since it had the lowest expectations. This accomplishment put the Soviets in a strong position to "bury" the results of the conference, double down on its commitment to peaceful coexistence, and expand its influence over liberation movements strapped for material support. While the Soviet Union grew more assertive in Africa, adds Friedman, Moscow's aversion to revolutionary activism in the Western Hemisphere, combined with eventual Soviet-Cuban rapprochement, made OSPAAAL increasingly irrelevant in Latin America.

Gettig endorses Friedman's view that the Tricontinental Conference exacerbated differences between Moscow and Havana, which worked at "cross-purposes" in Latin America for a time thereafter. But Gettig adds yet another explanation for Tricontinental's limitations: US hostility. Efforts to undermine radical impulses of the Third World movement had been a constant feature of American foreign policy for many years by 1966. Washington particularly worked to encourage friendly Third World governments such as Iran and Pakistan to blunt the anti-Americanism that often ran powerfully through Third World forums. So there was, as Gettig notes, nothing particularly new about US efforts to sow divisions at the Havana meeting. The most striking part of Gettig's analysis is his judgment that Washington's counterrevolutionary efforts "certainly deserve some modest share of the credit or blame for the solidarity movement's failure to support and achieve armed revolution in the Americas, Africa, or Asia." Even though Washington's behavior cast it in precisely the nefarious role decried by the radicals, the Tricontinental Conference was, on the whole, suggests Gettig, a propaganda victory for the United States.

For other authors, however, the Tricontinental and the movement that it generated achieved notable successes. These authors suggest, with varying degrees of explicitness, that the movement succeeded in inspiring precisely the sort of revolutionary commitment espoused in the conference's statement of purpose. At least implicitly, these chapters rebut critiques about the narrow ideological scope of Tricontinentalism by suggesting that such narrowness was precisely the point; the movement should be judged, that is, more by the ideological unity and political connections that it forged among committed adherents than by its geographical breadth or fractious tendencies. Perhaps unsurprisingly, the most favorable assessments of Trincontinentalism come in chapters focused on Africa, where armed revolutions gained ground after the Havana conference and Cuba's professions of solidarity carried tangible implications for the continent's liberation movements. Irwin argues in no uncertain terms that the Tricontinental movement provided crucial support for the ANC at a time of doubt and uncertainty. Shifting the focus to Guinea-Bissau, Parrott notes Cabral's caution about accepting large-scale Cuban support but leaves no doubt he drew inspiration, legitimacy, and even a modicum of material aid from his association with the larger Tricontinental movement. Covey, too, highlights the impact of Cuban interventions in Africa, especially in Angola, and the broad persuasiveness of Cuban ideas, including those related to mercenaries. Taken together, these essays leave little doubt about the ways in which Cuban intervention, along with the larger tenets of Tricontinentalism, shaped Africa during the 1960s and 1970s.

Asselin's essay goes furthest in suggesting truly global impacts of Tricontinentalism. For one thing, North Vietnam's stand against the military might of the United States provided a model of revolutionary commitment and defiance that figured prominently in the rhetoric of Tricontinentalism. Che Guevara's appeal for "two, three, many Vietnams" stood out as a rhetorical high point of the conference and provided a slogan that has hung around the movement ever since. Charles de Gaulle demonstrated awareness of the war's capacity to stir action when in September 1966 he spoke out sharply against US policy in a speech aimed at currying favor in the Third World. But Asselin also hints at something more significant – that Tricontinentalism provided opportunities for the Hanoi government to gain support around the world for its military and political cause. Although Asselin does not explore North Vietnam's agency in connection with the Tricontinental Conference, he argues that Hanoi generally "weaponized" diplomacy and secured important political support by projecting the same blend of Marxism and Third Worldism that sat at the heart of Tricontinentalism. To demonstrate North Vietnam's status as a postcolonial nation in sync with radical strands of the larger Third World movement, leaders in Hanoi pressed for the end of colonial rule in Africa and granted quick recognition to newly independent nations.

With the crucial exception of Cuban interventionism in Africa, then, the strongest claims about Tricontinentalism's impact often lead into the intangible realms of rhetoric, inspiration, and persuasion. Mahler hits this point most strongly, asserting that OSPAAAL should be understood first and foremost as "an engine of radical cultural production that – for over four decades and in multiple languages – reflected, shaped, and distributed a shared worldview among a transnational community." All the way to its closure in 2019, adds Mahler, OSPAAAL continued to produce the "ephemera" – books, pamphlets, posters, and so forth – for which it was best known. The effect, she resoundingly concludes, was no less than "a major impact on the aesthetics, and ideologies of the contemporary Left." The power of Mahler's contention is perhaps nowhere as clear as in Gettig's chapter, one of the more critical assessments of the Tricontinental movement to appear in this collection. While contending that Cuban activism under the banner of Tricontinentalism ultimately made a concrete, enduring impact only in Southern Africa, Gettig concedes that the movement "gave voice to a transnational discourse of revolution that would continue to inspire revolutionaries around the world over the ensuring decades." The latter, he acknowledges, is no small thing.

The problem with such claims, of course, lies in the challenge of evaluating the impact of cultural production or the discourse it generates. How can we measure reception of propaganda or pin down the power of rhetoric? Several essays point out the cliched quality of grandiose statements of Third World solidarity, which flew off the presses in the 1960s and 1970s and circulated alongside propaganda generated by other political agendas. Yet Mahler and other authors who extol the enduring power of the Tricontinental's appeals for Third World solidarity undoubtedly speak to something real – rhetoric that, precisely because it emanated from relatively weak players on the international stage, plausibly carried weight far out of proportion to what one might expect from mere words and symbols. The ultimate moral valence of those words and symbols is perhaps a subject as much for philosophers as historians. The Tricontinental, after all, celebrated not only solidarity and social justice but also confrontational, often violent means of promoting change – violence that spawned bloodshed and terrorism while often promoting the agendas of communist superpowers that presided over staggering repression and bloodletting in the twentieth century. How to balance progress toward the liberation of colonized societies against the accompanying repression is a question that can never be answered definitively.

Questions that this book has delineated about the origins, trajectory, and effectiveness of the Tricontinental movement do, however, lend themselves to historical research that may enable us to engage in debate at a higher level of understanding. The preceding chapters, along with the body of earlier scholarship discussed in Parrott's Introduction, make bold steps forward in appreciating a fascinating and often-overlooked dimension of the global history of the twentieth century but also lay down a research agenda that invites new work. Pursuing this agenda promises to recover the agency of non-Western actors too often ignored in historical accounts because of the difficulties of accessing the necessary sources, the tendency of Western historians to examine more familiar ground, or both. Integrating Third World histories into the larger history of the Cold War era remains a vital task in fleshing out the global history of the twentieth century. (The Tricontinental is not even mentioned in two of the most prominent books to appear in recent years about the Cold War in the Third World.[5]) Even more important, addressing questions raised in this book promises to help expose the roots of a contemporary world order that continues to be profoundly shaped by power imbalances, economic exploitation, and social injustice. In the successes and failures, choices and missed opportunities, of earlier efforts to address these problems lie implications for the present and future.

---

[5] Robert B. Rakove, *Kennedy, Johnson, and the Nonaligned World* (New York: Cambridge University Press, 2013), and Odd Arne Westad, *The Global Cold War: Third World Interventions and the Making of Our Times* (New York: Cambridge University Press, 2005).

Select Bibliography of Secondary Sources

Adi, Hakim. *Pan-Africanism: A History.* London: Bloomsbury, 2018.

Anderson, Jon Lee. *Che: A Revolutionary Life.* New York: Grove, 2010.

Asselin, Pierre. *Hanoi's Road to the Vietnam War, 1954–1965.* Berkeley: University of California Press, 2013.

Aydin, Cemil. *The Politics of Anti-Westernism in Asia: Visions of World Order in Pan-Islamic and Pan-Asian Thought.* New York: Columbia University Press, 2019.

Bao, Ricardo Melgar. "The Anti-Imperialist League of the Americas between the East and Latin America." Translated by Mariana Ortega Breña. *Latin American Perspectives* 35:2 (March 2008): 9–24.

Berger, Mark T. and Heloise Weber. *Rethinking the Third World: International Development and World Politics.* New York: Macmillan, 2014.

Brands, H. W. *The Specter of Neutralism.* New York: Columbia University Press, 1990.

Brazinsky, Gregg A. *Winning the Third World: Sino-American Rivalry during the Cold War.* Chapel Hill: University of North Carolina Press, 2017.

Brown, Jonathan C. *Cuba's Revolutionary World.* New York: Oxford University Press 2017.

Byrne, Jeffrey James. "Beyond Continents, Colours, and the Cold War: Yugoslavia, Algeria, and the Struggle for Non-Alignment." *The International History Review* 37:5 (2015): 912–932.

Byrne, Jeffrey James. *Mecca of Revolution: Algeria, Decolonization, and the Third World Order.* New York: Oxford University Press, 2016.

Castañeda, Jorge G. *Compañero: The Life and Death of Che Guevara.* New York: Knopf, 1997.

Chamberlin, Paul Thomas. *The Cold War's Killing Fields.* New York: HarperCollins, 2018.

Chamberlin, Paul Thomas. *The Global Offensive: The United States, the Palestine Liberation Organization, and the Making of the Post-Cold War Order.* New York: Oxford University Press, 2012.

Chatterjee, Partha. *The Nation and Its Fragments*. Princeton: Princeton University Press, 1993.

Christiansen, Samantha, and Zachary A. Scarlett, eds. *The Third World in the Global 1960s*. New York: Berghan Books, 2013.

Citino, Nathan. *Envisioning the Arab Future: Modernization in US-Arab Relations, 1945–1967*. New York: Cambridge University Press, 2017.

Clayfield, Anna. *The Guerrilla Legacy of the Cuban Revolution*. Gainesville: University Press of Florida, 2019.

Colburn, Forrest D. *The Vogue of Revolution in Poor Countries*. Princeton: Princeton University Press, 1994.

Connelly, Matthew. *A Diplomatic Revolution: Algeria's Fight for Independence and the Origins of the Post-Cold War Era*. New York: Oxford University Press, 2002.

Dhada, Mustafah. *Warriors at Work: How Guinea Was Really Set Free*. Boulder: University of Colorado Press, 1993.

Dietrich, Christopher R. W. *Oil Revolution: Anticolonial Elites, Sovereign Rights, and the Economic Culture of Decolonization*. New York: Cambridge University Press, 2017.

Dinkel, Jürgen. *The Non-Aligned Movement: Genesis, Organization and Politics*. Leiden: Brill, 2018.

Drachewych, Oleksa and Ian McKay, eds. *Left Transnationalism: The Communist International and the National, Colonial, and Racial Questions*. Montreal: McGill-Queen's University Press, 2020.

Drew, Allison, ed. *South Africa's Radical Tradition*, vol. 2. Cape Town: University of Cape Town Press, 1997.

Dubinsky, Karen, Catherine Krull, Susan Lord, Sean Mills, and Scott Rutherford, eds. *New World Coming: The Sixties and the Shaping of a Global Consciousness*. Toronto: Between the Lines, 2009.

Dubow, Saul. "Were There Political Alternatives in the Wake of the Sharpeville-Langa Violence in South Africa?" *Journal of African History* 56:1 (2015): 119–142.

Elbaum, Max. *Revolution in the Air: Sixties Radicals turn to Lenin, Mao and Che*. New York: Verso, 2002.

Ellis, Stephen. *External Mission: The ANC in Exile, 1960–1990*. London: Hurst and Company, 2014.

Ewing, Cindy. "The Colombo Powers: Crafting Diplomacy in the Third World and Launching Afro-Asia at Bandung." *Cold War History* 19:1 (2019): 1–19.

Faligot, Roger. *Tricontinentale: Quand Che Guevara, Ben Barka, Cabral, Castro et Hô Chi Minh préparaient la révolution mondiale (1964–1968)*. Paris: La Découverte, 2013.

Field, Thomas, Stella Krepp, and Vanni Pettiná, eds. *Latin America and the Global Cold War*. Chapel Hill: University of North Carolina Press, 2020.

Frazier, Robeson Taj. *The East Is Black: Cold War China in the Black Radical Imagination*. Durham: Duke University Press, 2014.

Friedman, Jeremy. *Shadow Cold War: The Sino-Soviet Competition for the Third World*. Chapel Hill: University of North Carolina Press, 2015.

Garavini, Giuliano. *The Rise and Fall of OPEC in the Twentieth Century.* New York: Oxford University Press, 2019.

Gerhart, Gail. *Black Power in South Africa: The Evolution of an Ideology.* Berkeley: University of California Press, 1978.

Getachew, Adom. *Worldmaking After Empire: The Rise and Fall of Self-Determination.* Princeton: Princeton University Press, 2019.

Gettig, Eric. "'Trouble Ahead in Afro-Asia': The United States, the Second Bandung Conference, and the Struggle for the Third World, 1964–65." *Diplomatic History* 39:1 (January 2015): 126–156.

Gilman, Nils. "The New International Economic Order: A Reintroduction." *Humanity* 6:1 (Spring 2015): 1–16.

Gleijeses, Piero. *Conflicting Missions: Havana, Washington, and Africa, 1959–1976.* Chapel Hill: University of North Carolina Press, 2003.

Goebel, Michael. *Anti-Imperial Metropolis: Interwar Paris and the Seeds of Third World Nationalism.* New York: Cambridge University Press, 2015.

Gronbeck-Tedesco, John A. *Cuba, the United States, and Cultures of the Transnational Left, 1930–1975.* New York: Cambridge University Press, 2015.

Gupta, Pamila, Christopher J. Lee, Marissa J. Moorman, and Sandhya Shukla. "Editor's Introduction." *Radical History Review* 131 (May 2018): 1–12.

Harmer, Tanya. "Two, Three, Many Revolutions? Cuba and the Prospects for Revolutionary Change in Latin America, 1967–1975." *Journal of Latin American Studies* 45:1 (February 2013): 61–89.

Harris, Richard L. "Cuban Internationalism, Che Guevara, and the Survival of Cuba's Socialist Regime." *Latin American Perspectives* 36:3 (May 2009): 27–42.

Hashemi, Nader, and Danny Postel, eds. *Sectarianization: Mapping the New Politics of the Middle East.* New York: Oxford University Press, 2017.

Hatzky, Christine. *Cubans in Angola: South-South Cooperation and Transfer of Knowledge, 1976–1991.* Madison: University of Wisconsin Press, 2015.

Hernández, Rafael. "El año rojo. Política, sociedad y cultura en 1968." *Revista de Estudios Sociales* 33 (August 2009): 44–54.

Hosek, Jennifer Ruth. "'Subaltern Nationalism' and the Anti-Authoritarians." *German Politics and Society* 26:1 (2008): 57–81.

Irwin, Ryan. *Gordian Knot: Apartheid and the Unmaking of the Liberal World Order.* New York: Oxford University Press, 2012.

Jackson, Richard L. *The Non-Aligned, the UN, and the Superpowers.* Westport, CT: Praeger, 1983.

Jones, Matthew. "A 'Segregated' Asia?: Race, the Bandung Conference, and Pan-Asianist Fears in American Thought and Policy, 1954–5." *Diplomatic History* 29:5 (November 2005): 841–868.

Kalter, Christopher. *The Discovery of the Third World: Decolonization and the Rise of the New Left in France, c.1950–1976.* New York: Cambridge University Press, 2016.

Keller, Renata. *Mexico's Cold War: Cuba, the United States, and the Legacy of the Mexican Revolution.* New York: Cambridge University Press, 2015.

Kersffeld, Daniel. *Contra el imperio: Historia de la Liga Antimperialista de las Américas.* Mexico: Siglo XXI Editores, 2012.

Kimche, David. *The Afro-Asian Movement: Ideology and Foreign Policy of the Third World*. Jerusalem: Israel Universities Press, 1973.

Kullaa, Rinna. *Non-Alignment and Its Origins in Cold War Europe: Yugoslavia, Finland, and the Soviet Challenge*. London: I.B. Tauris, 2012.

Landau, Paul. "Controlled by Communists? (Re)Assessing the ANC in its Exilic Decades." *South African Historical Journal* 67:2 (2015): 222–241.

Latner, Teishan A. *Cuban Revolution in America: Havana and the Making of a United States Left, 1968–1992*. Chapel Hill: University of North Carolina Press, 2018.

Lee, Christopher J., ed. *Making a World After Empire: The Bandung Moment and Its Political Afterlives*. Athens: Ohio University Press, 2010.

Lewis, Su Lin and Carolien Stolte, "Other Bandungs: Afro-Asian Internationalisms in the Early Cold War." *Journal of World History* 30:1–2 (June 2019): 1–19.

Lissoni, Arianna. "Transformations in the ANC External Mission and Umkhonto we Sizwe, 1960–1969." *Journal of South African Studies* 35:2 (2009): 287–301.

Louro, Michele, Carolien Stolte, Heather Streets-Salter, and Sana Tannoury-Karam, eds. *The League Against Imperialism: Lives and Afterlives*. Leiden: Leiden University Press, 2020.

Louro, Michele. *Comrades against Imperialism: Nehru, India, and Interwar Internationalism*. New York: Cambridge University Press, 2018.

Lowy, Michael. *The Marxism of Che Guevara: Philosophy, Economics, and Revolutionary Warfare*. New York and London: Monthly Review Press, 1973.

Lüthi, Lorenz M. *Cold Wars*. New York: Cambridge University Press, 2020.

Lüthi, Lorenz M. *The Sino-Soviet Split: Cold War in the Communist World*. Princeton: Princeton University Press, 2008.

Macmillan, Hugh. *The Lusaka Years: The ANC in Exile in Zambia*. Johannesburg: Jacana, 2013.

Mahler, Anne Garland. "The Global South in the Belly of the Beast: Viewing African American Civil Rights Through a Tricontinental Lens." *Latin American Research Review* 50:1 (2015): 95–116.

Mahler, Anne Garland. *From the Tricontinental to the Global South: Race, Radicalism, and Transnational Solidarity*. Durham: Duke University Press, 2018.

Makalani, Minkah. *In the Cause of Freedom: Radical Black Internationalism, 1917–1939*. Chapel Hill: University of North Carolina Press, 2011.

McMahon, Robert J., ed. *The Cold War in the Third World*. New York: Oxford University Press, 2013.

Miskovic, Natasa, Harald Fischer-Tiné, and Nada Boskovska, eds. *The Non-Aligned Movement and the Cold War: Delhi – Bandung – Belgrade*. New York: Routledge, 2014.

Mortimer, Robert A. *The Third World Coalition in International Politics*. 2nd ed. Boulder: Westview Press, 1984.

Mortimer, Robert A. "Algerian Foreign Policy: From Revolution to National Interest." *The Journal of North African Studies* 20:3 (2015): 466–482.

Munro, John. *The Anticolonial Front: The African American Freedom Struggle and Global Decolonization, 1945–1960.* New York: Cambridge University Press, 2017.

Nguyen Thanh. *Bac Ho voi Chau Phi* [Uncle Ho and Africa]. Hanoi: Nha xuat ban Ly luan Chinh tri, 2005.

Nguyen, Lien-Hang T. *Hanoi's War: An International History of the War for Peace in Vietnam.* Chapel Hill: University of North Carolina Press, 2016.

Nunan, Timothy. "'Neither East Nor West,' Neither Liberal Nor Illiberal? Iranian Islamist Internationalism in the 1980s." *Journal of World History* 31:1 (March 2020): 43–77.

Parker, Jason. *Hearts, Minds, Voices: US Cold War Public Diplomacy and the Formation of the Third World.* New York: Oxford University Press, 2016.

Parrott, R. Joseph. "Boycott Gulf! Angolan Oil and the Black Power Roots of American Anti-Apartheid Organizing." *Modern American History* 1:2 (2018): 195–220.

Peters, Christabelle. *Cuban Identity and the Angolan Experience.* New York: Palgrave Macmillan, 2012.

Prashad, Vijay. *The Darker Nations: A People's History of the Third World.* New York: The New Press, 2008.

Prashad, Vijay. *The Poorer Nations: A Possible History of the Global South.* New York: Verso, 2013.

Prestholdt, Jeremy. "Resurrecting Che: Radicalism, the Transnational Imagination, and the Politics of Heroes." *Journal of Global History* 7:3 (2012): 506–526.

Pulido, Laura. *Black, Brown, Yellow, and Left: Radical Activism in Los Angeles.* Berkeley: University of California Press, 2006.

Qiang Zhai. *China and the Vietnam Wars: 1950–1975.* Chapel Hill: University of North Carolina Press, 2000.

Radchenko, Sergey. *Two Suns in the Heavens: The Sino-Soviet Struggle for Supremacy, 1962–1967.* Washington, DC: Woodrow Wilson Center Press, 2009.

Rakove, Robert B. *Kennedy, Johnson, and the Nonaligned World.* New York: Cambridge University Press, 2012.

Rodriguez, Besenia. "Beyond Nation: The Formation of a Tricontinental Discourse." PhD dissertation, Yale University, 2006.

Seidman, Sarah. "Venceremos Means We Shall Overcome: The African American Freedom Struggle and Cuban Revolution, 1959–79." PhD dissertation, Brown University, 2013.

Shen Zhihua and Xia Yafeng. "Leadership Transfer in the Asian Revolution: Mao Zedong and the Asian Cominform." *Cold War History* 14:2 (2014): 195–213.

Shen Zhihua and Xia Yafeng. *Mao and the Sino-Soviet Partnership, 1945–1959.* New York: Lexington Books, 2015.

Shubin, Vladimir. *ANC: A View from Moscow.* 2nd ed. Johannesburg: Jacana, 2008.

Slobodian, Quinn. *Foreign Front: Third World Politics in Sixties West Germany.* Durham: Duke University Press, 2012.

Soske, Jon. *Internal Frontiers: African Nationalism and the Indian Diaspora in Twentieth-Century South Africa.* Athens: Ohio University Press, 2017.

Sousa, Julião Soares. *Amílcar Cabral: Vida e Morte de um Revolucionário Africano*. Lisbon: Vega, 2011.

Sousa, Julião Soares. "Amílcar Cabral, the PAIGC and the Relations with China at the Time of the Sino-Soviet Split and of Anti-Colonialism." *International History Review* 42:6 (2020):1274–1296.

Suri, Jeremi. *Power and Protest: Global Revolution and the Rise of Détente*. Cambridge: Harvard University Press, 2005.

Tan, Seng and Amitav Acharya, eds. *Bandung Revisited: The Legacy of the 1955 African-Asian Conference for the International Order*. Singapore: National University of Singapore Press, 2008.

Telepneva, Natalia. "Our Sacred Duty: The Soviet Union, the Liberation Movements in the Portuguese Colonies, and the Cold War, 1961–1975." PhD dissertation, London School of Economics, 2015.

Thomas, Darryl. "The Impact of the Sino-Soviet Conflict on the Afro-Asian People's Solidarity Organization." *Journal of Asian and African Affairs* 3:2 (April 1992): 167–191.

Thomas, Scott. *The Diplomacy of Liberation: The Foreign Relations of the African National Congress since 1960*. London: I.B. Taurus, 2000.

Trnka, Jamie. *Revolutionary Subjects: German Literatures and the Limits of Aesthetic Solidarity with Latin America*. Berlin: De Gruyter, 2015.

Tulchin, Joseph. *Latin America in International Politics: Challenging US Hegemony*. Boulder: Lynne Rienner, 2016.

Tuong Vu. *Vietnam's Communist Revolution: The Power and Limits of Ideology*. New York: Cambridge University Press, 2017.

Vélez, Federico. *Latin American Revolutionaries and the Arab World: From the Suez Canal to the Arab Spring*. Burlington: Ashgate Publishing, 2016.

Vitalis, Robert. "The Midnight Ride of Kwame Nkrumah and Other Fables of Bandung." *Humanity* 4:2 (Summer 2013): 261–288.

Vo Kim Cuong. *Viet Nam va chau Phi trong su nghiep dau tranh giai phong dan toc* [Vietnam and Africa in the Struggle for National Liberation]. Hanoi: Nha xuat ban Chinh tri quoc gia, 2004.

Voß, Klaas. "Plausibly Deniable: Mercenaries in US Covert Interventions During the Cold War, 1964–1987." *Cold War History* 16:1 (2016): 37–60.

Westad, Odd Arne. *The Global Cold War: Third World Interventions and the Making of Our Times*. New York: Cambridge University Press, 2005.

Willetts, Peter. *The Non-Aligned Movement: The Origins of the Third World Alliance*. London: Frances Pinter Publishers, 1978.

Wu, Judy Tzu-Chun. *Radicals on the Road: Internationalism, Orientalism, and Feminism during the Vietnam Era*. Cornell University Press, 2013.

Yaffe, Helen. *Che Guevara: The Economics of Revolution*. London: Palgrave Macmillan, 2009.

Young, Cynthia A. *Soul Power: Culture, Radicalism, and the Making of the U.S. Third World Left*. Durham: Duke University Press, 2006.

Young, Robert J. C. *Postcolonialism: An Historical Introduction*. Malden, MA: Wiley-Blackwell, 2001.

Index

CPSIA information can be obtained
at www.ICGtesting.com
Printed in the USA
BVHW031709110122
626011BV00001B/13